manhattan

men[...]

The Great Res[...] [...]uide

Third Annu[...]

The most comprehensive and authoritative guide to the restaurants of New York. Where to Go, What it Costs, What to Expect

Edited by M. Archer Brown

 Manhattan Menus
New York

Library of Congress Catalogue Number: 77-2488

ISBN-0-931576-00-8

Cover Design by Shirley Langworthy

Manufactured in the United States of America
Third Edition. First printing.

CONTENTS

about this book

New York has more French restaurants than Lyon, more Italian restaurants than Venice, more restaurants of every size, type and description than just about anyplace else in the world. Even at the rate of two a day, it would take you at least twenty-five years to visit every dining place here; closer to *thirty* if you took time off for holidays and weekends.

Precisely because the choices are so numerous, restaurant guides are necessary. Yet most of those heretofore available have been long on opinion and short on fact—too often providing little more than a recital of a single reviewer's subjective opinions and personal experiences. Displays of the writer's craft, rather than objective evaluations, they have typically left the reader hungry for hard facts and real illumination. It is this hunger that *Manhattan Menus* is intended to satisfy.

Manhattan Menus is the only book of its kind, entirely different from other sources of restaurant information. A work of fact, *not* opinion, it takes *no* positions and prints *no* reviews. Rather, it features the full menu and prices of many of the area's best and best-known restaurants, along with a capsule description of each establishment, and such essential information as dress code, days closed, hours, location, telephone numbers, credit cards accepted, etc.

There will always be risks involved in trying new dining places—that the selection of dishes offered will not please, that the prices will not be right, that the ambience will be unsuitable or that the service will be poor. *Manhattan Menus'* aim is to limit those risks by giving you as much factual information as possible.

One final note. Change is inevitable. Menus change, prices change. New restaurants open and, sometimes, old standbys fade away. To keep the information in *Manhattan Menus* current, a completely revised and updated edition is published annually. Make it a point to ask for each year's new edition at your bookstore. If your dealer is out of stock, order direct from the publisher by filling out the order cards elsewhere in this book.

Some acknowledgements: Our thanks to the staff of Caffé Ferrara for their considerable assistance with the definitions of Italian pastries. The Caffé Ferrara is located at 195 Grand Street, New York City . . . Mihaly Vestergom for his kind help on German pastry definitions. Mr. Vestergom is the owner of Cafe Geiger, 206 East 86th Street, New York City . . . Guy Pascal for his contribution to the definitions of French pastries. Mr. Pascal is owner of Délices La Côte Basque, 1032 Lexington Avenue, New York City . . . Bill Todd Singer for his expert advice on wines and wine terms. Mr. Singer is the Executive Director of *Wine Line* Magazine, P.O. Box 766, Forest Hills, New York . . . and to Raymond L. Vaudard, Master Chef, for his significant and knowledgeable contribution to the descriptions of chefs' associations and awards. Mr. Vaudard's career in the culinary arts has been long and prestigious, but his own words describe him best: " chef on both the old and new continents, chef in the sky for Air France, chef on the sea with The French Line."

ON FRENCH CUISINE *By André Soltner*

There is, in France, a long tradition of gastronomy—a respect, even a reverence, for well-prepared meals that goes back at least as far as the reign of Henri IV. Many of France's most prominent public men have been known to be great gourmets—Rabelais, Louis XV, Danton—and many others have become well-known largely because they *were* gourmets—Brillat-Savarin, Grimod de la Reynière, the Duc de Luynes, and, more recently, Curnonsky. But even the ordinary Frenchman has historically regarded cooking as a fine art rather than just a necessity, and has typically made the appreciation of good food a major part of his life.

That is one reason why France has produced so many chefs of the first rank—a disproportionate number, in fact, for a country of its size and population.

After all, when an art is so esteemed by the people, by the nation as a whole, it is logical for a great tradition to develop around it. And there is no question that gifted young Frenchmen from ordinary families came to view careers in the kitchen as particularly honorable ones—and as a way to achieve a measure of upward mobility in what is, even today, a rather structured class society. Look, for example, at Carême. His circumstances were modest, yet he became the chef to Tallyrand, George IV, the Rothschilds. There are many others. I myself am the son of a carpenter.

Of course, opportunity alone is not the reason for the highly-developed state of the culinary arts in France. What is perhaps even more important are the raw materials. It is impossible to have a great cuisine without the finest fish, beef, butter, cream, produce and so forth. From the beginning, France has been fortunate in that everything was raised or grown right there—very little had to be imported. And the quality was good.

At one time transportation was more difficult than today, so the people cooked with what they had, with what was most available in the local area. This is what accounts for the regional differences in French cuisine. In the south, they used a lot of olive oil. In the east, mainly pork fat. In other places, butter. Then, little by little, it became easier to ship food from one region to another. The train and automobile came along, and refrigeration was invented. That was very important. Before that, it wasn't so easy to keep food fresh, so chefs had to use rich sauces to improve flavor. Sauces are still used today, but we do them differently than 50 years ago. We don't cook the bases for days, and we don't bind them. Today, people want to feel "light" after a meal. The fashion is to be thin, not fat. In the old days, being fat was a sign of great wealth and social position.

But none of this is to say that there is some great revolution taking place in the way the French prepare their food. What is called the "Nouvelle Cuisine" isn't so new, really. Certainly not a revolution or anything of the kind. It is simply the classic French cuisine that has evolved for the style of today. Paul Bocuse made it famous at Collonges-au-Mont-d'Or near Lyon. The idea is to serve meals that are "light" and natural. Not to overcook or undercook. And not to be tied down by the habits of the past.

Until 10 years ago, beef was almost always served with potatoes and carrots and stringbeans. But why? Why not cucumbers, for example? So today, we are more adventurous. But this does not mean that we don't use butter and cream. We just use less. Without butter and cream, there can be no French cuisine.

The new approach requires greater talent on the part of a chef. Salmon must taste like salmon, and beef must taste like beef. Mistakes can no longer be covered up with rich sauces. Neither can ingredients of less than superior quality. So now it is even more important to begin with the very best produce, fish, and meat. Without them, nothing worthwhile can follow.

André Soltner is Chef-Propriétaire of Lutèce.

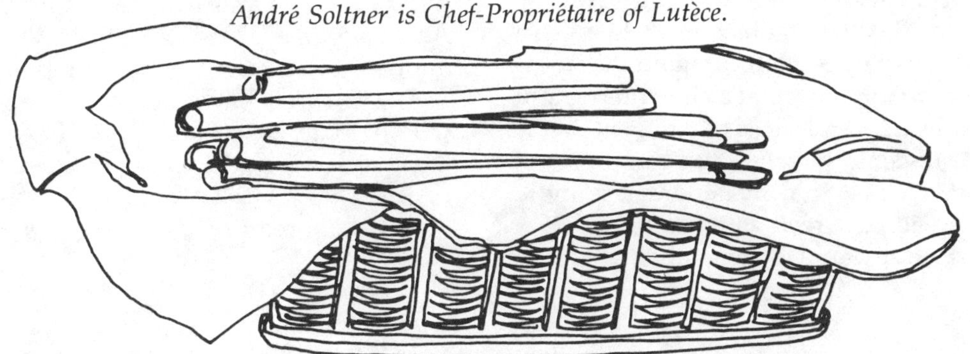

On Pâté *by Lozach Amede*

What is called *pâté* in the United States is often not pâté at all. If one follows the strictest definition of the word, a pâté is a pastry crust with a ground meat filling that may be served either hot or cold. It is rare to order a pâté in a restaurant in this country and be served with this kind of pâté. (Unless it is referred to on the menu as a *pâté en croute*—in a crust.) What one will usually be served is what is more accurately called a *terrine.* At La Côte Basque we refer to our *terrine Côte Basque* but it is what many think of as our pâté. A terrine or, if you will, a pâté, is very simply a dish of ground meat, often with a pork base, baked in a deep, straight-sided pan lined with pork fat and served cool.

Terrine is the name of the oblong clay dish that is used for baking the pâté or terrine. It is possible that some restaurants may even serve a *galantine* as a pâté but this is rare: a galantine is similar to a terrine but it is made with a duck or chicken that is boned, and the skin of the fowl is used as an apron or wrap for the stuffing or *farce.*

In France, every town, no matter how small, has at least one *charcuterie*—a store where pork products are prepared by a *charcutier.* Each charcuterie offers three or four varieties of pâté—a *pâté maison* which is the specialty of that particular charcuterie and other varieties that change with the season or the whim of the charcutier. In general one cooks what one likes to eat and a charcutier follows this same rule. If one is lucky, one may find a fresh *foie gras*—the delectable pâté made from the specially-fattened livers of geese. Since foie gras geese are not bred in the U.S. and it is not possible for France to export their foie gras (the actual livers) to the U.S., any foie gras that you will eat in the U.S. is grown and made in France and then exported to the U.S.

Other varieties of pâté and galantines that are often available in a French charcuterie are *pâté de lapin* (of rabbit), galantines de *volaille* (of chicken), *de dinde* (of turkey), *de canard* (of duck); and at times game pâtés made from hare *(lièvre)* or partridge *(perdrix)* or even thrushes *(grives).* It is rare to find a game pâté made in a U.S. restaurant because of the enormous expense and work involved—it takes so many birds to make a game pâté and so many people to prepare them.

In France it is common to stop at a charcuterie right before lunch and buy several slices of pâté. All that is needed then is a scenic picnic spot, bread, some cheese and a good wine. In a restaurant it is more likely that a pâté will be served as an appetizer.

I come from Brittany and I remember well my mother's pâté. I suppose one would call it a *pâté de campagne* (country pâté). It was much heartier than the pâté usually served in a restaurant; its texture was not as refined and it had a more rustic taste. Pâtés were popular in French households then because they kept for such a very long time. If made correctly from the start, they will last several weeks.

The terrine—or, if you will, pâté—that we make at La Côte Basque is from a recipe that has been perfected over many, many years. It is made with pork butt, *foie de volaille* (chicken livers), shallots, truffles, pistachio nuts, eggs, cognac, port, nutmeg and other seasonings. It, like any other pâté, is made the following way: first we place a layer of pork fat in the terrine, leaving some to hang over the sides of the dish so that it will eventually cover the loaf. Next we put in a layer of meat that has been ground together with the spices, cognac and port. On top of this layer we add some very thin strips of veal and pork to give the pâté an interesting texture and appearance. Usually there are three of these double layers when the pâté is ready to be wrapped with the pork fat lining.

To make a truly excellent pâté it is important to allow oneself at least one entire day but two days is preferred. It is best to marinate the meat in the seasonings and liquids before it is ground and, once it is cooked, the pâté must wait at least one day at room temperature before it can be eaten or stored. If there's not enough grease on the top of the pâté after it has been baked—and this happens often—it is necessary to spread either butter or *saindoux* (lard) on top to make the pâté airtight for storage.

On the day that the pâté is to be served, our staff arrives early in the morning, takes the grease off the pâté and replaces it with a gelatine topping.

A pâté of this sort must be served cool; it is often set on a plate in a base of ice if it is to be served from a buffet. It should *never* be served from the refrigerator.

I like my pâté served alone on a plate so that I can fully enjoy its taste and nothing else. Many people prefer their pâtés accompanied by a *cornichon* (gherkin) or diced gelatine. On a picnic you may want to put the pâté on a slice of bread but not in a restaurant. And no butter please. I prefer a good red wine with my pâté but many Americans prefer white.

A good pâté—whether it is actually a terrine, a pâté, a pâté en croute or even a galantine—is best when it is carefully prepared from the finest ingredients, spiced and flavored with finesse, served at the correct temperature and heartily enjoyed.

Lozach Amede is Chef of La Côte Basque.

On French Desserts *by Jean-Jacques Rachou*

By the time people reach the dessert course these days, they are thinking about calories. Fifty years ago people adored rich and heavy foods followed by rich and heavy desserts—they didn't worry about calories the way we do now. In fact, at one time the *entremets* or sweet course was served between the appetizer course and the main course—long before the end of the meal. Now the word entremets—which literally means "between dishes"—is best translated as sweets or desserts and is served after the salad and cheese course. Entremets are an important part of the meal—they are the finale, the diner's last memory of the meal.

Although desserts nowadays are much less elaborate than they once were—at times they must have looked as though they owed more to an architect than to a chef—they are still very special and no less delicious.

Desserts, like most other things, enjoy vogues. Some desserts which were popular ten years ago hardly ever appear on menus today. New desserts are being created all the time, too, making both the cooking and the eating of desserts enjoyable.

Perhaps it would be best to talk about sweets or entremets according to types and to give examples of some of the most popular and most interesting sweets in each type.

We can begin with batter sweets. These would include *crêpes* and *beignets*. Everyone has heard of *crêpes Suzette* but this has become a somewhat passé dessert. Most French restaurants in New York are too small for the drama involved in the preparation of a flaming crêpe. The kind of crêpes that I think are the most successful are *crêpes soufflé*—crêpes with a soufflé filling, flavored with apricot, strawberry, raspberry or calvados, and served with a fruit sauce. Beignets (or fritters) are no longer very popular as a dessert since they are deep-fried and considered too filling after a substantial meal.

Cooked creams and custards and rice desserts are probably best after a light lunch rather than a full dinner. Rich puddings like *riz à l'impératrice*—vanilla flavored rice mixed with candied fruit, custard and whipped cream—are not very popular now, here or in France. Perhaps there is a bit of snobbism involved—rice has never been considered very "special."

There are many types of sweets that are made with eggs and one of the most interesting is called *île flottante* or floating island. It was once extremely popular but is quite out of vogue now. The name floating island describes the dessert—the "island" is made with the whites of eggs and it is afloat on a base of *crème anglaise* made from the yolks. Dessert omelets are considered too rich these days, but at Eastertime an exception is made and omelets will appear as a last course. One dessert, called *omelette à la norvégienne* isn't an omelet at all; it is what is called a Baked Alaska in the U.S. and when it was created in 1895 it caused quite a bit of excitement. It is ice cream covered with *meringue* and baked in a very hot oven—hot enough so that the meringue bakes quickly but the ice cream stays frozen.

Fruit sweets are popular now since people feel much less guilty about finishing a meal with fruit than with a rich pastry or custard. A *compote*—fresh fruit poached in syrup—can be delicious. Pears or peaches make a good compote but I've found that apricots are best. One of my own favorite fruit desserts is a poached pear with a cream filling baked in a *brioche* dough. It is served with vanilla or apricot sauce and I call it *poire surprise*.

Two fruit desserts which appear on many New York menus are *poires Hélène* and *pêches Melba*. Poire Hélène is a pear poached in a vanilla-flavored syrup and served on vanilla ice cream with hot chocolate sauce. Pêche Melba is a peach on vanilla ice cream which is covered with raspberry purée. Any fruit can be served "Melba"—strawberries, pears and nectarines are all good prepared this way.

Meringue is a category of sweet that is not at all popular anymore. Twenty years ago, this was not true and people used to enjoy a dessert of two pieces of meringue with ice cream in between or meringue glacée. Diners seldom order a meringue dessert these days.

What they do order again and again, though, are desserts that are made with whipped cream. In French, whipped cream is called *crème Chantilly* and it is adored by both French and Americans alike. In France *crème fraiche*—a very heavy and delicious cream—will sometimes be served by itself with sugar for dessert.

A *mousse* is one of the best-liked desserts made with crème Chantilly; when made well it is both light and rich. A *mousse au chocolat* is the favorite dessert of so many Americans, but I think they should try, too, mousses made with Grand Marnier, raspberry, apricot and—my favorite—one made with the anise-flavored Ricard.

If I had to choose my own favorite dessert I would say that it is a *bombe*. I love bombes of any flavor—after a nice dinner a bombe is a refreshing and light dessert and a perfect ending to a meal. A bombe belongs in the category of ice cream desserts. It is made with crème fraiche and is placed in a mold. It is lighter than ice cream and more delicate. To make my bombe I use a *mélange* of egg yolk, cooked sugar, beaten egg whites and crème Chantilly. The bombe mold can be in any form at all, although originally it was a spherical shape. I like to flavor the bombes I make with *pralines* (almonds), raspberries and Grand Marnier.

Some people consider ice creams or *glaces* a bit too ordinary to serve as desserts, but it is possible to make ice cream quite out-of-the-ordinary. For instance, I make *glaces aux truffes,* which is vanilla ice cream with *essence de truffe du Périgord*. It is quite unlike any other ice cream I have ever tasted. A *coupe* is another ice cream dessert—it is what Americans call a "sundae."

Sorbets (or sherbets), as dessert, are very much in favor with people who want to keep their dessert course light. I find that *cassis* or lime (*citron vert*) are the most successful flavorings for sorbets. A sorbet flavored with lemon and mint is very popular in America, but the French would much prefer the flavor of Grand Marnier to the mint. Champagne sorbet is also very popular in France. I like to serve my sorbets right in their own fruit—this works well with lime, lemon or orange.

And finally we come to the *patisseries*—the very first thing that many Americans think of when they hear "French dessert." A pastry tray in a French restaurant should offer several delicious choices. There should definitely be two or three types of *tartelette* (what we call tarts in the U.S.). The flavor of the tartelette will depend on the season, of course, but pineapple, strawberry and cherry are usually available. You can make an excellent tart with the kiwi fruit, but not many restaurants have tried it.

Napoléons, the many-layered pastries with cream filling, should be on the tray, too, but they must be absolutely fresh. The same Napoléon should never be on a lunch and then a dinner tray. It will be soggy. Éclairs should be one of the choices—filled with chocolate, coffee or even Kirsch-flavored cream—and there should also be some *choux à la crème*—cream puffs. Both éclairs and choux à la crème are made with the same dough—called *pâte à chou.*

Palmiers are another specialty for the pastry platter—they're called that because they look like the leaves of palm. Finally, the tray should have a *genoise* or sponge layer cake with a *crème au beurre* (butter cream icing).

Whatever dessert you choose from all of the possibilities, be sure that it will complement the meal you have just eaten, and don't be afraid to experiment a bit with new flavors or new combinations.

Jean-Jacques Rachou is Chef-Propriétaire of Le Lavandou.

ON ITALIAN CUISINE *by Mario Giani*

Italy is a land of sharp geographical and cultural divisions, and each of its regions has its own unique approach to food. True, certain characteristics are common to all, or most, of the cuisines of Italy. For example, pasta, although prepared differently in different areas, is a staple throughout the country. So are seafoods, as one would expect in a nation surrounded on three sides by water. Furthermore, slow cooking and elaborately prepared sauces are the exception in Italy, the approach to food being more direct and practical than that taken by practitioners of French *"haute cuisine."*

But there are fundamental differences among the Italian regional cuisines. For instance, food in the southern regions is prepared with olive oil, while butter is the most common cooking fat of the north. The chief southern pastas, spaghetti and macaroni, are generally made without eggs, unlike the richer, generally flat northern varieties. And in northern Italy, meat is an important supplement to seafood, while in the south it is too expensive to be served as a matter of course. Throughout Italy, the range of raw materials and styles of preparation creates a wide variety of taste experiences.

Emilia-Romagna, centered on Bologna, is the culinary capital of northern Italy, and its cuisine is superbly *ingrassamento* ("fattening"). Butter, pork fat and olive oil are all locally available and used in cooking. This is a wheat-growing area, and pasta dishes abound, *tortellini, togliatelli* and *lasagne* being the most distinctive. From the coastal area around Ravenna come the ingredients for a noble fish chowder, *brodetto.* Parmesan cheese and *prosciutto,* the flavorful ham produced here, are famous throughout the world, as is the local sausage, *mortadella.*

Florence is the capital of Tuscany, Italy's largest region. Tuscany, it is said, was baptized in wine, and the region is the birthplace of Chianti. It also produces the finest beef in Italy, and is the home of famous bean dishes, such as *zuppa di fagioli* and *riso e fagioli.*

In medieval Milan, food had political impact. You could not sit on the Milanese parliament if you did not make your own wine and bread. The regional cuisine here is closely allied to French traditions. More time is taken in preparing foods, with slow cooking and elaborate sauces being characteristic. *Osso bucco* and other veal dishes are perhaps the most celebrated Milanese specialities. Lombardy, the province where Milan is located, produces many great cheeses, Gorgonzola and Bel Paese among them.

Venice, on the Adriatic, is famous for its seafood dishes. Scampi and eel, especially, are prepared in a host of different styles. As a staple, rice replaces pasta here.

The region of Piedmont, whose capital is Turin, has no sea coast, but rice and fish dishes are plentiful there as well. Piedmont is the mountainous source of the Po River. On its plains rice is the primary grain crop. Hence rice and such fresh water fish as trout and carp are basic foods. However, the best known Piemontese products are white truffles and fontina cheese. From these is made a *fondata,* a fondue containing truffles.

Rome stands out for the care its expert chefs lavish on the dishes of all the regions of Italy. But strictly, food prepared *alla romana* is singularly robust. One native dish is *porchetta*—suckling pig roasted whole on a spit.

Italian cuisine has traveled well. In New York City, the better Italian restaurants offer cooking as rich, varied and well-prepared as any in Italy. Here, the selective diner can sample the full range of Italian cuisine—from northern *calamari* to Neopolitan *spaghetti alla marinara*—without spending a penny for air fare.

Mario Giani is a partner in The Italian Pavilion.

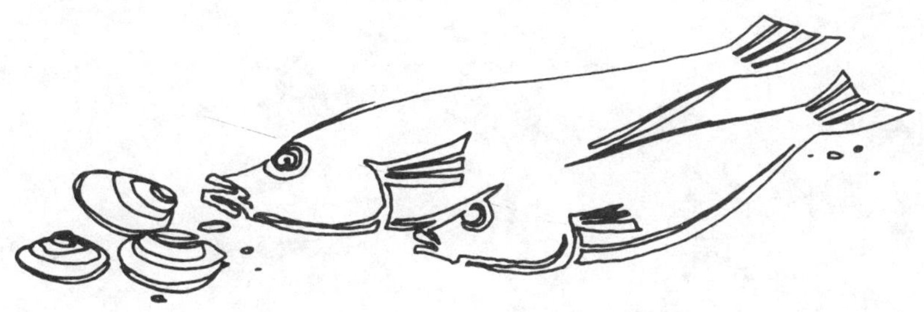

On Chinese Cuisine

By T.T. Wang & Michael Tong

Many Americans have come to associate Chinese cooking mainly with the Cantonese style of cuisine which immigrants from Canton in southern China brought to the eastern U.S. in the late 19th Century.

Even today the cuisine most frequently found in the U.S., Cantonese cooking features sweet and sour dishes, seafood specialities, dishes prepared with oyster sauce or black bean sauce, and little dumplings with a variety of fillings. These dumplings (dim sum) are an integral part of the daily routine in Canton, where people snack frequently at teahouses during the day and usually sit down to a full meal only in the evening.

Of course, Cantonese cooking is just one of many different culinary styles that are native to China.

The Mandarin and Pekinese cuisines, for example, have been developed from the basic ingredients found in the provinces of Hopeh, Shantung and Honan. In these northern areas, wheat—not rice—is the principal source of starch, while lamb and fowl provide much of the protein. Peking Duck originated here. And menus usually feature many kinds of noodles and breads. Mandarin and Pekinese dishes are generally mild, but are usually brought to the table very hot. Stewing, steaming and fire pot cooking are the favored methods of preparation.

In the eastern provinces, centered on Shanghai, rice replaces wheat as the basic grain. These are coastal areas, and so seafood, rather than poultry or red meats, makes up a substantial portion of the local diet. In these regions, dishes tend to be on the sweet side. Ingredients are usually shredded before preparation, in contrast to the custom in the north where larger pieces are served.

The major culinary regions in the west of China are Szechuan and Hunan. Hunan is rural with no large cities or restaurants. Its people are hardworking peasants with big appetites. Food there is generally cut into larger pieces than elsewhere in China and is served in one large bowl. Even the chopsticks are longer and heavier in Hunan. In both of these provinces, foods are usually highly seasoned.

Throughout China's history, food has always been very valuable. Perhaps that is why it is treated with particular respect and care. Great pains are taken to insure the eye-appeal of everything being served. Ingredients are selected not only for their taste, but for their color and texture. Food is cut and chopped into shapes that complement each other.

At home, all members of the family sit down together. There are fewer choices than at a more formal dinner—perhaps only rice and one or two other dishes along with soup. Rice is often the staple in family dining, and other things are served to add variety and flavor.

Since China is more than double the size of western Europe—in both area and population—it should be no surprise that the cuisines that have arisen there are at least as varied and complex as those to be found in the West. Just as in Europe one finds distinctively Italian, German, Russian, French and other culinary styles, so in China there are regional cuisines of equal, or even greater, diversity. Yet the rich culinary traditions of this vast and populous nation are only now being discovered in the United States.

T.T. Wang is the Proprietor and Master Chef, and Michael Tong is the Director, of the Shun Lee and Hunam Restaurants.

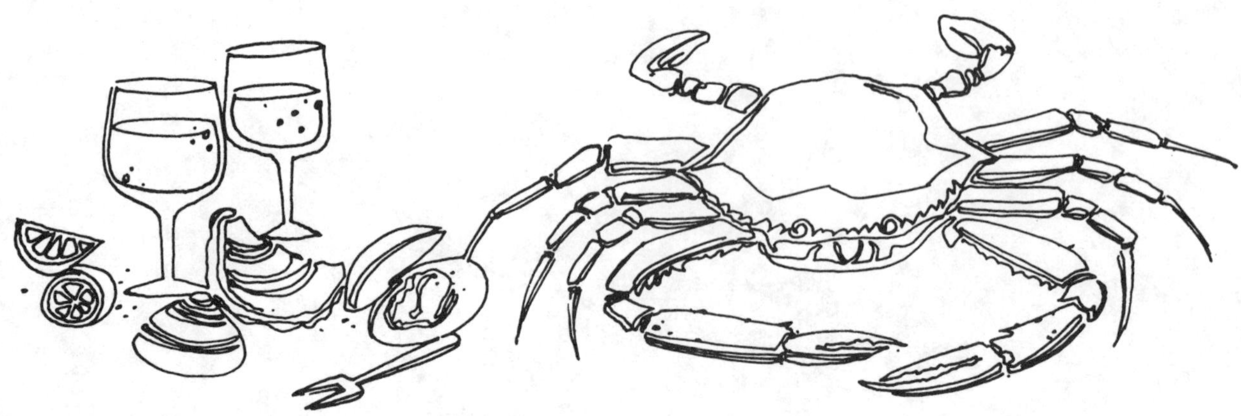

On Japanese Cuisine *by Tetsuzo Kaburaki*

Japanese cooking is beginning to be recognized in the United States as one of the major cuisines of the world. One reason is that there has been so much emphasis here in recent years on natural foods of high nutritional value.

For example, seafood has been proclaimed popularly in the West as the way to longer life and better health; but seafood has been a staple of the Japanese diet for centuries. Much of it we eat raw, or cooked very simply with salt; a stock called *dashi* (made from dried bonito) is virtually indispensable to Japanese cooking.

Another highly nutritious staple which Japanese use is the soybean. As *shoyu,* or soy sauce, it accompanies food in a number of ways—in marinades, cooking liquors, sauces and dips. In paste form it serves as a base, notably for the delicious soup known as *miso shiru.* As *tofu,* a bland custard-like cake known here as bean curd, it is excellent served with any number of sauces. Or it can be eaten plain, cooked or uncooked, and in the summer even iced.

If you went to a vegetarian restaurant in Japan, you would find soybeans transformed into likenesses of steaks, chops, patties, kebabs and other forbidden favorites.

The Japanese language is not very familiar to most westerners and so the terms we use in referring to our cooking are sometimes confusing. For example, though most westerners have come in contact with both *sashimi*—bite-sized portions of raw fish—and *sushi*—cold vinegared rice patties garnished with fish or vegetables—confusion between the two is very common. This is another reason that our cuisine is only now becoming better known in this country.

One way to understand Japanese cooking is to classify it according to cooking styles. One of the best loved Japanese dishes, *sukiyaki,* belongs to that class called *nabemono,* which literally means "pot things." Nabemono dishes correspond to casserole cookery, for everything is cooked in one pot, but there are differences. Nabemono dishes are cooked at the table and are usually simmered rather than baked.

Another nabemono dish is *shabu shabu.* Thin slices of beefsteak, followed by assorted vegetables including Chinese cabbage and mushrooms, are held with chopsticks and passed through a simmering broth of chicken or dashi (the soft swishing sound that results is what gives the dish its name) and then dipped in a soy-based sauce flavored with sesame or lemon or lime. The nabemono category also includes a popular chicken dish, *tori mizutaki,* and a seafood dish called *yosenabe.*

In the *agemono* ("fried things") group the favorite among many westerners is tempura. Just about any food may be used to make tempura: shrimp, squid, fish, mushrooms, peppers, eggplant or your own specialty. I like to use a blend of sesame, olive and camellia oils for the deep frying, but ordinary vegetable oil may be used. It is a combination of the light batter and the light frying at just the right temperature that gives this dish its wonderful delicacy, which is then enhanced by the dipping sauce. Interestingly, tempura came into our cuisine from the Portuguese.

Tofu makes an appearance in the agemono family as *agedofu,* and meats, fish and vegetables skewered on bamboo before deep-frying are called *kushiage.*

Yakimono, the "broiled things," include *yakitori* (in Japan the birds are often sparrows) and various kinds of *teriyaki*—chicken, pork and beef broiled in a delicious sauce made with *mirin,* a kind of sweet sake. A popular summer favorite in Japan is *kabayaki,* broiled eels, also in sweet sauce. Another kind of yakimono is *teppanyaki,* or meat and vegetables cooked on a metal grill.

In the noodle group—*menrui*—there are many different kinds and, like tofu, they appear with an astonishing variety of soups, sauces and garnishes, as well as plain, hot and cold. *Soba,* the most common variety, is perhaps the most popular lunch food in Japan, and there are soba shops everywhere catering to office workers. You can buy soba here; it makes a delicious and quick meal at home.

But it is rice—*gohan*—without which no Japanese meal is complete. It is most commonly served steamed and accompanies other dishes. However, it can be a meal in itself, cooked in an individual pot with vegetables, fish and meat, as *kamameshi.* Another such complete dish is *oyako* (mother and child) *domburi,* referring to rice served with chicken and egg.

Sake and beer are considered ideal accompaniments to a Japanese meal, and fruit a natural way to end the meal. And if you should overdo, there is a natural digestive remedy in *umeboshi,* a small, sour, shriveled plum.

Tetsuzo Kaburaki is the Manager of Inagiku.

ON INDIAN CUISINE by Jati Hoon

The tradition of Indian cooking is 5,000 years old, and in those 5,000 years Indian chefs have created what can be called the ultimate in health foods. You may not have ever thought of Indian foods in this way but it is true. Spices are important to Indian cooking not only because of the delicacy of their flavor but also because of their therapeutic value. The spices of Indian food are chosen for their taste, their aroma and, no less importantly, for their nutritive value. In the hot climate of India, it is vital that the food be easily digested as well as delicious. Spices, when mixed with food during the cooking process, chemically react in the digestive system, producing natural juices which help to maintain the normal functioning of the body.

Each spice is selected to correspond to a particular need of the body. For instance, saffron *(kesar)* which is sometimes called the king of spices, has more than just its delicate flavor and rich golden color to give to food. In India, saffron is used to treat colds. Cumin *(zeera)* which is often used in Indian cooking—in cookies, rice and with *dal* (lentils)—stimulates the appetite and the digestive system. Cardamom *(elaichi)* is added to many meat dishes and to some sweets; a tincture of cardamom is used to treat stomach upsets. Practically any Indian food that you will eat will have tumeric *(haldi)* in it—it is essential to curry. Tumeric has a preserving quality and is often used in Indian medicines. Everyone knows how much ginger can add to the flavor of a dish but it may come as a surprise to many that ginger mixed with tea and honey can cure a cold. I don't know why, but it always seems to work. Indian herbs—coriander leaves *(dhanyia)* and mint *(pudeena)*—also have healthful properties as well as exquisite taste and aroma.

Although many people characterize Indian food as spicy—or hot—this is definitely not true. In the south of India, where the climate is particularly tropical, the spices are used in greater quantity than in the north but still spices must *never* overpower an Indian dish in the south or north. The art of Indian cooking is the balancing of herbs and spices so one will never dominate; without a perfect balance, a dish is destroyed.

Indian food is naturally low in fat and high in protein. All meat that is used in Indian cooking is extremely lean. Yogurt, which is to Indian cooking as wine is to French cooking, provides a great deal of protein and is used in the preparation of practically any Indian meal you might have. Besides yogurt, one of the most important ingredients in Indian cooking is *ghee* or clarified butter. It is healthier than plain butter because it is both sediment-and-salt-free. Ghee also has a higher burning point than other oils and enables Indian chefs to fry food quickly at a high heat, avoiding the absorption of much of the oil. The vegetable oil that is most popular in India is mustard oil; it also has a high burning point and is good for the sinuses.

Since Indian cooking is somewhat of a mystery to many westerners, it may be wise to explain something about the kinds of food you will find in India or in an Indian restaurant in the United States, and about the way these foods are prepared. Indian food is not served in courses as western food is—all dishes are brought to the table at once and the diner decides on his own what he wants to eat and when. Most meals will include meat or poultry and/or a vegetable dish, rice, bread, a salad, pickles and chutneys and sweets. A majority of Indians are vegetarians and many of those who are not are restricted in the kinds of meat they may eat. You will never find beef in an authentic Indian restaurant but you will be able to enjoy lamb or chicken. Spices and herbs are used to bring out the best in the meat or poultry. I know a chef who used to say that he used spices to "wake the bird;" if he tasted the chicken and something was not right with the flavor, he would say: "the bird is sleeping."

Of course, most westerners think of curry when they think of Indian food. This is because the English chose curried dishes as their favorites. A curry is simply a stew with a sauce, and any meat or vegetable can be prepared in the curry style. Each curry has its own very special blend of spices and the idea of pre-mixed curry powder is out of the question. It is unheard of in India.

To my mind, the best way to prepare meat or poultry is in the tandoori—the unique barrel-shaped clay oven which uses white-hot charcoal and gives food cooked "tandoori" a special flavor derived from charcoal and the smoky fragrance of the clay. Tandoori chicken (chicken breasts and legs marinated for at least twelve hours in yogurt, herbs and spices and then put on a skewer and lowered into the tandoori pit) is, to me, the most delicious chicken of all. Chicken prepared in this way, and then served in a sauce prepared with tomatoes, ghee, yogurt, onions, coriander, tumeric, etc., is called *chicken tikka masala* and is also excellent.

Meat is often prepared as a kebab, a style of cooking which came to India from Central Asia. *Seekh kebab* is a popular version of this dish. To make it, ground lamb is marinated with yogurt, black pepper, green chilies, onions, coriander and cumin for twelve hours. It is then skewered and cooked over the coals of the tandoori. *Kofta* is ground meat, also marinated and rolled into a ball shape. *Kofta masala* is a delicious blend of ground meat balls in a flavorful sauce with onions, coriander, cumin, tumeric, cayenne and ginger.

Indian chefs can work magic with vegetables. The same vegetables can be cooked in a variety of ways—in the form of a curry, tandoori style, as *raita* (in a salad with yogurt) or even as a sweet. The most common vegetables in India are cauliflower, eggplant, tomatoes (introduced to India by traders in the 16th century), potatoes and green peas.

One type of vegetable in particular, lentils or *dal,* is extremely important to the Indian diet. All Indians eat dal; they may prepare it differently in different regions, but it is almost always on the table when Indians eat. Dal is an excellent source of protein and therefore especially important to vegetarians. Two excellent Indian vegetable dishes are *sag paneer* (spinach with cheese) and *bahar e paneer.* Sag paneer is fresh spinach leaves (all vegetables must be fresh in Indian cooking), spiced and deep-fried in ghee with small pieces of *paneer* or Indian-style cottage cheese; Bahar e paneer is a mixture of several vegetables cooked with cheese and nuts.

Pomfret, a flat fish from Bombay Bay, is a very tasty and popular Indian fish. It is good when prepared tandoori or it may also be fried. Jumbo shrimp or lobster can be prepared either tandoori or in a curry style.

Indian breads are unleavened and they all must be served hot. Some of the most popular are *naan,* a rather rich bread made of white flour in an oblong shape; *paratha,* a whole wheat bread popular in northern and central India which is made of dough that is rolled over and over again with ghee and then baked in the tandoori by slapping it on the wall; *alloo paratha,* paratha that is covered with cooked potatoes; onion *kulcha,* a bread with cooked onions inside; and *chapati,* a round flat bread made of whole wheat. It is said that the lighter and larger the chapati, the better the cook.

Rice is important to any Indian meal—especially in southern and central India—and the best rice of all is *basmati* rice which is grown in the Dehradun valley region of northwest India. It is long-grained, has a distinctive aroma and tastes better the longer it ages. Basmati rice is used to make *pullau*—rice that is fried in ghee and then simmered in liquid with saffron and other spices. Chicken, lamb, shrimp or vegetables may be added to pullau, making it almost a meal in itself—known as *biriyani.*

The most popular Indian salad of all is a *raita*—a yogurt salad made with chopped or shredded vegetables. One of the most refreshing raitas is made with cucumbers. Both pickles and chutneys are eaten as accompaniments to Indian food—usually with meat and vegetable dishes—and are served separately. Anything may be pickled but lime and mango pickles seem to be the favorite of most westerners. Pickles are hot and sour; chutney is sweet and sour. Mango and tomato chutneys are quite popular in the United States.

Sweets are very much a part of Indian cuisine but they are quite unlike most western desserts. One of the most delicious is *rasmalai*—homemade Indian cottage cheese in a ball-shape, served with a heavy cream and sugar syrup. The taste is subtle and not at all heavy. Another favorite is *bessan barfi,* squares that are made with chick pea flour (bessan) and pistachios, fried and sprinkled with rose water. Westerners may be surprised to find that some desserts are topped with incredibly thin sheets of silver foil. This silver foil, lighter than you can imagine, is meant not only to be decorative, but to be eaten, since it adds important minerals to the diet.

Indian food is quite different from western food and the differences are deliberate. One thing that Indian cooking demands from a diner is patience. No real Indian food can be prepared instantly. It must be made carefully and each dish may take hours. It is possible now, with technological advances, for restaurants to speed the process somewhat, but unless it takes 45 minutes for your meal to arrive in an Indian restaurant, you should be suspicious of its authenticity.

Indian cooking has been carefully developed over the years to provide food that is both healthy and delicious. Just one Indian meal will prove to you that food does not have to be uninteresting or bland to be good for you.

Jati Hoon is the owner of Gaylord (India) Restaurant.

On The American Steak House

by Leon and Stanley Lobel

America's unique contribution to the culinary arts is the beef-based diet developed on the western plains during the last century. The early colonists brought cattle to this country to provide both meat and dairy products. The quality of the meat was secondary to the hardiness of the breed and to its ability to serve the dual purpose.

Through generations of animal husbandry, however, beef quality was vastly improved. First the distinction was made between meat-producing breeds and dairy breeds. Next, selective breeding was used to improve yield and quality. Finally, cattle were taken off the range and fattened in feed lots on carefully contrived diets, based mostly on corn. As a result, the beef available in America came to be of immensely better quality than was ever before possible.

Unfortunately, not all beef purveyed in this country today is of a superior grade. So the merits of a Steak House depend to a large extent on the quality of the beef it serves. How, then, does the diner determine if a particular Steak House rates top marks?

First, the best Steak House will serve "prime" beef. Prime is the highest quality rating assigned by the U.S. Department of Agriculture. Prime beef comes only from steers weighing 900 to 1,300 pounds and slaughtered at an age of one to one and one half years. In view of the fact that a 1,000 pound steer yields only 75 pounds of steak, prime beef is scarce and expensive. If the restauranteur serves meat of this quality, you can be sure he'll let you know by so stating on his menu.

Second, the knowledgeable and responsible restauranteur will go to the market to select his own beef from the wholesaler and will age it himself, as these steps assure maximum quality control. Aging firms the meat's texture and permits natural enzymes to "tenderize" tougher portions. (Properly aged beef is beef that has been stored at temperatures ranging from 34 to 38 degrees for a period of from three to six weeks.) The better Steak Houses conform to commonly accepted nomenclature in describing their meat cuts. Look for standard names such as porterhouse, T-bone, filet mignon, shell, sirloin, club, etc. (New York strip or Kansas City strip are simply shell steaks by other names.) Beware of nonconformist or "cute" names. They are often used to disguise inferior cuts or grades.

Finally, to be doubly reassured, the diner might ask to see the specific steak which is to be served to him. A really good restaurant will not object to such a request. A prime steak will be marbled, with a fine skein of fat interlacing the red meat. (Lesser grades have coarser marbling indicating that the steer was overfed or overaged when slaughtered.) Prime beef will also be firm and fine textured with a thin layer of outside fat which is closer to white than to yellow in color.

If a Steak House meets these standards, the diner can be reasonably sure that the meal set before him will be a good one.

The Lobel Brothers, authors of Meat *and* All About Meat, *are the Proprietors of M. Lobel & Sons, Inc.*

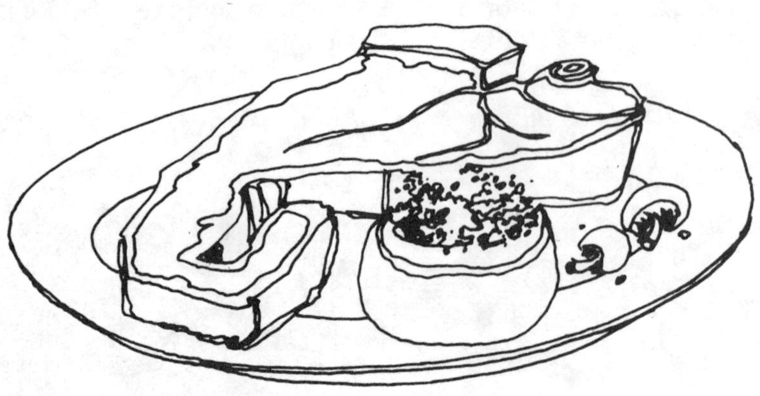

ON SPANISH CUISINE *by Jose Perez*

If someone were to ask me to give them a taste of Spain—of the *cocina* of Spain—in just one meal, I would choose a menu like this: I'd begin with *chorizos*—sliced and broiled. Chorizos is a pork sausage flavored with paprika, garlic and oregano and served everywhere in Spain. For a soup course I would choose one we make at our restaurant called Galician soup from my home region of Galicia. This hearty soup is made with beef, pork and vegetables, including mustard greens.

And for the main course—what else but *paella*, probably the most famous Spanish dish of all. Paella, which was actually created in Valencia, is now thoroughly Spanish and has crossed all provincial boundaries. The ingredients of a paella may vary considerably from place to place, but the one I would serve to someone wanting "a taste of Spain" would be made with chicken, shrimp, clams, scallops, chorizos, pepper, garlic, tomatoes—all cooked in a broth of saffron, chicken, onions and green peppers—and served on rice. As a drink, I'd offer either *sangria* (a red wine and fruit punch) or a dry white wine, and for dessert I'd serve *natillas*, a soft vanilla custard made with milk, eggs, sugar and cinnamon. After dessert I'd pour a coffee and with the coffee, *licor cuaremta y tres*—an orange-flavored liqueur made with 43 different herbs.

After enjoying a meal like this, my guest would understand some of the subtleties of Spanish cooking and would have enjoyed some of the most popular tastes of Spain. He or she would understand, too, after a meal like this, that the reputation Spanish food has for being spicy is undeserved—Mexican food is spicy and is often confused with Spanish food by people who have never been to Spain.

Like most of the countries of the world, Spain's cooking varies from region to region. Although certain ingredients are used everywhere—garlic, olive oil, seafood, green peas, chick peas, tomatoes—they appear in different combinations and are used differently depending on where you go in Spain.

It is usual for Americans who travel to Spain to spend most of their time in its capital city of Madrid, in the Castile region of the country. Since Madrid is such a cosmopolitan city, the cooking of Madrid represents the cooking of the entire country. *Madrileños* have their choice of restaurants that serve food from all the regions of the country, and one could sample the food of all of Spain if one had enough time to explore the restaurants of Madrid.

One of the favorites of the Madrileños is lamb and one of the finest dishes you can enjoy in Madrid is *costillas de cordero asadas*—a rack of lamb marinated in lemon, white wine, oil, garlic and oregano and then barbecued. Or, if you prefer a boiled dinner, you can order the *cocido madrileño*, a mixture of beef, chick peas *(garbanzos)*, cabbage, sausages and potatoes. Every part of Spain has its own favorite way of preparing cocido. Tripe is popular, too, in Madrid, and *callos a la madrileña*—tripe sauteed in olive oil with the spice *cominos* and paprika—often appears on menus. The restaurants of Madrid serve seafood from the North—the crabs *(centolla)*, lobsters *(langosta)*, shrimp *(gambas)* and hake *(merluza)* of Galicia that are the finest in the world.

Madrileños might have their large meal in the afternoon (*almuerzo*) between 1:00 pm and 3:00 pm or at night (*cena*) at 9:00 pm or 10:00 pm. At other times when they get hungry they like to stop at the bars and cafes that serve sherry or wine and *tapas*—appetizers. Tapas are popular everywhere in Spain—the variety is endless but two of the most popular are *gambas a la plancha* (grilled shrimp) and fried *calamares* (squid).

A visitor to Andalusia, the region of southern Spain where Seville, Cadiz, Cordoba and Granada are located, would find that here the sun is at its hottest and brightest. That is why in Andalusia the cooking is also the lightest of the entire country. Andalusians eat salads and lightly fried seafoods, and they are the ones who have created one of the best-known and most refreshing dishes —*gazpacho*. Gazpacho is a soup made from seeded tomatoes, garlic, oil, salt, bread, wine vinegar and water and is served chilled with cucumbers and green peppers as a garnish.

The east coast of Spain is called the Levante from the verb which means "to rise." This is the land of the sunrise—a land of rice and oranges and lemons; Valencia is its best known city and paella its best known dish. Paella began as a poor man's creation and has evolved into a rich man's delight. Originally it was cooked out-of-doors and with vegetables and rice. Traditionally it is eaten right from the pan—the paella.

Catalonia, the part of Spain which includes the Costa Brava and the city of Barcelona, has excellent seafood to offer visitors. Here you can enjoy *calamares a la plancha* and a tasty white fish called *rape* (rah-pay). In Catalonia, too, you can taste *sobrasada*, a soft sausage that is spread on bread and eaten as an appetizer.

To the west of Catalonia is the Basque country, which is well known for its cooking, and especially its sauces. *Bacalao,* or salt cod cooked *al pil-pil* or in oil and garlic, is a popular dish from this part of Spain. In San Sebastian, the largest city of the Basque provinces, visitors can buy seafood cooked right at the harbor—it is delicious.

Galicia, in the northwest corner of Spain, north of Portugal, is where you can find my own favorite—*cocido gallego*—the Galician version of a boiled dinner. This includes smoked ham, sausages, the head of a pig, chick peas, cabbage and potatoes. It is served in restaurants and is popular at home, too. Other specialties of the area are *lacon congrelos*—the foreleg of a pig boiled with mustard greens and potatoes—and *pulpo a la feria* (octopus) which is cooked, served and eaten at an outdoor market and is at its best when enjoyed with a glass of red wine.

The cooking of Spain is honest cooking. Whether you sit down to a Spanish meal in New York, in Madrid or in Barcelona, you can expect that Spanish food will be prepared in such a way as to bring out the best of its natural flavor.

Jose Perez is the Proprietor of El Faro.

On Wine *by Paul Kovi*

To my mind, wine is one of the most beautiful and complex expressions of nature. A great wine has a life span not unlike that of man. It begins as an unformed mass, then slowly, through maturation, develops a distinctive and multi-faceted personality which, after a period of time, fades away.

Fine restauranteurs recognize wine not only as an alcoholic beverage, but as a food—one which must be handled with care, love and restraint. When served in combination with other foods the effect can be synergistic—resulting in an orchestration of taste which is unsurpassable in nature. Just think of the combination of freshly shucked oysters and a glass of bone-dry Chablis, or a beautifully roasted duckling, its skin brought to a crackling crispness, accompanied by a glass of full-bodied Chambertin. This is sheer beauty and pleasure.

It is most satisfying to see the growing importance and beauty of the wines of California. I would like to pay particular tribute to our California vintners for their almost religious love of wine making and their obsession with perfection. The fine soil and sun provide ideal conditions which, when combined with the devotion of these California vintners, give us wines that do not have to take second position to any in the world. This does not necessarily mean that they are better than the noble French wines, merely different. The differences arise from the quality of the soil, the microclimate in which the grapes grow, and the method of vinification, all of which are expressed in what I call the "style" of the wine.

The glorified wine tastings which seem to give so much prestige to one wine while taking away previously earned honors from some others are misdirected. It must be understood that the best qualified, most honestly intentioned tasters will judge the wines according to the impression created at that particular moment only. Often they praise wines which have a big "punch" rather than those which have a refined subtlety and a noble character but are not particularly endowed with a "fighting virtue."

My feeling is that a restauranteur should carry one or two wines at a very reasonable price, to make them available to all, and several medium-priced wines that are good buys. Then if he charges $100 or even more for a particular wine of great reputation and outstanding vintage, it is understandable. Great, great wines are like diamonds. They can add an extra-special joy to those few, really unforgettable days in one's lifetime.

Paul Kovi, a recipient of The Medaille d'Honneur de Committee National des Vins de France, and a member of The Jurade de Saint Emilion, is co-owner of The Four Seasons.

In a constantly changing world, we don't.

Authentic.

DEWAR'S®

"White Label"®

Call it Dewar's or "White Label," you'll get the same great Scotch that never varies.

BLENDED SCOTCH WHISKY • 86.8 PROOF • ©SCHENLEY IMPORTS CO., N. Y., N. Y.

ALPHABETICAL INDEX

France's idea of a cocktail since 1846.

"Dubonnet"

Dubonnet Aperitif Wines. Product of U.S.A. Dubonnet Co., N.Y., N.Y. © 1977

BY CUISINE

BY LOCATION

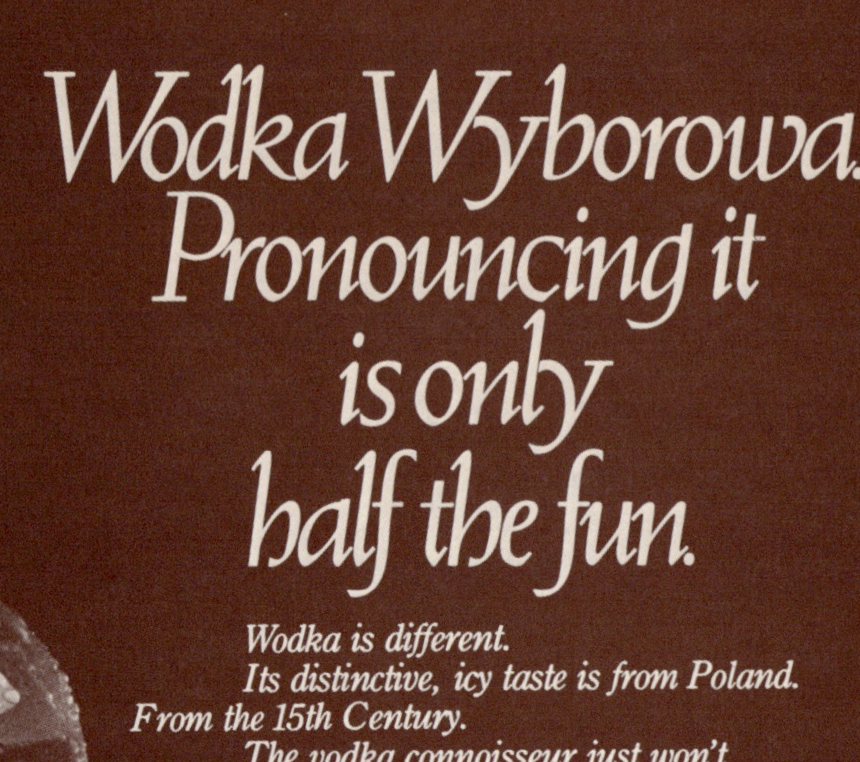

Wodka is different.
Its distinctive, icy taste is from Poland. From the 15th Century.
The vodka connoisseur just won't settle for anything less than the taste of Wodka.
The colder, the better. Straight. Or in a crystal clear martini.
Instead of vodka, ask for Wodka.

Wodka Wyborowa (Vib-a-rova) from Poland. Instead of Vodka.

Imported by Schenley Imports Co., N.Y. 80 and 100 Proof © 1977.

BY DRESS REQUIRED

BY SPECIAL MENU, ETC.

*After-theatre only
**Pre-theatre only
***Both pre- and after-theatre

Restaurants Serving Breakfast

Restaurants Serving Afternoon Tea

LATE DINING (RESTAURANTS SERVING MEALS AFTER 1:00 A.M.)

Weekends only

PARTY FACILITIES

RESTAURANTS WITH ENTERTAINMENT

Restaurants With Dancing

FREE PARKING

d = discount

OPEN SUNDAYS

**Evening only*
***Brunch/Lunch only*

RESTAURANTS WITH OUTSIDE CATERING FACILITIES

ROOFTOP, GARDEN AND OUTDOOR CAFE RESTAURANTS

r=rooftop
g=garden
c=outdoor cafe

INDEX TO WINE TERMS

INDEX TO CHEFS' ASSOCIATIONS AND HONORS

INDEX TO PASTRY DEFINITIONS

French

German

Italian

INDEX TO CHEESE DEFINITIONS

INDEX TO WINE DEFINITIONS

ACT I

Address: 1 Times Square
Location: 42nd Street at Broadway and Seventh Avenue
Telephone: 695-1880
Credit Cards: AE; V; DC; MC
Reservations: Recommended
Hours: 11:30 AM to 11:00 PM Monday thru Saturday
Days Closed: Sundays and major holidays
Liquor: Full bar service; "Front Row" Cocktail Lounge
Recommended or Listed in: Cue; Where
Maitre d': Flynn Rivenbark
Seating Capacity: 110
Cuisine: American and English
Specialties of the House: Ribs of Beef with Yorkshire Pudding; Flaming Duck a l'Orange
Entertainment: Live music and dancing

Act I is situated on the 15th and 16th floors of the old New York Times Building and offers, especially after dark, an exciting view of Times Square, midtown New York and the Hudson River. The decor is that of a well-run British pub in the days of Queen Victoria. Act I is conveniently located for pre-curtain dining and the intimate cocktail lounge on the 15th floor offers live music and dancing nightly.

LUNCHEON MENU

(a la carte)

(Representative of four luncheon menus offered on a rotating basis.)

APPETIZERS & SOUPS:
Homemade French Onion Soup au Gratin (.95); Fresh Fruit Cocktail (.95); Today's Freshly Prepared Soup (.95); Chilled Tomato Juice (.75); Gulf Coast Shrimp Cocktail (3.25).

ENTREES:
Filet Mignonette Claridge 5.95
(Tenderloin Steak with Maitre d'Hotel Butter)
Swedish Meat Balls 4.75
(Served with Buttered Noodles)
Roast Top Sirloin of Beef au Jus 5.95
Filet of Schrod 4.95
Chopped Sirloin Steak 5.75
French Fried Gulf Shrimp 6.80
Broiled 10 oz Sirloin Strip Steak 8.25
Sliced Turkey Divan 4.70
(Breast of Turkey and Asparagus Spears topped with Sherry Sauce)
Quiche Lorraine 3.95
Hot Roast Beef Sandwich 4.60
Caribbean Chicken Salad 4.95
(Creamy Chicken Salad with Pineapple Sticks and Strawberries)
Act I Salad Bowl 4.80
(Julienne Turkey, Ham and Muenster Cheese)
Fruit 'n Cheese Salad with Lime French Dressing 4.70

(Hot entrees include a choice of potato or vegetable, salad and loaf of bread.)

(A variety of sandwiches is available from 4.30 to 5.35.)

DESSERTS:
A dessert menu is available which includes daily specialties.

(Luncheon is also served in the Cocktail Lounge, Monday thru Friday. The special "Front Row" menu includes entrees, sandwiches and salads at prices ranging from 3.20 to 6.00.)

continued on next page

Act I

DINNER MENU

(a la carte)

APPETIZERS & SOUPS:
Fresh Fruit Cocktail (1.25); French Onion Soup Gratinee (1.75); Herring Filets in Sour Cream (1.75); Gulf Shrimp de Jonghe (3.95); Clams Casino (3.95); Tureen of Soup (.95); Crabmeat Cocktail (3.95); Chicken Livers wrapped in Bacon (2.25); Assorted Canapes for Two (4.50); Shrimp Cocktail (4.25).

ENTREES:
Roast Prime Ribs of Beef au Jus with Yorkshire Pudding 11.95
Baked Stuffed Rainbow Trout Filled with Shrimp and mild Seafood 9.75
Fresh Fish of the Day 9.25
Filet Mignon a la Henri IV Topped with a Bearnaise-filled Artichoke 13.50
14 oz New York Strip Steak 13.50
Broiled Spring Lamb Chops 12.95
Steak a la Maison with Cognac Mustard Sauce 14.50
Shish Kebab with Curry Sauce 10.50
(Marinated Spring Lamb, Bacon and Green Pepper)
Sea 'n Shore Grill .... (...)
(Filet Mignonette and Lobster Tail)
English Mixed Grill 10.95
(Broiled Lamb Chop with Sauteed Calf's Liver and Crisp Bacon Slices)
Lobster Tails with Drawn Butter .... (...)
(Entrees include a choice of potato or vegetable, salad and a loaf of bread.)

DESSERTS:
A dessert menu is available which includes daily specialties.

(Complete dinners are also available at 9.95.)

BARQUETTES AUX MARRON: *These pastries are in the shape of little row boats. They are made from a pâte sucrée or sweet dough and are filled with chestnut cream mixed with pure butter and a drop of rum. On top, there's an icing of chocolate.*

ADAM'S RIB

Address: 23 East 74th Street
Location: 74th Street between Madison Avenue and Fifth Avenue
Telephone: 535-2112
Credit Cards: AE; DC; CB; MC; V
Reservations: Recommended
Hours: Lunch from 12:00 Noon to 3:00 PM, Monday thru Saturday; Dinner from 5:00 PM to 11:00 PM, Monday thru Saturday; from 4:30 PM to 10:30 PM, Sunday
Days Closed: None
Liquor: Full Bar Service
Recommended or listed in: Cue; New York Times; New York Magazine
Maitre d': Robert
Seating Capacity: 80
Cuisine: American
Specialties of the House: Prime Ribs of Beef; Chicken Kiev; Alaskan King Crab Snug Harbor

This is a simple restaurant, run by one man, N. A. Nicholas. His philosophy: serve the best. Always. The menu is limited. The reason is a belief in superb quality. One cannot prepare everything well. The non-beef entrees are frankly a compromise. Order one only if you are unable to enjoy roast beef. It's Prime Ribs of Beef that this restaurant is famous for.

LUNCHEON MENU
(a la carte)

APPETIZERS & SOUPS:
Onion Soup Gratinee (1.75); Shrimp Cocktail (3.75).

ENTREES:
Chef Salad Bowl 4.75
Gourmet Seafood Salad 5.95
Omelettes 3.95
(Cheese, Ham, Bacon, Onions or Combination)
Quiche Lorraine with Caesar Salad 5.50
Sandwiches 2.95
(Grilled Bacon and Cheddar, Ham and Swiss Cheese, Turkey Club, Roast Beef)
Roast Beef Sandwich Special 4.75
Old Fashioned Steak Sandwich 4.75
Caesar Salad 3.75
Roast Prime Ribs of Beef, au Jus ..... 8.25 & 10.50
Prime Rib Steak 10.50
London Broil with Mushroom Sauce and Grilled Tomato 6.25
Breast of Chicken Kiev 5.95
Seafood Crepes Mornay 7.95
Supreme of Chicken Marechale 5.95
King Crab Snug Harbor 7.95
Broiled Filet of Lemon Sole 8.50

DESSERTS:
Chocolate Pie Suisse (1.60); Peach Combinage Bavarian Cream (1.60); Sedutto's French Ice Cream (1.60).

DINNER MENU
(a la carte)

ENTREES:
Roast Prime Ribs of Beef au Jus ..... 9.25 & 11.50
(Served with Yorkshire Pudding, Fresh Broiled Mushrooms and a Horseradish Sauce)
Prime Rib Steak 11.50
Broiled Filet of Lemon Sole 9.50
South African Lobster Tails 12.95
Breast of Chicken Kiev 6.95
King Crab Snug Harbor 8.95
Supreme of Chicken Marechale 6.95
Seafood Crepes Mornay 8.95
Shrimp on a Skewer 8.95
(All entrees are served with Caesar Salad, Loaf of Hot Bread and Baked Potato with Butter and/or Sour Cream and Chives.)

DESSERTS:
Chocolate Pie Suisse (1.60); Sedutto's French Ice Cream (1.60); Peach Combinage Bavarian Cream (1.60).

AKBAR INDIAN RESTAURANT

Address: 475 Park Avenue
Location: Park Avenue at 57th Street
Telephone: 838-1717 or 838-1718
Credit Cards: AE; V ; DC; MC; CB
Hours: Lunch from 11:30 AM to 3:00 PM; Dinner from 5:30 PM to 11:00 PM
Days Closed: Closed for lunch on Sundays
Liquor: Full bar service
Recommended or Listed in: New York Times; New York Post; Gourmet; Cue; WQXR Radio; New York Magazine
Seating Capacity: 100
Cuisine: Indian
Specialties of the House: Chicken Ginger Kebab; Prawn Kebab, Chicken Patiala; Chicken Tikka Muglai; Sag Meat
Party Facilities: Private room; capacity: 40

The specialty at Akbar is the Muglai cuisine of Northern India and, in fact, this fine restaurant has brought many Muglai dishes to New York for the first time. The dining room is appropriately Indian in decor and motif. A stained glass ceiling and stained glass portraits are much in evidence while white beams and mirrors lend expansiveness to the dimly lit room. The soft Indian music is pleasant and unobtrusive.

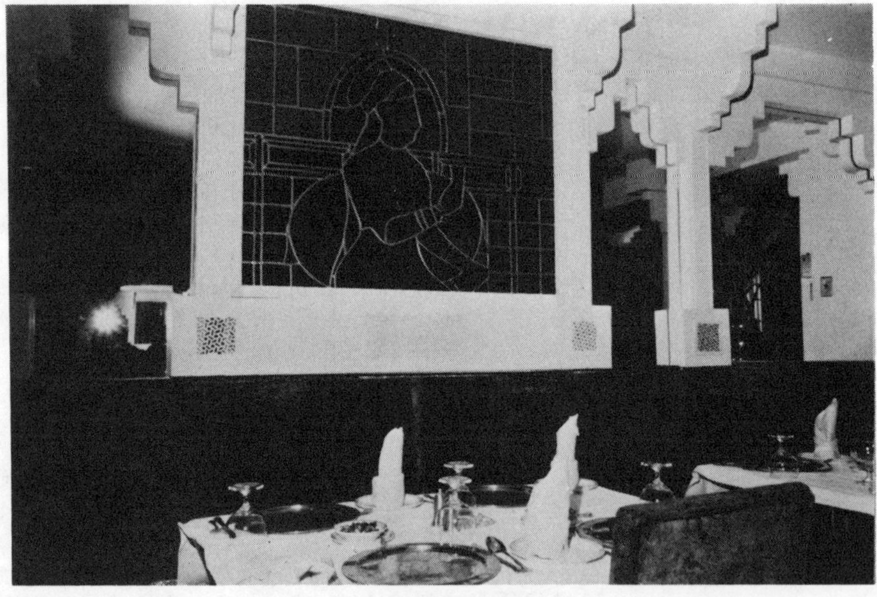

Akbar Indian Restaurant

DINNER MENU

(a la carte)

(Akbar offers an extensive selection of Indian dishes. The following are representative.)

APPETIZERS & SOUPS:
Special Hors d'Oeuvres: (Chicken Tikka, Seekh Kebab, Samosa,Pakora, Papadum) (2.95); Vegetable Samosa (Crisp spiced patties with vegetable stuffing) (1.25); Chicken Pakora (Delicately spiced and deep fried chicken fritters) (2.50); Vegetable Pakora (Fritters stuffed with assorted vegetables) (1.50); Alu Chat (Potatoes and onions marinated in a tangy sauce) (1.50); Tomato Soup (1.50); Bombay Shorba (Tasty broth garnished with diced chicken) (1.50).

ENTREES:

Shrimp Bhuna 6.95
(Shrimp cooked in specially selected herbs and spices with a touch of ginger and garlic)

Fish Begum Behar 5.50
(Fish cooked in delicately prepared spices and fresh cream)

Fish Masala 5.50
(Fish with mildly spiced gravy)

Tandoori Chicken .... (Full) 6.50

Tandoori Chicken .... (Half) 3.75
(Chicken marinated in yogurt and mild spices, roasted in our traditional clay oven)

Chicken Ginger Kebab 5.25
(Succulent portions of tender chicken roasted in our Tandoor)

Chicken Masala 4.95
(Delectable chicken cooked in mild spices and gravy)

Boti Kebab 5.25
(Cubed leg of lamb roasted in our clay oven)

Seekh Kebab 5.25
(Minced lamb with onions and herbs roasted on skewers)

Mixed Grill 7.25
(Assorted Tandoori varieties)

Fish Tikka 5.25
(Cubes of fish roasted on special Indian grill)

Prawn Kebab 7.95
(King size prawns roasted with Indian spices)

Chicken Tikka 5.25
(Boned chicken marinated with spices and fresh cream)

Chicken Patiala 4.95
(Chicken with Indian spices and fresh cream)

Chicken Makhani 4.95
(Pieces of tandoori chicken with butter and mild gravy)

Chicken Tikka Masala 5.25
(Tandoori diced chicken in mild gravy & Indian spices)

Rara Meat 5.25
(Lamb cubes cooked in freshly ground spices and tomato gravy)

Lamb Pasanda 5.25
(Lamb marinated in yogurt and spices and cooked in cream sauce)

Sag Meat 5.25
(Tender lamb cooked in delicate spices with creamed spinach)

Lamb Vindaloo 5.25
(Highly spiced lamb in a sharp and tangy sauce)

DESSERTS:

Rasmalai (Sweet made from Cottage Cheese & Milk sprinkled with Rose Water)(1.50); Kulfi (Authentic Indian Ice Cream with Saffron and Nuts delicately flavoured) (1.50); Selection from Trolley (Two pieces) (1.50).

(A variety of Indian breads, rice specialties and vegetarian entrees are also offered.)

(Complete luncheons priced from 4.00 to 4.95 are available every day except Sunday.)

ALSATIAN: *Fragrant, dry, usually white wines from an ancient French province bordering the Rhine. Alsatian wines are usually shipped in green "flutes" – tall, slender bottles like those used in the nearby Moselle Valley of Germany.*

AMONTILLADO: *The most popular of the Spanish sherries, with an unmistakably nutty bouquet and flavor. The unique flavor is said to mimic that of the wines of Montilla, in the province of Cordoba; hence, the name.*

BARDOLINO: *A very light Italian red wine, almost a rośe in color, produced near the town of the same name close by Verona in northeastern Italy. This wine is usually drunk quite young (one to three years old) and has a charming, fruity flavor.*

BAROLO: *Considered one of the great European wines, this powerful, deep-colored Italian red is produced in Piemonte, the Italian province closest to France. Sometimes heavily sedimented (even after three years in a cask) this wine is stored standing up, in "Burgundy" bottles.*

ALFREDO, "THE ORIGINAL OF ROME"

Address: 152 East 53rd Street
Location: The Atrium at the Market Place, Citicorp Center
Telephone: 371-3367
Credit Cards: AE; V; DC; MC
Hours: 11:30 AM to 11:30 PM, daily
Days Closed: None
Liquor: Full bar service
Seating Capacity: 164
Cuisine: Italian
Specialty of the House: Fettuccine Alfredo

Fettuccine Alfredo is one of the most popular menu choices at New York's Italian restaurants. Alfredo Di Lelio, whose family recipe for fettuccine elevated this flat little noodle to gastronomic stardom is, now for the first time in the United States, preparing and serving this famous dish as well as a wide variety of his other Italian specialties. All the fettuccine is made on the premises, using the same techniques perfected by Mr. Di Lelio at his well-known restaurant in Rome. Alfredo's is a sophisticated and elegant dining establishment. The style is Italian modern—combining the warm beige tones of the fabric covered walls with solid oak panelling to create a warm and inviting ambience. Given the richness of the decor and the quality of the cuisine, the moderately priced menu is a welcome and unexpected bonus to dining at Alfredo, "The Original of Rome."

MENU

(At the time of this printing, the menu for Alfredo, "The Original of Rome", had not yet been finalized. The following is representative of the restaurant's menu selections; prices are moderate.)

The world-famous "Fettuccine Alfredo"

An extensive selection of pasta dishes, made with special Alfredo sauces

Four varieties of veal dishes prepared and served with gourmet vegetables

The famous Alfredo "Golden Turkey"

Special Alfredo Roman Pizza

Alfredo Garden Salad with choice of Alfredo's special dressings

A variety of Italian pastries, ice cream and coffees

Alfredo, "The Original of Rome"

ALGONQUIN HOTEL

Address:	**59 West 44th Street**
Location:	**44th Street between Fifth Avenue and Avenue of the Americas**
Telephone:	**687-4400**
Credit Cards:	**DC; AE; CB; V; MC**
Reservations:	**Recommended**
Hours:	**Breakfast from 7:30 AM to 11:45 AM; Lunch from 12 Noon to 3:00 PM; Tea from 3:00 PM to 5:00 PM; Dinner from 5:30 PM to 9:30 PM; Supper Buffet from 9:30 PM to 12:30 AM; Sunday Brunch from 12 Noon to 2:15 PM**
Days Closed:	**Sundays after 2:15 PM and major holidays**
Liquor:	**Full bar service**
Recommended or Listed in:	**Town & Country; New York; New Yorker; Mobil Guide; Cue; New York Times; Playbill**
Maitre d':	**Robert**
Seating Capacity:	**150**
Cuisine:	**Continental/American**
Specialties of the House:	**Roast Prime Ribs of Beef au Jus with Yorkshire Pudding; Veal Paillard a la Limon with Chanterelles; Broiled Prawns in Beer Batter; Chicken Pot Pie with Garden Vegetables**
Dress:	**Jackets required**
Party Facilities:	**Stratford Suite; capacity: 30 (luncheons), 100 (receptions)**
Parking:	**Complimentary garage parking for dinner guests**

For more than 50 years The Algonquin has been garnering fame not only as a gathering place for literary and theatrical notables but also as a bastion of mellow old world charm and excellent Continental cuisine. The three dining rooms and the lounge have carefully preserved the decor and the luxurious appointments which characterized an earlier and more relaxed era. Oak paneling, rich carpeting, comfortable couches and chairs all contribute to the aura of charm and warmth.

DINNER MENU

(a la carte)

(The menus change daily. Items below are a sample selection from one evening's menu.)

APPETIZERS & SOUPS:

Bluepoint Oysters (4.25); Seafood Pancake, Maison (4.25); Little Necks or Cherrystone (4.25); Escargot Bourguignon (4.75); Marinated Herring in Cream (4.25); Cape Cod Oysters (4.25); Mussels in Green Sauce (4.25); Pate Maison, Aspic au Port (3.75); Fresh Fruit Cocktail (2.75); Shrimp Cocktail (6.95); Marinated Fresh Mushrooms a la Grecque (3.50); Onion Soup au Gratin (3.00); Cold Cream Vichyssoise (2.25); Algonquin Cold Senegalese Soup (1.95); Jellied Madrilene (1.75).

HOT ENTREES:

Roast Prime Ribs of Beef au Jus, Yorkshire Pudding 12.50
Lump Maryland Crabmeat a la Dewey 10.50
Steak Tartare, Garni 8.25
Seafood Mixed Grill, Algonquin 12.50
Poached Filet of Sole, Waleska, au Gratin ... 9.25
Venison Cutlet with Mandarin Sections, Wild Rice 10.50
Scallopini of Veal Sautee with Artichokes and Green Asparagus 9.50
Brochette of Beef Filet with Risotto Piemontese Sauce Diable 9.95
Scampi Fra Diavolo, Fettuccine 10.95
Mignons of Beef Filet Sautee, Marchand de Vin, Wild Rice 10.50
Sauteed Sweetbread, Maryland, Sherry Cream Sauce 8.50

(Choice of two vegetables, salad or potatoes is served with hot entrees.)

continued on next page

Rose Room (Algonquin Hotel); Original Home of the Algonquin Round Table

COLD BUFFET:

Special Fish Salad Bowl: Lobster, Crabmeat, Tunafish, Anchovy, Cheese, Tomato, Egg, Russian Dressing 8.95
Chef's Salad, Algonquin 6.50
Fresh Fruit Salad with Cottage Cheese, Sour Cream or Yogurt 6.25
Fresh Seafood Algonquin 9.25
Tomato Stuffed with Shrimp or Lobster, Garni 8.25
Breast of Chicken Salad with Kumquats 6.75

DESSERTS:

Algonquin Deep Dish Apple Pie (2.50); Meringue Glace (2.35); Parfait Algonquin (2.50); Cherries Jubilee (3.75); Coupe au Marrons (2.75); Snow Ball Kahlua (3.00); Assorted French Ice Creams (2.00); Macedoine of Fresh Fruits (2.50); Fresh Poached Pears a l'Orange (2.85); Boysenberry Sherbet (1.75); Bread and Butter Pudding (2.50); Frozen Ice Cream Cake, Melba (2.75); Imported Macaroons (2.50).

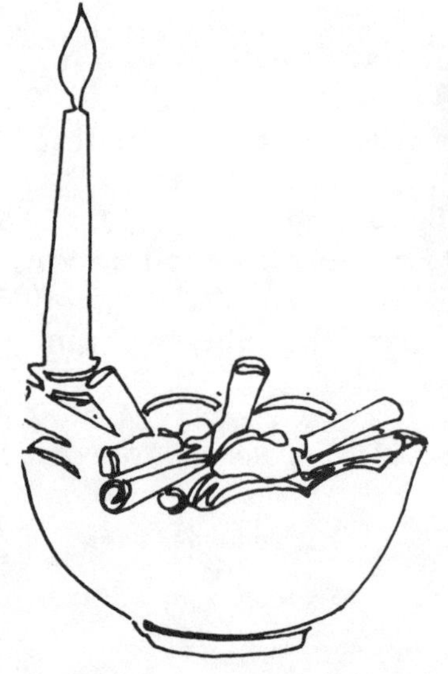

ACADEMIE CULINAIRE DE FRANCE *The U.S. branch of this French organization has a membership limited to 50 elite chefs; it is probably the most prestigious organization of all for French chefs and restaurateurs in this country. As one member explained: "More reference you cannot give to a chef." Members must have an excellent reputation and can remain members only as long as they maintain this reputation. The Académie was founded in 1883 by Joseph Favre, the author of the* Dictionnaire Universel de Cuisine; *at its founding it was called the Académie de Cuisine. The Président Actif of the U.S. branch of the Académie is Jean-Jacques Rachou, Chef-Propriétaire of Le Lavandou restaurant in New York.*

THE AMBASSADOR GRILL

Address: One United Nations Plaza
Location: 44th Street between First Avenue and Second Avenue (in United Nations Plaza Hotel)
Telephone: 355-3400
Credit Cards: AE; CB; V; DC
Reservations: Recommended
Hours: Breakfast from 7:00 AM to 11:00 AM; Lunch from 12 Noon to 3:00 PM; Dinner from 6:00 PM to 11:30 PM; Sunday Brunch from 11:30 AM to 3:00 PM
Days Closed: None
Liquor: Full bar service
Seating Capacity: 200
Cuisine: Continental
Specialties of the House: Filet of Sole in Puff Pastry; Chicken Calvados; Veal Oskar; Oysters Rockefeller
Dress: Jacket required
Entertainment: Pianist from 5:00 PM to closing every evening
Party Facilities: 3 private rooms; capacity: 25-200

This restaurant, located in Hyatt International's new and innovative United Nations Plaza Hotel, features an award winning design by Roche-Dinkaloo Associates. A mirror prism ceiling which gives the effect of a clear and starry night, luscious burgundy velvet banquettes and dark green and white patterned marble floors create an aura of low-key elegance. The single red rose which graces each table exemplifies perfectly the air of composed luxury. To the right of the dining room is the comfortable Ambassador Lounge, a favorite meeting place for UN diplomats.

DINNER MENU
(a la carte)

APPETIZERS & SOUP:
Oysters on the Half Shell (4.00); Oysters Rockefeller (4.50); Smoked Perthshire Salmon (6.00); Snails in Mushroom Caps (4.50); Marinated Shrimps (6.25); Lump Crabmeat Cocktail (6.00); Chef's Terrine (4.00); French Onion Soup Gratinée (3.00); Fresh Lobster Bisque (4.50); Double Consommé Sherry (2.50); Chilled Cucumber Soup with Caviar Toast (2.50).

ENTREES:
Sautéed Trout Almondine 9.00
Baked Trout Beaulieu 11.00
Broiled Striped Bass 12.50
Poached Bass in Fresh Dill Sauce 12.50
Filet of Sole in Puff Pastry 15.00
Bouillabaisse 15.00
Broiled Prawns with Garlic Butter 14.00
New York Sirloin Steak 12.50
Grilled Filet Mignon 12.50
Peppersteak Prepared at Table 14.00
Rack of Lamb for Two 28.00
Long Island Duckling in Orange Sauce 10.00
Chicken Calvados 7.50
Veal Oskar 13.00

SALADS:
Caesar Salad for Two (5.00); Ambassador Salad (3.00); Spinach Salad (3.00).

DESSERTS:
Chocolate Mousse Cointreau (2.50); Strawberries Romanoff (3.50); Cherries Jubilee for Two (6.00); Caramel Custard (2.00); Fresh Fruit Salad with Kirsch (2.75); Choice of Ice Cream (1.75); Berries in Season with a Double Cream (2.50); Selection of Cakes from the Pastry Table (2.00); Irish Coffee (2.75); Café Marco (2.75).
(An a la carte luncheon menu is also offered with entrees ranging in price from 4.75 to 8.00.)

continued on next page

The Ambassador Grill

AVGERINOS

avgerinos

Address:	**153 East 53rd Street**
Location:	**The Market at Citicorp Center; 53rd Street between Lexington and Third Avenues**
Telephone:	**688-8828**
Credit Cards:	**MC; AE; V**
Reservations:	**Not necessary**
Hours:	**11:00 AM to 11:00 PM, Monday thru Saturday; 12:00 Noon to 8:00 PM, Sunday**
Days Closed:	**None**
Liquor:	**Wine and beer**
Recommended or Listed in:	**New York Times; Cue; Time**
Seating Capacity:	**50**
Cuisine:	**Greek and Middle Eastern**
Specialties of the House:	**Melitzanosalata; Saganaki; Mezedakia; Moussaka; Lamb Casserole; Greek Desserts**
Dress:	**Informal**
Party Facilities:	**Upon request**

Avgerinos offers the best in home-style Greek cooking, prepared before your eyes and served by friendly waiters in colorful costumes. The three-level restaurant, designed by Anestis Demou, is located in the popular Market at Citicorp Center. White stucco walls decorated with rugs, cookware and other Greek handicrafts, arched doorways and a ceramic tile floor create a warm and colorful Aegean atmosphere. Customers come back not just for the food, but for the fun.

Avgerinos

DINNER MENU

(a la carte)

APPETIZERS & SOUPS:

Avgolemono Soup (1.25); Taramosalata (Fish Roe Salad with Lemon, Olive Oil) (1.95); Melitzanosalata (Eggplant Salad) (1.95); Dolmades Yalanzi (Stuffed Grape Leaves) (1.95); Tzatziki (Cucumbers, Yogurt, Garlic and Dill) (1.95); Greek Antipasto (Taramosalata, Melitzanosalata, Tzatziki, Fassolia, Dolmades, Feta Cheese) (4.25); Saganaki (Kasseri Cheese Sauteed with Lemon) (2.25); Spanakotiropitta (Spinach-Cheese Pie) (2.25); Tiropitta (Cheese Pie) (2.25); Kolokithakia Scordalia (Fried Zucchini with Mashed Garlic Potatoes) (2.75); Mixed Hot Mezedakia (Greek Meat Balls, Spinach-Cheese Pie, Cheese Pie, Sweetbreads, Liver, Sausage) (4.75).

continued on next page

Menu continued

ENTREES:

Moussaka 5.25
(Layers of Eggplant and Beef Topped with Bechamel Sauce)

Pastitsio 5.25
(Macaroni and Ground Beef Topped with Bechamel Sauce)

Exochiko 5.75
(Chunks of Lamb, Cheese and Vegetables Baked in a Crust)

Kalamarakia 5.75
(Fried Baby Squid)

Dolmades Avgolemono 5.95
(Stuffed Grape Leaves with Egg-Lemon Sauce)

Chicken Souvlaki 5.25
(Marinated Breast of Chicken Broiled on a Skewer)

Souvlaki 6.50
(Marinated Beef Chunks Broiled on a Skewer)

Seafood Souvlaki 6.95
(Scallops, Shrimp and Fish Fillet, Marinated and Broiled on a Skewer)

(Entrees are served with two vegetables and a salad.)

DESSERTS:

Flogera (Rolled Baklava) (1.50); Galactoboureko (Filo Leaves with Custard Filling) (1.50); Bougatsa (Cream-Filled Pastry) (1.50); Yogurt with Honey (1.50).

(Similar luncheon menu is available at prices ranging from 3.25 to 4.95; a selection of Greek wines is available at both lunch and dinner. Lunch minimum per person: 3.25; Dinner minimum: 5.25.)

(All menu selections are available for take out).

LE BEC FIN

Address: 232 East 58th Street
Location: 58th Street between Second Avenue and Third Avenue
Telephone: 758-5665
Credit Cards: AE
Reservations: Recommended
Hours: Lunch from 12:00 Noon to 3:00 PM, Monday thru Saturday; Dinner from 6:00 PM to 10:15 PM, Monday thru Saturday; Sunday dinner from 5:00 PM to 10:00 PM
Days Closed: None
Liquor: Full Bar Service
Recommended or Listed in: New York Times; Gourmet; Forbes; New York Magazine; Cue; Madison Avenue Magazine
Maitre d': Yves Lelan
Seating Capacity: 65
Cuisine: French
Specialties of the House: Canard aux Pêche; Striped Bass Béarnaise; Moules Marinière
Dress: Casual

Le Bec Fin translates into a "sophisticated beak," or one who knows where to eat well. This bistro appears to live up to its translation, but seems to attract the younger set rather than older coupon-clipping gourmets. With sensible ordering, you can come out with a bill which leaves you on the safe side of bankruptcy, after a serene dinner. A Left Bank atmosphere is engendered by low ceilings and Parisian art.

LUNCHEON MENU
(table d'hote)

APPETIZERS & SOUPS:

Tomato Juice; Half Grapefruit; Herring in Sour Cream; Melon in Season; Sardines à l'Huile; Avocado Vinaigrette; Champignons à la Grecque (.75); Terrine du Chef; Saucisson Sec; Escargots de Bourgogne (6 for 3.00); Maquereaux au Vin Blanc; Oeuf en Gelée; Poireaux Vinaigrette (1.50); Anchois Niçoise; Shrimps Cocktail (3.25); Potage du Jour; Vichyssoise; Onion Soup (.50).

ENTREES:
Plat du Jour 6.50
Filet de Sole Meunière 6.95
Saumon Froid 6.95
Moules Marinière 6.75
Salade Niçoise 6.50
Escalopine de Veau à la Française 9.50
Calf's Brain au Beurre Noir 6.50
Foie de Veau Meunière or Lyonnaise 8.25
Minute Steak 9.25
Tripes à la Mode de Caen 6.75
Omelette du Jour 6.50
Salade "Bec Fin" 6.95

DESSERTS:
Mousse du Chef; Crème Caramel; Poire au Vin; Fruit Cup; Gâteau de Riz; Glaces Assorties; Pêche Melba (1.50); Pâtisseries Françaises (1.00); Les Fromages (.50); Cheese Cake.

DINNER MENU
(table d'hote)

APPETIZERS & SOUPS:
Artichaut Vinaigrette (.75); Half Grapefruit; Melon in Season; Champignons à la Grecque; Marquereaux au Vin Blanc; Little Neck Clams (1.75); Saucisson Chaud; Poireaux Vinaigrette (2.00); Truite au Naturel Sauce Verte (2.00); Sardines à l'Huile; Shrimps Cocktail (3.50); Baked Clams (2.00); Escargots de Bourgogne (6 for 3.50); Avocado Vinaigrette; Coquille St. Jacques (2.75); Oeuf en Gelée; Terrine du Chef; Potage du Jour; Vichyssoise; Soupe à l'Oignon Gratinée (.95); Quiche Lorraine.

continued on next page

Menu continued

ENTREES:

Le Plat du Jour 11.00
Filet de Sole Amandine 11.25
Frogs Legs Provençale 11.50
Darne de Bass Grillée Béarnaise 11.50
Saumon Froid 11.50
Moules Marinière 11.25
Rognon de Veau Bercy 11.00
Escalope de Veau "Bec Fin" 12.00
Calf's Liver Meunière 12.00
Ris de Veau Financière 11.50
Canard Bigarade 11.50
Poussin Roti au Jus 11.25
Poussin Grillé à la Diable 11.25
Tournedos Rossini 15.00
Steak au Poivre 14.50
Carré d'Agneau Antiboise 13.25
Entrecôte Maître d'Hôtel 13.50
Tripes à la Mode de Caen 11.25
Filet Mignon Marcan de Vin 13.75

DESSERTS:

Mousse de Chef; Crème Caramel; Meringue Glacée (.75); Gâteau de Riz; Poire au Vin; Glaces Assorties; Fruit Cup; Coupe aux Marrons (1.50); Pêche Melba (1.50); Patisserie Françaises (1.00); Crêpe "Bec Fin"; Les Fromages (1.00); Cheesecake.

BARSAC: *A delicate and fruity white Bordeaux, named after the largest and northernmost township in the Sauternes district in southwestern France. A true Sauternes by its grapes and vinting, it is typically far less sweet than its southern neighbors.*

BEAUJOLAIS: *An uncomplicated yet fruity, full-bodied red wine produced in Burgundy, north of Lyon. It is usually served cool – at cellar temperature – and drunk very young, sometimes as early as mid-November of the harvest year.*

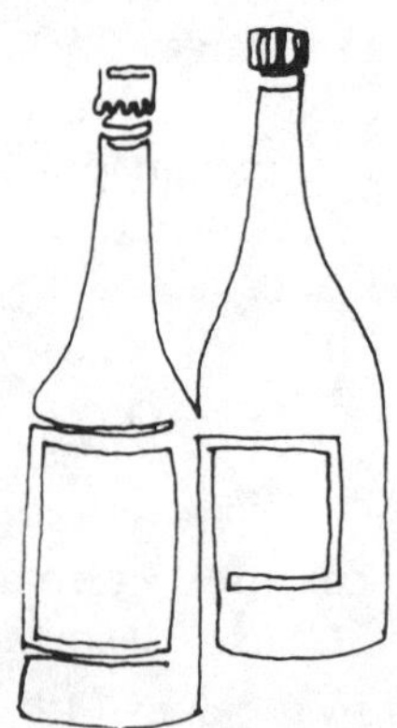

BEAUNE: *Distinctive, graceful Burgundies, both red and white (but more often the former) from the southern half of the Côte d'Or – and especially from the area to the west of the town of the same name. Also, the commercial center of the Burgundy wine trade.*

BLANC DE BLANCS: *Literally, a white wine made from white grapes. Traditionally used only to identify a distinctively made champagne (which is usually produced from a blend of white and black grapes) the term is now frequently employed by the white grape vintners of some of the secondary wine areas (such as Provence or the Loire Valley) to add prestige to their labels.*

ALLGÄUER CHEESES: *Cheeses made in the Bavarian Alps, particularly the district of Allgäu which adjoins Switzerland's Emme Valley. Hence, Allgäuer Bergkäse closely resembles Emmenthal, being of firm texture and nutty flavor with the "eyes" characteristic of "Swiss" cheese. Allgäuer Rahmkäse is softer and more strongly flavored, having a closer resemblance to Limburger.*

Nominate your favorite restaurants for inclusion in Manhattan Menus. Send cards or letters to: Manhattan Menus, P.O. Box 5217, FDR Station, New York, N.Y. 10022.

BERRY'S

Address: 180 Spring Street
Location: Spring Street at corner of Thompson Street
Telephone: 226-4394
Credit Cards: V; MC; AE
Reservations: Recommended
Hours: Lunch from 12:00 Noon to 3:00 PM Tuesday thru Friday; Dinner from 6:00 PM to 11:30 PM Tuesday thru Saturday and 5:00 PM to 11:30 PM Sunday; Brunch from 12:00 Noon to 3:00 PM Saturday and 11:00 AM to 4:00 PM Sunday
Days Closed: Monday and Christmas Day
Liquor: Full bar service
Recommended or Listed in: Gourmet; New York Times; Village Voice; Soho Weekly News
Maitre d': Berry
Seating Capacity: 40
Cuisine: Continental
Dress: Casual

Aside from a massive old mahogany bar, Berry's more closely resembles a private home than it does a restaurant. The decor features hanging plants, sundry antiques, wainscoting and downhome wallpaper and the cheerful warmth usually found only in a family setting. The menu is limited but changes every week with different specials offered daily. The chef reports that no entrees have been repeated in six months' time.

LUNCHEON MENU

(The lunch menu changes frequently. The following is representative.)

Omelette a la Berry's 4.00
Poached Eggs, Burgundy Style 3.75
Casserole du Chef 3.75
Fresh Fish 4.25
Salade du Jour 3.75
Dessert 1.75

DINNER MENU

(a la carte)

(The dinner menu changes frequently. The following is representative.)

APPETIZERS:
Salmon Muscovite (3.25); Moutabel (2.50); Venison Pate (3.25); Ham and Cucumber Sushi (2.00); Salad (1.50).

ENTREES:
Filet of Beef Andalouse 9.25
Ballotine of Rock Cornish Hen Chinoise 8.00
Lamb Chops Fillo 8.25
Troutlings Grenobloise 7.00
Steak Tartare 6.50
Bastilla Morocaine 9.75

DESSERTS:
Daquoise (2.00); Pithivier (2.00); Berry's Chocolate Surprise (2.00); Grand Marnier Mousse Cake (2.00); Austrian Torte (2.00); Mocha Macaroon Mousse (1.75); Tarts: Strawberry, Apricot, Apple (1.75).

BRUNCH MENU

(The brunch menu changes frequently. The following is representative.)

ENTREES:
Fried or Scrambled Eggs 3.25
Omelettes: Ham; Mushroom; Cheese; or Fines Herb 3.50
Omelette Special: Agnes Sorell or a la Berry's 4.25
Calf's Liver Saute 5.25
Troutlings — Devil Style 3.25
Belgian Waffle 3.00
Brioche French Toast 3.75

SIDE ORDERS:
Smoked Nova Scotia Salmon (2.50); Potatoes Saute (.75).

BIANCHI & MARGHERITA

Address: 186 West 4th Street
Location: 4th Street between Seventh Avenue and Avenue of the Americas
Telphone: CH2-2756
Credit Cards: AE; CB; V; DC; MC
Reservations: Recommended
Hours: 5:30 PM to 2:00 AM; Music starts at 7:30 PM
Days Closed: Sundays
Liquor: Full Bar Service
Recommended or listed in: New York Times; Esquire; Cue; New York Post
Proprietors: Joe d'Amico; Fred Fagnani; Fillipo Fornari
Seating Capacity: 125
Cuisine: Italian/French
Entertainment: Professional musicians provide operatic renditions and continental singing from 7:30 PM
Party Facilities: Private parties can be arranged between 5:00 PM and 7:30 PM for up to 100 persons. A special party menu is available.

This authentic Italian restaurant combines antipasto and arias; diners are loudly regaled by professional singers as they enjoy the excellent cuisine. The decor of this long established Village landmark is comfortable and pleasant, well suited to an evening of fun and relaxation. If a glass of wine or two causes you to wax musical, then you'll surely enjoy Bianchi & Margherita.

DINNER MENU

(table d'hote)

APPETIZERS & SOUPS:
Tomato Juice; Macedonia di Frutta; Shrimp Cocktail (2.25); Vongole (2.25); Prosciutto con Melone (2.25); Scampi Margherita (2.50); Vongole al Forno (2.25); Antipasto (2.25); Minestrone alla Milanese; Consomme Domenico; Soupe a l'Oignon; Soupe du Jour.

ENTREES:
Cannelloni alla Crema 11.50
(Meat-filled pasta with cream sauce)
Fettuccine all'Alfredo 11.50
Lasagne alla Bolognese 11.50
Melanzane alla Parmigiana 11.00
(Eggplant with melted cheese and tomato sauce)
Pollo a la Champagne - Fettucine Alfredo - Veal Marsala 13.25
(Combination plate of chicken in Champagne sauce and veal with Marsala wine sauce served with noodles in cheese sauce, Roman style)
Filetti di Pollo Giuseppe Verdi 13.25
(Boneless chicken with mushrooms served on green spinach noodles)
Rollatini di Vitello Via Veneto 12.25
(Stuffed rolled veal in wine sauce)
Pollo alla Parmigiana 12.25
Scallopine di Vitello alla Pizzaiola 12.50
(Thinly sliced veal sautéed in tomato sauce with garlic)
Cotoletta di Vitello alla Bolognese 13.25
(Veal cutlet sautéed with fontina cheese and prosciutto)
Vitello alla Parmigiana 12.50
(Filets of veal with melted cheese and tomato sauce)
Escalopes de Veau Cordon Bleu 13.25
Scallopine di Vitello al Marsala con Funghi . 12.25
(Thinly sliced veal sautéed in Marsala wine sauce, served with mushrooms)
Piccata di Vitello al Limone 12.25
(Thinly-sliced veal in a butter and lemon sauce)

Bianchi & Margherita

Medaillon de Boeuf a la Chambertin 15.00
(Filet of beef in red wine sauce)
Broiled Double Lamb Chops 14.00
Sirloin Steak or Filet Mignon 15.00
Broiled Lobster or Diavolo .... (. . .)
Sogliola Filippo 12.25
(Sole in a sauce of butter and lemon juice)
Vongole e Cozze alla Riviera 12.00
(Clams and mussels in garlic and tomato sauce)
Scampi Fra Diavolo or Margherita 14.00

(Entrees are served with a mixed green salad.)

DESSERTS:
Melone di Stagione (Melon in season); Spumoni Gateau Millefoglie (Napoleon); Gateau au Rhum (Rum Cake); Tortoni Dolce del Giorno (Dessert of the day); Assorted Cheeses.

(An a la carte dinner menu is also available with prices of entrees ranging from 6.50 to 12.00.)

BORDEAUX: *Elegant and aesthetic red and white wines, produced in the Province of Gironde, surrounding the port city of Bordeaux, in southwestern France. Shipped in the traditional straight sided, high-shouldered bottle. Also, the largest of the great wine areas of France.*

BROUILLY: *The most typical and most attractive of the Beaujolais district red wines. Drunk early because it is short-lived, the wine is grapy, full-bodied and full-flavored.*

BURGUNDY: *Rich and sensual red and white wines, produced in the ancient Duchy of Burgundy southeast of Paris and always shipped in a distinctive, slope shouldered bottle. Since Burgundies are often made from a blend of wines from a given area, the shipper's reputation is critical.*

LA BIBLIOTHÈQUE

Address: 341 East 43 Street
Location: 43rd Street between First Avenue and Second Avenue
Telephone: 661-5757
Credit Cards: AE; CB; V; DC; MC
Reservations: Recommended
Hours: 12:00 Noon to 12:00 Midnight
Days Closed: Sundays
Liquor: Full Bar Service
Recommended or Listed in: New York Times; Gourmet; Cue; New York Times "Guide to Dining Out;" New York Magazine
Maitre d's: Mr. Gordon and Mr. Meisels
Seating Capacity: 80
Cuisine: French
Specialties of the House: Prime Filet of Beef William Shakespeare; Roast Long Island Duckling; Paupiettes de Veau Viroflay; Eggs Benedict
Dress: Casual
Entertainment: Live piano music every evening, Monday thru Saturday
Party Facilities: 3 private rooms; capacity: 10-180
Parking: Reduced-rate parking at Econo-Car on 43rd Street between Second and Third Avenues

Decorated in rich brown tones, this lively bistro looks fresh and beautiful. The mirrored cathedral ceiling, raw brick walls and book-filled bookcases give the main dining room a warm and comfortable feeling. But the most unique feature of La Bibliothèque is the magnificent view of the flag-festooned UN Plaza from its windows. A handsome second floor dining room can accommodate up to 180 for private parties and banquets. The outdoor café is charming and offers another stunning view of the United Nations. For those demanding good food and gracious service, La Bibliothèque is perfect on any occasion.

LUNCHEON MENU

(a la carte)

APPETIZERS & SOUPS:
Fresh Fruit Supreme (1.50); Hearts of Artichokes Vinaigrette (1.50); Avocado remoulade (2.25); Melon en Saison (1.95); Shrimps aux Câpres (3.50); Champignons à la Grecque (3.25); Onion Soup au Gratin (2.25); Consommé Celestine (1.95); Chilled Cream Vichyssoise (2.25); Potage du Jour (2.25).

ENTREES:
Poached Eggs Benedict 5.95
Crêpes au Poulet 5.95
L'hamburger à Cheval 6.25
Veal Scallopine, "Voltaire" 6.50
Mixed Grill "Bibliothèque" 7.95
Mignonette of Prime Beef, "Hemingway" ... 8.50
Poached Bass, Beurre d'Echalote 7.25
Boston Sole, Sauté Meunière 7.25
Scallops Boniface 7.25
Broiled Red Snapper Amandine 8.95
Sliced Steak, Pommes Frites 10.50
Blue Ribbon Minute Steak, Maître d'Hôtel .. 10.50
French Lamb Chops Vert Pré 11.50
Prime Filet Mignon "Camus" 11.95
Sirloin Steak "Bibliothèque" 11.95
Chicken Salad Niçoise 5.95
Chef's Salad 6.25
Assorted Cold Vegetable Salad, Mustard Hollandaise Sauce 6.25
Half Alligator Pear Stuffed with Chicken 6.25
Half Alligator Pear Stuffed with Crab Meat .. 6.95
Cold Poached Salmon à La Royale, Hollandaise Sauce 8.50
Spinach, Bacon and Mushroom Salad (Demi: 3.50) 5.95

(A variety of vegetables, potatoes and salads are offered a la carte at prices ranging from 1.00 to 2.75.)

DESSERTS:
Assorted Ice Cream or Sherbet (1.50); Crème Caramel (1.50); Plateau de Fromages (1.50); Peach Melba (1.75); Gâteau au Chocolat (1.75); Cheese Cake (2.00); Mousse au Chocolat (2.00); Fresh Strawberries Romanoff (2.25); Mousse au Citron Givreé (2.25); Bombe Pralineé "Bibliothèque" (2.50).

La Bibliothèque

DINNER MENU
(a la carte)

APPETIZERS & SOUPS:
Fresh Fruit Supreme (1.95); Hearts of Artichoke Vinaigrette (1.95); Melon en Saison (2.50); Seafood Crepes (3.25); Champignons Cèvenols (3.75); Smoked Brook Trout, Horseradish Sauce (3.75); Shrimp aux Câpres, Fonds d'Artichauts (3.95); Prosciutto with Melon (4.25); Escargots Bourguignons (4.50); Consommé Celestine (2.25); Petite Marmite "Bibliothèque" (2.25); Chilled Cream Vichyssoise (2.50); Potage du Jour (2.50); Onion Soup au Gratin (2.50).

ENTREES:
Poulet Grillé à la Moutarde 8.25
Veal Cutlet "Jean Paul Sartre" 8.75
Paupiettes de Veau Viroflay 8.95
Filet of Prime Beef, "William Shakespeare" . 11.50
Plat du Jour . . . . (. . .)
Poached Filet of Sole Veronique 8.25
Broiled Red Snapper Amandine 9.95
Saumon, Sauce Dijonaise 9.75
Broiled Calf Liver with Bacon 10.75
Blue Ribbon Minute Steak Maître d'Hôtel . . . 11.75
French Lamb Chops Vert Pré 12.95
Sirloin Steak "Bibliothèque" 13.75
Prime Filet Mignon "Marsaillaise" 13.75
Steak Au Poivre 14.25
Tournedos Rossini 14.95
Chicken Salad Niçoise 6.75
Salade de Tourteau 8.00
Cold Poached Salmon à la Royale, Hollandaise Sauce 9.75
Steak Tartar Mirabeau 10.25
Roast Long Island Duckling aux Cerises Noires, Sauce Airelles 9.50
Truite Farcie 8.50
Suprême de Volaille au Citron 7.95

(A variety of vegetables, potatoes and salads are offered a la carte at prices ranging from 1.25 to 3.25.)

DESSERTS:
Assorted Ice Cream and Sherbet (1.75); Crème Caramel (1.75); Plateau de Fromages (1.75); Gâteau au Chocolat (2.25); Cheese Cake (2.50); Mousse au Chocolat (2.75); Fresh Strawberries Romanoff (2.75); Bombe Pralinée "Bibliothèque" (2.95); Dessert du Jour (. . .).

(A special pre-theater dinner is served from 5:00 PM to 7:30 PM at prix fixe 11.50.)

BIENVENUE

Address: 21 East 36th Street
Location: 36th Street between Fifth Avenue and Madison Avenue
Telephone: 684-0215
Credit Cards: Not accepted
Reservations: Recommended for dinner
Hours: Lunch from 11:30 AM to 2:30 PM Monday thru Friday; Dinner from 5:30 PM to 10:00 PM Monday thru Saturday
Days Closed: Sunday and major holidays
Liquor: Wine and beer only
Recommended or Listed in: New York Times; New York Magazine; Gentlemen's Quarterly; Esquire; Women's Wear Daily
Seating Capacity: 48
Cuisine: French
Specialties of the House: Quiche Lorraine; Two specialties are featured each evening at dinner, e.g., Veal Chop with Madeira Sauce; Breast of Chicken Calvados; Turbot with Hollandaise Sauce
Dress: Casual

The decor in this delightful little restaurant draws its inspiration from the countryside of Normandy with stucco walls, wood paneling, bentwood chairs and natural wood tables. The color scheme is red, white and blue in the manner of the French tricolor. In the front windows hang a collection of unusual plates. Family owned and operated, Bienvenue offers a limited, but choice, selection of expertly prepared French dishes.

DINNER MENU

(a la carte)

APPETIZERS:
L'Oeuf en Gelee (Poached Egg in Aspic) (1.20); Les Champignons a la Grecque (Mushrooms, Greek Style) (1.40); Le Pate du Chef (Chef's Pate) (1.50); Le Melon en Saison (Melon in Season) (1.60); Le Melon avec Jambon Fume (Prosciutto Ham and Melon in Season) (3.00); Les Moules Ravigote (Mussels in Ravigote Sauce) (1.50); L'Oeuf a la Russe (1.20); La Quiche Lorraine (Lorraine Tart) (1.75); Le Saucisson en Croute (Garlic Sausage in Crust, Potato Salad) (1.85); Les Escargots de Bourgogne (Snails, Burgundy Style) (6 for 3.50) (12 for 5.95).

SOUPS & SALADS:
La Vichyssoise (Cold Potatoes and Leeks, Cream with Chives) (1.20); La Soupe du Jour (Soup of the Day) (1.10); Le Soupe a l'Oignon Gratinee (Onion Soup) (1.50); La Salade Maison (Green Salad, House Dressing) (.95); La Salade d'Epinards aux Champignons (Fresh Spinach Salad with Mushrooms) (1.50).

ENTREES:
La Crepe Royale 5.25
(Chicken Pancake)
Le Coq au Vin 6.50
(Chicken in Wine Sauce)
La Supreme de Volaille Cordon Bleu 7.25
(Breast of Chicken Cordon Bleu)
Le Canard Roti du Jour 8.25
(Roasted Duck)
Le Filet de Sole Bonne Femme 7.50
Le Steak Maitre d'Hotel 8.75
(Steak Maitre d'Hotel Butter)
Le Steak au Poivre 9.75
(Steak with Crushed Pepper)
La Coquille St. Jacques 7.25
Le Steak d'Agneau aux Champignons with Sauce Menthe 7.00
(Lamb Steak with Mushrooms, Mint Sauce)

DESSERTS:
La Mousse au Chocolat (Chocolate Mousse) (1.30); La Peche Melba (Peach Melba) (1.50); La Coupe aux Marrons (Vanilla Ice Cream with Candied Chestnuts) (1.50); La Creme Caramel (Cream Custard) (1.30); Les Glaces (Ice Cream) (1.10); Les Patisseries Maison (Home Made Pastries) (1.40); Fraises Fraiches en Saison (Fresh Strawberries in Season) (. . . .); Melon en Saison (Melon in Season) (. . . .).

(Complete dinners, priced from 8.25 to 13.25 are also available.)
(An a la carte luncheon menu is also offered.)

THE BLACK ORCHID

Address:	**81 Lexington Avenue**
Location:	**Lexington Avenue at 26th Street**
Telephone:	**889-0960**
Credit Cards:	**AE; MC; V; DC**
Reservations:	**Required for parties of 6 or more**
Hours:	**Lunch from 11:30 AM to 3:00 PM, Monday thru Friday; Dinner from 6:00 PM to 11:30 PM, Monday thru Sunday; Bar open to 1 AM; Sunday Brunch from 12:00 Noon to 4:00 PM**
Days Closed:	**Saturday Lunch**
Liquor:	**Full bar service**
Recommended or Listed in:	**Women's Wear Daily; Murray Hill Press; Gramercy Herald**
Seating Capacity:	**Lunch, 60; Dinner, 48**
Cuisine:	**Continental**
Dress:	**Informal**
Entertainment:	**Live piano or guitar music**

The Black Orchid is located a few short blocks from Gramercy Park, New York's bastion of a bygone age. The restaurant invites you to rediscover this gracious past in an eclectic decor combining authentic mahogany paneling with stylish chrome and black leather appointments. Art-deco lighting and an elegant piano add the finishing touches to an altogether pleasant room. In addition to an imaginative menu (which changes every Wednesday), The Black Orchid features a Sunday Brunch with a pianist whose repertoire is as varied as the choice of food. Copies of The Sunday Times *are available for patrons who want to read or do the puzzle as they enjoy the cuisine, the music and the surroundings.*

DINNER MENU

(a la carte)

(Menu changes every Wednesday; the following is representative)

APPETIZERS & SOUPS:
Mushroom and Barley Soup (1.50); Cucumber and Zucchini Soup (1.50); Mussel and Scallion Strudel (1.75); Snails in Pasta Shells (2.50); Onion Soup with Cheese Croutons (1.50); Cream of Broccoli Soup (1.50); Spinach, Mushroom and Cheese Strudel (1.75); Clams Casino (2.75).

ENTREES:
Veal Scallops with Mushrooms, Capers and Lemon 7.00
Sea Trout, Baked with Shallots and White Wine 6.50
Poached Chicken Breast with Sauteed Zucchini, Onion and Mushrooms, Mornay Sauce 6.75
Spaghetti with Bacon, Cheese and Cream Sauce 5.00
Chicken Fricassee with Mushrooms and Onions 5.50
Broiled Mushrooms, Candied Carrots, Spinach and Rice 5.00
Broiled Marinated Pork Chops 6.75
Sole Meuniere 6.75
Chicken Breasts with Watercress Sauce 6.75
Short Ribs of Beef with Horseradish 6.50
Fettuchine, Peas and Proscuitto with Cream Sauce 5.50
Noodles with Poppy Seeds, Creamed Spinach and Baked Tomato 5.00
Shell Steak with Herbed Butter 9.25
(All entrees are served with salad.)

BLACK ORCHID SALADS:
Spinach, Bacon, Mushroom, Onion and Green Pepper (4.50); Artichokes, Olives, Peppers, Ham, Turkey, Salad Greens and Herb Dressing (4.50).

DESSERTS:
Cranberry Apple Pie; Pineapple Upside Down Cake; Coffee Mousse with Chocolate; Chocolate Grand Marnier Cake; Pumpkin Pie, Banana Mousse; Cheese and Fruit. (Each dessert is 1.50.)

continued on next page

The Black Orchid

CABERNET SAUVIGNON: *A strong red wine from the grape of the same name, produced in the North Coast counties of California. This long-lived, slow maturing red wine is considered by many wine experts to be America's finest. It is often compared to the red wine of Médoc, in which the Cabernet Sauvignon grape also predominates.*

CHABLIS: *A dry white Burgundy, produced near the town of the same name southeast of Paris. Made exclusively from the Chardonnay grape, it has a pale straw color and a distinctive "flinty" flavor. The name has been widely appropriated in the U.S. and other wine-producing countries to describe a variety of white wines using some proportion of Chardonnay grapes.*

CHAMBERTIN: *One of the truly great red Burgundies, produced in very limited quantity in the northern portion of the Côte d'Or. This rich, long-lasting (and frequently expensive) wine has a long tradition dating back to 600 A.D. It was a favorite of both Napoleon and Alexander Dumas.*

BEL PAESE: *Made in the town of Melzo near Milan, Bel Paese is among the most popular Italian table cheeses. It is a soft, mild cheese with a pale yellow hue. An excellent Bel Paese is also made in the United States.*

BLEU: *A generic term embracing a variety of blue-green or green veined cheeses which are soft and crumbly in texture and, typically, strong, even biting, in flavor. Among the better known bleus are Roquefort, Gorgonzola, Danablu and Stilton.*

BLUE MILL TAVERN

Address:	**50 Commerce Street**
Location:	**West of Seventh Avenue, 2 blocks south of Sheridan Square**
Telephone:	**243-7114**
Credit Cards:	**AE; MC; V**
Reservations:	**Not necessary**
Hours:	**Lunch from 12:00 Noon to 2:00 PM, Monday thru Friday; Dinner from 5:00 PM to 9:30 PM, Monday thru Thursday and 5:00 PM to 10:30 PM, Friday and Saturday**
Days Closed:	**Sunday**
Liquor:	**Full bar service**
Recommended or Listed in:	**Village Voice; Mobil Travel Guide; WOR/Radio**
Maitre d':	**Alcino Neves**
Seating Capacity:	**110**
Cuisine:	**American; Portuguese**
Specialties of the House:	**Steak Frango à Mamarrosa; Fried Butterfly Shrimp; Homemade Portuguese Soups**
Dress:	**Casual**
Parking:	**Free parking at Morton Street Garage (2-hour limit)**

The Blue Mill Tavern is justifiably a neighborhood institution, offering a congenial atmosphere and exceptionally good value for its reasonably priced menu. Located on a charming, old world street in Greenwich Village, the Blue Mill's interior decor provides as warm a welcome as the proprietors. The Blue Mill has been owned and managed by the Neves family for more than 35 years, and they are always there to ensure the comfort of their loyal clientele. Convenient to many off-Broadway theatres, this is an ideal spot for pre-theatre dinner or drinks in the congenial barroom adjoining the restaurant.

Blue Mill Tavern

continued on next page

LUNCHEON AND DINNER MENU

(a la carte)

SOUPS:
Portuguese Caldo Verde; Portuguese Minestrone; Clam Chowder: (cup .75) (bowl 1.25).

ENTREES:

Chef's Salad	3.95
Broiled Blue Fish	3.95
Fried Scallops	4.95
Filet of Sole	4.75
Fried Butterfly Shrimp	5.95
Blue Mill Burger	1.95
Omelettes	1.95
Potted Steak	3.95
Fried Chicken	3.95
Veal Cutlet	4.95
Pork Chops	4.95
Small Steak	4.95
Filet Mignon	5.95
Vegetable Dinner	1.95
Chopped Sirloin	2.95
Liver and Bacon or Onions	3.95
Steak Bits	4.75
Beef en Brochette	4.95
Frango à Mamarrosa	4.95
Lamb Chops	5.95
Sirloin Steak	6.95

(Entrees are served with potatoes and two vegetables or salad.)

DESSERTS:
Spumoni, Tortoni, Vanilla and Chocolate Brick Ice Cream (1.00); French Pastry (1.00); Homemade Cakes (1.25); Cheesecake (1.50); Pecan Pie (1.50); Apple Cake (1.50); Orange Grimbletorte (1.75).

CHAUSSON AUX POMMES: *This special Parisian puff pastry is quite like the American apple turnover. It is made with a circle of puff pastry dough, covered with freshly cut apples that have been cooked first in butter and sugar. The dough is folded over into a semi-circle before it is baked. It has an apricot glaze on top.*

CONVERSATIONS: *These tarts begin with a round shell of puff pastry—pâte feuilletée. The shell is filled with* frangipane *(almond cream) and then a second sheet of pastry is placed over it. A* glâce royale *or royal icing, made from sugar and beaten egg whites, is layered on the crust and topped with a criss-cross pattern of dough.*

ECLAIR: *This small pastry is one of the "classiques" of French pastry. It is a long, thin pastry made with "pâte à chou" dough and filled with cream that may be flavored with vanilla, coffee, chocolate or mocha. An éclair is iced with a fondant icing; éclairs iced with caramel sugar instead of icing are called* batons de Jacob.

LE GANACHE A LA SUISSE: *This is a chocolate cream filling that is often used in a variety of pastries. It is made with sweet chocolate, heavy cream and a vanilla bean and, if made properly, it is the texture of a mousse au chocolat. It is particularly difficult to make since the chocolate and cream must be just the right temperature when it is whipped.*

GATEAU DE SAVOIE: *This is a sponge cake made with the egg yolks and whites beaten separately. It is a very light cake and is popular at teatime. It may be used as the basis for other, fancier cakes and is often used to make a rolled cake.*

CAN YOU NAME THESE 6 NEW YORK RESTAURANTS?

1. This chic new place is one of the current hangouts for high-fashion models. (Hint: It's a converted saloon on Third Avenue, in the 70's.)

2. Hand-painted cartoons cover the walls here—and 5-pound lobsters overflow the platters they're served on.

3. The menu at this very-French restaurant features over 500 different omelettes—and the luncheon crowd often includes stars like Paul Newman and Joanne Woodward.

4. This third-floor West Side walk-up has the feeling of a Roaring 20s speakeasy. Its menu includes some of the thickest steaks in town.

5. New York's most fashionable Chinese restaurant. Ultra-modern decor, 4-star cuisine, and a jet set clientele.

6. An East Side workingman's bar that's become an "in" Italian restaurant. Has a backroom bocce court with tables alongside it.

These are the kinds of places that everyone wants to go to — but that relatively few people know about.

You'll rarely, if ever, see them advertised anywhere. (Why should they pay for advertising? They do plenty of business without it.)

You'll rarely find them written up in newspapers or magazines.

And you'll only rarely be lucky enough to hear about them from a friend, or to happen into them accidentally.

All of which explains why you need The New York INSIDER.

The INSIDER is a fact-filled bimonthly newsletter that reviews and recommends the best that New York has to offer.

The best restaurants. The best bars. The best clubs. The best discos. The best singles places.

The best places to go for a business lunch, a haircut, a discount, an unusual gift.

The best places to go very late or in the wee hours for everything from a stamp to a steak, a shirt to a shoelace, a book to a bouquet of flowers.

In short, The INSIDER sends you to places that mainly insiders know, and where mainly insiders go.

So you'll always be able to have a really good time in the world's most exciting city.

Without ever winding up in a tourist trap. Or in a clip joint. Or even in a place that's overrated.

Special Offer! Save 35%

Subscribe to The INSIDER using the special reply cards at right, and you'll get a 35% saving — plus exclusive INSIDER reviews of the exciting places described above, if you enclose a check with your order.

THE NEW YORK INSIDER™

An unconventional guide to a good time in New York.

Yes! Please send me a 1-year (6 issue) subscription, and bill me at the special introductory price of just $9 — a saving of $5 (35%) off the regular subscription price. I understand that I will get my money back *in full* if I am not completely satisfied.

☐ Payment enclosed. Please send me, as a free bonus, INSIDER information about the 6 places described.

☐ Bill me ☐ Bill my company

☐ I'd like to save even more! Enclosed is my check for $17, for a 2-year (12 issue) subscription. Please send me, absolutely free, the following bonus gifts: 1. INSIDER reviews of the 6 exciting places described; and 2. The New York INSIDER's Midhattan Map.

Name

Company Name

Address

City State Zip M2

THE NEW YORK INSIDER™

An unconventional guide to a good time in New York.

Yes! Please send me a 1-year (6 issue) subscription, and bill me at the special introductory price of just $9 — a saving of $5 (35%) off the regular subscription price. I understand that I will get my money back *in full* if I am not completely satisfied.

☐ Payment enclosed. Please send me, as a free bonus, INSIDER information about the 6 places described.

☐ Bill me ☐ Bill my company

☐ I'd like to save even more! Enclosed is my check for $17, for a 2-year (12 issue) subscription. Please send me, absolutely free, the following bonus gifts: 1. INSIDER reviews of the 6 exciting places described; and 2. The New York INSIDER's Midhattan Map.

Name

Company Name

Address

City State Zip M1

CAN YOU NAME THESE 6 NEW YORK RESTAURANTS?

1. This chic new place is one of the current hangouts for high-fashion models. (Hint: It's a converted saloon on Third Avenue, in the 70's.)

2. Hand-painted cartoons cover the walls here—and 5-pound lobsters overflow the platters they're served on.

3. The menu at this very-French restaurant features over 500 different omelettes—and the luncheon crowd often includes stars like Paul Newman and Joanne Woodward.

4. This third-floor West Side walk-up has the feeling of a Roaring 20s speakeasy. Its menu includes some of the thickest steaks in town.

5. New York's most fashionable Chinese restaurant. Ultra-modern decor, 4-star cuisine, and a jet set clientele.

6. An East Side workingman's bar that's become an "in" Italian restaurant. Has a backroom bocce court with tables alongside it.

These are the kinds of places that everyone wants to go to — but that relatively few people know about.

You'll rarely, if ever, see them advertised anywhere. (Why should they pay for advertising? They do plenty of business without it.)

You'll rarely find them written up in newspapers or magazines.

And you'll only rarely be lucky enough to hear about them from a friend, or to happen into them accidentally.

All of which explains why you need The New York INSIDER.

The INSIDER is a fact-filled bimonthly newsletter that reviews and recommends the best that New York has to offer.

The best restaurants. The best bars. The best clubs. The best discos. The best singles places.

The best places to go for a business lunch, a haircut, a discount, an unusual gift.

The best places to go very late or in the wee hours for everything from a stamp to a steak, a shirt to a shoelace, a book to a bouquet of flowers.

In short, The INSIDER sends you to places that mainly insiders know, and where mainly insiders go.

So you'll always be able to have a really good time in the world's most exciting city.

Without ever winding up in a tourist trap. Or in a clip joint. Or even in a place that's overrated.

FIRST CLASS
PERMIT NO. 53760
NEW YORK, N.Y.

BUSINESS REPLY MAIL

NO POSTAGE STAMP NECESSARY IF MAILED IN THE UNITED STATES

POSTAGE WILL BE PAID BY

THE NEW YORK INSIDER

P.O. Box 2083
Grand Central Station
New York, N.Y. 10017

FIRST CLASS
PERMIT NO. 53760
NEW YORK, N.Y.

BUSINESS REPLY MAIL

NO POSTAGE STAMP NECESSARY IF MAILED IN THE UNITED STATES

POSTAGE WILL BE PAID BY

THE NEW YORK INSIDER

P.O. Box 2083
Grand Central Station
New York, N.Y. 10017

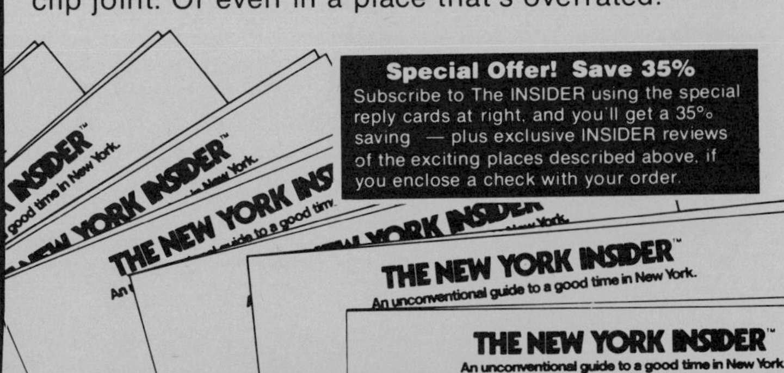

BONDINI'S

Address:	**62 West 9th Street**
Location:	**9th Street, between Fifth Avenue and Avenue of the Americas**
Telephone:	**777-0670**
Credit Cards:	**AE; CB; V; DC**
Reservations:	**Recommended**
Hours:	**Lunch from 12 Noon to 2:30 PM, Dinner from 5:30 PM to 11:30 PM**
Days Closed:	**Mondays**
Liquor:	**Full Bar Service**
Recommended or listed in:	**Cue; New York Magazine; Gourmet**
Maitre d':	**Anselmo**
Seating Capacity:	**75**
Cuisine:	**Northern Italian**
Specialties of the House:	**Costoletta al Valdostana; Adriatic Fish Soup; Rack of Spring Lamb (for two); Squab with Grapes**
Entertainment:	**Strolling guitarist, Tuesday thru Sunday**

Bondini's is a very intimate eating spot in the heart of Greenwich Village, with an excellent Italian cuisine at moderate prices. The Mediterranean atmosphere is accented by white stucco walls, magenta carpeting, and very subtle wall lighting. Tables are well spaced for dining ease. There are fresh cut flowers on each table. The Mediterranean motif is furthered by a balcony overlooking the main dining area.

LUNCHEON MENU

(Luncheon includes choice of fresh fruit, roast pepper, pasta del giorno, soup or juice, entree, vegetable or salad, ice cream or sherbet and coffee.)

ENTREES:

Cannelloni 4.50
Eggplant Parmigiana 4.50
Linguine Clam Sauce 6.00
Fettucini Alfredo 6.00
Shrimp a la Marinara 7.00
Broiled Striped Bass 7.00
Scaloppini of Veal Limone or Marsala 7.00
Chicken Francese 6.50
Veal Parmigiana 7.00
Liver Veneciana 7.00
Eggs Benedictine 6.50
Antipasto della Casa 6.50
Shrimp Salad 7.00
Omelette with Cheese 6.50
Sliced Steak with Mushrooms 7.00
Sole Meuniere 6.50
Spaghetti Bolognese or Carbonara 5.50

DINNER MENU

(Dinner includes soup or pasta del giorno, vegetables, salad, dessert and coffee or tea.)

ENTREES:

Broiled Scampi Bondini's 11.50
Adriatic Fish Soup 10.75
Sea Food Fra Diavolo .... (...)
Bay Scallops Provencale 10.75
Madaglione of Filet Beef 11.50
Chateaubriand Sauce Bernaise For Two 29.00
Rack of Spring Lamb Roasted For Two 29.00
Milk-Fed Veal Paillard 11.00
Scaloppini of Veal Marsala with Mushrooms 10.50
Costoletta di Vitello Valdostana 11.00
Petti di Pollo Bolognese 9.75
Veal Chop Millanese 10.50
Fegato Alla Veneziana 11.00
Veal Cutlet Parmigiana 10.50
Squab with Grapes 11.75
Breast of Capon Bondini 10.00
Fresh Striped Bass Cooked in its own Broth 11.00
Fresh Fillet of Sole Meuniere 10.00
Prime Sirloin Steak 14.25

(An a la carte dinner menu is also offered, with the prices of entrees ranging from 5.50 to 12.00.)

LA BONNE SOUPE

Address: 48 West 55th Street
Location: 55th Street between Fifth and Sixth Avenues
Telephone: 586-7650
Credit Cards: Not accepted
Reservations: Recommended for parties of 4 or more
Hours: 11:30 AM to 12:00 Midnight, 7 days a week
Days Closed: None
Liquor: Full bar service
Recommended or Listed in: New York Times; New York Magazine; Cue
Seating Capacity: 105
Cuisine: French
Specialties of the House: Onion Soup; Mushroom and Barley Soup; Steak au Poivre; Fondues
Dress: Informal
Party Facilities: 3 private rooms; capacity: 30/22/20

The accent is French at La Bonne Soupe—from the red and white checked tablecloths and the French-speaking waitresses to the attractive menu. The fare is basic and well-prepared, the portions hearty and the prices more than reasonable. Wood-beamed ceilings, colorful art on the fabric-covered walls and soft light from the wrought iron lamps add warmth to the decor of this pleasant and intimate restaurant.

MENU
(a la carte)

SOUPS:
(served with bread, dessert and wine or coffee)

Soupe Paysanne à l'Orge 3.75
(Mushroom and Barley Soup with Lamb)
Crème Andalouse 3.75
(Cream of Vegetable Soup)
Soupe à l'Oignon 3.75
Soupe aux Choix à la Russe 3.75
(Sweet and Sour Cabbage Soup)

ENTREES:
Omelette Ratatouille 3.50
(Eggplant, Zucchini and Tomatoes)
Omelette Paysanne 3.50
(Onions, Ham and Potatoes)
Omelette au Fromage 3.50
Quiche Lorraine 3.50
Croque Monsieur 3.50
(Toasted Bread topped with Swiss Gruyere, Ham and Mornay Sauce)
Les Escargots de Bourgogne, served with Salad 3.85
Omelette aux Epinards, served with Salad ... 3.50
(Spinach and Mushrooms)
Salade Niçoise 3.95
Salade du Chef 3.95
Salade Popeye 3.95
Steak Haché Sauce Maison 3.75
(Broiled Ground Sirloin Steak with Chef's Sauce)
Steak Haché au Fromage 3.75
(Broiled Ground Steak with Mornay Sauce)
Steak Haché Paysan 3.75
(Ground Sirloin Steak with Garlic Butter Sauce)
Steak Haché Pizzaiola 3.75
(Ground Sirloin Steak with Mozzarella Cheese and Tomato Sauce)
Poulet Basquaise 5.75
(Chicken sauteed with Onions, Green Peppers, Tomatoes and Herbs)
Boeuf Bourguignon 5.95
Lasagne Maison 3.95
Filet Mignon "au Poivre" 9.95
Filet Mignon Nature, served with Salad and French Fries 8.95
Fondue au Fromage 3.95
Fondue au Fromage for Two 7.95
Fondue Bourguignonne, served with Salad .. 6.95
Fondue Bourguignonne for Two, served with Salad 12.95

DESSERTS:
Crème Caramel (1.25); Pudding du Chef (Seminola cooked with Currents and Raisins; topped with "Crème Anglaise") (1.25); Mousse au Chocolat (1.25); Gâteau Maison (2.00); Ice Cream: Vanilla Coffee, Chocolate, Strawberry (1.25); Fromage (1.25); Fondue Chocolat (2.75; for Two, 4.75).

(Minimum Charge: 3.00 per person)

BOODLE'S

Address: 1478 First Avenue
Location: First Avenue and 77th Street
Telephone: 628-0900
Credit Cards: All major credit cards accepted
Reservations: Not accepted
Hours: 12:00 Noon to 4:00 AM, daily; Brunch served 11:45 AM to 4:00 PM, Saturday and Sunday
Days Closed: None
Liquor: Full bar service
Recommended or Listed in: Restaurant Business; Cue; New York Times Backstage
Seating Capacity: 65
Cuisine: Continental
Specialties of the House: Tortellini with Cream and Wild Mushrooms; Fish du Jour; Deviled Chicken Breast, Sauce Diable; Specialties of the Day
Dress: Casual

A relative newcomer to the upper eastside, Boodle's has already established a reputation for good food, nicely served, in pleasant, leisurely surroundings. A glass-enclosed sidewalk cafe is decorated with hanging plants. The main dining area is raised and separated from the cafe by a highly polished brass railing. Warm interior lighting provided by crystal and brass fixtures is reflected in attractive mirrored columns. Vases of fresh flowers on each table complete the decor which is warm and inviting.

DINNER MENU

(a la carte)

APPETIZERS & SOUPS:
Mushrooms à la Grecque (1.75); Shrimp Cocktail (3.95); Escargots (3.95); Quiche (1.75); Eggplant Orientale (1.75); Carpaccio (2.95); Broiled Shrimp with Lemon, Butter and Garlic (3.95); Baked French Onion Soup au Gratin (2.50); Soup du Jour (1.75).

ENTREES:
Manicotti Pomodori 4.95
Tortellini with Cream and Wild Mushrooms . 5.95
Fettucini Alfredo with Green Noodles 4.95
Broiled Fresh Fish of the Day 5.95
Scampi Griglia Pescatore 7.95
Deviled Chicken Breast, Sauce Diable 6.50
Rack of Lamb, Vert Pré with Waffled Potatoes 9.95
Broiled Shell Steak, Dill Butter Sauce 8.95
Hamburger with Steak Fries 2.95
Gruyèreburger 3.25
(Entrees are served with fresh vegetables.)

SALADS:
House Salad (Garlic or Yoghurt and Blue Cheese Dressing) (1.25); Salade Niçoise (4.50); Chef Salade Parisienne (4.75).

DESSERTS:
Mocha Cheesecake (1.95); Almond Délice (2.25); Lemon Mousse with Raspberry Sauce (1.50); Dessert Cart (...).

BRUNCH MENU

FRUITS & JUICES:
Orange Juice (.75); Spiced Tomato Juice with Lime (.75); Fresh Fruit with Rum Lime Sauce (1.75); Melon in Season (1.75).

ENTREES:
Eggs Benedict 4.50
Poached Eggs Mexican 3.75
Steak and Eggs 5.75
Scrambled Eggs with Onions and Lox 4.75
French Toast with Irish Bacon 4.50
Gruyere and Irish Bacon Omelette 4.50
Omelette Provençal 4.50
Quiche 2.95
Salade Niçoise 4.50
Hamburger 2.95
Swiss Cheeseburger 3.25
Bacon Cheeseburger 3.75

continued on next page

continued

Boodle's (Photo by David Franzen)

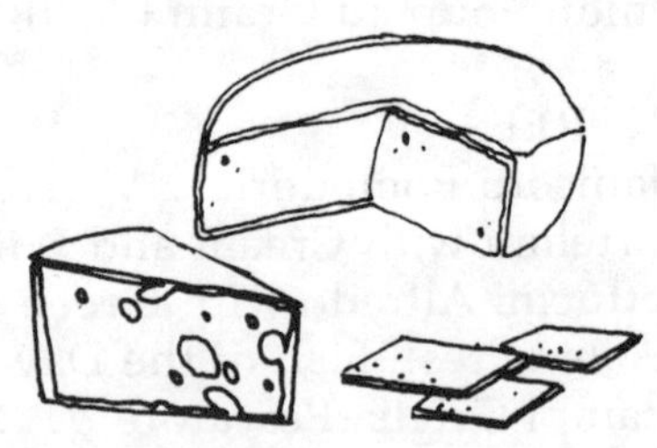

BRICK: *First made in the United States, Brick Cheese is semi-soft with a sharp and pungent flavor. It is stronger than Cheddar but milder than Limburger with which it is often compared.*

BRIE: *Often called the "Queen of cheeses", Brie is made in the department of Seine et Marne just to the southeast of Paris. It is made in wheels less than an inch thick with tough crusts and pale, soft centers. When properly aged, the center is very soft and the color of ivory. The flavor is both mild and delicate.*

CHAMPAGNE: *Generally, a sparkling wine. In France, a specific dry, white sparkling wine, made by a special process (using only certain varieties of grapes) in a legally limited area east of Paris. The unique shape of its bottle and cork have evolved from the fermenting process, which involves the removal of accumulated sediment from the neck of the overturned bottle.*

CHÂTEAUNEUF-DU-PAPE: *A sturdy Rhône Valley red wine, deep crimson in color, produced from a mixture of grape varieties grown in an extraordinary pebble-like soil north of the Provencal town of the same name. This wine's popularity soared in the 1920's when one of its growers initiated the system of legally defining French wine producing areas which was eventually applied nationally.*

BRETT'S

Address: 304 East 78th Street
Location: 78th Street between First and Second Avenues
Telephone: 628-3725
Credit Cards: AE; MC; V; CB; DC
Reservations: Recommended (for Dinner)
Hours: Lunch from 12:00 Noon to 3:00 PM, Monday thru Friday; Dinner from 5:30 PM to 11:00 PM, Monday thru Thursday, to 12:00 Midnight on Friday and Saturday; Saturday Brunch from 12:00 Noon to 4:00 PM.
Days Closed: Sunday
Liquor: Full bar service
Recommended or Listed in: Manhattan East; New York Times; Park East; Cue; Key Host
Maitre d': Andy Cavaciuti
Reservations Manager: Maria Reidy
Seating Capacity: 32
Cuisine: Continental
Specialties of the House: Tortellini with Wild Mushrooms; Tripe Lyonnaise; Fresh Trout Amandine; Special Requests Cooked to Order
Dress: Informal; Jackets preferred

Brett's could well be one of the prettiest restaurants in the city—the white china and sparkling crystal place settings on pink tablecloths, the deep rose and grey fabric accents throughout the dining room, and the fresh flowers and candles on each table combine to create a decor and mood that is intimate, inviting and warm. The menu is selective and changes each week; although the choice of entrees is limited to five or six selections, these are imaginatively prepared and always include chicken, veal, fish and beef. Regular patrons of Brett's know that they are welcome to make special menu requests in advance—and you can too. The service is very professional and at the same time relaxed and friendly.

DINNER MENU

(a la carte)
(The menu changes weekly; the following is a representative selection.)

APPETIZERS: *(Prices from 2.00 to 3.95.)*
Pimento and Anchovies; Smoked Trout; Manicotti; Shrimp Basque; Mussels Ravigote; Fettucine Alfredo; Escargots.

SOUPS: *(Prices from 1.75 to 2.25.)*
Cream of Vegetable; Cream of Mushroom; Straciatella.

PASTAS: *(Prices from 6.75 to 7.50.)*
Tortellini with Wild Mushrooms; Cannelloni; Fettucine Alfredo; Paglia e Fieno.

ENTREES: *(Prices from 7.50 to 11.50.)*
Chicken Marengo
Scallopine Saltimbocca
Tripe Lyonnaise
Chicken au Noix
(Breast of Chicken with Ground Walnuts)
Tournedo Antoine
Bay Scallops Sauteed in White Wine
Coq au Vin

SALADS: *(Prices from 1.75 to 3.75.)*
Spinach, Bacon and Mushroom; Endive and Watercress; Escarole and Hearts of Artichoke; Salad Maison.

DESSERTS: *(Prices from 1.25 to 3.75.)*
Coupe aux Marrons; Creme Caramel; Zabaglione (prepared at the table); Fresh Fruit; Baked Apple; Chocolate Mousse; Ice Cream or Sherbet; Gateau Maison.
(All desserts are baked on the premises.)

(An a la carte luncheon menu similar to the dinner menu is also offered.)

continued on next page

Brett's

AMERICAN CULINARY FEDERATION *This organization's Big Apple Chapter is now devoting a great deal of its energy to setting up an apprenticeship system in New York for graduates of culinary institutes. Among its other activities, this organization selects the U.S. culinary crews or "equipes" for international culinary competitions; the most recent was in Israel. Its function can be compared to that of the U.S. Olympic Committee—it selects the culinary "teams" that are to represent the U.S. in culinary "olympics" throughout the world. Arno Schmidt, Executive Chef of the Waldorf Astoria, is the current President of the New York chapter.*

AMITIES GASTRONOMIQUES INTERNATIONALES *This organization is devoted to "rallying friends of good fare" all over the world. A U.S. group of this organization has just been established under the direction of Mrs. Frances D. Robotti, author of books on history and co-author, with her husband Peter, of* French Cooking in the New World.

Shouldn't your company's library own a copy of Manhattan Menus? Have the librarian write to: Manhattan Menus, P.O. Box 5217, FDR Station, New York, N.Y. 10022.

BUFFALO ROADHOUSE

Address: 87 Seventh Avenue South
Location: Seventh Avenue South, between Grove and Barrow Streets
Telephone: 675-9875
Credit Cards: Not accepted
Reservations: Required
Hours: 11:00 AM to 3:00 AM, Bar until 4 AM; seven days a week
Days Closed: Christmas
Liquor: Full bar service
Recommended or Listed in: New York Times; New York Magazine; Esquire
Manager: O. Joan Breck
Seating Capacity: 65
Cuisine: American
Specialties of the House: Chinese Chicken Cashew; Stuffed Filet of Sole; Stuffed Breast of Chicken; Steak Tartare; Homemade Soups
Dress: Casual

This charming restaurant might well have been named Greenwich Village Oasis. Its exposed brick walls, lush greenery and easy informality make it a delightful place to relax and enjoy good food, whether it be an early brunch or a quiet post-midnight supper. During warm weather, the Buffalo Roadhouse offers outdoor facilities as well. You'll find it a pleasant dining experience and a chance to watch an interesting world go by. When there, ask to see the wine list, which is very reasonably priced.

LUNCHEON MENU
(a la carte)

APPETIZERS & SOUPS:
Gazpacho (.85); Steamed Clams (2.50); Snails Florentine (2.25); Spinach Quiche (1.75); Quiche Lorraine (1.65); Soup of the Day (1.10).

SALADS:
Waldorf Salad and Quiche Lorraine 3.00
Chef Salad 3.50
Spinach Salad 3.25

ENTREES:
Eggs Sardou 3.25
Eggs Benedict 3.25
Eggs Florentine 3.00
Steak and Eggs 3.75
Mushroom, Ham or Cheese Omelette 2.75
Apple, Swiss Cheese and Raisin Omelette 3.25
Watercress and Sour Cream Omelette 3.00
Cucumber Delight 2.50
Club Sandwich - Ham, Turkey Breast, Swiss Cheese 3.00
Hamburger on English Muffin 1.85
Cheeseburger on English Muffin 1.95
Sliced Steak Sandwich - Mushroom Sauce 3.75
Side Order of French Fried Idaho Potatoes .... .85

DESSERTS:
Orange Grand Marnier Cake (1.50); Hot Apple Pie with Fresh Whipped Cream (1.50); Hot Pecan Pie with Fresh Whipped Cream (1.35); Cheesecake (1.35); Rum Chocolate Pudding with Fresh Whipped Cream (1.10).

continued on next page

Buffalo Roadhouse

DINNER MENU

(a la carte)

(Appetizers and Desserts similar to Luncheon Menu)

ENTREES:

Almond Shrimp with Orange Sauce 5.00
Deepwater Sole 4.50
Barbeque Spare Ribs 4.00
Shell Steak 6.50
Marinated Steak Tidbits 4.50
Sliced Steak Sandwich - Mushroom Sauce ... 3.75
Waldorf Salad and Quiche Lorraine 3.00
Chef Salad 3.50
Spinach Salad 3.25
Chicken and Ribs 5.00
Hamburger Platter 3.00

AFTER TWELVE MENU

(a la carte)

(Appetizers, Salads and Desserts similar to Luncheon Menu)

ENTREES:

Club Sandwich 3.00
Sliced Steak Sandwich with Mushroom Sauce 3.75
Mushroom, Ham or Cheese Omelette 2.75
Apple, Swiss Cheese and Raisin Omelette ... 3.25
Watercress and Sour Cream Omelette 3.00
Hamburger on English Muffin 1.85
Cheeseburger on English Muffin 1.95

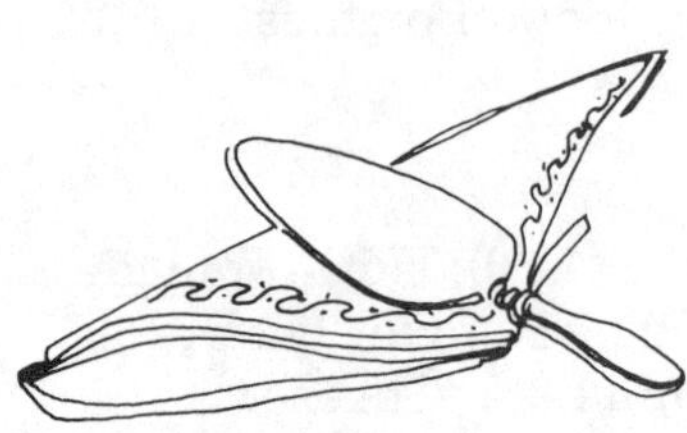

NAPOLEON: *This pastry is made with a* mille feuille *dough—a puff dough that, when baked, looks like many individual layers or, as mille feuille literally means, a thousand leaves. The napoléon has two layers of custard between three layers of mille feuille crust and a marbled white and chocolate icing on top. One pâtissier suggests that this pastry got its name because it is to pastries as Napoléon was to generals—one of the most spectacular.*

PAIN AU CHOCOLAT: *This used to be a favorite with school children who would bring it to school for their afternoon recess. It was a privilege of rich children, primarily, since chocolate was such a luxury. It is a bar of chocolate rolled in croissant dough and baked.*

CAFÉ DE LA PAIX at The St. Moritz

Address: 50 Central Park South
Location: 59th Street and Avenue of the Americas
Telephone: PL 5-5800, ext. 196 or 208
Credit Cards: All major credit cards accepted
Reservations: Recommended
Hours: 11:30 AM to 2:00 AM, Monday thru Friday; 11:00 AM to 2:00 AM, Saturday and Sunday
Days Closed: None
Liquor: Full bar service
Seating Capacity: 150
Cuisine: French/ Continental
Specialties of the House: Canard Roti au Citron Flambe au Grand Marnier; Paillard de Veau Flambe au Cognac; Steak au Poivre Madagascar Flambe au Cognac
Dress: Casual
Entertainment: Pianist; Sunday from 12:00 Noon to 3:00 PM
Party Facilities: Quadrille—capacity: 300; Penthouse (Park View)—capacity: 75; Sky Garden—capacity: 150; other private rooms—capacity: 10-50

New York has few things that remain unchanged through the years, and the quiet elegance of the Café de la Paix is one of them. Located in the prestigious St. Moritz Hotel, the restaurant faces Central Park and is particularly attractive in the warm weather months when the sidewalk café, one of New York's first, is open. But winter or summer, the restaurant means quality. The interior is similar to a fine French café, with subtle shades of red and peach accenting the leather chairs and banquettes. The walls are panelled and tastefully hung with mirrors which enhance the indirect lighting. Food for any palate is available and the buffet is quite simply a triumph of culinary display. Long a favorite of European visitors, the Café de la Paix deserves its reputation as one of New York's special places.

DINNER MENU
(a la carte)

(The menu changes daily; the following is a representative selection.)

APPETIZERS:
Imported Pate de Strasbourg (4.25); Melon with Prosciutto Ham (4.75); Chilled V-8 or Tomato Juice (1.25); Blue Point Oysters on Half Shell (3.95); Fresh Fruit Cocktail (2.50); Little Neck or Cherrystone Clams (3.75); Smoked Nova Scotia Salmon (4.75); Supreme of Shrimp Cocktail (4.50); Filet of Marinated Herring, Sour Cream (3.95).

SOUPS:
Potage Ambassadeur (1.60); Petite Marmite (1.95); French Onion Soup Gratinee (1.95); Chilled Vichyssoise (1.25); Consomme Nicoise (1.60); Potage St. Germain (1.60); Cream of Tomato Soup (1.60); Jellied Consomme Madrilene (1.25).

ENTREES:
Poached Stuffed Filet of Sole Bonne Femme . 8.45
Broiled Long Island Deep Sea Scallops 8.55
Shish Kebab of Marinated Tender Lamb 8.65
Breaded Veal Cutlet Parmesan 8.75
Broiled Medaillon of Tenderloin of Beef Rossini 11.20
Roast Prime Ribs of Beef au Jus 11.75
Chateaubriand Bouquetiere (for two), Bearnaise 31.00
Prime Filet Mignon 14.50
St. Moritz Steak Sandwich 10.25
Calf's Liver Steak Cressoniere 9.75
Half Spring Chicken 8.50
Double Sirloin Bouquetiere 31.00

continued on next page

Menu continued

Jersey Pork Chops (2) 9.75
Prime Minute Steak 13.00
Imported Dover Sole Saute Amandine...... 11.00
Frogs' Legs Provencale 8.75
Deep Sea Scallops, Sauce Tartare 8.95
Broiled Rainbow Brook Trout Veronique or Amandine................................ 8.50
Fried Louisiana Shrimps, Sauce Tartare 8.95

(All entrees are served with two vegetables.)

(A variety of Cold Buffet selections is also available, at prices ranging from 5.75 to 9.75.)

DESSERTS:

Cherry Tart (1.95); Diplomat Pudding (1.75); Home Made Apple Pie (1.95); Linzer Tart (1.75); Pear Helene (2.50); St. Moritz Cheese Cake (1.95); Baked Apple (1.75); Fresh Melon (2.75); Compote of Fruit (2.50); Mont Blanc (2.75); Macedoine of Fresh Fruit (2.75); French Pastry (1.25); Sherbets (1.95); Fresh Berries in Season (2.75); Ice Cream (1.95).

(A special Buffet Luncheon (8.25) is available Monday thru Friday. Le Grand Buffet (10.75), served on Sunday, includes a choice of omelettes, assorted crepes, roasts, smoked trout and Nova Scotia salmon, croissants, antipasto, imported cheeses, and a variety of pastries.)

PALMIERS: *This is a Parisian specialty. It is made from a puff pastry rolled with granulated sugar and is shaped in such a way that when it is baked it looks like the leaf of a palm tree. Some people refer to these pastries in English as butterflies since they do, in fact, look as much like the wings of a butterfly as the leaves of a palm.*

PAVE AU CHOCOLAT: *This is a layer cake made of* genoise *or chocolate sponge and chocolate butter cream filling. It is in a square shape and iced with chocolate frosting. Pavés may be made in many flavors—coffee, almond, chestnut, fruit, etc.*

PROFITEROLES AU CHOCOLAT: *This is a miniature, round version of an éclair. It is made with a pâte à chou pastry, filled with chocolate-flavored cream and served with hot chocolate sauce. Profiteroles may also be filled with whipped cream—then they are more like miniature cream puffs.*

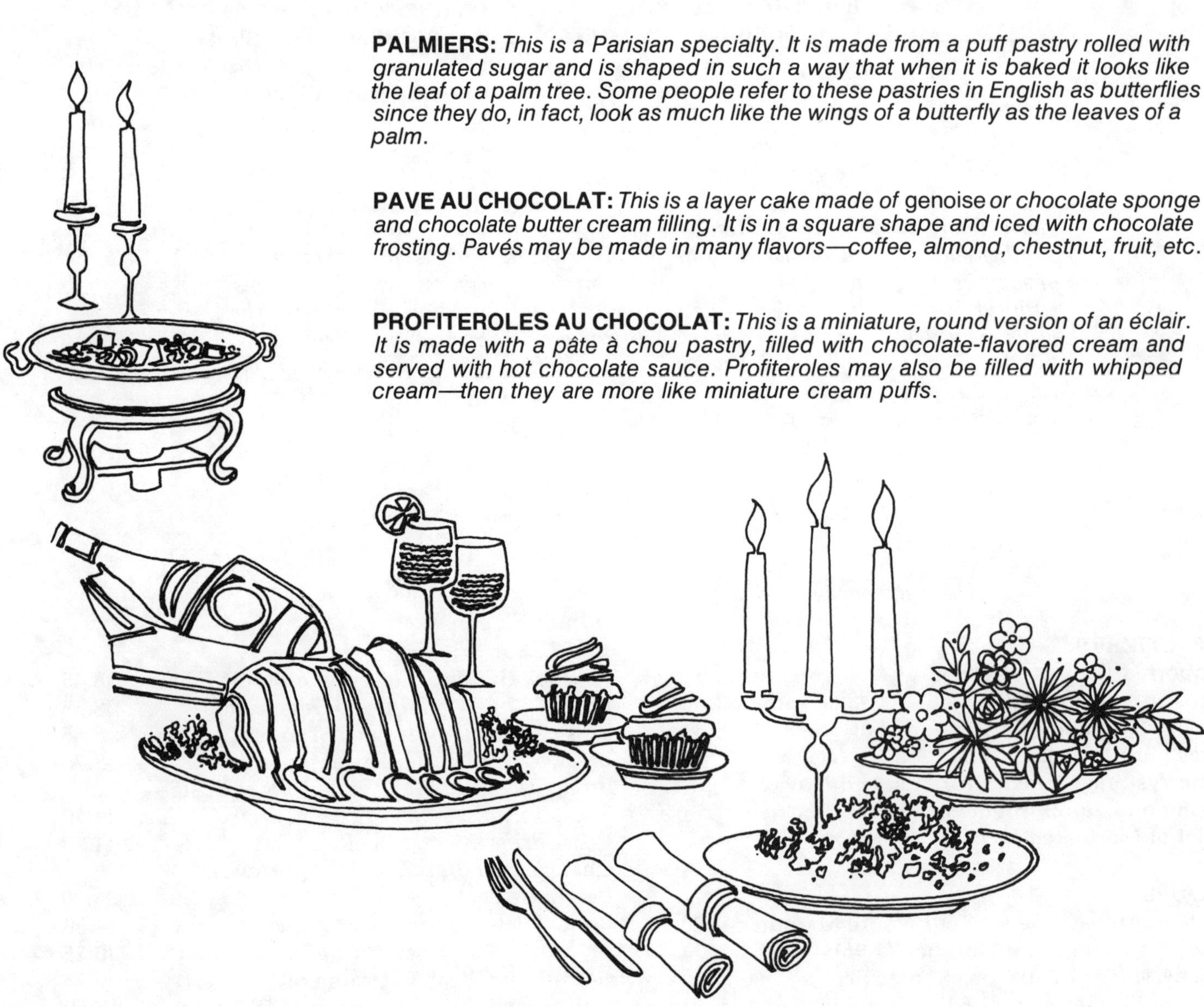

CAFE DU SOIR

CAFE
DU
SOIR

Address:	**322 East 86th Street**
Location:	**86th Street between First Avenue and Second Avenue**
Telephone:	**289-9996; 427-3900**
Credit Cards:	**AE; DC; MC**
Reservations:	**Not Necessary**
Hours:	**12 Noon to 2:30 PM, and 5:00 PM to 12 Midnight, Tuesday thru Saturday; Sunday from 1:00 PM.**
Days Closed:	**Mondays**
Liquor:	**Full Bar Service**
Recommended or Listed in:	**New York Times; Cue; Where; Gourmet**
Maitre d':	**Marcel**
Seating Capacity:	**146**
Cuisine:	**French**
Specialties of the House:	**Shrimps Mode Cafe du Soir; Coq au Vin de Chambertin; Half Duckling Flambé**
Dress:	**Informal**

Cafe du Soir is a delightful restaurant serving French cuisine and graced by murals of French country life, yet located in the heart of German Yorkville! The tables are dimly lit and white napkins give notice that you are dining correctly but not necessarily formally. A very lively spot at dinner but quiet at lunch.

DINNER MENU

(table d'hote)

(Includes appetizer, soup, entree, salad, dessert and beverage.)

APPETIZERS:
Hors d'Oeuvres Varies; Pate Maison; Crepe Farcie; Jambon de Bayonne; Tomato Juice; Salami de Gene; Tomates aux Filet d'Anchovies; Half Grapefruit; Coquille Saint Jacques; Bismark Herring; Fruit Cup; Assiette du Chef; Imported Sardines; Oeuf a la Russe; Coeurs d'Artichauts Vinaigrette; Maquereaux au Vin Blanc; Saumon Fume (1.75); Cherrystone Clams (1.25); Shrimp Cocktail (2.00); Escargots de Bourgogne (6 for 2.75)

SOUPS:
Onion Soup, Consome en Tasse; Potage du Jour.

ENTREES:

Filet of Sole Meuniere	9.25
Shrimps Mode Cafe du Soir	11.00
Truite de Ruisseau, Amandine	8.50
Frogs Legs Saute Provencale	12.50
Scampis, Garlic Sauce	12.25
Tranches de Noix de Boeuf Maison	9.25
Le Coq au Vin de Chambertin	8.50
Veal Scaloppine au Madere	9.50
Rognons de Veau, Marchand de Vin	8.50
Sliced Filet of Beef, Mushroom Sauce	12.00
Half Duckling Flambe, Sauce Bigarrade	9.75
Cervelles au Beurre Noir	8.75
French Pot Roast a la Bourgeoise	8.50
Steak Saute Bordelaise	11.25
Ris de Veau a l'Ariegeoise	10.75
Tripes a la Mode de Caen	9.25
Boeuf Bourguignon	9.75
Calf's Liver and Bacon	9.50
Poulet Chasseur	8.50
Broiled Spring Chicken	8.50
Pork Chops, Apple Sauce	8.50
London Broil du Chef	8.50
Lamb Chops Grille Vert Pre	12.00
Filet Mignon, aux Champignons	14.00
Prime Sirloin Steak	13.75
Entrecote for Two	28.00

DESSERTS & CHEESES:
Assorted French Pastries, Apple Pie a la Mode; Mousse au Chocolat; Cuope aux Cerises Noires; Caramel Custard; Poire Maison; Cheese Cake; Peche au Vin; Spumoni; Peche Melba; Coupe aux Marrons; Babas a la Glace; Poire au Vin; Biscuit Tortoni; Orange or Raspberry Sherbet; Chocolate, Coffee, Vanilla Ice Cream; Port Salut, Blue and Brie Cheese.

(A la carte dinner service is also available.)
(A table d'hote luncheon menu is also offered.)

CAFE NEW AMSTERDAM

Address:	**284 West 12th Street**
Location:	**12th Street between Seventh and Eighth Avenues**
Telephone:	**242-7929**
Credit Cards:	**AE; MC; V**
Reservations:	**Recommended**
Hours:	**6:00 PM to 11:00 PM, Tuesday thru Sunday**
Days Closed:	**Monday**
Liquor:	**Full bar service**
Recommended or Listed in:	**Village Voice; Wisdom's Child; The Trib**
Proprietors:	**Lavinia Watkins and Arthur Rudick**
Reservations Managers:	**Lavinia Watkins and Arthur Rudick**
Seating Capacity:	**40**
Cuisine:	**International**
Specialties of the House:	**Broiled Lamb Chops with Hazelnuts; Salmon in Brioche; Duckling Glazed with Armagnac; Brook Trout Stuffed with Mushrooms and Shallots; Chocolate Cake**
Dress:	**Casual**

Cafe New Amsterdam is one of the newest and best dining discoveries in the Village. Located on a residential street of gracious brownstones, this restaurant combines a warm, rich color scheme, candlelit sconces and dark oak to create an ambience of comfortable well-being. The menu is very selective—limited to four or five entrees which change weekly—and a testimonial to the culinary imagination of Chef Arthur Rudick. The quality of the Cafe New Amsterdam's cuisine is outstanding, and the menu very reasonably priced.

DINNER MENU

(a la carte)

(The menu changes weekly; the following is a representative selection.)

APPETIZERS & SOUPS:
Smoked Salmon Quiche (2.00); Duck Liver Mousse in Barquettes (1.75); Watercress and Garlic Soup (1.50); Deep Fried Crêpes with Three Cheeses (1.75); Wild Rice in Pastry (2.00); Sausage in Brioche (1.75).

ENTREES:
Spinach Stuffed Sole with Lobster Sauce 7.00
Broiled Loin Lamb Chops with Hazelnuts ... 8.25
Braised Beef with Margaux 7.25
Scallops of Veal in Champagne 7.50
Mustard and Crumb-Coated Leg of Lamb 7.00
Fettuccine with Prosciutto 5.50
Bay Scallops and Lobster in Puff Pastry 8.00
Stuffed Shrimp New Amsterdam in Hazlenut Batter 7.75
Roast Loin of Pork with Port and Cream 7.25
Rabbit Chartreuse 7.50
Cassoulet 7.00
Sauté of Chicken with Coriander and Vinegar 6.00

(Entrees are served with vegetables and salad.)

DESSERTS:
Bittersweet Chocolate Cake (2.00); Lemon Champagne Syllabub (1.75); Raspberry Dacquoise (1.75); Strawberry Whipped Cream Cake (1.75); Praline Almond Bavarian Cream (1.75); Hazelnut Torte (1.75).

(A complete dinner, including choice of appetizer and dessert, is offered at an additional cost of 2.75.)

IL CAMINETTO

Address: 202 East 50th Street
Location: 50th Street between Second and Third Avenues
Telephone: 758-1775; 758-1780
Credit Cards: All major credit cards accepted
Reservations: Recommended
Hours: Lunch from 12:00 Noon to 3:30 PM; Dinner from 5:30 PM to 10:30 PM, 11:30 PM on weekends
Days Closed: Sunday
Liquor: Full bar service; large selection of French wines
Recommended or Listed in: Women's Wear Daily; Daily News; Town & Country; Madison Avenue; ABC/TV
Maitre d': Marcello
Seating Capacity: 65-70
Cuisine: Northern Italian
Specialties of the House: Homemade Pasta and Desserts; I Golosi del Caminetto; Green Tortelloni; Fish Soup; Veal Chop "Sassi"
Dress: Jackets required

Il Caminetto, a fine Italian restaurant located in midtown, reflects the very personal touch of its owner and Chef de Cuisine, Nino Ruzzier—the attractive art that decorates the walls of the restaurant was painted by Mr. Ruzzier, and the pasta and desserts are all homemade on the premises under his supervision. Even the decor of the restaurant was created by Mr. Ruzzier—and blends in well with the inviting fireplace in the dining room. Il Caminetto has often been cited for its excellent Northern Italian cuisine; the menu as well as the ambience attracts a celebrity clientele.

DINNER MENU

(a la carte)

APPETIZERS & SOUPS:

Cold Steamed Mussels with Green Sauce (3.00); Clams on the Half Shell, Cocktail Sauce (3.25); Baked Clams "Della Casa" (3.75); Shrimp Cocktail (3.75); Prosciutto and Melon (3.50); Hearts of Palm and Artichokes Vinaigrette (3.25); Coquille of Seafood Gratinated (4.00); Nova Scotia Smoked Salmon (5.00); Soup du Jour (2.25); Minestrone Soup (2.25); Egg Drop Soup with Spinach (Stracciatella) "Mille Fanti" (2.25); Onion Soup (2.25).

PASTA:

"I Golosi del Caminetto" 7.00
Linquine or Spaghetti with Red or White Clam Sauce 6.50
Home-Made Egg Noodles, Any Style 7.50
Macaroni Shells with Broccoli 6.00
"Trenette" with Pesto Sauce 6.00
Green "Tortelloni" with Cream Sauce 7.00

ENTREES:

Boned Breast of Chicken "Sorrentina" 8.00
Boneless Chicken "Scarpariello" 7.50
Boneless Chicken "in Tecia" with Artichokes and Prosciutto 7.75
Saltimbocca alla Romana 8.25
Veal Scaloppine "Francese" 7.75
Veal Piccata with Lemon Sauce 7.75
Veal Chop "Sassi" 9.25
Golden Sweetbreads with Mushrooms or Capers 8.50
Calf's Liver Sauteed with Onions "Veneziana" 8.50
Mignonette of Beef with Mushrooms and Peppers 11.00
Filet of Beef "Rossini" 12.00
Broiled Filet Mignon 11.50
Veal Paillard 9.25
Beef Paillard 11.00
Calf's Liver English Style 8.50
Sirloin Steak 11.00
Shrimp Casserole "Americana" 8.00
Fish Soup "Nino" 8.75
Broiled Shrimp with a hint of Garlic 9.00
Sea Scallops "Meuniere" or "Marinara" 7.25
Striped Bass "Golfo di Napoli" 8.00
Filet of Sole "Meuniere" 7.00

DESSERTS:

Zabaglione (2.50); Pastries (2.00); Ice Cream (1.75); Strawberries in Wine (in season) (2.50); Melon (in season) (2.00).

CARMEN'S CAFE

Address: 750 Barclay Avenue, Staten Island
Location: Barclay Avenue and Hylan Boulevard
Telephone: YU 4-9786
Credit Cards: AE; MC; DC
Reservations: Recommended
Hours: 12:00 Noon to 11:00 PM; 7 days a week
Days Closed: None
Liquor: Full bar service
Maitre d': Eddy Ramos
Reservations Manager: Joseph Ramos
Seating: Capacity: 150
Cuisine: Spanish; Mexican; American
Specialties of the House: Carmen's Paella; Seafood ala Jerez; Carmen's Mexican Platter
Dress: Casual
Parking: Restaurant parking lot

You could be on the Mediterranean or dining in a villa on Spain's Costa Brava, but you've really gone to Carmen's on Staten Island, complete with a panoramic view of the Atlantic Ocean. The white stucco archways adorned with delicate Spanish ironwork create an atmosphere that combines the grace of old Castile with all the amenities of a well-staffed restaurant. The menu at Carmen's offers a wide variety of Spanish and Mexican dishes. Some—like the paella or arroz con pollo—are familiar favorites, but there is also a broad selection of authentic and lesser known dishes from which to choose. Carmen's unusual and choice location creates the illusion of a meal at a top seaside resort. For a distinctive and memorable dining experience, sample the real Spanish flavor of Carmen's Cafe.

DINNER MENU

(a la carte)

(The following is a representative selection.)

APPETIZERS & SOUPS:
Camarones a la Plancha (Scampi) (3.00); Jumbo Shrimp Cocktail (3.00); Fried Chicken Livers (2.75); Mexican Antipasto (Enchilada and Tacos) (2.50); Beef or Chicken Tacos (2.50); Pulpo (Octopus) (2.50); Guacamole (2.25); Special Mexican Antipasto for Two (5.75); Chorizos (2.00); Panadilla de Tacos (2.50); Callos ala Amaluza (3.50); Clams Oreganato (2.75); Jumbo Shrimp with Green Sauce (3.00); Little Neck Clams (1.75); Chilled Tomato Juice (.50); Chile con Carne (2.25); Platanos (1.00); Nachos (1.25); Stuffed Mushrooms (2.50); Gazpacho, Onion Soup or Spanish Garlic Soup (1.00).

MEXICAN SPECIALTIES:
Carmen's Special Mexican Platter 6.95
(Beef Tamale, Beef Enchilada, Beef Taco, Meat Ball with Hot Chili Sauce, Mexican Rice and Chile Beans, Carmen's Special Salad Bowl, Hot Garlic Bread)
Mexican Style Pork Chops 6.95
(With Fresh Mushrooms, Green Peppers, Tomatoes, Special Chili Sauce (hot), Mexican Rice, Salad Bowl, Hot Garlic Bread)
Mexican Style Filet Mignon 8.95

SPANISH SPECIALTIES:
Carmen's Paella (for Two) 15.95
(Chicken, Rice, Clams, Shrimp, Lobster, Mussels, Scallops, Spanish Sausage; Cooked with Safron in Casserole, Garnished with Green Peas, with Sherry Wine and Spanish Pimientos)
Seafood ala Jerez 8.85
(Lobster Tails, Clams, Mussels, Scallops, Shrimps, Crabmeat with Sherry Wine)
Zarzuela de Marisco 8.85
(Seafood a la Carmen, Served with Rice)
Terner ala Madrilena 6.95
(With Almond Sauce, Spanish Sherry)

Filet Mignon Solteado con Salsa de Vino 7.90
(Fried Peppers, Onions and Sherry Wine)
Pollo ala Castellana 6.95
(Chicken Breast, Button Mushrooms, Spanish Sausages, Green Peas; Cooked in Tomato Sauce with Spanish Sherry)

AMERICAN DISHES:
Broiled Lobster Stuffed with Crabmeat ...... (...)
Alaska King Crab 8.85

Surf & Turf 9.95
(Lobster Tail and Filet Mignon with Potato)
Broiled Filet Mignon with Baked Potato 8.95

(Carmen's also offers a daily special, priced at 7.95, which includes a Champagne Cocktail; Bowl of Salad with Olives, Cucumbers, Radishes, Peppers and Avocado; Bowl of Macaroni Salad, Cole Slaw and Chick Peas; Garlic Bread; Onion Soup; Roast Prime Ribs with Rice or Baked Potato; Flan or Ice Cream; Coffee.)

(A variety of desserts is available, ranging in price from .95 to 1.75.)

CHIANTI: *The best known Italian red wine. Produced in Tuscany, south of Florence. Refreshing and piquant, Chianti is made from a wide variety of grapes and bottled in squat flasks which, until recently, were usually wrapped in straw. Even its better grades, bottled in Bordeaux-shaped bottles, are usually drunk young.*

CLARET (SEE BORDEAUX): *A red wine term used interchangeably with Bordeaux.*

COGNAC: *The highest quality French brandy, produced from local wine by the pot-still method in and around the town of the same name, north of the Bordeaux country in southwestern France. Cognac is usually aged in oak barrels after distillation (for a minimum of two years and up to five years or more) before being bottled and shipped.*

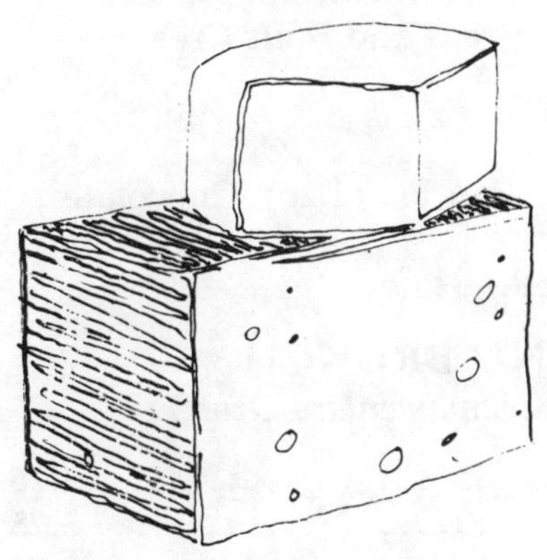

CAMEMBERT: *This cheese originated near the town of Vimontiers in the department of Orne but is now made throughout France and elsewhere as well. In France it is the most popular of all cheeses. Camembert comes in wheels about 4 inches thick which are crusty on the outside and soft in the center. It is a delicate cheese which is at its best during the winter months.*

CHEDDAR: *The term "Cheddar" originally referred to a cheese made in Somerset County in England but today it refers to a wide variety of cheeses made throughout the English speaking world. Typically, Cheddars are hard, sometimes crumbly cheeses which range from mild to very sharp in flavor. Colors vary from pale yellow to deep orange, the stronger hues being attained by adding vegetable dye. True English Cheddars are not sold in the United States.*

CENTRAL PARC

Address: 1024 Second Avenue
Location: Second Avenue at 54th Street
Telephone: 838-6360
Credit Cards: AE; V; MC
Reservations: Recommended for parties of 5 or more
Hours: 12:00 Noon to 4:00 AM, seven days a week
Days Closed: Thanksgiving and Christmas
Liquor: Full bar service
Seating Capacity: 70
Cuisine: American
Specialties of the House: 1¼ lb Maine Lobster; 16 oz New York Sirloin Steak; Roast Prime Ribs of Beef
Dress: Casual

The floor-to-ceiling windows flanking the entrance of this East Side restaurant reveal inviting warmth reflected by the wood and brick walls. Hanging plants and low-keyed lighting add to the picture of a comfortable, unpretentious place to have a drink or a sample of the inexpensively priced but tasty fare. Menu specials are available on Monday, Thursday and Saturday each week, and the Brunch, served all weekend, is particularly worthwhile. This Central Parc is located in the heart of New York's swinging single territory, so either as a participant or an observer, give it a try.

DINNER MENU

(a la carte)

APPETIZERS & SOUPS:
Shrimp Cocktail (2.50); Artichoke Hearts Vinaigrette (1.75); Pate Strasbourg (1.75); Quiche Lorraine (1.75); French Onion Soup (1.50); Beef Barley Soup (1.25); Bay Scallops Scampi (2.75); Crabmeat Cocktail (3.75).

SALADS:
Chef Salad (3.25; small, 2.25); Spinach Salad/Mushrooms and Bacon (2.95; small, 1.95); Mixed Green Salad (.75); Cucumber and Tomato with Onion (1.50); Fresh String Bean Salad Vinaigrette (1.75).

ENTREES:

New York Shell Steak 7.50
Baked Sugar Cured Virginia Ham with Mashed Potatoes 4.75
Baked Meat Loaf with Mashed Potatoes 3.95
London Broil with Mushroom Gravy 5.50
Chicken Parmigiana 4.95
Steak Sandwich 5.75
Filet of Sole, Broiled or Almondine 4.75
Shrimp Scampi 6.50
Veal Francese 5.75
Broiled Pork Chops 5.25
Chopped Beef Steak 3.95
Sauteed Liver with Onions and Bacon 4.25
Side Order of Chili 1.25
Side Order of French Fries .... .75
Side Order of Cottage Fries 1.00

(All entrees are served with salad, vegetable and potato.)

SPECIALS:
Monday: 1¼ lb Maine Lobster (5.95); Thursday: 16 oz New York Sirloin Steak (5.95); Saturday: Roast Prime Ribs of Beef (5.95).
(All of the above specials include a baked potato, salad and one glass of wine.)

SANDWICHES & OMELETTES:
Club Sandwich with French Fried Potatoes (2.95); Hamburger Platter (2.75); Open Grilled Cheese and Tomato with Bacon (2.00); Mushroom, Cheese, Bacon, Ham, or Watercress and Sour Cream Omelette (3.25).

DESSERTS:
Cheese Cake (1.50); Pecan Pie (1.25); Chocolate Cake (1.50).
(Minimum at table: 1.50.)

WEEKEND BRUNCH

(Served with a Complimentary Drink)

Steak and Eggs 4.75
Omelettes, any Style 3.25
Eggs Benedict 3.50
Blueberry Pancakes with Bacon 3.25
French Toast with Bacon 3.25

Central Parc

CHESHIRE: *A close relative of Cheddar, Cheshire is believed to have been made around the English city of Chester as long as 2,000 years ago. Cheshire is a hard table cheese and, since it keeps its flavor even when melted, is also used in cooking. In color Cheshires range from almost white to peach or even darker. Cheshires are best when aged but most sold today are only briefly cured.*

COTTAGE CHEESE: *Made throughout the world, cottage cheese is simply the curd formed when rennet is added to milk in the first stage of cheese making. Typically, it is sold with some whey retained and with some salt added. Tasting like slightly acid fresh milk, it has a short life and must be eaten fresh.*

CORTAILLOD: *The best Swiss wine, produced near the town of the same name on the north shore of Lake Neuchâtel in western (French-speaking) Switzerland. It is a pale, light wine – almost rose in color – made from the Burgundian Pinot Noir grape.*

COTE DE BEAUNE: *Red and white wines from the southern half of the celebrated Burgundian Côte d'Or. The better Côte de Beaune wines are known by their vineyard names (Montrachet, Meursault, Pommard, Beaune, etc.). A wine labeled Côte de Beaune is usually of only regional quality. All Côte de Beaune wines mature quickly into softness and refinement.*

LE CHAMPIGNON

Address:	**35 West 56th Street**
Location:	**56th Street Between Fifth Avenue and Avenue of the Americas**
Telephone:	**245-6335**
Credit Cards:	**AE; DC; MC; V; CB**
Reservations:	**Recommended**
Hours:	**Lunch from 12 Noon to 3:00 PM Monday thru Saturday; Dinner from 5:30 PM to 10:30 PM Monday thru Thursday, 5:30 PM to 11:00 PM on Friday and 5:30 PM to 11:30 PM on Saturday**
Days Closed:	**Sundays**
Liquor:	**Full bar service**
Recommended or Listed in:	**New York Times; Cue; Where; Women's Wear Daily**
Seating Capacity:	**155**
Cuisine:	**French**
Specialties of the House:	**Champignons Farcis; Bouillabaise du Vieux Port; Carre d'Agneau Persille; Filet de Boeuf en Croute**
Dress:	**Jackets recommended**
Party Facilities:	**Private room; capacity: 75**

Located in the handsome town house which was once the home of John Wanamaker, this lovely French provincial restaurant is popular for its intimate candlelit atmosphere as well as its fine cuisine. Decor in the three separate dining rooms features antique buffets, mahogany paneling and fireplaces. The attractive setting makes this an ideal place for parties, receptions and other social functions.

LUNCHEON MENU

(table d'hote)

(The appetizers, soups and desserts offered at lunch are similar to those on the dinner menu.)

ENTREES:

Les Plats du Jour 6.95
Oeufs Poches Benedict 6.95
Omelette Fines Herbes ou au Choix 4.95
Filet de Sole Saute Meuniere 7.50
Gougeonette de Sole Sauce Tartare 6.75
Boston Scrod Grille 6.95
Foie de Volaille a la Turque 5.95
Escalope de Veau Bergeret 8.50
Boeuf St. Emilion 6.95
Steak Minute Echalottes 8.95
Chef Salad 4.95

DINNER MENU

(table d'hote)

APPETIZERS & SOUPS:

Pamplemousse; Pate du Chef; Melon; Jus de Tomate; Oeufs Mimosa; Celeri Remoulade; Hareng Creme Sure; Champignons a la Grecque; Hors d'Oeuvres (1.50); Fruits de Mer Provencale; Escargots Bourguignonne (½ dozen 3.75) (1 dozen 6.25); Les Champignons Farcis Sauce Madere (1.50); Coupe de Fruits Fraisette (. . .); Prosciutto (2.00, with Melon 2.50); Saumon Fume (2.50); Bouquet de Crevettes (2.75); Moules Ravigote (1.25); Sardines Importees (1.25); Consomme Double; Madrilene Froid (.50); Soup a l'Oignon Gratinee (1.25); Vichyssoise (1.00); Potage du Jour.

ENTREES:

Contrefilet of Beef 11.50
Les Plats du Jour 8.95
Specialitee du Chef — Le Champignon Special 15.95
La Sole de Douvres Belle Meuniere 13.50
Cuisses de Grenouilles Provencale 12.95
Coq au Vin 7.95
Canard Roti Bigarade Flambe Grand Marnier .11.50
Le Ris de Veau Financiere Fleuron 11.95
Escalope de Veau Saute Marsala 12.25
La Piece de Boeuf Roti Bourguignonne 9.50
La Grand Entrecote Grille 14.95
Steak au Poivre Flambe 15.95
Filet Mignon 16.95

DESSERTS:

Patisseries Assorties; Creme Caramel, Fruits Frais Fraisette; Glaces et Sorbet; Mousse au Chocolat; Variete de Fromages (1.50); Fraises en saison (1.50), au Kirsch (1.75); Peches aux Cognac (1.75); Cherries Jubilee (2.00); Baba au Rhum; Crepe Suzette (3.50); Poires Cuites au Vin (1.50); Parfait Liqueur (1.50).

(A pre-theatre dinner priced at 6.95 is also available.)

ACIDITY: *The "tang" or "bite" of a wine. The right amount of acidity is necessary to all wines—without enough, a wine is weak and uninteresting; with too much, it is sharp and unpalatable.*

ALCOHOL CONTENT: *Most table wines have an alcoholic content of between 9 and 13 per cent. In lower percentages are many Moselles; in the higher, Chateauneuf-du-Pape or Barolo. While wines with higher alcohol content tend to be heavier bodied, they can lack the delicacy of those with lower proof. Wines with low alcohol levels are meant to be consumed as soon as possible since they do not age well.*

AROMA: *This key term, when combined with bouquet, refers to the "nose," or the composite of all the fragrances found in a wine. A wine's aroma specifically describes the varietal character of the grape—it is, very simply, its unique grape smell.*

AUSTERE: *This is a flattering term and it refers to the crispness and dryness of a white wine. Initially, an austere wine is too "sharp" for pleasurable consumption; connoisseurs use the phrase to indicate a positive aging potential. Especially used in conjunction with Chablis Grand Cru and other leading white Burgundies.*

BALANCE: *This is the harmony of the basic elements of a wine—its dryness, acidity, aroma, bouquet, body and finish. In a good wine one element must complement the other; none should be overpowering. For instance, a wine with a light, soft bouquet should have a relatively light body; a wine with an intense bouquet should have a more substantial body.*

CHARLEY O'S

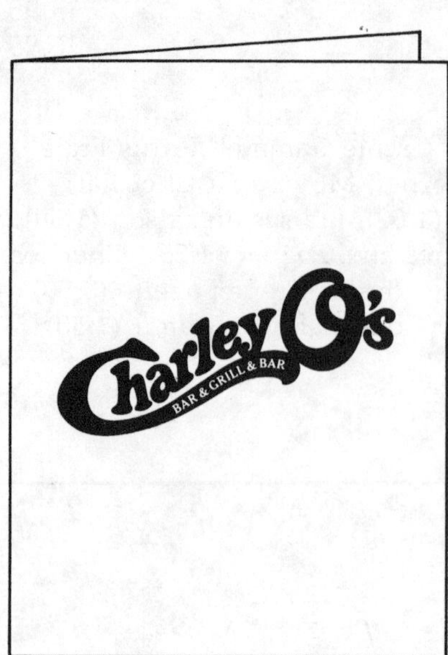

Address:	**33 West 48th Street**
Location:	**48th Street between Fifth Avenue and Avenue of the Americas (in Rockefeller Center)**
Telephone:	**582-7141**
Credit Cards:	**AE; DC; CB; V; MC**
Reservations:	**Recommended**
Hours:	**11:30 AM to 1:00 AM, Monday thru Thursday and Sunday, to 2:00 AM, Friday and Saturday; Saturday and Sunday Brunch from 11:30 AM to 3:00 PM**
Days Closed:	**None**
Liquor:	**Full bar service**
Recommended or Listed in:	**New York Times; New York Magazine; Cue; Promenade; Where**
Seating Capacity:	**150**
Cuisine:	**Irish and American**
Specialties of the House:	**Corned Beef and Cabbage; Irish Lamb Stew; Prawns in Ale Batter; Irish Coffee**
Dress:	**Casual**
Party Facilities:	**2 private rooms; capacity: 500**

Not only is the food at Charley O's of top notch quality, but you can enjoy it at lunch, brunch, dinner and supper. Famous for hearty Irish-American fare, this restaurant has produced a menu which runs the gamut from Irish Lamb Stew to Frozen Irish Coffee Mousse. The decor here is a successful combination of modern and turn-of-the-century motifs. The bar, which serves sandwiches at all hours, is always crowded and lively while the raised platforms in the front and rear offer alcoves for quieter dining.

DINNER MENU

(a la carte)

APPETIZERS & SOUPS:
Charley O's Bean Soup (1.50); Pea Soup (1.50); The Chef's Soup (1.50); Country Pâté (1.95); Sliced Tomatoes with Onions (1.95); Chilled Melon (1.50); Melon with Prosciutto (2.50); Local Oysters or Clams (3.25); Charley O's Soused Shrimp (4.50); Shrimp Cocktail (4.50).

ENTREES:
Charley O's Corned Beef and Cabbage 7.25
Irish Lamb Stew 6.95
Thick Prime Sirloin Steak 12.95
Sliced Beefsteak on Toast 7.95
Grilled Chopped Steak 6.95
Roast Prime Ribs of Beef 11.95
Brandied Skillet Steak 13.95
Barbecued Beef Bones 6.95
Lamb Chops 11.95
Calf's Liver with Onions 7.50
Chicken Pot Pie 7.25
Fish of the Day 7.50
Scallops Broiled or Fried 7.50
Fried Jumbo Prawns in Ale Batter 7.50
Fish and Chips 6.95

(A variety of potatoes, vegetables and salads is offered at prices ranging from 1.10 to 3.95.)

DESSERTS:
Hot Deep Dish Apple Pie (1.95); Frozen Chocolate Mousse Pie (1.95); Cheese Cake (1.95); Ice Cream or Sherbet (1.50); Fresh Strawberries with Sweet Cream (2.50); Chocolate Cake (1.95); Bassett's Irish Coffee Ice Cream (1.50); Hot Fudge Irish Coffee Sundae (2.95); Homemade Irish Coffee Pie (2.25); Frozen Irish Coffee Mousse (1.95).

SUPPER MENU

(a la carte)

(Appetizers, soups and desserts on the Supper Menu are identical to those served at Dinner.)

ENTREES:

Corned Beef and Cabbage	7.25
Irish Lamb Stew	6.95
Irish Potato Pancakes	4.50
Corned Beef Hash	5.50
Fried Prawns in Ale Batter	7.50
Quiche and Salad	5.50
Sliced Beefsteak on Toast	7.95
Thick Prime Sirloin Steak	12.95
Fresh Fish of the Day	7.50
Hamburger	3.95
Hamburger with Cup of Chili	4.75
Cheeseburger	3.95
Cheeseburger with Cup of Chili	4.75
Charley O's Corned Beef Sandwich	4.50
Roast Beef Sandwich	4.50
Turkey Sandwich	4.50
Club Sandwich	4.50
Cold Roast Beef Platter	6.95
Chef's Salad	5.50
Spinach Salad	3.95
Fried or Scrambled Eggs with Bacon, Ham, Sausage	4.50
Irish Omelette	4.75
Omelette with Jam, Ham, Tomato, Cheese, Mushroom or Fines Herbes	4.50
Eggs Benedict	5.25

L'ASSOCIATION DES JEUNES CUISINIERS DE FRANCE *Members of this organization are young French and American chefs who work together to promote the future of "the new cooking." The U.S. representative is Jean Yves Piquet, Executive Chef of Le Cygne restaurant, New York.*

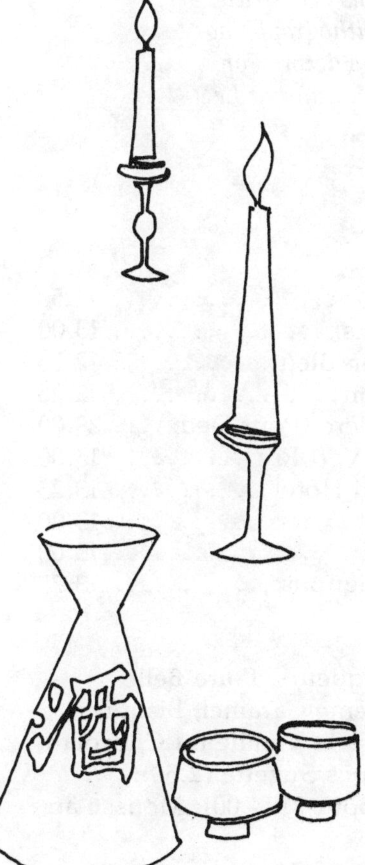

L'ASSOCIATION DES MAITRES CUISINIERS DE FRANCE *This organization is similar to L'Académie for the prestige accorded to its members but its membership is restricted to chef-restaurateurs only. There are approximately 30 members of the U.S. branch of this French association—they represent restaurants in New York, Chicago, Washington, D.C., New Jersey and California. The aim of the organization is "Maintien et diffusion de l'art culinaire Français, encouragement a l'apprentisage et perfectionnement professionel." The U.S. representative to the Association in France is André Soltner, Chef-Propriétaire of Lutèce. It is the Maîtres Cuisiniers who present the coveted Toque d'Argent, or Chef-of-the-Year Award. The Toque d'Argent—a Chef's hat of silver—has been awarded since 1967 and was established by M. André Surmain. The award is one of the most important of all for chefs since it represents the recognition and admiration of colleagues. It is awarded at a special dinner each January.*

Les Chefs de l'Année since 1967 have been:

1967—André Soltner, M.O.F., Lutèce, New York
1968—André René, Windows on the World, New York
1969—Roger Fessaguet, La Caravelle, New York
1970—Raymond L. Vaudard, Retired
1971—Marcel Haentzler, Retired
1972—Claude Bouchet, Bouchet Restaurant, Washington, D.C.
1973—Pierre Orsi, Orsi Restaurant, Lyon, France
1974—André Surmain, Relais Mougin, Provence, France
1975—Joseph Castaybert, Retired
1976—Jean Banchet, Le Français Restaurant, Chicago
1977—Willy Krause, Le Périgord Park, New York
1978—Jean Vergnes, Le Cirque, New York

LE CHEVAL BLANC

Address:	**145 East 45th Street**
Location:	**45th Street between Third and Lexington Avenues**
Telephone:	**MU 2-9695**
Credit Cards:	**AE; MC; DC; CB**
Reservations:	**Recommended**
Hours:	**Lunch from 12:00 Noon to 2:30 PM, Monday thru Friday; Dinner from 5:30 PM to 10:00 PM, Monday thru Saturday**
Days Closed:	**Sunday (Saturday and Sunday during July and August)**
Liquor:	**Full bar service**
Recommended or Listed in:	**Cue; Where; New York Times**
Maitre d':	**Louise Jeannine**
Reservations Manager:	**Louise Jeannine**
Seating Capacity:	**70**
Cuisine:	**French**
Specialties of the House:	**Moules Cheval Blanc; Cassolette de Fruits de Mer Cardinal au Gratin; Escalope de Veau, Cordon Bleu; Poulet à l'Estragon; Crêpes Suzette; Mousse au Chocolat**
Dress:	**Jackets required**

Its convenient midtown location and fine French cuisine have made Le Cheval Blanc the popular dining choice of its many loyal patrons. The menu selections are varied, prepared in traditional French style and pleasantly served. Original lithographs by Daumier, Matisse and Toulouse Lautrec contribute dramatically to the decor. For authentic French cooking in a very French ambience, try luncheon or dinner at Le Cheval Blanc.

DINNER MENU

(table d'hote)

APPETIZERS & SOUPS:

Moules Cheval Blanc (Hot Mussels, Garlic, Butter); Saumon Fumé (1.50); Sardines à l'Huile; Rillettes de Tours; Oeufs aux Anchois; Coeurs d'Artichauts Parisienne; Crevettes (1.25); Pâté Maison; Saucisson; Melon; Jus de Tomate; Escargots de Bourgogne (2.50); Vichyssoise; Consommé; Soupe à l'Oignon.

ENTREES:

Soft Shell Crabs Amandine	12.50
Filet de Sole Bonne Femme	11.75
Sole de la Manche, Meunière	12.25
Grenouilles Provençale	12.25
Cassolette de Fruits de Mer Cardinal au Gratin *(Lobster, Shrimps, Scallops, White Wine, Cream)*	13.00
Cold Salmon Parisienne	12.25
Coq au Vin Mode de Bourgogne	9.50
Poulet à l'Estragon	10.25
Canard à l'Orange	11.50
Ris de Veau des Gourmets	13.00
Escalope de Veau, Cordon Bleu	12.25
Foie de Veau Sauté, Bacon	12.25
Carré d'Agneau Bouquetière (Pour Deux)	29.00
Côtes d'Agneau Grillées Vert Pré	13.00
Entrecôte Grillée Maître d'Hôtel	13.25
Tournedos Forestières	13.00
Filet de Boeuf Strogonoff	13.00
Filet Mignon aux Champignons	13.75

DESSERTS:

Pêches Rafraîchies aux Liqueurs; Poire Belle Hélène; Pêche Melba; Crème Caramel; Bisquit Tortoni; Spumoni; Glace à la Vanille ou Chocolat; Cerises Jubilé (2.00); Crêpes Suzette (2.50); Omelette Norvégienne (pour 2) (4.00); Mousse au Chocolat; Fromages.

(Minimum per person: 9.50.)

CHEZ PASCAL

Address:	**151 East 82nd Street**
Location:	**82nd Street between Lexington Avenue and Third Avenue**
Telephone:	**249-1334**
Credit Cards:	**AE**
Reservations:	**Required**
Hours:	**Two dinner seatings: 7:00 PM and 9:30 PM, daily**
Days Closed:	**Sunday during July and August**
Liquor:	**Full bar service**
Maitre d':	**Marc Saccone**
Reservations Manager:	**Jacques Vermeulen**
Seating Capacity:	**65**
Cuisine:	**French**
Specialties of the House:	**Bouillabaisse "Chez Pascal"; Bass en Croute au Beurre Blanc; Medaillons de Veau aux Morilles; Canard a la Vasco de Gama**
Dress:	**Jackets required**
Party Facilities:	**Private dining room; capacity: 18**

Without doubt one of the very finest haute cuisine restaurants in New York, Chez Pascal is also exceptionally attractive in its decor and appointments. The polished bare wood floor, exposed brick walls, and antique ceiling are complemented by plush gray banquettes, white framed chairs and a plethora of fresh flowers. The overall effect is one of both warmth and elegance. Chef Emmanuel Sender creates masterpieces in the kitchen which are more than worthy of the magnificent surroundings in which they are served.

DINNER MENU

(a la carte)

(The menu changes every three months; the following is a representative selection.)

APPETIZERS & SOUPS:

Escargots en Croute (5.25); Asperges Maltaise (4.95); Artichaut and Champignons Remoulade (4.50); Poire d'Avocat Calypso (4.25); Salade Haricots Verts Truffee (5.75); Salade Royale (9.00); Nos Terrines Maison (5.50); Saumon Fume d'Ecosse (7.50); Foie Gras Frais de Canard au Poivre Vert (9.00); Caviar Beluga et sa Garniture (22.00); La Creme du Jour (3.00); Soupe de Poisson Provencale (3.50).

ENTREES:

Bouillabaisse "Chez Pascal"	18.00
Bass en Croute au Beurre Blanc	15.75
Canard a la Vasco de Gama	14.50
Medaillons de Veau aux Morilles	16.50
Truite Farcie au Champagne	14.50
Sole de Douvre Dijonnaise	15.00
Mousse de Homard Pascal	17.50
Escalope de Saumon a l'Oseille	14.50
Supreme de Bass au Chablis	14.00
Carre d'Agneau "La Reserve" (For Two)	35.00
Cote de Boeuf Grillee Bordelaise (For Two)	35.00
Entrecote Flambee au Poivre	17.50
Steak de Gigot d'Agneau Grille Des Alpes	14.50
Poussin Grille aux Aromes de Provence	13.50
Rognons de Veau a Votre Choix	13.50

SALADS:

Salade d'Endives et Cresson (4.00); Salade Verte Maison (3.00).

(A separate dessert menu is available.)

(Specialties not on the menu are prepared daily.)

CHIN-YA JAPANESE RESTAURANT

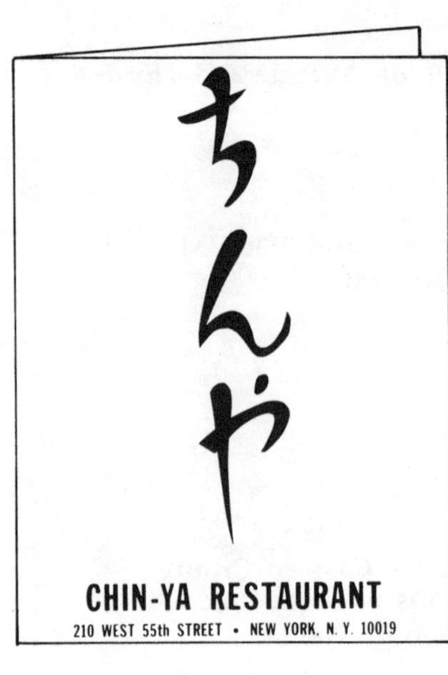

Address: 210 West 55th Street
Location: 55th Street between 7th Avenue and Broadway
Telephone: 586-0160
Credit Cards: AE; DC; MC; V; CB
Reservations: Recommended
Hours: 6:00 PM to 6:00 AM Monday thru Saturday; 6:00 PM to 5:00 AM Sunday
Days Closed: None
Liquor: Full Bar Service
Recommended or Listed in: Cue; New York Times; Genesis
Seating Capacity: 75
Cuisine: Japanese
Specialty of the House: Fresh fish
Dress: Casual
Party Facilities: Tatami Room; capacity: 25

Situated in the Woodward Hotel in the heart of the theater district, Chin-ya is a popular late night spot for musicians, entertainers and executives from television and the Broadway stage. It is also frequented by restauranteurs who close their own doors at earlier hours. Chin-ya's decor is simple and features a sushi bar. The tatami room is especially popular and can be reserved for groups numbering up to twenty-five. The kitchen is open until 5:00 AM for late snacks and dinners.

MENU

Full Course Dinner

Sukiyaki Dinner 7.25
(Clear or Soya Bean Soup; Tempura or Sashimi; Beef, Pork or Chicken Sukiyaki with Vegetables; Rice; tea; pickles; dessert)

Tempura Dinner 7.00
(Clear or Soya Bean Soup; Tempura (Fried Shrimp and Vegetables); Rice; tea, pickles; dessert)

Teishoku Dinner 7.50
(Clear or Soya Bean Soup; Tempura or Sashimi; Three Course Entrees of the Day; Rice; tea; pickles; dessert)

Teriyaki Dinner 8.75
(Clear or Soya Bean Soup; Beef, Pork or Chicken Teriyaki; Rice; tea; pickles; dessert)

a la carte Entrees

Sukiyaki 6.25
(Tender Beef, Pork or Chicken Prepared at your Table with Fresh Garden Vegetables, Bamboo Shoots, Tofu and Saifun Noodles)

Beef Teriyaki 7.75
(Tender Japan Style Beef Broiled with Piquant Tare Sauce)

Chin-ya Pepper Steak 9.00
(Broiled Tender Steak smothered with Vegetables and Seasoned with Tare Sauce)

Chin-ya Special Steak Toyo-fu 15.00
(Broiled Tender Prime Shell Steak Smothered with Vegetables and Seasoned with Tare Sauce)

Steak Toyo-fu 13.75
(Broiled Tender Prime Shell Steak Seasoned with Tare Sauce)

Yaki Niku Korean Style 5.25
(Broiled Tender Pieces of Beef Seasoned Korean Style)

Tempura 6.00
(Shrimps and Assorted Fresh Vegetables Gently Fried with Uniquely Delicate Batter, Served with Specially Prepared Tempura Sauce)

Tonkatsu 5.75
(Pork Cutlet Prepared Japanese Style, Served with House Special Sauce)

Fried Lobster Tail 8.25
(African Lobster Tail, Fried Tenderly and Served with House Special Sauce)

Yaki Tori 4.75
(Tender Morsels of Chicken Broiled on Skewer and Served with Lemon)

Kushiyaki 4.25
(Tender Chunks of Beef, Marinated and Broiled on Skewer and Served with Delicate Sauce)

Fish Shioyaki .... 3.50 up
(Salted Filet of Fresh Fish Broiled and Served with Lemon and Ginger Sauce)

Sashimi .... 5.50 up
(Sliced Fresh Fish Served with Hot Wasabi and Soya Sauce)
Sushi .... 6.00 up
(A Famous Japanese Delicacy — Thin Slices of Fresh Fish and Seafood Served with Hot Wasabi and Soya Sauce)
Fuguzukuri 5.00
(Fresh Fish Sliced Paper-thin and Served with Special Sauce)
Oyster Fry 4.00
(Deep Fried Tender Juicy Oyster Served with Special Sauce)
Kushi Katsu 4.00
(Deep Fried Tender Pieces Skewered Beef and Vegetables)
Ebi Fry 3.75
(Deep Fried Shrimps Served with Special Sauce)
Ishi Yaki 7.00
(Thin Slices of Tender Beef Broiled on Hot Stone at your Table)

(A variety of a la carte side dishes are offered priced from .65 to 3.75.)

DESSERTS:
Ice Cream (.80); Melon in Season (1.35); Yokan (Japanese Sweetened Bean Cake) (1.00).

LATE SNACKS-DONBURI MONO:
Nori Chazuke 2.50
(Large Bowl of Rice Topped with Seaweed, Sesame Seed and Served with Hot Delicately Seasoned Seaweed Sauce)
Sake Chazuke 3.00
(Prepared Salted Salmon, Broiled, Flaked and Served on Rice with Hot Japanese Tea)
Tai Chazuke 3.00
(Fresh Sliced Morsel of Fish, Topped on Rice and Served with Hot Japanese Tea)
Tarako Chazuke 3.00
(Broiled Preserved Cod Fish Roe, Topped on Rice, Served with Hot Japanese Tea)
Su Udon 2.25
(Noodles in Soup)
Tanuki Udon 2.50
(Noodles in Soup, Sprinkled with Age)
Kitsune Udon 2.65
(Noodles in Soup, Sprinkled with Age Kasu)
Mori Soba 2.65
(Cold Soba Noodle Served with Special Noodle Sauce)
Tsukimi Udon 2.65
(Noodles in Soup with Egg)
Nabeyaki Udon 4.00
(Cooked Japanese Noodle, Vegetable, Chopped Meat, Shrimp and Egg in Delicately Seasoned House Special Soup)
Tempura Udon 3.50
(Noodles in Soup with Deep Fried Shrimp and Vegetables)

ROSE GRAND MARNIER: *This pastry is from Nice and is made from a* pâte sucrée *shell filled with almond cream* (frangipane). *On top of the cream is a butter cream rose—as large as the whole pastry—which has been flavored with Grand Marnier.*

SAVARIN: *This cake, made in a ring mold, is similar to a baba in taste. Made with a yeast dough—somewhat like a brioche but with more eggs—it is soaked in a syrup flavored with either rum or kirsch. A Savarin Chantilly is a Savarin that is served with whipped cream heaped in the middle; a Savarin Montmorency is one that has semi-sweet cherries stewed in kirsch in its center.*

TARTE AU CITRON: *To make a true lemon tart, one must use pure lemon juice and grated lemon rind mixed with a blend of eggs and sugar. This fresh lemon filling is placed in a* pâte sucrée *(sweet dough) and covered with almond paste.*

TARTES AUX FRUITS A L'ALSACIENNE: *This one-crust pie or flan is usually made with plums, apples and cherries. After the fruit mixture is placed in the shell, it is covered with custard or a light pastry cream. Other tartes that are often made à l'Alsacienne are cherry and apricot* (cerises *and* abricots).

P.J. CLARKE'S AT MACY'S

P.J. CLARKE'S
AT MACY'S

Address: 135 West 34th Street
Location: 34th Street between Broadway and Seventh Avenue
Telephone: 564-5690
Credit Cards: AE; Macy's Charge
Reservations: Recommended
Hours: Daily from 11:00 AM to 11:00 PM
Days Closed: Major holidays
Liquor: Full bar service
Maitre d': Christine
Seating Capacity: 170
Cuisine: American
Specialties of the House: Eggs Benedict; Mushroom and Spinach Salad; Hamburgers; Chili; Apple Pie

Thirty-fourth street shoppers have discovered a welcome addition to Macy's Cellar—P.J. Clarke's at Macy's. A charming replica of the well-known eastside Irish pub of the same name, P.J. Clarke's handsome polished bar, wood-paneled walls and red and white checked table cloths create a comfortable and informal ambience for dining—from early lunch to late supper. Antique lighting fixtures, ornate clocks and the photographs and paintings of another era contribute to the turn-of-the-century feeling. P.J. Clarke's at Macy's provides a peaceful respite from the activity of this shoppers' mecca and a congenial meeting place for its downtown patrons.

MENU

(a la carte)

SOUPS & SIDE DISHES:
Beef Barley Soup (cup: 1.20); Mixed Green Salad (1.00); String Beans and Beets Vinaigrette (1.30); Spinach and Potatoes (1.60); Broccoli (1.10); Lentil Soup (Dinner only) (1.30); Chili (cup: 1.90).

ENTREES:
Eggs Benedict 3.20
Fillet of Lemon Sole 3.90
Steak Diane 5.30
Tartar Steak 3.90
Broiled Chopped Steak 4.20
Prime Shell Steak 7.40
Chicken Breast Nicoise 3.40
Mushroom and Spinach Salad 3.20
Special Chef's Salad 3.00
Chicken Salad 3.70
Vegetable Casserole 3.50
Prime Hamburger 2.40
Prime Cheeseburger 2.50
Bernaise Burger with English Muffin 2.60
Cadillac 2.90
Bowl of Chili 2.30
Chicken Divan (Dinner menu only) 3.90
Chicken Tarragon (Dinner menu only) 3.80

DESSERTS:
Homemade Apple-Walnut Pie (1.30); Lemon Mousse (1.30).

THE COACH HOUSE

Address: 110 Waverly Place
Location: Waverly Place between Avenue of the Americas and Washington Square
Telephone: SP 7-0303; SP 7-0349
Credit Cards: AE; CB; DC; MC
Reservations: Essential
Hours: Dinner from 5:30 PM to 11:00 PM, Tuesday thru Saturday; 4:30 PM to 10:30 PM, Sunday
Days Closed: Mondays and major holidays
Liquor: Full Bar Service
Recommended or listed in: Gourmet, New York Times, many others
Maitre d': Paul Wilkins
Seating Capacity: 125
Cuisine: American
Specialties of the House: Prime Ribs of Beef; Mignonettes of Veal; Seafood Mediterranee; Rack of Lamb

The Coach House has for 30 years built a solid reputation for sustained excellence, and has become a Village landmark. Its menu, combining as it does both American standbys and more gourmet-geared fare, will please virtually every palate. The gracious Colonial decor, the quiet and serene atmosphere and attentive and efficient service, also help to make dining at the Coach House a memorable experience.

DINNER MENU

(table d'hote)

APPETIZERS & SOUPS:
Fresh Mushrooms à la Grecque; Fresh Eggplant Provencale; Fresh Clams (1.50); Smoked Wild Turkey; Quiche Lorraine; Paté Maison; Chilled Tomato Juice, Herring in Cream; Fresh Fruit; Escargots de Bourgogne Sauteed with Croutons in Garlic Butter (for two) (7.00); Fresh Melon; Fresh Oysters (3.50); The Coach House Black Bean Soup Madeira; Soup of the Day.

ENTREES:
Long Island Duckling — Brandied Quince .. 19.85
Fresh Oysters Coach House 22.85
(Stuffed with Lump Crab Meat and Baked with Mornay Sauce)
Fresh Striped Bass Vin Blanc 22.50
Baby Lobster Tails Skorpios with Feta Cheese 22.85
Prime Ribs of Beef, Natural 22.00
Rack of Spring Lamb, Roasted to a Crisp ... 22.85
Mignonettes of Veal à la Campagne with Glazed Chestnuts 22.85
Veal Piccate à la Francaise 20.50
(Medaillons of Milk-Fed Veal Sauteed in a Delicate Wine Sauce)
Fresh Lump Crab Meat Baltimore with Julienne Ham 22.50
Delightful Striped Bass Cooked in its own Court Bouillon with Vegetables 22.50
Baby Lobster Tails Sauteed in Garlic Butter . 22.00
(All entrees served with choice of vegetable, potatoes or salad.)

DESSERTS:
The Coach House Chocolate Cake; Dacquoise; Fresh Apple Tart; Coupe aux Marrons; Fresh Melon; Fresh Strawberries; Grand Marnier Bavarois; American Pecan Pie; Lemon Sherbet; Hot Fudge Ice Cream Cake; Chef's Custard; Ice Cream; Imported Cheeses.

(a la carte)

APPETIZERS & SOUPS:
Fresh Oysters (4.00); Onion au Gratin (2.50). Fresh Lump Crab Meat Cocktail (6.50); Fresh Clams (2.75); Baked Clams Provencale (for two) (7.00); Escargots de Bourgogne Sauteed with Croutons in Garlic Butter (for two) (7.00); Fresh Melon (2.50); Fresh Melon with Prosciutto (6.00); The Coach House Black Bean Soup Madeira (2.50);

continued on next page

Menu continued

ENTREES:

Fresh Striped Bass Poached with Fresh Vegetables and Broth 13.50
Veal Paillard 12.85
Carpetbag Steak Stuffed with Oysters (for Two) 37.50
Giant Loin Lamb Chop 10.50
Heavy Western Steer Sirloin Steak 14.00
(Boneless and Trimmed)
Steak au Poivre 15.50
(A French Black Pepper Steak)
Fresh Chicken Livers and Mushrooms Sauteed, Sauce Chasseur 8.50
American Chicken Pie 8.50
Roast Prime Ribs of Beef 13.75

(All entrees served with choice of potato or salad.)

DESSERTS:

Coupe aux Marrons (3.50); Coupe Chartreuse (4.50).

(Minimum cover per person: 5.00.)

CREAM CHEESE: *Cream cheese is made by draining the whey from cottage cheese and adding cream. The result is a firm, mild, fresh cheese which is used as a spread or in making pastries. Gum arabic is usually added to cream cheese to thicken it.*

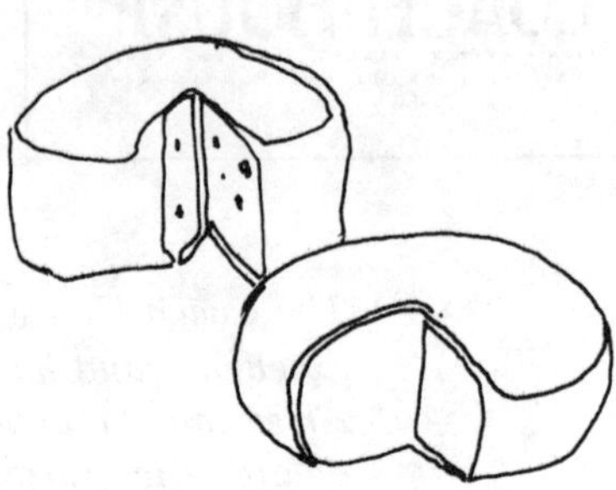

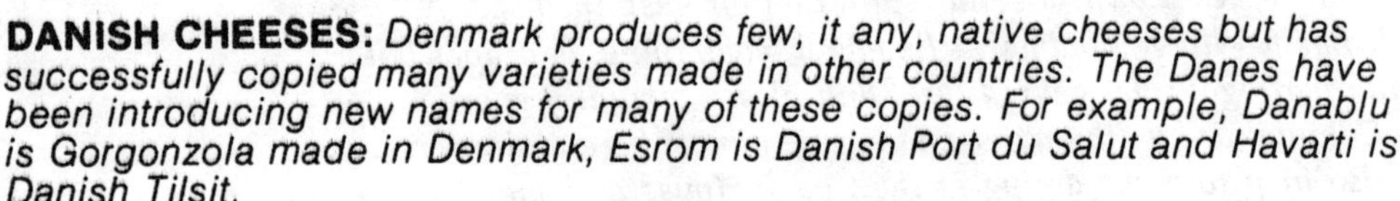

DANISH CHEESES: *Denmark produces few, it any, native cheeses but has successfully copied many varieties made in other countries. The Danes have been introducing new names for many of these copies. For example, Danablu is Gorgonzola made in Denmark, Esrom is Danish Port du Salut and Havarti is Danish Tilsit.*

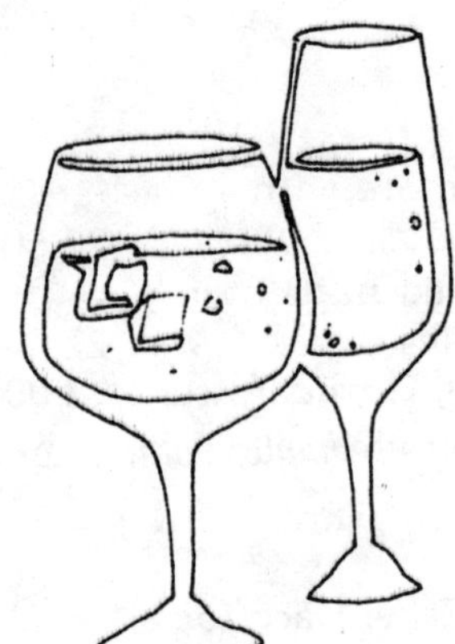

COTE DE NUITS: *Red wines from the northern half of the celebrated Burgundian Côte d'Or. The better Côte de Nuits wines are known by their commune or vineyard names (Chambertin, Musigny, Nuits-Saint-Georges, etc.). The regionally labeled wines are deeper-colored and longer-lived than their southern brethren in the Côte de Beaune.*

COTES DU RHONE: *The general name of the red wines bottled in Burgundy-style bottles that are produced on both banks of the Rhône river between Lyon and Avignon. These wines are deep red and somewhat heady; the best are known by their vineyard names, such as Côte Rôtie, Hermitage and Châteauneuf-du-Pape.*

DEZALEY: *One of the best Swiss white wines; a dry, gentle and fruity wine produced from grapes grown in a famous, city-owned vineyard on the north shore of Lake Geneva east of Lausanne.*

COMPANY

Address:	**365 Third Avenue**
Location:	**Third Avenue between 26th and 27th Streets**
Telephone:	**532-5222**
Credit Cards:	**AE; V; DC; MC; CB**
Reservations:	**Recommended**
Hours:	**Lunch from 12:00 Noon to 3:30 PM; Dinner from 6:00 PM to 1:00 AM; Friday and Saturday Dinner to 1:30 AM; Sunday Brunch from 12:00 Noon to 5:00 PM**
Days Closed:	**None**
Liquor:	**Full bar service**
Recommended or Listed in:	**New York Times; Gentleman's Quarterly; Where; After Dark; Michael's Thing; ABC/TV; Show Business**
Maitre d's:	**Jeffrey Croland; Scott MacClelland**
Reservations Manager:	**Jeffrey Croland**
Seating Capacity:	**80**
Cuisine:	**American/Continental**
Specialties of the House:	**Veal Cordon Bleu; Chicken Kiev; Steak au Poivre; Roast Duckling a l'Orange; Roast Prime Ribs of Beef; Mixed Seafood Casserole**
Dress:	**Casual**
Entertainment:	**Live music nightly, from 9:30 PM to 3:30 AM**
Party Facilities:	**Private room; capacity: 25**

Quality cooking and delightful service at a price one can afford has brought to Company a reputation as one of the more popular New York restaurants. The New York Times says, "Company is close to outstanding in the amount of good food—imaginatively prepared—you get for your money!" There is also an extensive wine list to merit approval. Company's attractive and comfortable bar is a popular meeting place for cocktails and the two dining rooms are well frequented from lunch through after-theatre supper. Fresh flowers, high ceilings, soft lights and nationally acclaimed songstress-pianists Pamela Stanley and Ava Williams add much character to this intimate, warm and romantic restaurant. The proprietor, Jeff Croland, is on hand to make sure your dining experience is a memorable one. It is definitely worth a visit. Company 2, a restaurant/flower shop, opens this summer at 228 West 10th Street, between Bleecker and Hudson Streets. Its two floors feature skylight dining and a cabaret.

DINNER MENU
(a la carte)

APPETIZERS & SOUPS:
Quiche du Chef (1.95); Escargot Bourguignon (3.25); Chopped Chicken Liver (1.50); Fettuccini Alfredo (2.75); Baked Stuffed Clams (2.50); Shrimp Cocktail (3.25); Chicken Livers in Bacon (2.25); Melon (1.50); Homemade Onion Soup (1.75).

ENTREES:

Breast of Chicken Parmigiana	6.25
Crisp Roast Duckling	7.95
Chicken Kiev	6.75
Chicken Francaise	6.50
Sliced Sirloin Steak	6.50

continued on next page

Company

Broiled Chopped Sirloin 5.25
Broiled Pork Chops, Apple Sauce 6.50
Sautéed Calf's Liver with Bacon and Onions . 6.50
Veal Cordon Bleu 7.50
Veal Parmigian 6.95
French Veal Cutlet 6.75
Veal Marsala 6.95
Prime Sirloin Steak 9.75
Roast Prime Ribs of Beef 8.75
Broiled Prime Filet Mignon 10.50
Mussels in White Wine or Marinara 5.95
Broiled Scampi 6.95
Broiled Filet of Sole Almondine 5.95
Ale Batter Fried Shrimp 6.75
Sea Scallops Broiled or Breaded 6.50
Baked Filet of Sole stuffed with Crabmeat ... 7.50
Mixed Seafood en Casserole 7.95

(All Entrees served with tossed green salad and choice of potato, rice pilaf or vegetable du jour.)

(Hamburgers and Salads are also available.)

DESSERTS:
Company's Cheesecake (1.50); Chocolate Mousse with Whipped Cream (1.75); Selection of Haagen Dazs Ice Cream (1.25); Company's Hot Apple Pie (1.25); Southern Pecan Pie with Whipped Cream (1.50); Fresh Strawberries with Cream (1.95); Chilled Melon (1.50).

SUNDAY BRUNCH

(12 Noon to 5:00 PM)
(prix fixe: 3.95)

(Includes a glass of Champagne, Bloody Mary or Screwdriver)

Three country fresh eggs with bacon, ham or sausage
Eggs Benedict
French toast
Chef's Salad
Three egg omelette - all kinds
Bagel with cream cheese, nova scotia lox, tomato and onion
Steakburger with steakhouse fries, garnished with tomato, onion and pickle
Triple Decker Club Sandwich
Fresh Spinach, Bacon and Mushroom Salad

If you own or manage a fine restaurant, and would like to see it included in the next edition of Manhattan Menus, please contact the publisher for information.

LA CÔTE BASQUE

Address: 5 East 55th Street
Location: 55th Street between Madison and Fifth Avenues
Telephone: 688-6525
Credit Cards: AE
Reservations: Required
Hours: Luncheon from 12:00 Noon to 3:00 PM; Dinner from 6:00 PM to 11:00 PM
Days Closed: Sunday; Saturday (August only); July; major holidays
Liquor: Full bar service
Recommended or Listed in: Forbes; Holiday
Maitre d': Gerard Loil
Reservations Manager: Gerard Loil
Seating Capacity: 186
Cuisine: French
Specialties of the House: Les Noisettes d'Agneau Éduard VII; La Côte de Veau aux Cèpes; La Sole Soufflée Walewska; Le Turbot Frais Poché Beurre de Truffe; Le Homard au Porto; Les Quenelles de Brochet Éminence; Les Côtelettes de Pigeonneau Sévigné
Dress: Jacket and tie; pant suits acceptable for ladies

By any standards, La Côte Basque is a beautiful restaurant—and the region it represents is beautifully depicted in original oil paintings by Bernard Lamotte. The decor is a blend of simplicity and elegance; the ambience combines comfort with sophistication, and the staff and the service is discreet while solicitous. The management of La Côte Basque was trained under the late Henri Soulé, and the menu is the creation of Chef Lozach Amede whose selections and their preparation reflect his own high standards and the pleasure he takes in the enjoyment of those who dine at La Côte Basque.

LUNCHEON MENU

(Prix fixe: 16.25)

(The menu changes frequently; the following is a representative selection.)

APPETIZERS:
Caviar Malossol (25.00); Hors d'Oeuvre; Terrine Côte Basque; Jambon de Bayonne; Saumon Fumé; Anguille Fumée; Melon, Grapfruit; Shrimps Cocktail; Coupe de Fruits; Cherrystones; Oysters in Season; Little Necks; Saucisson Tiède Franc-comtoise; Jus de Tomate; Artichaut Vinaigrette; Jambon Persillé; Oeuf en Gelée; Foie Gras Frais des Landes en Brioche Vieille France (12.00); Foie Gras Frais Prestige des Landes à la Gelée (12.00).

ENTREES:
Filet de Boeuf Financière
Blanquette de Veau à l'Ancienne
Cervelle au Beurre Noir
Jambon Madère aux Épinards
Omelette Côte Basque
Poularde Poêlée Beauséjour
Délices de Sole Véronique
Striped Bass Bretonne

DESSERTS:
Les Desserts Côte Basque; Les Fromages.

continued on next page

DINNER MENU

(Prix fixe: 28.50)

(The menu changes frequently; the following is a representative selection.)

APPETIZERS & SOUPS:
Caviar Malossol (25.00); Saumon Fumé; Jambon de Bayonne; Melon; Anguille Fumée; Hors d'Oeuvre; Cherrystones; Shrimps Cocktail; Melon Bayonne (1.75); Truite Fumée (1.50); Little Necks; Artichaut Vinaigrette; Oysters in Season; Grapefruit; Jambon Persillé; Consommé; Bisque de Homard; Vichyssoise; Saint Germain; Terrine Côte Basque; Madrilène en Gelée; Billy-By (1.75); Foie Gras Frais Prestige des Landes à la Gelée (12.00).

ENTREES:
Noix de Veau Rôtie Épinards au Jus
Poularde Poêlée au Champagne
Caneton Rôti aux Pêches
Filet d'Agneau en Brochette Côte Basque
Mignonnettes de Boeuf Sautées Vigneronne
Foie de Veau à l'Anglaise
Striped Bass Braisé aux Aromates
Délices de Sole des Gourmets
Sole Importée Meunière Doria

SPECIALTIES: *(7.00 supplement)*
Les Noisettes d'Agneau Édouard VII
Le Coeur de Filet Périgourdine
La Côte de Veau aux Cèpes
Les Quenelles de Brochet Éminence
La Sole Soufflée Walewska
Les Côtelettes de Pigeonneau Sévigné
Le Steak au Poivre
Le Turbot Frais Poché Beurre de Truffe
Le Poulet Reine Sauté Petit Duc
Le Homard au Porto

DESSERTS:
Les Desserts Côte Basque; Les Fromages; Spécialités: Les Soufflés Tous Arômes (4.50 p.p.), Les Crêpes Côte Basque (4.00).

EGRI BIKAVER: *One of the best red wines of Hungary, Bikaver ("Bull's Blood") is a rich, dark, long-lived wine produced northwest of Budapest near the old market town of Eger, one of Hungary's leading wine centers.*

FINO: *The finest of the Spanish sherries, Fino can be drunk relatively young but ages excellently. It is a very dry sherry, pale in color, with a sharp, intensely clean finish, and totally without bitterness.*

GRAVES: *Red and white Bordeaux from the gravelly districts on the left bank of the Garonne south of the city of Bordeaux. The whites are generally better known (the reds usually carry the chateau name); they run dry to medium sweet, pale yellow in color, with a distinctive metallic character.*

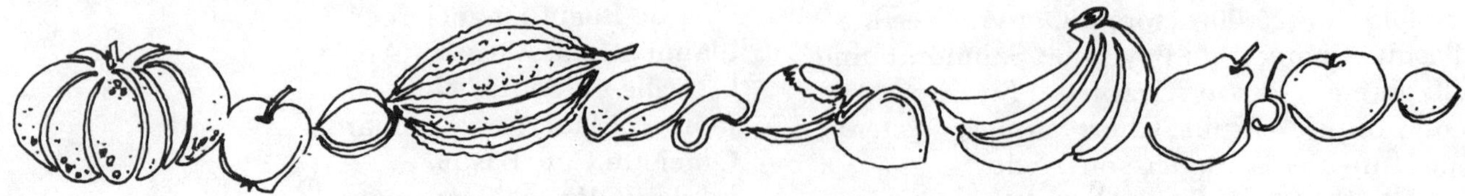

Inflation affects everyone, including restauranteurs. So look for the prices of menu items listed in this book to rise a bit during the year.

LA CRÊPE

Locations:	**East Side: 981 Third Avenue, at 58th Street** **Lincoln Center: 1974 Broadway, at 67th Street** **Midtown: 57 West 56th Street** **Times Square: 158 West 44th Street** **Village: 15 Greenwich Avenue** **Financial District: 59 Nassau Street** **Forest Hills, Queens: Austin Street** **Manhasset, L.I.: 2014 Northern Boulevard** **Cedarhurst, L.I.: 531 Central Avenue** **Massapequa Park, L.I.: 4924 Merrick Road** **White Plains, N.Y.: 51 Mamaroneck Avenue** **Hartford, Conn.: Civic Center** **Eatontown, N.J.: Monmouth Shopping Mall** **Princeton, N.J.: Quaker Bridge Mall** **Tom's River, N.J.: Ocean Mall** **Paramus, N.J.: Fashion Mall**
Credit Cards:	**AE; DC**
Reservations:	**Not necessary**
Days Closed:	**None, except that the Nassau Street location is closed on weekends**
Liquor:	**Full bar service except at 56th Street and Greenwich Village locations**
Recommended or Listed in:	**Cue; Women's Wear Daily; New York Times**
Cuisine:	**French (Brittany)**
Specialties of the House:	**110 varieties of crêpes in both wheat and buckwheat flour; soups; Quiche Lorraine; salads**
Party Facilities:	**Private or semi-private rooms at all locations; capacity varies**

La Crêpe, the first French crêperie in America, was opened by Countess Maya Poncet 13 years ago on West 56th Street in Manhattan. Her formula was to offer a variety of Brittany crêpes, cooked in the dining room in public view, in a restaurant decorated like a Brittany house dating back to 1490. The restaurant also featured waitresses dressed in the authentic costumes of Brittany. Today this formula is being duplicated throughout the metropolitan area, and the country, with the same high quality as was achieved in the very first crêperie.

MENU
(a la carte)

(The crêpes listed below are available made from either wheat or buckwheat flour.)

Crêpe with Sugar	.75
Crêpe with Snail Butter	1.15
Egg Crêpe	1.25
Ham Crêpe	2.35
Sausage Crêpe	2.35
Bacon Crêpe	2.35
Egg and Bacon Crêpe	2.80
Egg and Swiss Cheese Crêpe	2.60
Sausage and Swiss Cheese Crêpe	2.75
Ham and Swiss Cheese Crêpe	2.95
Bacon and Swiss Cheese Crêpe	2.95
Egg, Ham and Swiss Cheese Crêpe	2.95
Egg, Sausage and Swiss Cheese Crêpe	3.15
Egg, Bacon and Swiss Cheese Crêpe	3.10
Asparagus Crêpe	2.25
Asparagus and Swiss Cheese Crêpe	3.15
Tomatoes and Bacon Crêpe	2.85
Tomatoes "provencales" Crêpe	2.85
Tomatoes "provencales" and Ham Crêpe	2.85
Tomatoes and Sausage Crêpe	2.95
Sausage, Swiss Cheese, Tomatoes Crêpe	3.85
Creamed Mushrooms Crêpe	3.25
Egg and Creamed Mushrooms Crêpe	3.45
Creamed Chicken Crêpe	3.65
Ham and Creamed Chicken Crêpe	3.95
Crabmeat Supreme Sauce	5.35
Sea Food Thermidor Crêpe	5.25
Salmon Caviar Crêpe	6.25

LE COUP DE FUSIL

Address: 160 East 64th Street
Location: 64th Street between Lexington and Third Avenues
Telephone: PL 1-9110; PL 1-9155
Credit Cards: MC; V; DC; AE
Reservations: Recommended
Hours: Lunch from 12:00 Noon to 3:00 PM; Dinner from 6:00 PM to 11:00 PM.
Days Closed: Sunday
Liquor: Full bar service
Recommended or Listed in: Cue; Stagebill; Gourmet; New York Times; Women's Wear Daily
Reservations Manager: Mrs. de Brantes (Owner)
Seating Capacity: 55
Cuisine: Nouvelle Cuisine Francaise
Specialties of the House: Beouf au Fumet de Miel; Cailles aux Fruits; Saumon au Caviar; Homard aux Morilles Tarte au Citron; Tarte aux Pommes
Dress: Tie preferred and Jacket
Party Facilities: Private room; capacity: 35

The upper east side boasts its own French bistro in Le Coup de Fusil. Located in a townhouse, this art deco restaurant is small and intimate; the relaxing ambience and comfortable banquettes invite lingering conversation over coffee and a French pastry. The menu is selective and changes frequently; fresh fruits and vegetables of the season are always included. The nouvelle cuisine of Le Coup de Fusil has attracted a celebrity clientele and earned justifiable praise for its owner, Marina de Brantes.

LUNCHEON MENU

(a la carte)

(Menu changes twice each month; the following is a representative selection.)

APPETIZERS & SOUPS:
Soupe du Jour (3.00); Melon au Jambon Fumé (3.00); Avocat aux Champignons (3.00); Salade de Crevettes (3.00); Salade du Jour (2.00).

ENTREES:
Omelette au Fond d'Artichaut 6.00
Poulet au Cresson 7.50
Foie de Veau au Raisins..................... 8.50
Salade de Homard ....
Emince de Boeuf aux Echalottes Roses ....

DESSERTS:
Galette de Citron (3.00); Vacherin Coup de Fu (3.00); L'Assiette de Fraises (3.00); Les Sorbets Temps (2.50); Mousse au Chocolat (3.00); L'Ass de Framboises (3.50).

DINNER MENU

(a la carte)

(Menu changes twice each month; the following is a representative selection.)

(A prix fixe dinner menu is also available.)

APPETIZERS & SOUPS:
Soupe du Soir (4.00); Galantine de Canard en Gelée (4.00); Salade du Temps (4.50); Feuillete aux Ris de Veau (5.00); Salade du Soir (2.00).

ENTREES:
Boeuf au Trois Moutardes 17.00
Coquilles St. Jacques à la Nage............. 15.50
Civet de Canard aux Nouilles Fraiches .....
Loup à la Julienne de Legumes ....

DESSERTS:
Tarte Fine aux Pommes Acidulées (3.50); Les Sorbets du Temps (2.50); Vacherin Coup de F (3.00); Mousse au Chocolat (3.00); Le Fromag Brie (3.00).

Asparagus, Swiss Cheese and Ham Crêpe	3.95
Smoked Salmon and Sour Cream Crêpe	4.85
Imported Iranian Caviar Crêpe	7.25
"Ratatouille" Crêpe	2.85
Sausage and "Ratatouille" Crêpe	3.95
Egg and "Ratatouille" Crêpe	2.85
"Ratatouille" and Ham Crêpe	3.35
Egg, "Ratatouille" and Bacon Crêpe	4.35
Egg, "Ratatouille" and Sausage Crêpe	4.35
Egg, "Ratatouille" and Ham Crêpe	4.35
Ham and Mushrooms with Cream Crêpe	3.45
Tomatoes Provencales, Egg, Bacon Crêpe	3.45
Beef "Bourguignon" Crêpe	4.45
Beef and Garden Vegetables Crêpe	4.85
Creamed Spinach Crêpe	1.95
Egg and Creamed Spinach Crêpe	2.35
Egg, Ham and Creamed Spinach Crêpe	3.35
Blue Cheese Crêpe	2.05
Swiss Cheese Crêpe	2.25
Blue Cheese and Apples Crêpe	3.50
Swiss Cheese and Apples Crêpe	3.15
Ratatouille and Swiss Cheese Crêpe	3.75

(A variety of soups, salads and desserts are also available.)

(Prices may vary slightly according to location.)

BODY: *The body of the wine is the feel of it on the tongue—its roundness and its texture upon the palate.*

BOUQUET: *The bouquet differs from the aroma in that it refers to the scent of the wine, derived not from the grapes but from the process of aging, cooperage and fermentation.*

CHEWY: *Chewy is used to describe a good, full body for red wines. Once you have a chewy wine in your mouth, it feels good, rich and full-bodied. A Pinot Noir should be chewy as should Vintage Port and Barolo.*

COLOR: *A good wine's color should be clear and even throughout, exhibiting no cloudiness whatsoever. A dry white wine should have a greenish-yellow tint, and the sweeter types a golden hue. An oxidized white wine has a brown tinge, a bad sign, and is said to have "maderized." Red wine should be purplish when young, acquiring brownish tones as it ages.* Pelure d'oignon, *or onion skin, refers to the thin, light-brown band which is visible around the rim of healthy, vintage wines. Beware of any wine that has a muddy appearance.*

DALY'S DANDELION

Address: 1029 Third Avenue
Location: Third Avenue and 61st Street
Telephone: 838-0780
Credit Cards: AE
Reservations: Not necessary
Hours: 11:00 AM to 3:00 AM, Daily
Days Closed: None
Liquor: Full bar service
Maitre d': Tony Beacon
Seating Capacity: 140
Cuisine: American
Specialties of the House: Hamburgers
Dress: Casual
Entertainment: Occasional

Lazy ceiling fans, tile floors, fresh flowers on marble-topped tables, stained glass and dark wood beams set the tone for Daly's Dandelion—a bustling yet amiable favorite of those who frequent one of the City's busiest areas for shopping and the cinema. The beautiful wooden, turn-of-the-century bar attracts its own clientele as does the glass-enclosed sidewalk cafe. Inside or out, the service is pleasant and efficient and the menu selections ample and satisfying.

MENU

(a la carte)

SOUPS & SIDE DISHES:
Clam Chowder (on Friday) (cup .95) (bowl 1.80); Soup of the Day (Seasonal) (cup .95) (bowl 1.80); Gazpacho (Seasonal) (cup .95) (bowl 1.80); Chili (cup 1.00); Cottage Fries (1.00); Tossed Salad (1.00); Spinach, Mushrooms and Bacon Salad (2.75).

ENTREES:
Hamburger 2.75
Cheeseburger 3.00
Baconburger 3.25
Bacon Cheeseburger 3.50
Chili Burger 3.50
Chili, bowl 3.00
Eggs with Bacon or Ham with Salad 3.50
Omelettes with Salad 3.75
Southern Fried Chicken with Cottage Fries .. 4.75
Club Sandwich 3.75
Turkey Sandwich 2.75
Ham Sandwich 2.75
Grilled Cheese and Bacon 2.50
Chef's Salad 4.25
Cottage Cheese and Bacon Salad 3.95
Spinach, Mushrooms and Bacon Salad 3.75
Tuna Salad 4.25
Sardine Salad 4.25
Shell Steak with Potato Souffle and Salad .. 10.00
Chopped Sirloin with Potato Souffle and Salad 5.50
Chopped Sirloin Berlin with Green Peppers and Onions 6.00
Steak Tartare 5.50

DESSERTS:
Chocolate Cake (1.50); Cheese Cake (1.75); Carrot Cake (1.50); Chocolate Fudge Brownies (1.50); Daly's Golden Apple Pie (1.50); Pecan Pie (1.75); Lemon Pie (1.25); Peanut Chiffon Pie (1.25).

(A special Brunch Menu is available on Sunday.)

DAVID K'S

Address: **1115 Third Avenue**
Location: **Third Avenue between 65th and 66th Streets**
Telephone: **371-9090**
Credit Cards: **AE**
Reservations: **Recommended**
Hours: **12:00 Noon to 12:00 Midnight, Sunday thru Thursday; 12:00 Noon to 12:30 AM, Friday and Saturday**
Days Closed: **None**
Liquor: **Full bar service**
Managing Director: **Norman Chi**
Seating Capacity: **175**
Cuisine: **Chinese**
Specialties of the House: **Orange Beef; Peking Duck (no advance order necessary); Jumbo Shrimp Szechuen Style; Chinese Tea Lunch**
Entertainment: **Pianist and Singer from 9:00 PM to 2:00 AM, nightly**
Party Facilities: **Private room; capacity: 100**

David Keh opened his first restaurant 10 years ago and introduced New Yorkers to the unique style of Szechuen cooking. Several restaurants later, he created David K's—a spacious and sophisticated dining establishment about which James Beard has said: "My one and only choice for Chinese food would be David K's, a large restaurant on Third Avenue, where the cooking is extremely good, and there's entertainment at night in the bar." Floor to ceiling windows and banks of fresh flowers create an airy atmosphere and the unusual beauty of the crystal and china service adds elegance to the decor. Only authentic Chinese food is served at David K's, and only the freshest ingredients are used in its preparation. In addition to a full dinner menu, the restaurant also serves Chinese snacks in its upstairs dining room and offers a special Chinese Tea Lunch.

DINNER MENU

(a la carte)

(The following is a representative selection.)

APPETIZERS:
Assorted Delicacy Platter for two (6.25); Minced Chicken for two (6.50); Diced Boneless Squab for two (6.50); Hacked Chicken, Szechuen Style (6.25); Sliced Kidney in Chef's Special Sauce (6.25); Tasty Walnuts (6.25).

SOUPS:
Wonton (1.75); Hot and Sour (1.75); Minced Squab in Bamboo Container (2.95); Fresh Fillet of Fish in Chicken Broth (2.95).

ENTREES:
Da Chin Chicken 7.75
Chicken, Szechuen Style 7.75
Chicken in Garlic Sauce 7.75
Shredded Chicken with Bean Sprouts 9.50
Crispy Duck 9.25
Smoked Duck 9.25
Barbequed Squab 14.00
Peking Duck 26.00
Dry Sauteed Beef 8.75
Oyster Beef 8.25
Orange Beef 10.50
Hot Spicy Shredded Beef 8.50
Shredded Beef in Garlic Sauce 8.25
Twice Cooked Pork 7.25
Shredded Pork with Szechuen Cabbage 7.25
Moo Shu Pork 7.25
Jumbo Shrimp, Szechuen Style 9.50
Prawns in Brown Sauce 8.75
Velvet Shrimp 8.75
Frog's Legs, Szechuen Style 9.50

continued on next page

David K's (Photo by Dan Brinzac)

Scallops with Garlic Sauce 8.75
Pomfort Fish with Pepper/Salt 12.00
Sliced Fish with Wine Sauce 8.75
Catch of the Day in a Sweet and Sour Sauce . 9.50
Steamed Fish 12.00
Crab with Brown Sauce 9.50
Lobster, Szechuen Style 15.00
Fresh Lobster Sauteed with Fresh Vegetables 19.50

Bean Curd in Oyster Sauce 6.00
Dry Sauteed String Beans 5.50
Snow Peas and Water Chestnuts 6.50
Pan Fried Noodles 6.25

DESSERTS:
Fresh Fruit (5.00); Sesame Banana (3.50); Sesame Apple (3.50); Miniature Lemon Custard Tart (1.75).

TARTE VISIDANTINE: *This pastry originated in Provence and is made with almonds, an ingredient that is very popular in that part of France. The "tarte" or one-crust pie is made with a sweet dough – pâte sucrée – and is filled with frangipane or almond cream.(Frangipane is reputedly named for the Italian, Frangipani, who invented it.) The frangipane is covered with sliced almonds.*

TRANCHE DE MOCCA: *This cake is made with a genoise base—a genoise is a sponge cake made with eggs, sugar, butter and flour. The tranche de mocca has three layers of genoise and two layers of butter cream filling flavored with mocha. There's butter cream on top, too, and toasted almonds on the sides.*

TUILES A L'ORANGE: *These cookies are made of egg whites, sugar, butter, flour and grated orange rind. They are baked until they are golden brown, removed from the oven immediately and, while still warm, are rolled lightly around a rolling pin. The result is a curled cookie that looks like a curved tile or a "tuile." Tuiles may also be flavored with vanilla or almonds.*

DRESNER'S/DRESNER'S OTHER

Address: Dresner's—1479 York Avenue
Dresner's Other—1701 Second Avenue
Location: Dresner's—York Avenue and 78th Street
Dresner's Other—Second Avenue and 88th Street
Telepnone: 988-5153 (Dresner's); 534-7553 (Dresner's Other)
Credit Cards: AE; MC; V; DC
Reservations: Not necessary
Hours: 11:00 AM to 12:00 Midnight, Sunday thru Thursday; to 1:00 AM Friday and Saturday; Bar from 11:00 AM to 2:00 AM daily
Days Closed: Thanksgiving; Christmas
Liquor: Full bar service
Recommended or Listed in: Cue; New York Times; New York Post
Seating Capacity: Dresner's—90; Dresner's Other—121
Cuisine: American and Continental
Specialty of the House: Roumanian Steak
Dress: Informal
Party Facilities: Private Room (Dresner's Other); capacity: 40

These two Yorkville establishments are considered landmarks by the loyal clientele who early on discovered Dresner's excellent beef specialties, moderate prices and informal surroundings. Both restaurants offer courteous service and a friendly atmosphere. The Roumanian Steak Platter–Dresner's most popular dish–is an excellent meal and a real dining value. There are unusual daily specials as well.

MENU
(a la carte)

APPETIZERS & SOUPS:
Baked Stuffed Clams (1.75); Jumbo Shrimp Cocktail (3.25); Bismark Herring in Cream Sauce (1.75); Chilled Tomato, Grapefruit or Orange Juice (.95); French Onion Soup au Gratin (1.75).

ENTREES:
Surf 'n' Turf 7.95
(Stuffed jumbo shrimp and filet mignon)
Filet Mignon 7.95
Junior Filet Mignon 6.75
New York Cut Shell Steak 7.95
Junior New York Cut Shell Steak 6.75
Broiled Chopped Beef Steak 4.50
London Broil with Mushroom Sauce 4.75
Sauteed Fresh Chicken Livers with Mushrooms 4.50
Broiled Young Steer Liver with Hickory Smoked Bacon and Sauteed Onions 4.25
Broiled Pork Chops with Apple Sauce 4.95
Broiled Half Spring Chicken 4.25
Golden Brown Southern Fried Chicken 4.25
Boneless Breast of Chicken Parmigiana 5.25
Veal Cutlet Parmigiana 5.75
Fried or Broiled Jumbo Shrimps 6.25
Shrimp Scampi 6.75
Filet of Sole Almandine 5.25
Fisherman's Platter 6.75
Jumbo Shrimps Stuffed with Crabmeat 6.75
Broiled Whole Long Island Flounder 5.25
Broiled or Fried Fresh Sea Scallops 6.25

(Above Entrees include Dresner's Salad Bowl and choice of Potato, Rice, Linguini or Vegetable du Jour.)

Whole Jumbo Shrimp Salad 6.25
Tunafish Salad 4.25
Chef's Salad 4.75
Dresner's Burger Delight with Lettuce and Tomato, French Fried Potatoes 3.75
Hot Roast Beef or Roast Maryland Turkey Sandwich with Vegetable and Choice of Potato 3.95

DESSERTS:
Apple Pie (1.25); Peach Melba (1.95); Fresh Strawberries with Whipped Cream (2.00); Pure Cream Cheese Cake (1.50); Cheesecake with Strawberries (2.00); Haagen Dazs Ice Cream or Fresh Fruit Sherbet (1.50).

(A prix-fixe brunch (3.50-4.95) is served on Saturday and Sunday from 12:00 Noon to 4:00 PM.)

THE EAST SIDE CAFE

Address: 1546 Third Avenue
Location: Third Avenue and 87th Street
Telephone: 348-7660
Credit Cards: AE; MC; DC; V; CB
Reservations: Recommended
Hours: 12:00 Noon to 12:00 Midnight, daily
Days Closed: None
Liquor: Wine and beer; liquor license pending
Seating Capacity: 60
Cuisine: Near, Middle and Far Eastern
Specialties of the House: Adobo; Pancit; Patlican Guvech; Rellenong Manok; Paella a la Oriental
Dress: Casual

The Yorkville section of New York has its share of fine restaurants but The East Side Cafe may be the first to offer a combination of Near, Middle and Far Eastern cuisines. The imaginative menu provides a flavorful balance between these culinary traditions and the result is a complementary blend of tastes and textures. Sparkling tile, white stucco walls, warm brown and beige tones and flourishing greenery create a soothing setting for dining, the decorative Oriental accents lend an authentic and exotic touch to the decor, and the service is friendly and welcoming.

MENU

(a la carte)

APPETIZERS & SOUPS:
Hummus (Cold Chick Pea and Sesame Oil with Herbs) (1.50); Dolmeh (Steamed Grape Leaves with Rice and Nut Stuffing) (1.75); Lumpiang Shanghai (Deep Fried Mini Egg Roll with Ground Pork and Shrimps) (2.00); Midye Dolmasi (Fresh Mussels, Stuffed with Rice and Cooked in Olive Oil) (2.00); Escargot de Bourgogne (2.95); Imam Bayildi (Fresh Eggplant with Sliced Onion and Tomato Cooked in Olive Oil) (2.25); Tarima (Spiced Dried Beef) (2.25); Shrimp Cocktail (2.25); Red Caviar Dip (1.75); Borek (Spinach Pie and Feta Cheese) (1.50); Fresh Artichoke Harts (2.00); Selected Hors d'Oeuvres Platter (6.50); Sotanghon (Clear Noodles in Chicken Soup) (1.25); Soup of the Day (1.25); Yogurt Soup (1.25); Kaleh Joosh (Onion Soup Creamed with Cheese) (1.50).

ENTREES:
Broiled Sea Food a la Istanbul 6.50
Rellenadong Hipon 6.50
(Deep Fried Jumbo Shrimps with Ground Pork and Ham)
Steamed Fish 5.50
Steamed Mussels in Oriental Sauce 5.00
Shrimp Oriental 6.50
(Fried Jumbo Shrimps Stuffed with Kassari Cheese in Delicate Walnut Sauce)
Cardillo 4.50
(Fried Fish with Tomato and Egg Sauce)
Shish Kebob 6.50
Moussaka 5.75
Rib Lamb Chops 6.50
Sirloin Steak a la East Side 6.95
Grilled Meat Specialties 6.95
(Combination of Shish and Kofta Kebobs, Lamb Chops and Chicken)
Kari-Kari 5.75
(Oxtail Stew with Green Beans and Eggplant)
Shish Kofte 5.50
(Charcoal Broiled Chopped Meat on Skewer)
Paksiw Na Pata 5.00
(Pickled Pork Hocks)
Lengua 5.00
(Braised Fresh Beef Tongue with Mushroom Sauce)
Patlican Guvech 5.50
(Chunks of Eggplant and Sweet Fresh Lamb Nestled in Wine Sauce)
Adobo 5.50
(Braised and Fried Chicken, Chicken Livers and Pork)
Rellenong Manok 5,50
(Roast Boned Chicken with Eggs and Pork Stuffing)
Tinola 4.50
(Ginger Chicken Soup)
Fried Chicken a la Ahmet 4.50

(All entrees are served with Turkish Rice Pilaff, Tossed Salad, Bread and Butter.)

RICE & NOODLE SPECIALTIES:
Pancit Bijon Guisado 3.00
(Pork, Chicken and Sausage with Noodles)
Pancit Sotanghon 3.50
(Cellophane Noodles with Chinese Vegetables)
Paella a la Oriental 5.95
(Special Rice with Mussels, Chicken, Spanish Sausage and Shrimps)
Khumbi Matar Pullao 3.00
(Rice with Green Peas and Mushrooms)

SALADS:
Plato's Salad (3.50); Vegetarian's Delight (1.75); Spinach Salad (3.50); Atsara (1.50).

DESSERTS:
Lychees (1.25); Leche Flan (1.25); Halo Halo (1.25); Baklava (1.00); Maiz con Hielo (1.00); Macapuno Sweets (1.00); Cheesecake (1.00); Mango Preserves (1.00); Langka Especial (1.00); Fruit of the Season (1.00); Ice Cream (1.00); Homemade Fruit Salad (1.50).

HERMITAGE: *One of the finest Rhône Valley reds. Produced in one of France's oldest vineyards (it dates to the Roman era) above the town of Tain, about 50 miles south of Lyon. Known widely as a "manly" wine, Hermitage has the qualities of a port – it throws a sediment and requires decanting, and its scent and flavor become almost overwhelming as it ages.*

JOHANNISBERG: *The most renowned of the German Rheingau white wines, produced on the hillside running down from the 12th Century Schloss Johannisberg to the banks of the Rhine. Frequently drunk by itself, rather than as an accompaniment to a meal, the wine has far more power than a Moselle, with an extraordinary grace, breed and bouquet.*

LACRIMA CHRISTI: *The celebrated and often quite pleasant Graves-like Italian white wine (its name means "Tears of Christ") produced at vineyards on the slopes of Mount Vesuvius near Naples. The words "del Vesuvio" on the label distinguish the original from sparkling versions produced elsewhere in Italy.*

LAMBRUSCO: *A slightly sparkling Italian red wine, produced just west of Bologna in northeast Italy. Vivid and grapy, Lambrusco has little subtlety; it is extremely fruity and somewhat sweet, with an intense bouquet.*

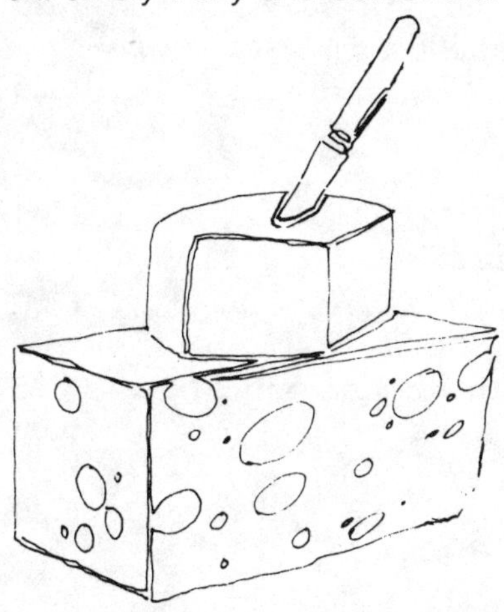

DOUBLE GLOUCESTER: *This cheese is a close relative of English Cheddar but matures faster and is of a moister and softer consistency. It has a clear yellow hue, with veins of blue mold, and a distinctly pungent flavor. True Double Gloucester is rarely found in the United States.*

EDAM: *Named for the town in northern Holland where it was first made, this popular cheese is now mass produced not only in its native land but throughout much of the world. It is a semi-soft table cheese with a bland taste and a smooth consistency. Edam is sold in the form of slightly flattened balls which are dipped in red wax.*

Inflation affects everyone, including restauranteurs. So look for the prices of menu items listed in this book to rise a bit during the year.

EL FARO

Address: 823 Greenwich Street
Location: Greenwich Street at Horatio Street (two blocks west of Eighth Avenue; two blocks north of 12th Street)
Telephone: WA 9-8210
Credit Cards: Not accepted
Reservations: Not accepted
Hours: 10:00 AM to 12 Midnight
Days Closed: None
Liquor: Full bar service
Recommended or Listed in: New York Times; Village Voice
Maitre d's: Pepe and Andres
Seating Capacity: 50
Cuisine: Spanish
Specialties of the House: Chicken Villarroy; Lobster with White Sauce; Paella a la Valenciana; Shrimps a la Faro
Dress: Casual
Party Facilities: Private room (lunchtime only); capacity: 50

El Faro is a Greenwich Village landmark, having been in its present location as long as most of us can remember. The decor is as distinctively Spanish as the cuisine with the barroom and dining room featuring murals in oil of flamenco dancers and scenes in Spain. You might have to wait for a table as this is a very popular dining spot and reservations are not accepted.

DINNER MENU
(a la carte)
(A partial listing)

APPETIZERS & SOUPS:
Shrimp Ajillo (2.00); Shrimp Cocktail (2.25); Ham and Olives Spanish Style (2.25); Salpicon (Seafood Salad) (2.75); Broiled Chorizos (Spanish Sausages) (2.25); Galician Soup (Beef, Pork, Vegetables) (1.50); Gazpacho (Cold Vegetable Soup) (1.50).

ENTREES:
Shrimp a la Faro 6.25
(Broiled with Wine Sauce)
Paella a la Valenciana 7.00
Paella a la Valenciana with Lobster 9.00
Paella a la Marinera 7.00
(Rice, Clams, Scallops and Shrimps)
Paella a la Marinera with Lobster 9.00
Mariscada with Egg Sauce 7.00
(Mixed Seafood)
Mariscada al Ajillo 7.00
(Hot Sauce with Garlic)
Mariscada with Green Sauce 7.00
(Olive Oil, Parsley, Garlic, Onions)
Crab-Meat with Green Sauce 8.50
Lobster with White Sauce 8.50
(Sherry Wine, Butter, Milk and Onions)
Lobster with Green Sauce 8.50
Shrimp a la Diablo 6.25
(Hot Sauce, Onions, Green Peppers and Tomatoes)
Shrimp with Green Sauce 6.25
Shrimp a la Criolla 6.25
Shrimp al Ajillo 6.25
(Hot Sauce with Garlic)
Beef Saute 6.25
(Oregano, Bay Leaves and Wine)
Filet of Pork Bar B.Q. with Almond Sauce 6.25
Spare Ribs Bar B.Q. with Fruit Sauce 6.50
Clams a la Marinera 6.25
(Olive Oil, Parsley, Garlic, Onions and Oregano)
Clams a la Burdalesa 6.25
(Hot Sauce)
Veal, Almond Sauce 6.00
Veal a la Corunesa 6.00
(With Tomato, Sherry and Butter)
Veal a la Extremena 6.00
(With Onions, Peppers and Sausages)
Duckling Bar B.Q. with Almond Sauce 6.75
Chicken and Rice 5.00
(Arroz con Pollo)
Chicken Villarroy 6.50
(Breast of Chicken with Bechamel Cream)
Fish of the Day 6.25
(Entrees are served with Spanish Rice or Spanish Potatoes and Salad.)
(A variety of desserts priced from 1.00 to 1.50 are also available.)

THE ENGLISH PUB

Address: 900 Seventh Avenue
Location: Seventh Avenue between 56th and 57th Streets
Telephone: 265-4360
Credit Cards: All major credit cards accepted
Reservations: Recommended
Hours: Daily, from 11:30 AM to 4:00 AM
Liquor: Full bar service
Recommended or Listed in: Cue; New York Times
Maitre d': Eduardo
Reservations Manager: Eduardo
Cuisine: English; American
Specialties of the House: Shepherd's Pie; Steak & Kidney Pie; Prime Ribs of Beef
Dress: Casual
Party Facilities: Private room; capacity: 80

The English Pub uses the newspapers of London as its theme and the fare is as authentically British as the classified ad pages of The Times. *The draught beers are special complements to any lunch or dinner; Whitbread's beer on tap is imported for your delectation, and stout—that robust brew held responsible for those wonderful British complexions—is also available. The hearty dishes include fish and chips, steak and kidney pie and a fabulous mixed grill. The atmosphere is friendly; the bar active. Stop in at The English Pub for a short visit to the land of Blighty.*

DINNER MENU

(a la carte)

APPETIZERS & SOUPS:
Melon in Season (1.50); Spare Ribs Appetizer (2.75); Escargot (3.50); Jumbo Shrimp Cocktail (3.50); Breaded Mushrooms (2.75); Baked Clams (2.95); Chile con Carne (2.00); Onion Soup au Gratin (1.50); Scotch Broth (1.00); Mulligatawny (1.00).

ENTREES:
Fish 'n' Chips 3.50
Shepherd's Pie 3.75
Steak and Kidney Pie 3.95
English Mixed Grille 7.95
Broiled Halibut Steak 5.95
Rainbow Brook Trout 5.75
Shrimp Scampi on Pilaf of Rice 7.25
Filet of Sole 6.95
Fried New Orleans Jumbo Shrimp 6.75
Fried Shrimp Stuffed with Crabmeat 6.95
Chicken in the Basket 4.50
Breast of Chicken Cordon Bleu 6.25
Boneless Breast of Chicken with Wine, Mushrooms and Chives 5.95
Duck l'Orange with Rice 6.25
English Pub's Chopped Steak 4.95
London Broil with Mushroom Sauce 4.75
Piccadilly Lamb Chops 7.25
Bar-B-Que Spare Ribs 5.25
Center Cut Pork Chops with Apple Sauce 6.50
16 oz Boneless Sirloin Steak 9.95
Prime Rib of Beef au Jus 9.50
Skewered Beef en Brochette 5.25
Filet Mignon 10.25

(All entrees are served with vegetable, choice of potato and mixed green salad.)

The Chef's Salad Bowl 3.95
Spinach Salad 3.75

DESSERTS:
Apple Pie (1.50); Hot Apple Pie with Cheddar Cheese (1.75); Chocolate Cream Cheese Cake (1.75); Plum Pudding in Hot Brandy Sauce (1.75); French Ice Cream (1.00); Cream Cheese Cake (1.75).

ENTRE NOUS

Address:	**396 Third Avenue**
Location:	**Third Avenue at 28th Street**
Telephone:	**679-0828**
Credit Cards:	**AE; DC; CB; V; MC**
Reservations:	**Recommended**
Hours:	**Lunch from 12:00 Noon to 3:00 PM, Monday thru Friday; Dinner from 6:00 PM to 11:30 PM, Monday thru Saturday**
Days Closed:	**Sunday**
Liquor:	**Full bar service**
Recommended or Listed in:	**New York Times**
Maitre d':	**Bernard Roy**
Reservations Manager:	**Bernard Roy**
Seating Capacity:	**49**
Cuisine:	**French**
Specialties of the House:	**Andouillettes des Halles; Rognons de Veau; Cornish Game Hen; Canard aux Navets; Civet de Lapin; Fresh Salmon Gravlax**
Dress:	**Casual**

Anyone who wants to broaden his knowledge of wines and certainly anyone who claims to be an aficionado owes Entre Nous a visit. For the cellar has been painstakingly assembled and boasts a breadth and depth of nearly 100 labels, growths and vintages, and at prices that are fair. But those more interested in food won't be disappointed. The French cuisine is masterfully prepared—often at your table—and seasonal specialties such as soft shell crab, lamb brains or shad roe are to be had in addition to the regular menu. Flower paintings repeat the motif created by the fresh cut flowers on every table. Entre Nous is an elegant restatement of the classic French restaurant.

LUNCHEON MENU

(a la carte)

APPETIZERS:

Fresh Fruits Macerated in Kirsch (1.75); Beansprout Crêpes - Sauce Cumberland (1.50); Oysters on the Half Shell - Brie Butter (3.00); Andouillettes des Halles (2.50).

ENTREES:

Endives Bruxelloises 5.50
Chopped Steak and Onions 4.75
Veal Cutlet à la Holstein 7.50
Roast Beef Hash - French Style 4.00
Sliced Roast Sirloin 6.75
Calf's Liver with Juniper and Bacon 6.50
Croque Monsieur 3.75
Junior Sirloin Steak 7.25
Omelette au Choix 4.00
Poached Eggs Florentines 4.20
Filet of Sole Meunière 6.25
Mussels Marinières 6.00
Salade Nicoise 6.00
Fresh Salmon Gravlax 7.70
Steak Tartare 8.70

DESSERTS:

Poire au Vin Rouge (Pear Poached in Red Wine) (2.50); Tarte à l'Orange (2.00); Glace ou Sorbet (1.25); Crêpes Suzette (for two) (5.50); Parfait Moccha et Menthe (2.75); Fromages ou Fruits (2.25); Pavé de Marrons (Chestnut Cake) (2.95); Pomme au Four (Baked Apple) (1.50); Frangipane aux Fruit (3.00).

DINNER MENU

(a la carte)

APPETIZERS:
Fresh Fruit Macerated in Kirsch (1.75); Crêpe Filled with Beansprouts - Sauce Cumberland (1.50); Braised Endive Rolled in Ham - Sauce Mornay (2.75); Oysters on the Half Shell - Brie Butter Bread (3.00); Grilled Sausage Topped with Breadcrumbs (3.50); Fresh Marinated Salmon (5.00); Mussels Poached in White Wine and Shallots (3.25).

ENTREES:
Canard aux Navets 9.75
(Roast Duckling Garnished with Glazed Turnips)
Rognons de Veau Christian X 7.95
(Flambeed Veal Kidneys - Oporto Sauce)
Poached Striped Bass au Fenouil 9.25
Carré de Porc aux Pruneaux 7.50
(Roast Loin of Pork stuffed with Marinated Prunes)
Civet de Lapin 8.50
(Rabbit in Red Burgundy Wine Sauce)
Paupiettes de Veau 8.25
(Braised Veal Birds in Tomato Sauce)
Aïoli Hyèrois 7.25
(Poached Cod and Garden Vegetable - Garlic Sauce)
Flambeed Sirloin Steak - Shallots and Red Wine 10.50
Roast Cornish Game Hen - Cognac and Grapes 8.95
Steak Tartare 8.75
(All entrees are appropriately garnished with potatoes and vegetable.)

Entre Nous

We've spared neither effort nor expense to make this edition of Manhattan Menus *as useful, accurate and up-to-date as possible. If you have suggestions or comments, we'd like to hear them. Drop us a note at: P.O. Box 5217, FDR Station, New York, N. Y. 10022.*

EXETER'S

Address: 1444 First Avenue
Location: First Avenue at 75th Street
Telephone: 535-3383
Credit Cards: AE; DC; CB; MC; V
Reservations: Recommended for Dinner
Hours: 12 Noon to 2:00 AM
Days Closed: None
Liquor: Full bar service
Recommended or Listed in: Cue; New York Magazine; Village Voice
Maitre d's: Craig and David
Reservations Managers: Craig and David
Seating Capacity: 55
Cuisine: American and Continental
Specialties of the House: Prime Sirloin Steak; Fresh Fish; Daily Specials
Dress: Jackets suggested

Casual elegance is the hallmark of this fine East Side establishment. A turn-of-the-century motif keynotes the decor with a long copper bar and antique fixtures lending authenticity to the theme. Fresh flowers add a bright note to the warm and intimate atmosphere. Fine cuisine at reasonable prices makes Exeter's a good choice for the discriminating.

MENU
(a la carte)

APPETIZERS & SOUPS:
Melon and Prosciutto (3.25); Shrimp Cocktail (3.50); Artichoke Hearts (2.75); Clams Oreganate (2.95); Avocado with Shrimp Salad (3.95); Cold Mushrooms in Mustard Sauce (2.75); Onion Soup au Gratin (1.50); Gaspacho (1.50).

ENTREES:
U.S.D.A. Prime Steak 10.95
Club Steak 6.95
Sliced Sirloin Steak 6.95
Beef Kabob on a Bed of Rice 7.50
Chopped Steak 5.50
Southern Style Spareribs 5.95
Filet Mignon 11.50
Surf and Turf 11.95
Roasted Half Chicken 5.95
Chili with Rice 3.50
Omelettes 3.95
Hamburger Platter 3.50
Fettuccine Alfredo 4.95
Tortellini alla Panna 5.50
Linguine with White Clam Sauce 4.95
Broiled Filet of Sole 6.50
Shrimp Scampi with Rice 6.95
Lobster Tails 11.95
Fish of the Day .... (...)
Bluefish 7.25
Barbecued Shrimp 6.95

SALADS:
Salad Nicoise (4.25); Chef Salad (3.95); Chicken Salad (3.25); Spinach, Bacon and Mushrooms (3.95); Shrimp Salad (3.75); Tomatoes and Onions (1.75); Tossed Salad (.95).

DESSERTS:
Chocolate Cake (1.75); Pecan Pie (1.50); Selected Ice Cream (1.50); Cheesecake (1.50); Ricciardi Sherbet (1.50).

THE FARM HOUSE RESTAURANT

Address: 175 Second Avenue
Location: Second Avenue and Eleventh Street
Telephone: 677-8807
Credit Cards: V; MC
Reservations: Recommended
Hours: 5:00 PM to 2:00 AM; Dinner from 6:00 PM to 12:00 Midnight, Tuesday thru Thursday, to 1:00 AM, Friday and Saturday
Days Closed: Monday
Liquor: Full bar service
Recommended or Listed in: New York Times; Cue; Daily News; The Villager; Unique New York
Reservations Manager: Mr. Wright
Seating Capacity: 50
Cuisine: Southern
Specialties of the House: Pork Chops; Southern Fried Chicken; Barbequed Ribs; Homemade Sweet Potato Pie, Apple Pie, Peach Pie
Dress: Casual

The Farm House Restaurant offers New Yorkers an opportunity to sample the best of Southern regional cooking. Mr. Wright, owner of The Farm House and a Georgia native, does most of the cooking himself—to order; you may have to wait a bit longer but it is well worth it. Knotty pine paneling, green hanging plants and candlelit tables create a comfortable atmosphere conducive to relaxed dining. In the five years since the restaurant was first opened, Mr. Wright has gotten to know most of his patrons personally, and you can be assured of the same warm welcome when you go.

DINNER MENU

(a la carte)

ENTREES:

Vegetable Plate (Pick any three vegetables) .. 4.00
Ground Steak with Peppers and Onions 4.25
Fried Fish 4.25
Ham Hocks 4.00
Roast Turkey 4.50
Country Fried Chicken 4.75
Smothered Pork Chops 6.75
Barbecued Spare Ribs 6.75

(All the above entrees are served with corn bread, salad and choice of two of the following vegetables: kidney beans, string beans, collard greens, rice, black eyed peas, potato salad, candied yams.)

Beef Stew, Served with Corn Bread and Salad 4.00
Chuckburger 1.40
Cheeseburger 1.60
Garden Salad 3.10
Tuna Salad 3.80

SIDE DISHES:

Small Green Salad (.90); Vegetable Side Orders (.90); Split Pea Soup (cup .70) (bowl .90).

DESSERTS:

Pie (Sweet Potato, Peach, Apple) (.90); Vanilla Ice Cream (.50).

FONDA LA PALOMA

Address: 256 East 49th Street
Location: 49th Street Between Second Avenue and Third Avenue
Telephone: 421-5495
Credit Cards: AE; MC; DC; CB; V
Reservations: Recommended
Hours: 11:30 AM to 12 Midnight Monday thru Thursday; 11:30 AM to 1:00 AM on Friday; 5:00 PM to 1:00 AM on Saturday; 5:00 PM to 11:00 PM on Sundays
Days Closed: Major holidays
Liquor: Full bar service
Recommended or Listed in: New York Times; Gourmet; Cue; New York; Where; Esquire; New York Post; Women's Wear Daily
Proprietors: Dinna and Salvador Hernandez
Seating Capacity: 120
Cuisine: Mexican
Specialties of the House: Camarones a la Fonda; Puerco Adovado; Mole Pablano-Pollo; Mole Verde-Pollo; Ceviche; Carne Asada
Dress: Jacket required
Entertainment: Guitarists
Party Facilities: Tequila Room; capacity: 60

This authentic Mexican restaurant occupies three floors in a lovely old townhouse just two blocks from the United Nations. There's a warm, romantic atmosphere here accented by the exposed brick walls, the richly varied Mexican paintings and the strolling guitarists who entertain every evening except on Sundays. The Proprietors, Dinna and Salvador Hernandez, take justifiable pride in their restaurant and in its reputation as the leading exponent of Mexican cuisine in New York. If you're looking for the best in Mexican fare, try Fonda La Paloma.

LUNCHEON MENU

(Dessert and coffee or tea included with lunch.)

APPETIZERS & SOUPS:
Sopa de Pollo y Tortilla con Cilandro (Chicken and Tortilla Soup with Coriander) (1.50); Sopa de Frijoles (Mexican Black Bean Soup) (1.75); Guacamole (2.25); Nachos (2.25); Ceviche (Marinated Mackerel Delicacies) (2.25); Nopalitos (Baby Cactus) (2.25).

ENTREES:
Enchilada, Taco, Tostada, Tamal, Arroz, Frijoles Combination 6.50
Enchilada, Taco, Tostada, Arroz, Frijoles Combination 6.00
Taco, Tostada, Tamal, Arroz, Frijoles Combination 6.00
Enchilada, Taco, Tamal, Arroz, Frijoles Combination 6.00
Stuffed Pepper, Taco, Enchilada, Arroz, Frijoles Combination 6.50

Mole Poblano — Pollo — Arroz 6.50
(Mole Sauce with Fine Spices, Chicken Breast, Rice, Tortillas)
Mole Verde — Pollo — Arroz 6.50
(Green Mole Sauce with Fine Spices, Chicken Breast, Rice, Tortillas)
Tamales de Carne (3) — Arroz — Frijoles 5.25
(Beef Tamales, Rice, Beans)
Tacos de Pollo (3) 5.25
(Chicken Tacos, Rice, Beans)
Tacos de Carne (3) 5.50
(Beef Tacos, Rice, Beans)
Enchiladas de Carne (3) — Arroz 5.50
(Beef Enchiladas, Rice)
Enchiladas de Pollo (3) — Arroz 5.25
(Chicken Enchiladas, Rice)
Enchiladas de Queso (3) 5.75
(Cheese Enchiladas with Rice and Beans)

Fonda La Paloma

Enchiladas Suizas — Arroz 6.25
(Swiss Enchiladas, Rice)
Tostadas Compuestas de Pollo (3) 5.00
(Chicken Tostadas)
Tostadas Compuestas de Carne (3) 5.50
(Beef Tostadas)
Burritos (2) 6.00
(Tortilla rolled around Beef or Pork)
Huevos Rancheros — Arroz — Frijoles 5.00
(Eggs Ranchero Style, Rice, Beans)
Carne Asada — Enchilada — Frijoles — Arroz 6.50
(Broiled Top Round Steak Tampico, Enchilada, Beans, Rice)
Carne Maya — Arroz — Frijoles 6.25
(Mayan Braised Pot Roast, Rice, Beans)
Chiles Rellenos 6.50
(Beef Stuffed Peppers, Rice, Beans, Tortillas)

Picadillo a la Criolla 5.25
(Chopped Beef Mexican Style, Rice, Beans, Tortillas)
Arroz con Pollo 5.00
(Double Breast of Chicken and Rice)
Arroz con Camarones 7.25
(Shrimps and Rice)
Arroz con Calamares 5.95
(Squid and Rice)

DESSERTS:
Flan; Natilla (Rummed Spanish Cream); Guayaba con Queso de Crema (Guava Shell with Cream Cheese) (.50); Helado (Ice Cream); Cafe con Piquete (Mug of Coffee with Benedictine and Whipped Cream) (2.00).

DINNER MENU

(a la carte)

APPETIZERS & SOUPS:
Sopa de Frijoles Negros (Mexican Black Bean Soup) (2.25); Sopa de Pollo y Tortilla con Cilandro (Chicken and Tortilla Soup with Coriander) (2.00); Nachos con Frijoles Refritos (Tortillas with Refried Beans and Melted Cheese, Jalopeno Peppers) (3.25); Camarones a la Fonda (Shrimps Saute in Wine and Fine Spices) (3.95); Guacamole (3.00); Nachos (3.00); Shrimp Cocktail with Mexican Sauce (3.75); Ceviche (Marinated Mackerel Delicacy) (3.00); Nopalitos (Baby Cactus) (2.95); Don Nacho Tortilla with Beans, Cheese and Green Sauce (2.50); Chorizos (Broiled Sliced Spanish Sausages) (3.00).

ENTREES:
Enchilada, Taco, Tostada, Tamal, Arroz y Frijoles Combination 8.50
Enchilada, Taco, Tostada, Arroz y Frijoles Combination 8.00
Taco, Tostada, Tamal, Arroz y Frijoles Combination 8.00
Enchilada, Taco, Tamal, Aroz y Frijoles Combination 8.00
Stuffed Pepper, Taco, Enchilada, Arroz, Frijoles Combination 8.00
Stuffed Pepper, Taco, Enchilada, Carne Asada, Arroz, Frijoles Combination 8.50
Mole Poblano — Pollo 8.50

continued on next page

(Mole Sauce with Fine Spices, Double Breast of Chicken, Rice, Tortillas)

Mole Verde — Pollo 8.25
(Green Mole Sauce with Fine Spices, Double Breast of Chicken, Rice, Tortillas)

Puerco Adovado 8.50
(Chunks of Pork prepared with our Special Sauce, served with Rice, Tortillas)

Tamales de Carne (3) 6.50
(Beef Tamales, Rice, Beans)

Tacos de Pollo (3) 7.25
(Chicken Tacos, Rice, Beans)

Tacos de Carne (3) 7.50
(Beef Tacos, Rice, Beans)

Enchiladas de Queso (3) 7.75
(Cheese Enchiladas with Rice and Beans)

Enchiladas de Carne (3) 7.50
(Beef Enchiladas with Rice and Beans)

Enchiladas de Pollo (3) 7.25
(Chicken Enchiladas with Rice and Beans)

Enchiladas Suizas (3) 8.00
(Swiss Enchiladas with Rice and Beans)

Tostadas Compuestas de Pollo (3) 7.00
(Chicken Tostadas)

Tostadas Compuestas de Carne (3) 7.25
(Beef Tostadas)

Burritos 7.00
(Flour Tortilla Rolled around Beef or Pork)

Carne Asada 8.50
(Broiled Top Round Steak Tampico with Enchilada, Beans, Rice, Tortillas)

Carne Maya 8.50
(Mayan Braised Pot Roast with Rice, Beans, Tortillas)

Chiles Rellenos 8.50
(Beef Stuffed Peppers with Rice, Beans, Tortillas)

Picadillo a la Criola 6.75
(Chopped Beef Mexican Style with Rice, Beans, Tortillas)

Arroz con Pollo 6.75
(Double Breast of Chicken and Rice)

Huevos Rancheros 6.00
(Eggs, Ranchero Style with Rice and Beans)

Arroz con Calamares 6.75
(Squid and Rice)

Arroz con Camarones 8.50
(Shrimp and Rice)

Camarones a la Fonda 8.50
(Shrimps sauteed in Wine and Fine Spices)

DESSERTS:
Flan (2.00); Guayaba con Queso de Crema (Guava Shells with Cream Cheese) (2.00); Natilla (Rum Spanish Cream) (2.00); Helado (Ice Cream) (1.75); Chocolaterias (Mexican Chocolate Cake with Whipped Cream Topping) (2.00); Cafe con Piquette (Mexican Coffee with Benedictine and Whipped Cream) (3.25).

(Typical Mexican side orders are available, a la carte, at both lunch and dinner.)

We'd like to make Manhattan Menus even more useful to you, and would welcome hearing any comments or suggestions you may have. Write to: Manhattan Menus, P.O. Box 5217, FDR Station, New York, N.Y. 10022.

THE "411" BLEECKER STREET RESTAURANT

Address:	**409-411 Bleecker Street**
Location:	**Between Bank and Eleventh Streets**
Telephone:	**CH 2-2117**
Credit Cards:	**DC; AE; MC**
Reservations:	**Recommended during the week; required on weekends**
Hours:	**6:00 PM to 11:30 PM, Sunday thru Thursday; 6:00 PM to 12:00 Midnight, Friday and Saturday**
Days Closed:	**None**
Liquor:	**Full bar service and cocktail lounge**
Recommended or Listed in:	**New York Times; Cue; Long Island Press; Daily News**
Maitre d':	**John Simmons**
Seating Capacity:	**70**
Cuisine:	**Continental**
Specialties of the House:	**Bobotie; Ballotine of Veal; Roast Venison; Cassoulet; Tortiere**
Dress:	**Casual**
Party Facilities:	**Semi-private room; capacity: 20**

"411" Bleecker is a Village restaurant with style. Its decor—a warm and inviting blend of raw brick, open fireplace and hanging colored glass lamps—matches the imagination and verve of the menu. There's a young, high-spirited feeling about "411," a feeling you'll be invited to share with its large and loyal following.

The "411" Bleecker Street Restaurant

DINNER MENU

(a la carte)

(Menu changes weekly; the following is a representative selection.)

APPETIZERS & SOUPS:
Stuffed Clams (2.25); Shrimps Remoulade (3.95); Eggplant and Anchovies (1.95); Coquille St. Jacques (3.95); Pickled Mushrooms (2.25); Pate Maison (2.25); Escargot Forrestier (. . .); Fresh Melon in Season (1.95); "Tian" (2.25); Venison Pate (3.50); Today's Soup (.75).

continued on next page

Menu continued

ENTREES:

The Steak 9.95
The Chopped Steak a la Helen 4.95
Pork Chops Broiled with Fruit 7.95
Shrimp Scampi 7.95
Chicken and Broccoli en Casserole 4.25
Broiled Calves Liver and Bacon or Onions ... 6.95
Broiled Filet of Flounder Amandine 6.95
East Indian Curry Maison 4.95
Alaskan King Crab and Asparagus Mornay .. 7.95
"Armenian" Lambsteak 8.95
Sesame Pork en Brochėtte 7.95
German Mushroom Ragout 5.50
Piece de Resistance (Daily Special) 7.95
(All entrees are served with salad and house vegetables.)

DESSERTS:

Peach Melba (1.95); Homemade Cakes and Pies (1.75-2.50); Ice Cream and Fruit Ices (1.50-1.75).

(Dinner minimum per person: 4.25.)

BRUNCH MENU

(Saturday and Sunday, from 12:00 Noon to 3:30 PM)

(Served with a Bloody Mary or Screwdriver)

ENTREES:

Corn Fritter, Sausages, Maple Syrup 4.25
Waffles with Apricots 3.25
Farmers Omelet 3.95
(Sausage meat, potatoes, onions and peppers)
Eggs Divan 3.95
(Eggs and broccoli with cheese sauce en casserole)
"411" Burger 3.75
Creamed Seafood Omelet 4.95
(Shrimps, scallops and mushrooms in a cream sauce)
Coconut Waffles, Sausages, Honey 4.25
Curried Eggs en Casserole 3.95
(Eggs and vegetables baked in curry sauce)
Eggs "Foo Yong" 4.25
(Omelet stuffed with Chinese vegetables, served with a Chinese brown sauce)
Omelet with White Asparagus 4.50
Piperade 4.50
(Provencale vegetables, ham and eggs en casserole)

SIDE ORDERS:

Today's Soup (.75); Mixed Green Salad (1.00); Bacon, Ham or Sausages (1.25).

DESSERTS:

Peach Melba (1.75); Homemade Cakes and Pies (1.75-2.00); Ice Cream and Fruit Ices (1.25-1.50).

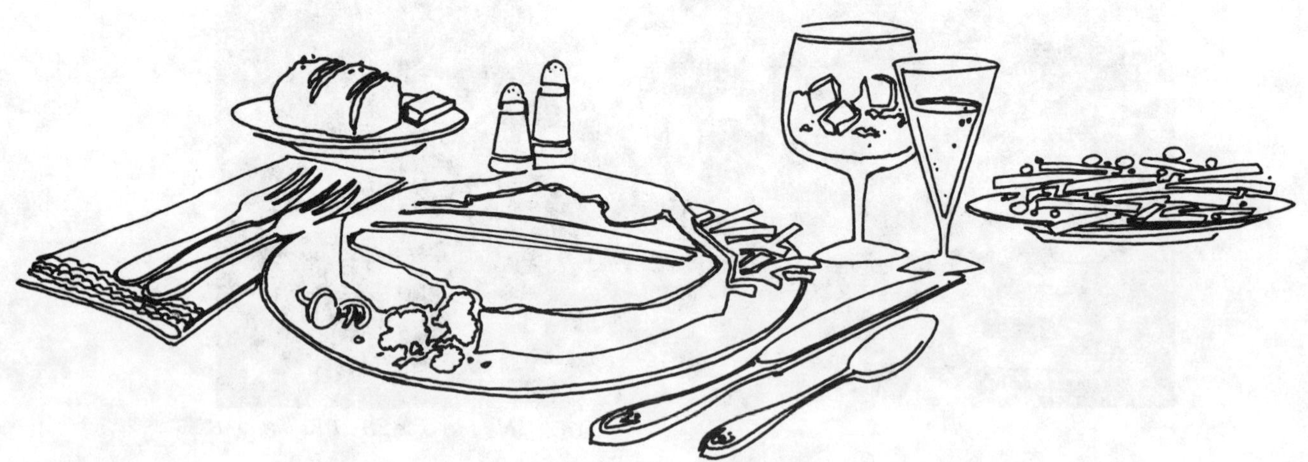

Nominate your favorite restaurants for inclusion in Manhattan Menus. Send cards or letters to: Manhattan Menus, P.O. Box 5217, FDR Station, New York, N.Y. 10022.

THE FOUR SEASONS

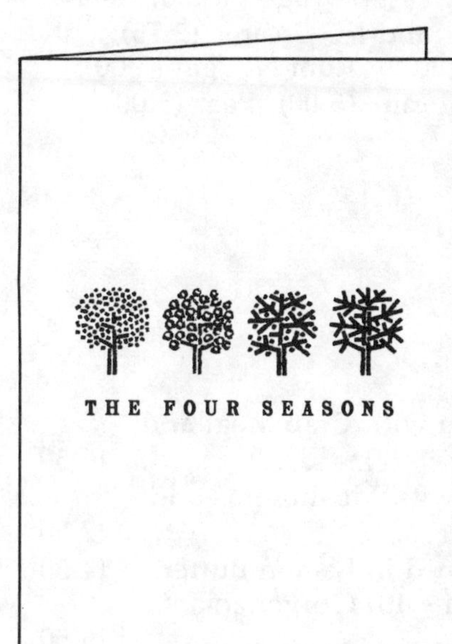

Address: 99 East 52nd Street
Location: 52nd Street between Park Avenue and Lexington Avenue
Telephone: PL 4-9494
Credit Cards: AE; CB; V; DC; MC
Reservations: Recommended
Hours: 12:00 Noon to 3:00 PM, and 5:00 PM to 11:30 PM, Monday thru Saturday
Days Closed: Sundays and major holidays
Liquor: Full Bar Service
Recommended: Gourmet, New York Times, Travel & Leisure, many others
Maitre d': Oreste
Reservations Manager: Francois
Seating Capacity: 300
Cuisine: International
Specialties of the Seasons: Specialties vary with each season; the Four Seasons' own menu identifies the selections created by its chefs for the particular season.
Dress: Jacket and tie required

The decor at this posh, carriage-trade restaurant is both contemporary and elegant. Featured are a 20-foot marble pool, original works by such famous artists as Picasso, Miro, and Chagall and elaborate displays of flowers and shrubs. Appointments, color schemes and plantings change with the seasons, as do the menus. High priced and high styled, the Four Seasons offers an international cuisine and a wine list geared to merit the approval of even the most blasé boulevardier.

LUNCHEON MENU

(a la carte)

APPETIZERS & SOUPS:
Small Clams with Green Onions and Truffles (5.50); Salmon and Pike Pâté (5.75); A Service of Shrimp (6.00); Louisiana Crab Lump Cocktail (8.00); Cotuit or Blue Point Oysters (5.50); Terrine of Game (5.75); Prosciutto with Melon or Pear (5.50); Smoked Scottish Salmon (12.50); Cherrystone Clams (5.00); Little Necks, a Platter (5.00); Caviar, per serving (. . .); Oysters with Horseradish and Ginger (6.00); Goose Rillette (5.50); Calf's Brains in Mustard Crumbs (6.00); Baked Clams with Almonds and Herbs (5.50); Feuilletage of Crab Meat and Oysters (6.50); Snails in Pot, Burgundian Style (4.50); Duckling Consommé (3.00); Onion Soup with Calvados, Gratinée (3.50); Lobster Bisque (4.00); A Winter Vegetable Potage (3.00).

ENTREES:
Omelette with Berries 7.50
Eggs Benedict 8.50
Scrambled Eggs with Scotch Salmon and Creamed Spinach 12.50
The Four Seasons Lobster Soufflé 16.50
Prosciutto and Zucchini Omelette 7.50
A Ragout of Shrimps and Scallops, Lobster Sauce 14.50
Crisped Shrimp with Mustard Fruits 11.50
The Classic Truite au Bleu 10.50
Dover Sole, Sauté Meunière 15.00
Crayfish Tails au Gratin 14.50
Steamed Calf's Liver with Mushrooms and Shallots 12.00
Cutlet of Veal Sautéed with Lemon Butter .. 14.50
Three French Lamb Chops 12.50
Filet of Plume de Veau with Crab Meat and Mushrooms 16.50
Medaillons of Venison with Chestnut Purée 15.00
The Four Seasons Pot au Feu 12.50
Civet of Pheasant with Spaetzle 13.50
Smoked Loin of Pork, Champagne Kraut ... 11.50
Steak Paillard 14.50
Sirloin Steak or Filet Mignon 15.00
Chopped Sirloin with Winter Vegetables ... 10.00
Minute Steak Four Seasons 13.50
Skillet Steak Smothered with Onions 15.50

continued on next page

Menu continued

Two Roast Quails with Sage and Fried Grapes 13.50
A Chef's Salad 10.50
Planked Steak Tartar 12.50
Avocado and Shrimp, Louis 11.50
The Four Seasons Shellfish Platter 18.50
(A variety of vegetables and petite salads is offered at prices ranging from 2.00 to 4.00.)

DESSERTS:
A selection from The Dessert Wagon (3.00); The Four Seasons Sherbets and Ice Creams (2.75); Soufflés: Coffee Cup (3.00), Rum Nougat (3.00); Soufflés for Two: Tangerine (5.00), Pear (5.00); Petits Fours (1.50).

DINNER MENU

(a la carte)

APPETIZERS & SOUPS:
Small Clams with Green Onions and Truffles (6.00); Scottish Smoked Salmon (12.50); Louisiana Crab Lump Cocktail (8.00); Prosciutto with Melon or Pear (5.50); A Service of Cold Shrimp (6.00); Salmon and Pike Pâté (6.25); Cotuit or Blue Point Oysters (6.50); Little Necks, a Platter (5.00); Cherrystone Clams (5.00); Caviar, per Serving (. . .); Oysters with Horseradish and Ginger (6.00); Terrine of Game (6.50); Goose Rillette (6.25); Crisped Shrimp Filled with Mustard Fruits (7.50); Baked Clams with Almonds and Herbs (6.00); Feuilletage of Crab Meat and Oysters (7.50); Calf's Brains in Herb Mustard Crumbs (6.00); Snails in Pots, Burgundian Style (5.75); A Civet of Wild Duck (7.50); Duckling Consommé (3.50); Onion Soup with Calvados, Gratinée (3.50); A Winter Vegetable Potage (3.50); Lobster Bisque (4.50).

ENTREES:
The Four Seasons Lobster Soufflé 18.50
Striped Bass for Two: Flamed on Fennel with Pernod 26.50
Striped Bass for Two: Poached in White Wine and Herbs 24.50
The Classic Truite au Bleu 11.50
A Ragout of Shrimps and Scallops, Lobster Sauce 15.50
Coho Baby Salmon with Herb Sauce 13.50
Crayfish Tails au Gratin 15.50
Broiled or Poached Maine Lobster ....
Dover Sole, Sauté Meunière 16.00
Grilled Filet of Red Snapper 14.50
Filet of Plume de Veau with Crab Meat and Mushrooms 16.50
Steamed Calf's Liver with Mushrooms and Shallots 12.50
Escalope of Veal Sautéed in Lemon Butter .. 14.50
Epigrams of Wild Boar with Gorgonzola Polenta 16.50
Breast of Pheasant with Apple Roesti 15.00
Medaillons of Venison with Purée of Chestnuts 16.00
Calf's Liver — Thick, Sage Butter 12.50
Sirloin Steak or Filet Mignon 15.00
Twin Double Lamb Chops 15.50
Skillet Steak Smothered with Onions 16.50
Two Roast Quails with Sage and Fried Grapes 14.50
The Four Seasons Farmhouse Duck: au Poivre or Served Very Crisp 13.50
Rosemary Roasted Rack of Lamb 16.50
Chateaubriand and Mangetout 18.50
Saddle of Venison with Pear and Pistachio . 17.50
Lobster and Sweetbread Salad 16.50
Planked Steak Tartar 13.50
Avocado and Shrimp, Louis 12.50

(A variety of vegetables, potatoes and salads is offered at prices ranging from 2.00 to 4.50.)

DESSERTS:
A Selection from The Dessert Wagon (3.50); The Four Seasons Sherbets and Ice Creams (2.75); Soufflés: Coffee Cup (3.00), Pear (3.00); Soufflés for Two: Tangerine (5.00), Rum Nougat (5.00).

CHEFS DE CUISINE ASSOCIATION OF AMERICA *This is an organization of some of the best chefs, sous-chefs and pastry chefs in this country—chefs who represent many nationalities. There are approximately 250 members who must undergo a very rigorous selection process before they are accepted for membership in the Association. The Chefs de Cuisine Association lends its support to two culinary schools—the New York City Community College's School of Hotel and Restaurant Management and the Culinary Institute of America in Hyde Park. The Association, founded in 1916, is a co-founder of the American Culinary Foundation and a co-sponsor of Les Amis d'Escoffier Gourmet Society. The President is Joseph J. Melz, Executive Chef-Steward of the Stock Exchange Club.*

FRAUNCES TAVERN

Address:	**Corner of Broad and Pearl Streets**
Telephone:	**269-0144**
Credit Cards:	**All major credit cards accepted**
Reservations:	**Recommended**
Hours:	**11:45 AM to 9:00 PM, Monday through Friday**
Days Closed:	**Saturday and Sunday**
Liquor:	**Full bar service**
Seating Capacity:	**400**
Cuisine:	**American Colonial Recipes**
Specialties of theHouse:	**Baked Chicken a la Washington; Fishhouse Punch; Daily Specials: Eggs Benedict; Paella Valenciana; Yankee Pot Roast; Tavern Beef Goulash; Crepes de Mer**
Dress:	**Jacket required**
Party Facilities:	**2 private rooms (Day); capacity: 35/75 Additional room (Evening); capacity: 150**

Fraunces Tavern, located on the intersection of Broad and Pearl Streets, is New York's, indeed the nation's, oldest continually operated restaurant. Robert Norden is tenth in an unbroken chain of tavern keepers that began with Samuel Fraunces, named by George Washington first Steward to the White House in 1789. For 215 years, Fraunces Tavern has offered discerning diners the best in authentic American cuisine. Crackling fires in winter.

Fraunces Tavern continued on next page

continued

MENU

(a la carte)

APPETIZERS & SOUPS:
Special Mixed Seafood Cocktail with Crab Meat, Lobster Meat, Clam, Oyster and Shrimps with Cocktail Sauce (5.25); Chilled Tomato Juice (.75); Fillets of Herring in Sour Cream with Onions (1.75); Cup of Fresh Seasonal Fruits (1.25); Iced Cherrystone Clams on Half Shell (2.75); Iced Bluepoint Oysters on Half Shell (2.50); Jumbo Shrimp Cocktail (3.95); Chilled Lobster Meat Cocktail (3.45); Jumbo Lump Crab Meat Cocktail (4.65); Soup of the Day (1.25); French Onion Soup Baked with Cheese and Crouton, en crock (1.50); Double Consomme with Rice (1.00); Escargots Bourguignon (3.85).

ENTREES:
Broiled Prime Sirloin Steak 12.95
Old Fashioned Sliced London Broil with Mushroom Sauce 7.95
Surf & Turf 10.95
(A tender broiled lobster tail & sliced beefsteak)
Fraunces Tavern Sliced Beefsteak Sandwich . 8.25
Prime Chopped Beefsteak.................. 5.95
Sauteed Calves Liver 7.95
Broiled Lamb Chops 10.95
English Mixed Grill........................ 8.25
Roast Prime Rib of Beef.................. 10.85
Cutlet of Veal, Cordon Bleu................ 8.65
Baked Chicken à la Washington 7.25
(Cubes of tender chicken and mushrooms in a light cream sauce, baked in casserole au gratin)
Hot Turkey Sandwich 5.25
Broiled Fresh Red Snapper................ 10.95
Whole Dover Sole Amandine............... 11.65
Long Island Bay Scallops, Broiled or Fried ... 8.75
Broiled Shrimp Scampi 8.95
New Orleans Shrimp Creole 8.75
Curry of Shrimp Indienne 8.75
Broiled Fillet of Grey Sole 7.25
Broiled Lobster Tails 11.25
Baked Avocado Pear Stuffed with Jumbo Lump Crab Meat au Gratin 10.95

(A selection of salads and cold platters is offered, ranging from 4.25 to 10.95. A selection of vegetables is also available.)

DESSERTS:
Chocolate Mousse (1.85); Strawberry Bavarian Cream Pie (1.75); Georgia Pecan Pie (2.00); Fresh Seasonal Melon (1.50); Fresh Seasonal Melon with Ice Cream (2.50); Apple Cake Montecello (1.75); Apple Cake Montecello with Ice Cream (2.50); Old Fashioned Rice Pudding with Whipped Cream (1.25); Parfait of the Day (1.75); French Ice Cream — Chocolate, Vanilla, Rum Raisin, Praline or Lemon Sherbet (1.50); Roquefort or Camembert Cheese with Crackers (1.25); Cheese with Glass of Ruby Port Wine (1.85); Light French Cheese Cake (1.75); Fresh Berries in season, Whipped Cream (1.50).

LIEBFRAUMILCH: *An adulterated German wine name for a generally sweet, heavy, seldom exceptional white. Originally the name (Milk of the Blessed Mother) applied to the produce of the vineyard around the Liebfraukirch in the town of Worms on the Rhine.*

MACON: *A solid, bourgeois wine produced north and west of the town of the same name on the River Saone in southern Burgundy. Macon reds are sound and pleasant, but less fruity and not as firm as a good neighboring area Beaujolais. Macon whites are frequently known by their district, most notably, Pouilly Fuissé.*

MADEIRA: *A fortified wine processed and matured on the Atlantic island of Madeira, a Portuguese possession off the west coast of North Africa. Its uniqueness was originally created by the combination of high temperature and slow motion that the wine was exposed to on long sea voyages paralleling the Equator. Madeiras vary from the very dry, pale straw Sercial to the very sweet, dark brown Malmsey. Madeiras are famed in cooking and, in the highest quality, as extra ordinary aperitif or dessert wines.*

MANZANILLA: *A pale, Sherry-like Spanish wine produced west of Jerez, Manzanilla has a characteristic dry bite. Like sherries, it grows darker while aging in the barrel. Manzanilla has a flavor thought to be the driest on earth.*

GAGE & TOLLNER

Gage & Tollner.

Address:	372 Fulton Street, Brooklyn
Location:	Fulton Street near Jay Street and Boro Hall
Telephone:	875-5181
Credit Cards:	MC; DC; V; AE
Reservations:	Required
Hours:	11:30 AM to 9:00 PM, Monday thru Friday; 4:00 PM to 11:00 PM, Saturday
Days Closed:	Sunday
Liquor:	Full bar service
Recommended or Listed in:	Mainliner
Seating Capacity:	200
Cuisine:	Seafood
Specialties of the House:	Crabmeat Virginia; Lobster Maryland; English Mutton Chop
Dress:	Casual
Party Facilities:	2 private rooms; capacity: 25-75

Gage & Tollner deserves its designation as "Brooklyn's Landmark Seafood and Steak House." Founded in 1879, the restaurant has traditionally attracted a clientele ranging from flamboyant millionaires such as Diamond Jim Brady to politicians, first families, celebrities and countless others who value the made-to-order excellence of the more than 100 menu selections. Gage & Tollner was officially designated as an historic landmark in 1975; its interior design and ambience have been preserved almost intact since the 1890's and are an authentic evocation of New York's La Belle Epoque—the good old days of a fabulous bygone era.

MENU
(a la carte)

(The following is a representative selection.)

SOUPS & BISQUES:
Soft Clam Soup (cup 1.75) (plate 2.00); Cream of Chicken (cup 1.25) (plate 1.50); Clam Soup or Broth (cup 1.25) (plate 1.50); Chicken Broth & Rice (cup 1.25) (plate 1.50); Fish Chowder (cup 1.25) (plate 1.50); Clam Chowder (cup 1.25) (plate 1.50); Soft Clam Bisque (cup 2.50) (bowl 3.50); Lobster Bisque (cup 3.25) (bowl 5.50); Clam Bisque (cup 2.00) (bowl 3.00); Oyster Bisque (cup 2.00) (bowl 3.00); Shrimp Bisque (cup 2.50) (bowl 3.50).

ENTREES:

Oyster Cocktail	3.25
Steamed Oysters	5.50
Oyster Stew	5.50
Oyster Cream Stew	6.00
Oyster Fry	5.50
Oyster Chicago Fry	5.75
Oyster Baltimore Fry	5.50
Oyster Seasoned Fry	5.50
Oyster Broil	5.50
Oyster Chicago Broil	5.75
Oyster Milk Broil	5.75
Oyster Cream Broil	6.00
Oyster Celery Broil	5.75
Oyster Celery Cream Broil	6.25
Seasoned Oyster Broil	5.50
Shell Roast Oysters	5.50
Shell Roast Oysters (Casino)	5.75
Pan Roast Oysters	5.50
Oysters En Brochette	5.50
Creamed Oysters	6.00
Shrimp Cocktail	5.25
Fried Shrimp	9.00
Shrimp Creole (with Rice)	9.25
Shrimp a la Newburg	9.75
Curried Shrimp (with Rice and Chutney)	9.25
Shrimp au Gratin	9.50
Shrimp Salad	9.25

continued on next page

Menu continued

(The extensive Gage & Tollner menu includes similar preparations of crabmeat, clams, scallops and lobster. A variety of fresh fish dishes and seafood salads is also available. Steaks, lamb chops and other meats, chicken, egg dishes and Welsh Rabbits are among the other menu selections. A la carte vegetables, side salads, potatoes and seafood appetizers are offered at prices ranging from .75 to 6.50.)

Gage & Tollner

GALLAGHER'S

Address: 228 West 52nd Street
Location: 52nd Street, just west of Broadway
Telephone: CI 5-5336
Credit Cards: DC; AE; MC; V; CB
Reservations: Recommended
Hours: 12:00 Noon to Midnight, seven days a week
Days Closed: None
Liquor: Full bar service
Recommended or Listed in: New York Times; Gourmet; many others
Seating Capacity: 225
Cuisine: American/Steak House
Specialties of the House: U.S. Prime Beef Aged on Premises; Hickory Broiled Sirloin Steak & Chops; Fresh Maine Lobster; Roast Prime Ribs of Beef
Dress: Casual
Party Facilities: The Trophy Room; capacity: 25-100

Broadway, beef and baseball are Gallagher's 3B's. The steak and prime ribs served at Gallagher's have made it a favorite with sports and theatrical figures for almost fifty years. You'll see their pictures literally covering the walls of this New York institution. One wall, however, is a window to Gallagher's refrigerator wherein is hung some of the best beef you'll ever taste. The portions are huge, and the service congenial. Located in the heart of the theatre district, Gallagher's is a steakhouse par excellence.

DINNER MENU
(a la carte)

APPETIZERS & SOUPS:
Jumbo Shrimps (3.95); Cherrystone Clams (2.95); Chopped Chicken Livers (2.45); Sliced Great Tomato and Bermuda Onion (3.25); Marinated Herring (2.45); Blue Point Oysters (3.25); Grapefruit (1.50); Ox-Tail Soup (1.50); Gazpacho (1.50); Jellied Madrilene (1.50); Onion Soup (1.50); Vichyssoise (1.50); The Other Soup (1.50).

ENTREES:
Sirloin Steak 12.75
Roast Prime Ribs of Beef 10.95
Filet Mignon 12.75
Calf's Liver Steak 8.50
Lamb Chops 11.75
Pork Chops 7.85
Boiled or Grilled Large Lobster 18.75
Broiled Boston Scrod 8.50
Broiled Spring Chicken 6.25
Filet of Sole with Almonds 9.50
Sliced Beefsteak on Toast 8.75
(with Gallagher's Mustard Sauce)
Mulligan Stew 5.95
Hamburger Steak 5.85
Broiled Scallops 8.50
Tartare Steak 7.50
Fried Shrimp in Beer Batter 8.95

SIDE DISHES:
Crisp Spinach Salad (2.25); Mixed Green Salad (1.95); French Fried Onion Rings (1.75); Baked Potato (1.25); Baked Potato Shell (1.10); French Fried Potatoes (1.25); Spinach, Creamed or Plain (1.75); Buttered String Beans (1.75); Creamed Corn (1.75); Corn and Tomato Combination (1.75); Hash Brown or Lyonnaise Potatoes (1.25); Broiled Mushroom Caps (1.90); Gallagher's own potatoes (1.25).

DESSERTS:
Ice Cream & Sherbets (1.50); Cheesecake (2.25); Fresh Strawberries (2.75); Apple Pie, Mel Ott (1.95); Rice Pudding Lefebre (1.95); Melon in season (1.75); Strawberry Shortcake (2.50); Gallagher's Irish Coffee (2.50).

GAYLORD

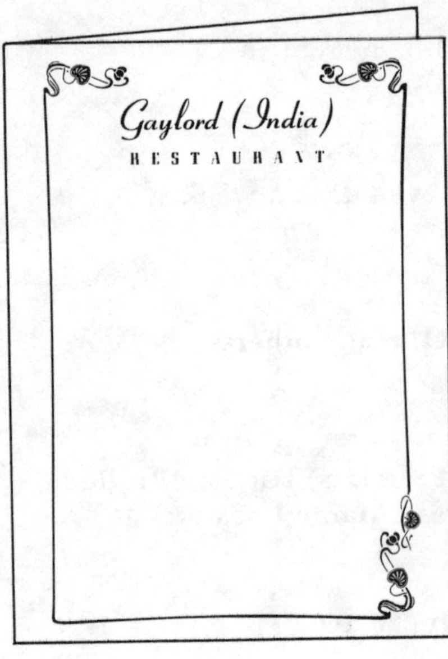

Address: 50 East 58th Street
Location: 58th Street between Madison and Park Avenues
Telephone: 759-1710
Credit Cards: AE; DC; V; MC; CB
Reservations: Required
Hours: Lunch from 11:30 AM to 3:00 PM, Monday thru Friday; Dinner from 5:30 PM to 11:00 PM, Monday thru Sunday
Days Closed: None
Liquor: Full bar service
Recommended or Listed in: New York Times; New York Magazine; Cue; Playbill; Village Voice; Gourmet
Reservations Manager: Mann
Seating Capacity: 145
Cuisine: North Indian
Specialties of the House: Chicken Tikka Masala; Boti Kebab Masala; Bahar-e-Paneer
Dress: Informal
Entertainment: Occasional live Indian music; palmist
Party Facilities: Private room; capacity: 35-40
Parking: Discount parking at 150 East 58th Street

With restaurants located in the major cities of India as well as in London, Gaylord has a deserved international reputation for its "dishes of a million tastes." Gaylord patrons watch Punjabi chefs cook the regional specialties of Northern India in a glass-enclosed kitchen. Gaylord was the first restaurant in the U.S. to use the Tandoor, an urn-shaped clay oven, fired by charcoal, that gives Tandoori cuisine its distinctive flavor. Gaylord offers a feast for the senses as well. Subdued lighting in the main dining room illuminates the brilliantly colored beaded murals created by Indian craftsmen. Hand-carved teak, hammered brass lamps and raw silk upholstery are subtly evocative of the beauty of India—in midtown Manhattan.

MENU

(a la carte)

(The following is representative of an extensive selection of Northern Indian dishes including seafood delicacies, rice and vegetarian delights.)

ENTREES:

Chicken Masala 5.75
(Chicken pieces cooked in mild spices)

Badshahi Korma 5.75
(Chicken delicately spiced with yogurt)

Murgh Musallam 5.75
(Chicken marinated in cream, mildly spiced, with boiled egg)

Chicken Makhanwala 5.75
(Tandoori chicken with spices, tomatoes and butter)

Chicken Tikka Masala 5.75
(Chicken Tikka kebab with tomatoes and butter)

Lamb Pasanda 6.15
(Lamb marinated in yogurt with cream and spices)

Rogan Josh 6.15
(Cubes of lamb in mildly spiced gravy)

Gobhi Meat 6.15
(Lamb cooked in spices with cauliflower)

Prawn Masala in sharp spices, gravy 6.50

Prawn Chilli Masala with green peppers and onions 6.50

Special Vegetarian Thali 7.50
(Vegetables, Samosa, Pullao, Dahi Raita, Purees, Papadum and Dessert)

Gaylord

Special Tandoori Mix 9.50
(Tandoori Chicken, Boti Kebab, Sheekh Kebab, Chicken Tikka, Tandoori Prawn and Lamb Pasanda, with Nukti Biryani, Mixed Vegetable or Dal, Onion Kulcha)

Tandoori Chicken Half-4.50 Full-7.25
(Chicken marinated in yogurt and mild spices)

Chicken Tikka.............................. 6.25
(Boneless chicken pieces marinated and roasted Tandoori style)

Boti Kebab 6.25
(Cubed leg of lamb roasted on a skewer)

Tandoori King Prawns 8.95

Fish Tikka Kebab 6.25
(Fish pieces marinated and roasted Tandoori style)

Sheekh Kebab 6.25
(Lamb with onions and herbs roasted on skewers)

Tandoori Mixed Grill 8.50

Navrattan Curry 4.50
("Nine Gems" vegetables, nuts and spices)

CLUB PROSPER MONTAGNE *This club of gastronomes honors Prosper Montagné, one of France's great chefs. It sponsors a competition among chefs; the winner receives the Coupe Prosper Montagné. The Board of the Club selects the dishes that it wants prepared by the entrants; any chef wishing to compete sends his recipe to the Board. From this collection of recipes, the Board selects six that they consider most worthy. The chefs then prepare their dishes for the judges and the one that is considered most successful is awarded the Coupe. The U.S. representative to the Club is Yves Menes, Executive Chef, Shoreham Hotel, Washington, D.C.*

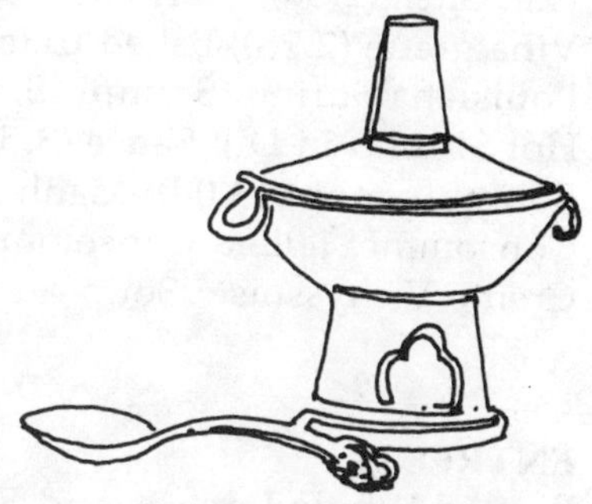

LA GRANGE INN

Address: Montauk Highway; West Islip, N.Y.
Location: Corner of Montauk Highway and Higbie Lane
Telephone: (516) 669-0765
Credit Cards: AE; V; CB; DC; MC
Reservations: Recommended
Hours: Luncheon 12 Noon to 3:00 PM; a la carte 3:00 PM to 5:00 PM. Dinner from 5:00 PM to 11:00 PM, a la carte to 12:00 Midnight
Days Closed: Tuesdays
Liquor: Full Bar Service
Recommended or listed in: Cue
Maitre d's: Jack Flathmann and Charley Hirsemann
Seating Capacity: 90
Cuisine: Continental
Specialties of the House: Fresh Maryland Lump Crab Meat au Gratin; Roast Half Boneless Long Island Duckling, Bigarade. Weekends: Prime Ribs of Beef au Jus
Party Facilities: Private room; capacity: 10-500

La Grange Inn is said to have been a licensed place as early as 1750. Rightly so that it has remained the watering and eating spot for discerning gourmets for more than 225 years. The Inn, impeccably maintained over the years, has always been famous for its cheery atmosphere, cordiality and excellent cuisine. The service is without fault, the ambience relaxing, and the food superb. Reservations on weekends are strongly recommended.

DINNER MENU

(table d'hote)

APPETIZERS & SOUP:
Herring Salad; Chilled Tomato Juice; V-8 Cocktail; Chilled Grapefruit Juice; Chopped Fresh Chicken Livers; Freshly Cut Florida Fruit Cocktail; Home Made Head Cheese Vinaigrette; Prosciutto and Melon (2.75); Fillets of Imported Herring in Sour Cream (1.25); Fresh Maryland Lump Crabmeat Cocktail (4.50); Jumbo Louisiana Shrimp Cocktail (3.25); Smoked Nova Scotia Salmon, Garni (3.00); Iced Blue Point Oysters on Half Shell (in season) (3.25); Iced Little Neck or Cherrystone Clams on Half Shell (2.50); Marinated Baby Brook Trout Vinaigrette (2.25); Baked Clams a la Maison (3.25); Louisiana Shrimp Scampi, Sauce Piquante (3.75); Hot Shrimp in Dill Sauce (3.50); Escargots Bourguignonne (3.00); Manhattan Clam Chowder; Consommé; Jellied Consommé Madrilene; Chilled Creme Vichyssoise; Soup du Jour.

ENTREES:
Broiled Whole Long Island Flounder, lemon butter sauce 9.50
Broiled Fillet of Sole, Amandine 9.50
Broiled Fresh Peconic Bay Scallops, lemon and tartar sauce 10.50
English Dover Sole, Sauté Meuniere, with Parsleyed Potato 11.75
Jumbo Louisiana Shrimp Scampi, sauce piquante 11.50
Fresh Maryland Lump Crabmeat au Gratin, en casserole au sherry 11.50
Broiled Stuffed Live Lobster, Crabmeat Dressing, drawn butter (according to size) .. (. . .)
Frogs Legs, Sauce Marseillaise, sauteed in butter with garlic 10.50
Twin Broiled New Jersey Pork Chops, spiced apple sauce 10.50
Twin Broiled Spring Lamb Chops, mint jelly . 13.00
Veal Cordon Bleu, stuffed with Ham and Imported Swiss Cheese, sauce supreme 11.00
Schnitzel a la Holstein, Fried Egg, Anchovy and Capers 10.75
Jaeger Schnitzel, sautéed in savory cream sauce, with Mushrooms; served with Spaetzle 10.25
Veal Cutlet a la Parmigian, with Spaghetti .. 10.75

La Grange Inn

Roast Turkey, Giblet Dressing, Cranberry Jelly 9.25
Deep Fried Jumbo Louisiana Shrimp, tartar sauce 10.50
Fried Fresh Peconic Bay Scallops, tartar sauce 10.50
Sautéed Twin Breasts of Chicken Polignac, boned and sautéed in sauce supreme 10.50
Roast Half Boneless Long Island Duckling, Bigarade, crisp and crackling, garnished with tiny Mandarin Oranges, Sage Stuffing 11.00
Broiled Prime Sirloin Steak, French Fried Onion Rings, Mushroom Cap 13.00
Broiled Prime Filet Mignon, Onion Rings, Mushroom Cap 13.00
Planked Chateaubriand Bouquetiere, ringed with Fresh Garden Vegetables, Onion Rings, crowned with sauce Bearnaise (for two) 30.00
Broiled Sirloin Steak Sandwich, open style . 12.00
Sliced Steak Thumbits 12.00
Broiled Chopped Tenderloin Steak, sautéed Onions 9.25
La Grange Mixed Grill: Lamb Chop, Small Filet Mignon, Calf's Liver, Sausage and Bacon Strip 13.00
Sauté of Fresh Calf's Liver, Rasher of Bacon or Sautéed Onions 10.50
Sauerbraten, fluffy Potato Dumpling, Red Cabbage 10.50

(Four daily dinner specials are also featured.)

SALADS:

Fresh Maryland Lump Crabmeat Salad Platter 10.50
Louisiana Shrimp Salad Platter 10.50
Fresh Chicken Salad Platter 8.50
Chef's Salad Bowl 8.50

(A variety of vegetables and salads are offered on a table d'hote basis)

DESSERTS AND CHEESES:

Strawberry Shortcake; Rice Pudding; Parfait a la Grange; Lemon Chiffon Pie; Peach Melba; Cheese Cake; Jello-O with Whipped Cream; Mousse au Chocolat; Angel Food Cake a la Mode; Sherbet; Ice Cream; Ice Cream Sundaes; Cheeses: Choice of imported Swiss Cheese, Camembert, Liederkranz or Bleu Cheese, served with selected crisp crackers.

To add greatly to your dining pleasure, La Grange offers a complete list of fine imported and domestic wines and beers. La Grange banquet facilities are available to make your next affair or business function a complete success.

(A complete luncheon menu is also available with prices ranging from 5.85 to 7.50.)

Inflation affects everyone, including restauranteurs. So look for the prices of menu items listed in this book to rise a bit during the year.

GRASS

Address: 1445 First Avenue
Location: First Avenue at 75th Street
Telephone: (212) PERFECT
Credit Cards: AE; DC; MC; V
Reservations: Recommended
Hours: Lunch from 11:30 AM to 5:00 PM, Monday thru Friday; dinner from 5:00 PM to 12:45 AM Sunday, Monday, Tuesday and Thursday, and from 4:30 PM to 1:45 AM, Wednesday, Friday and Saturday. Brunch from 11:00 AM to 3:30 PM, Saturday and Sunday
Liquor: Full bar service
Seating Capacity: 100
Cuisine: Gourmet Natural Foods
Dress: Casual
Entertainment: Live music

The menu, cuisine and decor of this refreshing restaurant have all been created with a "natural" flair. The menu definitely takes a gourmet slant – the food is brought in fresh daily, prepared to order with no chemicals or tenderizers and served with sauces and dressings made on the premises. Grass looks like a handsomely decorated greenhouse – tables made from tree trunks, hand-carved oak bar, colorful wall murals, all-year-round cafe and plants galore hanging throughout the restaurant. It is a city gardener's paradise.

DINNER MENU

(a la carte)

APPETIZERS & SOUPS:
Jumbo Shrimp with Dill and Lemon Mayonnaise or Red Cocktail Sauce (4.50); Fresh Cut Fruits Served with Honey and Shredded Coconut (1.75); Grass' Guacamole (1.95); Agaricus Mushrooms Stuffed with Snails with Bordelaise Sauce and Walnuts (3.95); Baked Clams Oreganato (3.25); Clams on the Half-Shell (2.75); Spinach, Bacon or Mushroom Quiche (2.95); Artichoke Served with Hollandaise Sauce (3.25); Onion Soup des Halles (1.95); Soup of the Day (1.75).

ENTREES:
Aged Boneless 14 oz Prime Sirloin Steak ... 11.75
The Grass Special Cut Steak, Served on Garlic Bread topped with Sauteed Mushrooms, Green Pepper and Onions ... 7.95
Sliced Steak Smothered in Barbecue Sauce .. 7.50
Chopped Steak Smothered with Sauteed Onions ... 6.95
Breast of Young Chicken a la Parmigiana 6.50
Crisply Roasted Boneless Long Island Duckling Served with a Grand Marnier Orange Sauce ... 7.95
Selection of Freshly Caught Fish ... 6.95
Sauteed Jumbo Shrimp Served with White Wine, Garlic and Herb Sauce ... 8.50
Sauteed Filet of Sole Served with Honeyed Banana and Almond Slivers ... 7.95
Spare Ribs Served with a Gingered Sweet Sauce and Pineapple or Barbecue Sauce 7.95
Veal Cutlet a la Parmigiana ... 7.75
Real Southern Fried Chicken Maryland 7.50
Home Made Lasagne a la Milanese ... 5.75
Fresh Vegetables, Sesame Seeds and Bean Sprouts Prepared in the Oriental Manner 5.25
Eggplant a la Parmigiana ... 4.95
Spinach, Bacon and Mushroom Quiche Served with Grass' Natural Salad ... 5.75

SALADS:
Spinach, Bacon and Mushroom Garnished with Egg and Special Spinach Salad Dressing ... 4.75
Fresh Fruit Cornucopia (Fresh Fruits and Berries Served with Creamy Cottage Cheese or Natural Sherbet and Yogurt Dressing, Honey and Sunflower Seeds) ... 4.95
Salade Nicoise ... 5.25
Avocado Stuffed with Chunks of Jumbo Shrimp, Egg Mixed with Russian Dressing ... 7.50
The Grass Chef Salad Bowl ... 6.25
The Grass Cheese and Fruit Board ... 7.50
Steak Tartare Lausanne ... 7.50
Caesar Salad ... 5.50

(There are daily specials in addition to the regular menu.)

DESSERTS:
Super Creamy Cheesecake (1.75); With Berries (2.25); Crepe Stuffed with Freshly Whipped Cream, Chopped Nuts, Kirschwasser, Topped with a Thick Hot Fudge Sauce and a Scoop of Haagen Daz Vanilla Ice Cream (2.75); Old Fashioned Hot Fudge, Berry, Banana, Peanut Butter Crunch or Nesselrode Sundae made with Haagen Daz Ice Cream, Chopped Nuts and Smothered with Freshly Whipped Heavy Cream (2.75); Fresh Large Strawberries Served with Creme de Cassis and Topped with Freshly Whipped Heavy Cream (2.50); A Dish of Haagen Daz Ice Cream or Boysenberry Sherbet (1.75); Grass Crepes Suzette with Crushed Strawberries, Grand Marnier Sauce and Vanilla Ice Cream (2.75); Pies, Cakes and Puddings from the Grass Dessert Table (1.95).

BRUNCH MENU

(prix fixe - 5.95)

COCKTAILS, JUICES OR FRUITS: (choice of one)
Champagne Orange; Bloody, Bloody Mary; Rum Milk Punch or Selection of Fruit and Vegetable Juices.

APPETIZERS: (choice of one)
Fresh Sliced Orange with Honey and Shredded Coconut; Rolled Oats with Bananas and Bee Honey; Chilled Melon with Lime Wedge.

ENTREES: (choice of one)
Three Flour Pancakes Served with Maple Syrup or Honey
Southern Style Waffles Served with Bananas or Berries and Syrup or Honey
Chalah French Toast Served with Fruit and Yogurt Compote and Maple Syrup or Honey
Scrambled or Fried Eggs with Imported Danish Ham or Crisp Bacon and Hash Browns
Scrambled Eggs with Smoked Nova Scotia Salmon & Onions
The Grass Omelette (tomatoes, agaricus mushrooms, green peppers, onions and jack cheese)
Three Cheese or Agaricus Mushroom Omelette
Giant Burgers with Fried Potatoes
Bagel with Smoked Nova Scotia Salmon, Sliced Bermuda Onion and Cream Cheese
Cheese Blintzes Served with Sour Cream or Blueberry Sauce
White Meat Tuna Salad Bowl Garnished with Black Olives, Egg, Crisp Greens and Capers
Spinach, Bacon and Mushrooms Salad Bowl Garnished with Egg and Grass' Special Dressing

---

THE HEADLESS HORSEMAN

Address: 142 West 10th Street
Location: 10th Street between Sixth and Seventh Avenues
Telephone: 989-9980
Credit Cards: AE; V; MC
Reservations: Recommended
Hours: 4:00 PM to 4:00 AM, Monday thru Saturday; Dinner from 6:00 PM to 12:00 Midnight; Sunday Brunch from 12:00 Noon to 6:00 PM. Closed for Sunday Dinner
Days Closed: None
Liquor: Full bar service
Recommended or Listed in: New York Times
Seating Capacity: 70
Cuisine: American; Continental
Specialties of the House: The Headless Horseman Seafood Chowder; Rack of Lamb; Stuffed Calves Liver
Dress: Casual
Entertainment: Piano music every evening from 9:30 PM to 2:30 AM and during Sunday Brunch from 1:30 PM to 6:30 PM
Party Facilities: Private room (for luncheons); capacity: 70

If you want to enjoy a good dinner in a warm and comfortable atmosphere, then join the singers and actors—'gypsies,' stars, and those 'between shows'—who have made The Headless Horseman a favorite after-theatre spot. Join, too, in the nightly, impromptu sing-alongs at the piano. Exposed brick walls, brass chandeliers, and the polished mahogany and teak bar contribute to the welcoming decor of The Headless Horseman. The Sunday Brunch has attracted its own following among this restaurant's clientele, but whenever you go, you'll enjoy your visit.

DINNER MENU

(a la carte)

APPETIZERS & SOUPS:
Paté (2.75); Shrimp Cocktail (3.75); Escargots (3.50); Clams Casino (3.50); Mussels Cold in Vinaigrette Sauce or Hot in Our Own Cream Sauce (3.00); Stuffed Mushrooms (2.95); The Headless Horseman Seafood Chowder (2.25); Soup of the Day (2.00).

ENTREES:
Braised Beef in the Grand Manner with Vegetable Paté and Marsala Sauce 8.50
Glazed Pork Chops stuffed with Apples, Raisins, Bread Crumbs and Herbs 8.75
Fresh Snapper Soufflé with Hollandaise Sauce 8.95
Boneless Breast of Chicken in Champagne and Truffle Sauce 6.95
Skewered Rollatini of Veal Sicilian Style 10.25
Rack of Lamb in Piquant Sauce 10.75
Stuffed Calves Liver with Bacon 8.50
Boneless Duck with Fresh Peaches 9.75
Sirloin Steak or Filet Mignon Served au Poivre, Bearnaise or with Herb Butter 13.50

(All entrees served with fresh vegetables.)

DESSERTS:
Fresh Strawberry Mousse (2.75); Viennese Dobos Cake (2.50); Brandy Alexander Cream Pie (2.50); Espresso Ice with Whipped Cream and Sliced Orange (1.75); Fresh Fruit Flambé (2.75); Crêpe du Jour Flambé (3.25).

SUNDAY BRUNCH

(Prix Fixe Brunch includes choice of Bloody Mary, Screwdriver, Sidecar, Champagne and Orange Juice, N.Y. Sour or Bullshot.)

(Prix fixe — 5.95)

Eggs Benedict
Ham, Bacon or Sausage with Eggs, Any Style
Quiche of the Day
Creamed Dried Beef with Mushrooms and Peppers on Toast
Western, Mushroom or Cheese Omelette
Spinach Salad with Bacon and Mushrooms
Buck Rarebit

(Prix fixe — 7.95)

Boneless Sirloin Steak and Eggs
Mixed Grill—Lamb Chop, Sausages, Bacon and Veal Kidneys
Calf's Liver Sauteed with Shallots
Veal Francese
Mixed Seafood Crêpe with Mornay Sauce
Steak Tartare

(All entrees served with Lyonnaise potatoes, grilled tomato, and choice of tea or coffee.)

MARGAUX: *The southernmost district of the Médoc, celebrated for its chateau bottled red Bordeaux wines. Margaux are considered the most refined and exquisite of the Médoc wines, with a delicate, silky texture and a sweet, haunting perfume.*

MARSALA: *The best-known of Italy's fortified wines, produced in the town of the same name on the west coast of Sicily. Sherry-like in texture, and usually served as an aperitif, Marsala is deep red and vaguely molasses-like in flavor.*

MEDOC: *The generally superior red wines produced in the region of Médoc on the left bank of the Gironde estuary north of Bordeaux. The best Médocs are usually known by the name of their commune (St. Julien, Pauillac, etc.) or of their chateau (Lafite, Latour, Mouton-Rothschild, etc.).*

MEURSAULT: *The dry, nutty white Burgundy produced around the towns of Meursault and Volnay in the Côte de Beaune. Green-gold in color, Meursault is full bodied, yet tangy; it is among the best white Burgundies.*

MONTILLA: *A naturally strong, and therefore unfortified, Spanish aperitif wine produced near Cordoba about 100 miles inland from the Sherry area. This wine has an exceptionally delicate flavor, given its high alcoholic content, and is occasionally served as a table wine.*

MONTRACHET: *The classic white Burgundy, Montrachet is probably the most celebrated and expensive dry white wine of France. Produced in the Côte de Beaune, solely from the Chardonnay grape, Montrachet is pale gold, with a hint of green, and has a soft, yet extraordinary bouquet and flavor.*

HERMITAGE

Address:	251 East 53rd Street
Location:	53rd Street between Second Avenue and Third Avenue
Telephone:	421-5360
Credit Cards:	AE; DC
Reservations:	Recommended
Hours:	12 Noon to 2:30 PM and 6:00 PM to 10:30 PM
Days Closed:	Sundays and major holidays
Liquor:	Full bar service
Recommended or Listed in:	New York Times; Cue; Women's Wear Daily
Maitre d':	Joseph
Seating Capacity:	100
Cuisine:	French
Specialty of the House:	Seafood
Dress:	Jackets required
Party Facilities:	Semi-private room; capacity: 50

Opened in late December, 1976, Hermitage is a new and brilliant star in the galaxy of New York's French restaurants. The proprietors, Julian Luthi and Joseph Reyers, earned their credentials at La Caravelle, La Goulue and Le Lavandou, guaranteeing their mastery of haute cuisine. The decor matches the excellence of the kitchen. The two spacious dining rooms feature exposed beams, mirrors, comfortable leather banquettes and an array of antiques. On the white clothed tables are fresh flowers. Rate Hermitage a beautiful and sophisticated new home for gourmets.

Hermitage

DINNER MENU

(a la carte)

APPETIZERS & SOUPS:

Saumon Romanoff (15.50); Terrine de Poisson (4.25); Moules à la Russe (2.95); Artichaut Vinaigrette (3.25); Anguille Fumé (3.75); Truite Fumée (4.25); Cocktail de Crevettes (4.75); Melon and Jambon (4.50); Bluepoints (3.75); Little Necks (3.75); Hors d'Oeuvres Variés (5.50); Le Bass Froid, Sauce aux Herbes (4.50); Caviar de Beluga (22.00); Crabmeat Hermitage (8.50); Barquette de Fruits de Mer (4.75); Potage du Jour (2.75); Soupe de Poisson (3.75); Bisque de Homard (3.75); Cressonière Froide (3.00); Mousse de Brothet au Poivre Vert (5.25); Paté de Campagne (4.75).

ENTREES:

La Timbale de Homard Robert 17.50
L'Escalope de Saumon Hermitage 15.75
La Coquille St. Jacques au Poivre 11.50
Red Snapper, Sauce Bearnaise 14.00
La Sole Belle Meunière 14.50
Le Bass Rayé du Jour 11.75
L'Entrecôte au Vinaigre 16.50
L'Escalopine au Cêpes 12.75
La Poularde à l'Estragon 11.75
La Crevettes Espagnole Provençale 15.50
Le Tourbot poché Hollandaise 16.50

DESSERTS:

Les Glaces et Sorbets (2.75); Tarte aux Fruits (3.00); Mousse au Chocolat (3.00); Le Gateau du Jour (3.50); La Macédoine de Fruits (2.75); Le Brie et le St. André (3.25); Le Gateau au Fromage (3.50); Coupe Hermitage (3.50).

(The luncheon menu is similar to the dinner menu. Prices at lunch are lower, with entrees priced from 6.50 to 12.50.)

COMMANDERIE DE CORDON BLEU DE FRANCE *This is an organization of "gastronomes"—members may be doctors, lawyers, chefs, restaurateurs—any individual, regardless of profession, who is deemed a true gastronome by the Board. There are approximately 100 members in the American group and each spring they assemble for a spectacular dinner. The menu for the dinner is chosen by the Board and prepared by the chef of the host restaurant or hotel. In 1978 the dinner's host was the New York City Community College's School of Hotel and Restaurant Management in Brooklyn. The President is Paul Sureau, Vice-President of The Vatel Club.*

LA FONDATION AUGUSTE ESCOFFIER *This organization honors the memory of Auguste Escoffier, who has been called "The King of Chefs and the Chef of Kings." His career spanned 62 years—from 1859 to 1921—and during that time he directed the kitchens at the Savoy and the Carlton Hotels in London. His motto was "good cooking is the basis of true happiness." The Foundation sponsors the Musée de l'Art Culinaire which is located in the house where Escoffier was born in Villeneuve-Loubet, a town on the Riviera, 15 minutes from Nice and Cannes.*

Every large city in the U.S. has a group called Les Amis d'Escoffier—for gastronomes and "admirateurs" of the great chef. Each year Les Amis sponsors a dinner. The following rules apply at this dinner: (1) The napkin must be tucked under the collar—"serviette au cou." (2) The wines, carefully selected to accompany the delicacy of each course, must be drunk during the course for which they are intended. (Glasses are removed, even if full, at the end of each course.) (3) Smoking is absolutely forbidden up to the time dessert is served. And, this warning appeared on the menu at one of the dinners: "Since 'Les Amis d'Escoffier' Society is dedicated to the art of good living only, it is forbidden, under the threat of expulsion, to speak of personal affairs, of one's own work or specialty and more particularly to attempt to use the Society as a means of making business contacts . . . Furthermore at these dinner-meetings reference will never be made on the subjects of: politics, religious belief, personal opinions of either members or guests irrespective of their professional or social status." The President-Founder of the Society is Mr. Joseph Donon.

HUNAM

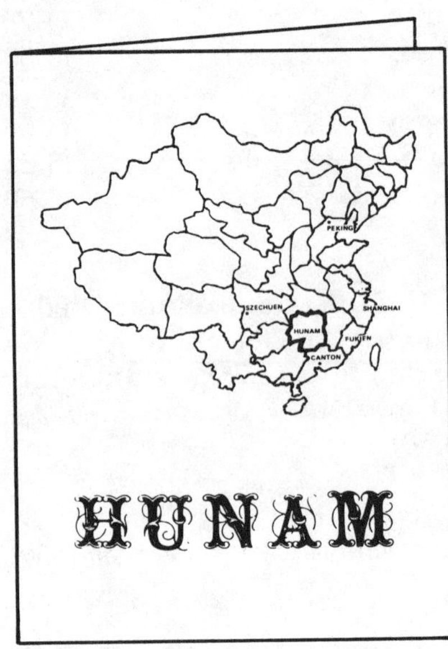

Address:	**845 Second Avenue**
Location:	**Second Avenue at 45th Street**
Telephone:	**MU 7-7471**
Credit Cards:	**AE; DC; CB**
Reservations:	**Recommended**
Hours:	**11:30 AM to 11:30 PM, Sunday thru Thursday; 11:30 AM to 1:30 AM, Friday and Saturday**
Days Closed:	**None**
Liquor:	**Full bar service**
Recommended or Listed in:	**New York Times; Gourmet; Forbes; Cue**
Maitre d':	**Paul Tang**
Seating Capacity:	**116**
Cuisine:	**Chinese (Hunam and Szechuan)**
Specialties of the House:	**Sliced Leg of Lamb, Hunam Style; Lake Tung Ting Shrimp; Hunam Beef; Spicy Crispy Whole Sea Bass; General Gau's Duckling; Peking Duck**
Dress:	**Casual**
Party Facilities:	**3 rooms; capacity: 100**
Parking:	**Free two-hour parking after 6:00PM at Park Swift Lot (Second Avenue between 46th and 47th Streets)**

It was the Hunam Restaurant which first introduced Hunamese cuisine to New Yorkers. It has had a lasting success and many imitators, but for authentic Hunamese dishes this restaurant still ranks at the top of the list. The decor in the two dining rooms is simple but attractive. The upstairs room, papered in red and deep gold, is dimly lit while the downstairs dining room, done in a patterned gold paper, is more brightly illuminated. Hunam is a very popular spot so it's best to make reservations.

DINNER MENU

(a la carte)

APPETIZERS:
Crisp Chicken with Peanuts (4.25); Shrimp Puff with Sesame Seeds (4.95); Pearl Balls (3.75); Curry Stuffed Crepe (4.25); Turnip Cake (4.25); Fried Dumplings (4 for 2.75); Steamed Dumplings (4 for 2.75); Spring Roll (.95); Egg Roll (.95); Spareribs (4.95); Roast Pork (4.95); Shrimp Toast (2.75); Hot Appetizers for two (6.50); Marinated Duck in Five Spices (5.50); Corned Pork (5.50); Hacked Chicken in Hot Sauce (5.50); Spicy and Tangy Chicken (5.50); Two Delicacy Combination Platter (8.00); Three Delicacy Combination Platter (10.75); Four Delicacy Combination Platter (12.95).

SOUPS:
Egg Drop (1.25); Hot and Sour (1.50); Won Ton (1.50); Hot and Sour Fish Broth (1.85); Winter Melon Soup (1.75); Sizzling Rice Soup (Shrimp, Chicken) (1.85).

ENTREES:

Sliced Leg of Lamb, Hunam Style 7.25
(Choice spring lamb with scallions and hot pepper sauce)

General Ching's Chicken 6.95
(General Ching, the renowned General of the Chung Dynasty, trained the famous Hunam Army. Chicken chunks with tingling hot sauce)

Lake Tung Ting Shrimp 7.95
(Giant Shrimp marinated with broccoli, ham, bamboo shoots and mushrooms in a white sauce. Lake Tung Ting is the largest lake in China)

Hunam Beef 7.75
(Fillet of beef garnished with fresh watercress in a hot sauce)

Bamboo Steamer's Spareribs 7.25
(An authentic Hunam specialty. Baby spareribs marinated in hot sauce coated with rice flour. Steamed in a bamboo steamer)

Hunam's Honey Ham 8.75
(China's finest preserved ham, honey glazed with lotus nuts)
Spicy Crispy Whole Sea Bass 10.50
(Sea Bass, deep fried till crisp coated with Hunam hot sauce)
Neptune's Platter 9.75
(An assortment of culinary sea treasures with crisp Chinese vegetables)
Hunam Preserved Duck 7.75
(Young preserved duckling steamed on a bed of marinated lean pork patties)
Fillet of Sea Bass with Shrimp Roe Sauce 7.75
Shredded Lamb Tripe 6.50
(Authentic Hunam country style cooking. Shredded lamb tripe sauteed in hot Hunam sauce)
General Gau's Duckling 7.75
(Boned Duckling with button mushrooms and Chinese five spices in red hot sauce. General Gau was a famous Governor of Hunam during the Chung Dynasty.)
Shredded Chicken with Hunam Pickle 6.50
Spicy and Tangy Chicken 6.50
Slippery Chicken 6.50
Chicken Floating in Red Wine 6.50
Tung-Goo Chicken 6.50
Sauteed Smoke Chicken 6.50
Orange Flavor Beef 7.50
Shredded Beef, Hunam Style 7.50
Tangy Spicy Beef 7.50
Mandarin Beef 7.50
Hunam Duckling with Smoked Flavor 8.75
Crisp Fried Boneless Duck with Chinese Vegetable 6.95
Peking Duck 19.00
Fresh Pork Hunam Style 6.50
Mo-Shu Pork 6.50
Preserved Pork with Hearts of Cabbages 6.50
Pork with Sea Bass Flavor 6.50
Lobster Hunam Style 10.50
Shrimp Puff in Ginger Sauce 8.25
River Shrimp with Sizzling Rice 6.95
Shrimp with Peanuts 8.25
Baby Shrimp with Pine Nuts 6.50
Fresh Scallops Hunam Style 7.50
Poached Whole Sea Bass in Hot Sauce 10.50
Translucent Fish Fillets 7.95

VEGETABLES, RICE & NOODLES:
Eggplant Family Style (5.50); Buddha's Delight (5.50); Tangy and Spicy Green Beans (5.50); Minced Pork Sauteed with Bean Cake (5.25); Tung-An Bean Cake (5.25); Roast Pork Fried Rice (3.50); Yang Chow Fried Rice (4.25)); Hunam Pan Fried Noodles (4.95); Subgum Lo Mein (4.95).

DESSERTS:
Stuffed Honey Crisp Banana (1.50); Assorted Chinese Fruits (1.50); Ice Cream (.85).

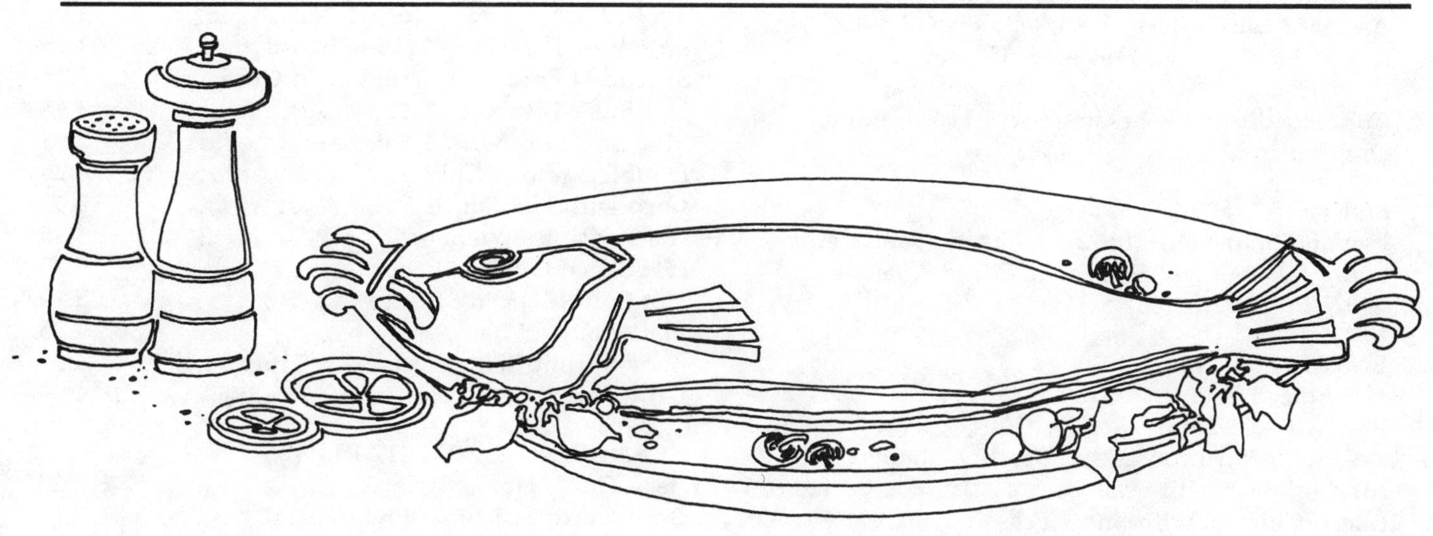

HWA YUAN SZECHUAN INN

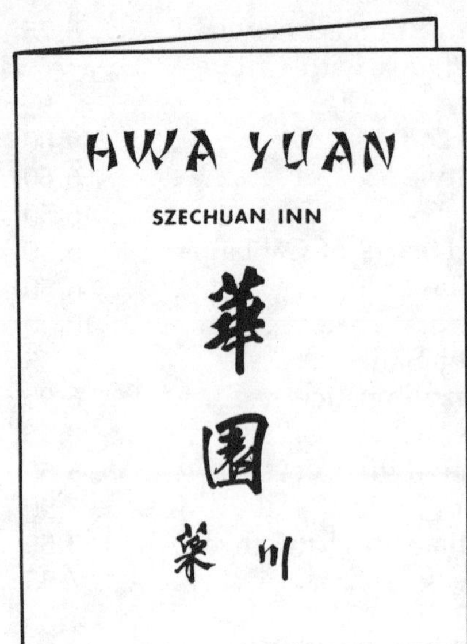

Address:	40 East Broadway
Location:	East Broadway between Catherine Street and Market Street
Telephone:	966-5534 or 966-5535
Credit Cards:	AE; DC; CB; MC; V
Reservations:	Recommended for parties of more than 8
Hours:	12 Noon to 10:00 PM Sunday thru Thursday; 12 Noon to 11:00 PM Friday and Saturday
Days Closed:	None
Liquor:	Beer only
Recommended or Listed in:	Cue
Seating Capacity:	250
Cuisine:	Chinese (Szechuan and Mandarin)
Specialties of the House:	Sizzling Beef with Scallops; Diced Chicken with Hot Pepper Sauce; Hot Sliced Ginger Shrimp; Dry Sauteed String Beans
Dress:	Casual
Party Facilities:	Downstairs dining room; capacity: 100

The decor at this Szechuanese eatery is simple yet distinctively Chinese. Featured are colorful papier mache masks, a carved wedding screen with the traditional phoenix and dragon symbols and silk screened calendars which are for sale during the New Year season. There are three separate dining rooms with the large downstairs room being available for parties of up to 100.

MENU

(a la carte)

(a representative selection)

APPETIZERS (Cold Dishes & Noodles):
Shredded Chicken with Pepper Sauce (3.25); Aromatic Sliced Beef (3.50); Jelly Fish (3.50); Smoked Fish (3.25); Hot Spicy Chinese Cabbage (2.75); Noodles with Hot Brown Meat Sauce (2.25); Cold Noodles with Sesame Sauce (1.75); Fried Dumplings (2.75).

SOUPS:
Hot and Sour Soup (for 2) (1.75); Pork and Radish Soup (for 2) (2.00); Soup with Sliced Abalone and Chicken (for 2) (2.00).

ENTREES:

Hot Spiced Beef	3.95
Beef with Scallions	3.95
Beef with Mushrooms and Bamboo Shoots	4.25
Sizzling Beef with Scallops	6.25
Sliced Chicken with Snow Peas	4.25
Diced Chicken with Hot Pepper Sauce	4.25
Diced Chicken with Walnuts	4.25
Diced Chicken with Pine Nuts	4.50
Smoked Duck with Camphor and Tea Flavor (Half)	6.25
Crispy Duck (Half)	6.25
Peking Duck (Order in Advance)	17.00
Sliced Pork Home Style	3.95
Shredded Pork with Peking Sauce	3.95
Shredded Pork with Dried Bean Curd	3.75
Hot Spiced Pork	3.95
Moo Shu Pork with 4 Pancakes	3.95
Double Sauteed Chinese Ham	4.25
Carp with Hot Sauce	5.45
Carp with Brown Sauce	5.25
Hot Sliced Ginger Shrimp	5.75
Hot Spiced Sliced Shrimp	5.75
Plain Sauteed Baby Shrimp	4.25
Baby Shrimp with Black Bean Sauce	4.25
Baby Shrimp with Hot Pepper Sauce	4.25

BEAN CURD & VEGETABLES:

Bean Curd, Home Style	3.25
Bean Curd, Szechuan Style	3.25
Bean Curd with Mushrooms	3.50
Hot Spiced Egg Plant	3.25
Egg Plant with Bean Sauce	3.25
Dried Sauteed String Beans	3.25
Mixed Vegetables	3.50

"How Many of New York's Great Menus Have You Held in Your Hands"

A Special Supplement to Manhattan Menus

BRASSERIE
BRASSERIE
BRASSERIE
BRASSERIE
BRASSERIE
BRASSERIE
BRASSERIE
BRASSERIE
BRASSERIE
BRASSERIE
BRASSERIE
BRASSERIE
BRASSERIE
BRASSERIE
BRASSERIE
BRASSERIE
BRASSERIE
BRASSERIE
BRASSERIE
BRASSERIE
BRASSERIE
BRASSERIE
BRASSERIE
BRASSERIE
BRASSERIE
BRASSERIE
BRASSERIE
BRASSERIE
BRASSERIE
BRASSERIE
BRASSERIE

BRASSERIE

100 EAST 53rd STREET, N.Y. — PLAZA 1-4840

OUVERTE A TOUTE HEURE

DINER

POUR COMMENCER — AVEC NOS COMPLIMENTS
LA TAPENADE AUX CRUDITES

HORS D'OEUVRE OU POTAGES

Melon en Saison *Pâté du Chef Sauce Cumberland*
Galantine de Sole, Sauce Verte *Coupe de Fruits Frais*
Les Délices de Gruyére, Sauce Tomate
Escargots de Bourgogne (les Six 1.50 extra)
Clovisses (.95 extra) *Clovisses Casino (1.95 extra)* *Cocktail de Crevettes (1.75 extra)*
Potage du Jour *Consommé Célestine* *Potage Froid Maison*

Soupe a L'Oignon Gratinee (.75 extra)

ENTREES

Mousse de Sole, Sauce Nantua.................. 7.85
La Truite Farcie Maison...................... 8.50
Surprise de Volaille Vigneronne.............. 8.25
Escalope de Veau Cordon Bleu................. 8.45
Paupiette de Boeuf Nouilles au Beurre........ 7.45
Civet de Chevreuil Grand Mère................ 8.75

POMMES ET LEGUMES

Pommes Frites ou Croquettes ou Vapeur ou Gratin Dauphinois
Légume du Jour

DESSERTS

Assorted Sherbets and Ice Creams *Kugelhopf* *Fromage and Fruit*
Meringue Glacé Melba *French Pastries* *Caramel Custard*
Mousse à l'Orange Maison *Orange Surprise* *Mousse au Chocolat* *Fruit Salad*

Café *Tea* *Lait*

VINS EN CARAFE

Ecu Royal Rouge ou Blanc

Un Verre	1.25
1/4 Litre	2.25
1/2 Litre	3.95
Litre	5.95

BIERES

Michelob on Draught	1.25
La Blonde de France	1.50
Cardinal de Fribourg	1.50
Hofbrau	1.50
Perrier	.85

VINS EN BOUTEILLE

	FULL	HALF
RED BORDEAUX: Château Monbousquet	9.50	5.50
RED BURGUNDY: Château des Tours Brouilly	9.50	5.50
WHITE BURGUNDY: Meursault, J.P. Bardot	11.50	6.50
ROSE: Rosé d'Anjou, Camille de Leger	5.50	
ALSACE: Sylvaner	7.50	4.50
AMERICAN: Sterling, White or Red	5.50	
CHAMPAGNE: Mumm's Cordon Rouge Brut N.V.	18.50	9.50
CHAMPAGNE: American: Gold Seal N.V.	10.00	5.50

PRIVATE ROOM AVAILABLE FOR GROUPS OF 10 TO 50

A LA CARTE

HORS D'OEUVRE

Pâté du Chef, Sauce Cumberland 1.95 — *Galantine de Sole, Sauce Verte 1.95*
Melon en Saison 1.50 — *Salade Savoyarde 2.25* — *Clovisses Casino 3.50*
Brochette Brasserie 2.50 — *Clovisses, les Six 2.95* — *Cocktail de Crevettes 3.75*
ESCARGOTS DE BOURGOGNE: les Six 3.50; la Douzaine 6.75

Potage du Jour *1.50*
Consommé Célestine *1.35*
Potage Froid Maison *1.50*

SOUPE A L'OIGNON GRATINEE 1.95 LA GRANDE 2.50

Bread and Butter when ordering Soup alone .... *.50*

LES SPECIALITES

La Crêpe de Volaille à la Crème 5.25
La Quiche Brasserie, Salade 5.50
Darne de Saumon Pochée, Sauce Mousseline 8.75
Les Crevettes Jacqueline 8.25
Medaillons de Veau aux Morilles 7.75
Côte de Porc au Poivre Vert 6.75
Sirloin of Beef Stroganoff and Rice 7.75

CHOUCROUTE A L'ALSACIENNE 7.25

GRILLADES

Sirloin Steak, Sauce Béarnaise 9.50 — *Filet Mignon with Mushrooms 9.50*
Steak Sandwich "Brasserie" 7.95 — *Brochette de Boeuf, Bordelaise 7.25*
Foie de Veau à l'Anglaise 7.75
Servi avec Légume et Pommes de Terre ou Salade

SANDWICHES

"Brasserie" Club 4.75 — *Monte Cristo 4.50*
Croque Madame 4.50 — *Sandwich Tartare 5.25* — *Croque Monsieur 4.50*

LES OEUFS A NOTRE FACON

Les Oeufs au Plat ou Brouillés avec Jambon, Bacon, Sausages, Tomatoes, Saucisson Lyonnaise 4.25
Les Oeufs Florentine 4.75 — *Les Oeufs Bénédictine 5.50*

LES OMELETTES

Prince Igor (Caviar de Saumon, Sour Cream) 4.95 — *Champignons 4.50*
Lorraine (Bacon - Cheese - Chives) 4.50 — *Piperade 4.50*
Provençale (Tomatoes - Garlic) 4.50
Smoked Salmon 4.75 — *Saint Laurent 4.75*
à la Môde du Chef 4.95

LES HAMBURGERS DE LA MAISON

Provençale, Ratatouille Niçoise 4.75
Basquaise, Piperade 4.75 — *Gruyère, Pommes à l'Huile 4.75*
Served on Garlic Bread

LE STEAK HAMBOURGEOIS, SAUCE CHAMPIGNONS 5.95

NOS SALADES A LA CARTE

Belgian Endives, Lemon Dressing 1.50 — *Watercress and Sliced Mushrooms 1.50*
Sliced Tomatoes and Fresh Basil 1.50 — *Romaine with Caesar Dressing 1.75*

BUFFET FROID

La Salade de Crabe Tina 6.95 — *La Salade aux Epinards et Champignons 4.50*
Assiette de Saumon Fumé, Garni 6.85 — *La Salade du Chef 5.25*
Le Steak Tartare, Garni 6.95 — *Salade Niçoise 5.75*
La Truite de Rivière Fumée, Sauce Raifort 6.50 — *La Salade Crinoline 5.25*

DESSERTS ET PATISSERIE

Kugelhopf 1.50 — ***Meringue Glacé Melba 1.95*** — ***French Pastries 1.75***
Mousse à l'Orange Maison 1.75 — ***Cheese 1.65; with Fruits 2.00***
Mousse au Chocolat 1.75 — ***Crème Caramel 1.65*** — ***Salade de Fruits 1.50***
Sorbets: Citron Framboise 1.30 — ***Ice Cream Sundaes 1.85*** — ***Orange Surprise 1.85***
Chocolat, Vanille, Butter Pecan, Mocha, Burgundy Cherry 1.30
Ice Cream Sodas, Malteds, Frosteds au Goût de Chacun 1.60

BEVERAGES

Café .75 — ***Pot de Thé .65*** — ***Cafe Viennois .95*** — ***Cappuccino 1.25***
Milk .70 — ***Chocolat Chantilly .95*** — ***Espresso .95*** — ***Cola .75***

10-77

Prices, Items and Hours Subject to Change

Brasserie

Address: 100 East 53rd Street
Location: Between Park Avenue & Lexington Avenue
Telephone: 751-4840
Credit Cards: All Major Credit Cards Accepted
Hours: Open 24 hours, 7 days a week
Liquor: Full Liquor Service at Tables Only
Recommended or listed in: Cue, Where Magazine, Host, Theatre & Events
Seating Capacity: 349
Private Rooms: Private room for up to 50 persons
Outside Catering: Call 997-1406 Take-out Picnic Baskets
Cuisine: French-Alsatian

BRASSERIE Where else can one have breakfast, Sunday brunch, lunch, dinner and all night-dining but here at midtown's busiest and happiest eatery. The Brasserie's menu is large its cuisine French-Alsatian, its prices moderate. Brioche, croissant and other unforgettable French pastries baked on premises. Vive la Brasserie! 24 hours a day, 7 days a week. Tables or a spacious counter with comfortable seats.

"Una Cena – Senza Vino – é come una Giornata Senza Sole."

Mamma Leone's

FAMOUS DINNER

$10.95
SERVED UNTIL CLOSING

Complete dinner consists of choice from
ANTIPASTI, PASTA, PESCE O ARROSTO, BUGIE, DESSERT and COFFEE

Celery, Olives, Tomatoes and our Famous Cheese on every Table

FAMOSI ANTIPASTI DELLA MAMMA

Shrimp Cocktail Leone — Fresh Chicken Liver Paté — Tomato Juice
Veal Caponata — Melon with Prosciutto — Anchovies and Peppers
Fruit Cocktail Leone — Sardines with Ricotta

Mamma's Suggestion: ANTIPASTO SUPREME

PASTA

We serve only Imported Spaghetti — Primo Brand

Minestrone — SPAGHETTI, CLAM SAUCE — Spaghetti Leone — Homemade Ravioli
Fresh Chicken Soup — Onion Soup alla Fiorentina — Fettuccine all'Alfredo or Meat Sauce
BAKED HOMEMADE LASAGNA — Homemade Fresh Manicotti, Meat Sauce

PESCE O ARROSTO

Filet of Sole alle Mandorle — Spaghetti with Meatballs — Mamma's Chicken Cacciatora
Baked Homemade Lasagna — Osso Buco alla Milanese
MAMMA'S WHOLE ROAST CHICKEN
VEAL CUTLET PARMIGIANA
VEAL SCALOPPINE AL MARSALA
Roast Duckling, Orange Sauce — Roast Stuffed Turkey
Italian Sausage with Peppers — Broiled Chopped Steak
Cornish Game Hen, The Italian Way — Broiled Thick Pork Chop
Fresh Chicken Livers and Mushrooms Brochette
Homemade Fresh Manicotti, Meat Sauce
Broiled Tenderloin of Pork
BONELESS CHICKEN PARMIGIANA
Broiled Half Chicken all'Italiana
BAKED EGGPLANT PARMIGIANA

TAKE HOME A TREAT!
TASTY PASTRIES OR CAKES FROM MAMMA'S OWN BAKE SHOP! OR AN ITALIAN GIFT!

SUPPER A LA CARTE

FROM 9:30 UNTIL CLOSING

Celery, Olives, Tomatoes and our Famous Cheese on every Table

Mamma's Antipasto Supreme 6.00 — Melon with Prosciutto 4.00
Fruit Cocktail Leone 1.75 — Shrimp Cocktail Leone 3.50
Anchovies and Peppers 2.50 — Fresh Chicken Liver Paté 3.50
Tomato Juice 1.25 — Sardines with Ricotta 3.00
MINESTRONE, ONION OR CHICKEN SOUP 2.50

PASTA

Served with Mamma Leone's Mixed Green Salad

Homemade Baked Lasagna or Manicotti or Ravioli	6.50
Homemade Fettucine all'Alfredo or Meat Sauce	6.50
Spaghetti Leone or with Clam Sauce	6.50
Spaghetti with Meat Balls	6.75

Entrees Below Served with Side Order of Spaghetti and Mamma Leone's Mixed Green Salad

Veal Scaloppine al Marsala	8.50
Osso Buco alla Milanese	8.50
Filet of Veal Piccata	9.50
Veal Cutlet Parmigiana	8.50
Chicken Parmigiana or Cacciatora	8.00
Baked Eggplant Parmigiana	7.00
MAMMA'S WHOLE ROAST CHICKEN	8.50
Saltimbocca alla Romana	9.50
Italian Sausage with Peppers	8.25
Half Roast Chicken	7.00
Broiled Half Chicken all'Italiana	7.50
Roast Duckling, Orange Sauce	8.50
Cornish Game Hen, The Italian Way	8.00
Filet of Sole alla Mandorle	8.00
Broiled Fresh Fish of the Day	9.00
Broiled Cold Water Lobster Tails	13.00
Roast Stuffed Turkey	8.00
Broiled Chopped Steak	8.00
Broiled Thick Pork Chop	9.00
Broiled Double Rib Lamb Chop	10.50
Roast Prime Ribs of Beef	11.00
Sliced Steak Basketball	10.50
Sliced Steak Pizzaiola	10.50
Broiled Sirloin Steak	11.00
Broiled Filet Mignon	11.00

Tortoni	.95
Ice Cream	.95
Lemon Ice	.95
Zabaglione	2.25
Rum Cake	1.00
Leone's Cheese Cake	1.25
Choice: Assorted Pastry Tray	1.25
Mamma's Special Ice Cream with Fruit and Brandy Sauce	2.25

BUGIE

Caffè Espresso	.75
Coffee	.60
Tea .50 Milk	.50
Cappuccino	.75
Irish Coffee	2.00
Caffè Romano	2.00
Ramazzotti Caldo	1.50

For Youngsters Under 12 Years of Age
FRUIT CUP
SPAGHETTI, MANICOTTI OR RAVIOLI with Meatballs
BUGIE - TORTONI and COCA-COLA OR MILK
$5.50

Mamma Leone's

Address: 48th Street West of Broadway
Location: Between 8th Avenue and Broadway
Telephone: 586-5151
Credit Cards: All Major Credit Cards Accepted
Reservations: Suggested
Hours: Monday through Friday: 11:30 a.m. to 11:30 p.m.
Buffet lunch 11:30 to 3 p.m.
Saturday: 2:30 p.m. to 11:30 p.m.
Sunday: 2:00 p.m. to 10 p.m.
Parking: Lot located next door
Liquor: Full Liquor Service
Recommended or listed in: Cue, Where Magazine, Host, Theatre & Events
Seating Capacity: 1200
Private Rooms: Facilities available for small and large groups
Outside Catering: Inquire of management
Cuisine: Italian

MAMMA LEONE'S The Italian dinner of the year every night. This colorful restaurant has been a favorite of tourists and New Yorkers alike since 1906. Come and see what you've been missing. We treat everyone like family, good Italian food and plenty of it and people just keep coming.

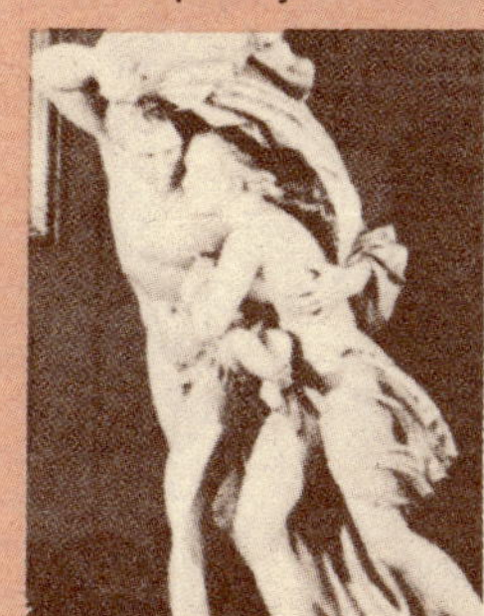

Specialità della Casa

Complete dinner consists of choice from
ANTIPASTI, PASTA, PESCE O ARROSTO, BUGIE, DESSERT and COFFEE

BROILED COLD WATER LOBSTER TAILS 14.00
BROILED FRESH FISH OF THE DAY 13.25
BROILED DOUBLE RIB LAMB CHOP 11.75
FILET OF VEAL PICCATA 11.75
SALTIMBOCCA ALLA ROMANA 12.00
Roast Prime Ribs of Beef 13.50
Sliced Steak Pizzaiola 13.00
Broiled Filet Mignon 13.50
Broiled Sirloin Steak 13.50
Filet Mignon con Barolo 13.50
Filetto di Bue alla Bruno 14.00

Mixed Green Salad and Potato

HOMEMADE TORTE, GELATI, FRUTTA FRESCA

Mamma's Italian Style Ice Cream: Chocolate, Vanilla, Strawberry
RUM CAKE LEMON ICE TORTONI
Fresh Pear or Apple 1.00 Zabaglione 2.00
LEONE'S CHEESE CAKE 1.00
Choice from Assorted Pastry Tray 1.00
Mamma's Special Ice Cream with Fruit and Brandy Sauce 2.00

BUGIE

Coffee Tea Milk Caffè Espresso Ramazzotti Caldo 1.50
Irish Coffee 2.00 Caffè Romano 2.00 Cappuccino .75

Lunch from 11:30 A.M. to 2:30 P.M. — Monday thru Friday.
Weekdays: Cocktails from 3:00 P.M.; Dinner from 3:30 P.M.
Saturdays: Cocktails from 2:30 P.M.; Dinner from 2:30 P.M.
Sundays and Holidays: Cocktails from 1:30 P.M.;
Dinner from 2:00 P.M. to 10:00 P.M.

FACILITIES FOR LUNCHEON AND DINNER PARTIES — 25 to 500 PERSONS

WINES

ITALIAN STILL WINES

	Bottle	½ Bot.
Spanna Red	7.75	4.50
Barolo Red	7.75	4.50
Bardolino Red	7.75	4.50
Chianti Red	7.75	4.50
Valpolicella Red	7.75	4.50
Draceno Siciliano Red & White	7.75	
Moscato Passito Red (Sweet)	7.75	4.50
Soave White (Dry)	7.75	4.50
Verdicchio White (Dry)	7.75	4.50
Rose Collameno	7.75	4.50
Orvieto White (Dry & Sweet)	7.75	4.50
Frascati White (Dry)	7.75	
Vino Nobile di Montepulciano Red	7.75	

ITALIAN SPARKLING WINES

	Bottle	½ Bot.
Asti Spumante White (Sweet)	10.50	6.50
Lacrima Christi White (Dry)	10.50	6.50
Spumarosa Pink	10.50	6.50
Lambrusco Red (Sweet)	9.50	6.00
Bracheto Red (Sweet)	10.50	6.50

FRENCH STILL WINES

	Bottle	½ Bot.
Beaujolais Red	8.00	5.00
St. Julien Red	8.00	5.00
Sauterne White	8.00	5.00
Chablis White	8.00	5.00

AMERICAN SPARKLING and STILL WINES

	Bottle	½ Bot.
Villa d'Este Sparkling Burgundy	8.75	5.25
Villa d'Este Champagne	9.25	5.75
Villa d'Este Burgundy	5.75	3.75
Villa d'Este Chablis	5.75	3.75

PORTUGUESE WINE

	Bottle	½ Bot.
Lancer's Sparkling	8.75	5.25

FRENCH SPARKLING WINES

	Bottle	½ Bot.
Sparkling Burgundy	11.00	6.25
Chauvenet Red Cap, Red	11.00	6.25
Mumm's Cordon Rouge	18.75	10.25
Piper Heidsieck White	19.75	
Moet & Chandon White	19.75	

GERMAN STILL WINES

	Bottle
Liebfraumilch	9.25
Piesporter	8.25
Niersteiner	8.25

BEERS and ALE

Heineken	1.35
Imported Beer	1.35
American Beer and Ale	1.10

Prices, Items and Hours Subject to Change

PRANZO DELLA SERA

APERITIVI
COCKTAILS

Americano	1.70
Negroni	1.75
Trattoria Cocktail	1.50
Campari & Soda	1.65
Punt e Mes	1.60
Vermouth; Rosso o Bianco	1.50
Martini Cocktail	1.60
Manhattan Cocktail	1.60
Scotch Whiskey	1.60

VINI IN CARAFFA
WINES IN CARAFE

IMPORTED ITALIAN WINES
ROSSI O BIANCHI

Bicchiere	**.95**
½ Litro	**2.95**
Litro	**4.95**

VINI ROSSI
RED WINES

BOTTIGLIA 6.75 / HALF 3.75

Barolo · *Frecciarossa*
Barbera · *Chianti*
Rustego · *Bardolino*
Valpolicella · *Lambrusco*

VINI BIANCHI
WHITE WINES

BOTTIGLIA 6.75 HALF 3.75

Soave · *Orvieto*
Verdicchio · *Chianti*

VINO SPUMANTE
SPARKLING WINES

BOTTIGLIA 9.50 / HALF 4.75

Lacrima Christi, Secco
Asti Spumante, Dolce

VINI ROSATI
ROSE WINE

BOTTIGLIA 6.25 HALF 3.50

Chiaretto del Garda
Collameno

BIRRA
BEER

Michelob or Heineken 1.50
Budweiser 1.25

BIBITE
SOFT DRINKS

Anise Anise	.95	*Orzata* Almond	.95
Menta Mint	.95	*Coca-Cola*	.75

San Pellegrino 1 Litro 1.95
½ Litro 1.10

DIGESTIVI
BITTERS

Fernet Branca 1.65
Amaretto 1.75

LIQUORI TIPICI
ITALIAN LIQUEURS

Anisette · *Strega*
Galliano · *Grappa*
Fior d'Alpi · *Sambuca*
Ciao-Ciao

1.75

ANTIPASTI e MINESTRE
APPETIZERS AND SOUPS

Melone 1.25 *w. Prosciutto*	2.95
Fresh Cut Fruits	1.25
Vongole alla Casino, Clams Casino	2.75
Cozze alla Napolitana in Red or White Sauce,	2.95
Minestrone alla Contadina	1.50
Minestre del Giorno	1.75

PASTA
HOMEMADE PASTA

Spaghetti w. Meat Balls	4.75
w. Carbonara - Prosciutto, Onions and Cream	4.75
w. Primavera - Tiny Sliced Vegetable and Tomato	4.75
Lasagne Trattoria, House Specialty	4.95
Tortellini in Brodo, in Chicken Broth	4.25
Linguine Pesto w. Garlic, Cheese and Basil	4.95
Linguine alle Vongole, Red or White Clam Sauce	4.95
Cannelloni Piemontese, Crepe Filled with Meat, Cheese and Spinach	4.95
Manicotti alla Marinara, Spiced Tomato Sauce	4.50
Ravioli Bolognese, Meat Sauce	4.50
Ziti alla Siciliana, Baked with Eggplant	4.50
Fettuccine Alfredo, Cream, Cheese & Eggs	4.95

PASTA SERVED AS ANTIPASTO W. MAIN COURSE 2.00 LESS

Served w. Salad

PIZZA and HEROS

Trattoria, Cheese, Pepper, Tomato, Sausage	3.75
Classica, Cheese, Tomatoes	3.50
Sicilian Pizza	3.95
Calzone	3.95

HEROS

Meatball or Sausage, Peppers and Onions	3.95
Eggplant Parmigiana	4.25
Veal Cutlet Parmigiana	4.95

INSALATE e PIATTI FREDDI
SALADS AND COLD PLATTERS

Insalata dello Chef, Chef's Salad	4.95
Insalata di Pollo, San Remo, Chicken Salad	5.50
Torta Rustica, Italian Country Pate	4.50
Crostata Primavera Crepe Filled with Vegetables and Italian Meats	5.25
Pomodori con Cipolle, Tomatoes and Onion	1.25
Spinaci e Funghi, Spinach and Mushrooms	1.25

PESCE
FISH

Spigola alla Marinara Baked Striped Bass, Tomato Sauce	7.25
Zuppa di Pesce del Liguria Fresh Fish and Shell Fish in Bowl	6.95
Passerino al Forno Baked Baby Flounder	6.50
Scampi Trattoria Shrimp Sauteed in Garlic and White Wine	7.50

Served with Salad and Choice of Spaghetti or Linguine

DINNER

Antipasto from the Cibi Ronda

Step up to our exciting new display of Italian delicacies and create your own Antipasto

Stuffed Green Peppers
Red Pimentos with Anchovies
Marinated Mushrooms
Artichoke Hearts
Stuffed Zucchini
Veal Caponata
Mortadella
Coppa
Milano Salami
Calamari and Tiny Shrimp

Regular Portion 3.25 Large Portion 4.50

PIATTA del GIORNO

MAIN COURSES

Melonzana Parmigiana
Eggplant, Tomato Sauce, Mozzarella Cheese 5.50

Petto di Pollo, Valdostana
Double Breast of Chicken Stuffed w. Cheese 6.50

Pollo Trattoria
Braised Chicken w. Sauce of Chestnuts and Raisins 6.50

Vitello Parmigiana
Veal Cutlet, Tomato Sauce, Mozzarella Cheese 6.75

Scallopine di Vitello, Marsala
Veal, Fresh Mushrooms, Marsala Wine 6.95

Scallopine alla Limone
Veal with Butter and Lemon 6.95

Bocconcino di Vitello
Veal and Vegetables in Light Wine Sauce 6.50

Braciola alla Napoletana
Slices of Beef Rolled with Herbs and Spices 6.95

Specialita del Capo di Cucina
Chef's Special 6.95

Costata di Manzo alla Fiorentina
Bone-in Strip Steak, Bed of Spinach 8.95
Served with Salad and Choice of Spaghetti or Linguine

FRITTATE

OMELETTES

Trattoria, Onions, Peppers and Sausages
Di Spinaci, w. Spinach and Garlic 4.95
Al Formaggio, The Classic Cheese Omelette
Served w. Salad

DOLCI e GELATI

DESSERTS

Torte Fragole	1.50
Sacrapantina	1.50
Cannoli	1.50
Cioccolata Italiana	1.75
Torta Gianduia	1.50
Specialita del Giorno	1.75
Pannettone	1.50
Assorted Cheese w. Fresh Fruits	2.95

BEVANDE

BEVERAGES

Caffe Americano Unlimited	.60
Espresso	.75
Espresso Doppio, Romano	1.50
Espresso Siciliano, Speciale	1.50
Cappuccino	1.35
Cappuccino de Medici	1.50
Caffe Cioccolato *alla Vesuvio*	1.50
Iced Tea or Iced Coffee	.50
Pot of Tea	.60

Take Home Some of Trattoria's Homemade Pastry and Ice Creams

CROSTATA DI RICOTTA 1.75
Italian Cheese Cake

ZUPPE INGLESE 1.75
A rich combination of Rum Cake, Custard, Candied Fruits and Meringue Topped

HOMEMADE ICE CREAMS 1.50
Vanilla, Chocolate, Coffee, Pistachio, Strawberry, Peach Brandy, Amaretto

TARTUFO 1.50
Rich Chocolate Ice Cream with a sweet Center, Chocolate Shavings

In New York Do As the Romans Do

Picnic Italiano.

And Don't Forget Trattoria's Five Different Italian Picnics Call 661-3090

Prices, Items and Hours Subject to Change

The New Trattoria

Address: 200 Park Avenue in Pan Am Bldg.
Location: Between 44th & 45th Streets
Telephone: 661-3090
Credit Cards: All Major Credit Cards Accepted
Reservations: Accepted at Dinner Only
Hours: Monday through Friday: 7 a.m. (breakfast) to midnight; Saturday: 12 noon to Midnight
Liquor: Full Liquor Service
Recommended or listed in: Cue, Where Magazine, Host, Theatre & Events
Seating Capacity: 250
Private Rooms: No; special attention to groups
Outside Catering: Call 997-1406 Picnic Baskets and Homemade Pastries Available
Cuisine: Italian

TRATTORIA This new sleek Italian restaurant buzzes with excitement. The best antipasto, pizza, pasta and veal specialties this side of Italy. Fabulous pastries and gelati (ice cream) made on premises. A Lotta Mangia for Not a Lotta Lire.

Main Concourse, Pan Am Building.

Location: Between 44th & 45th , Pan Am Concourse
Telephone: 661-2520
Credit Cards: All Major Credit Cards Accepted
Reservations: Recommended at Lunch and Dinner
Hours: Monday through Friday: Lunch: 11:30 to 4:30 p.m.
Dinner: 4:30 p.m. to 10:30 p.m.

(Let's talk it over at Charlie Brown's.)

Main Concourse, Pan Am Building. MO1-2520.

Appetizers & Soups

Mussels in Curry Cream 2.25
Smoked Salmon with Capers and Onions 4.25
Pink Shrimp Cocktail 3.75 Local Clams 3.25
Oysters on the Half Shell 3.25 Soused Tiny Shrimp 2.95
Combination Shellfish Platter 4.25
Chilled Ripe Melon 1.75

Baked Clams 3.50
SIZZLING SNAILS in Garlic 3.75
Pink Shrimp Sauteed in Herbed Butter 3.75

Tonight's Soup Kettle 1.25
Onion Soup with Apple Jack 1.50

FROM OUR CALIFORNIA VINEYARDS

Red American Wines	
Cabernet Sauvignon Excellent Finesse and Bouquet	9.00/5.00
Pinot Noir Full Bodied, Delightful Aroma	7.50/4.00
Gamay Beaujolais Softly Engaging, Fruity Wine	7.50/4.00
Burgundy North Coast, Full Bodied, Smooth	6.00/3.25
White American Wines	
Pinot Chardonnay Dry, Superlative Aroma	9.50/5.00
Chenin Blanc Fruity, Medium Dry	7.00/4.25
Chablis North Coast, Pale Gold, Delightfully Dry	6.00/3.25
American Rosé Wine	
Gamay Rosé Light and Dry	6.00/3.25
Red or White by the Glass	1.50
Champagnes	
Korbel Brut, California	12.50
Gold Seal, New York State	10.00/5.50

Desserts

English Sherry Trifle 1.50
Oxford Chocolate Cake 1.35
Apple Crumb Cake 1.35
CHARLIE BROWN'S CHEESECAKE 1.50
Strawberries with Whipped Cream 2.25
Selection of Ice Creams or Sherbet 1.25

Coffee—All Colombian Blend .60 Tea .60
Irish Coffee 2.25
Iced Tea or Coffee .60

Liquor: Full Liquor Service; Bar & Cocktail Lounge open from 11:30 a.m. to 1 a.m.
Recommended or listed: Cue, Where Magazine, Host, Theatre & Events, Mobil Travel Guide
Seating Capacity: 175
Private Rooms: Private Room for up to 35 Persons
Outside Catering: Inquire of Management
Cuisine: English–American–Continental Specialties

CHARLIE BROWN'S Get off the beaten track at the "miss the train" place. The center of action just off Grand Central Station for people in the know. Liveliest bar in town. Our open hearth dining room is acclaimed for prime ribs, steaks and chops.

Dinner Entrees

All Main Courses Served with Salad

The Daily Fare

TWIN TOURNEDOS OF BEEF
with Mushrooms
and Bordelaise Sauce 10.50

JUMBO SHRIMP
Stuffed with Crabmeat 10.25

ROAST DOUBLE BREAST OF CHICKEN
Apple and Raisin Dressing 8.25

VEAL CUTLET
Filled with Ham and Cheese
with it's Own Vegetable Platter 9.25

SOUTH AFRICAN LOBSTER TAILS 10.50

Main Courses

Beefsteak, Kidney & Mushroom Pie 6.75

Crisp Roast Duckling with Orange Sauce
& Nutted Brown Rice 8.50

ROAST PRIME RIBS OF BEEF,
YORKSHIRE PUDDING 11.25

Fish

Shrimp Scampi with Rice Pilaf 7.95
FRIED PRAWNS IN ALE BATTER
Tangy Orange Sauce 7.95
Fish & Chips 6.95
Shrimp & Scallop Curry, Eastern Relishes 8.25
Bay Scallops — Broiled or Sauteed 8.25
Poached Filet of Sole
with Grapes and White Wine Sauce 7.95
English Dover Sole, Grilled or Sauteed
with Toasted Almonds 9.75

Grills

PLANKED CHOPPED SIRLOIN OF BEEF
Served with a Bouquet of Vegetables 7.25

DOUBLE LAMB CHOPS,
Fresh English Mint Sauce 10.50

SAUTEED CALF'S LIVER
Smothered with Onions or Bacon 8.50

MIXED GRILL — Sirloin, Lamb Chop, Kidney
Sausage & Bacon 8.95

Steaks

U.S.D.A PRIME BEEF
All Steaks served with Our Special Steak Sauce

12 oz. Sirloin Steak 11.50
16 oz. Sirloin Steak 12.75
Filet Mignon 12.75

CHARLIE BROWN'S
SKILLET STEAKS
Served Three Ways
Smothered with Onions 12.50
Red Wine Sauce 12.50
Cracked Peppercorns 12.50

POTATOES

Oversized Baked 1.25
Charlie's Hashed Browns 1.25

SALADS AND VEGETABLES

Spinach Salad 1.75
Caesar Salad (for two) 5.25
Beefsteak Tomato and Onion 1.75
Fried Onion Rings 1.75
Broccoli Hollandaise 1.75
Fresh String Beans 1.75

We Cater to Your Home or Office
Please Ask Our Manager

Prices, Items and Hours Subject to Change

Ma Bell's

Address: 45th Street West of Broadway
Location: On Shubert Alley, between Broadway & 8th Avenue
Telephone: 869-0110
Credit Cards: All Major Credit Cards Accepted
Reservations: Recommended; Matinee Days Excluded
Hours: Monday through Saturday: 11:30 a.m. to 12 midnight; Sunday: 11:30 a.m. to 8 p.m.
Liquor: Full Liquor Service; Large Bar Facility
Recommended or listed in: Cue, Where Magazine, Host, Theatre & Events
Seating Capacity: 183
Private Rooms: No; special attention to groups
Outside Catering: Call 997-1406
Cuisine: American/Continental

MA BELL'S Good food and drinks right on famous Shubert Alley. Real telephones on the tables, humorous captioned wall photos, some very special private booths and hearty portions attract an exciting crowd daily. Our 80 foot bar has the friendliest bartenders in town.

"Listen, cutie, I thought I told you never to call that dancer again."

"Yes, doctor, it's stuck in his ear."

Wiring into Wine

A CARAFE OF WINE, White, Red, or Rose 2.95

WHITE
Johannisberger 6.75
Inglenook Chablis 5.75
Pinot Chardonnay Ninot 5.95

RED
Mouton Cadet 8.75
Beaujolais, Brouilly 7.75 / 4.00

ROSE
Lancer's Rose 7.50
Almaden Rose 6.25

CHAMPAGNE
Gold Seal 8.50 / 4.50
Asti Spumante 7.95
Piper Heidsieck N.V. 14.50

PERRIER WATER 1.00

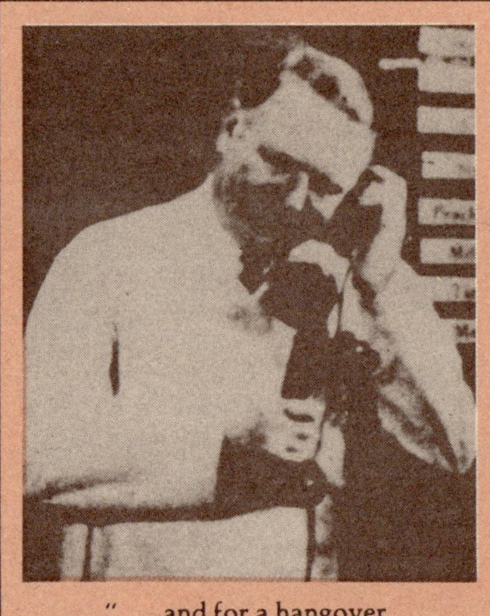

". . . and for a hangover, take the juice from two quarts of gin."

Ma Bells

Rousing First Courses

CLAMS, Shucked, Sherry-shallot-clam-meat Stuffing, placed back in the Shell and Baked 2.50

FRUITS, a Variety, Piquant, Divine 1.25

ICED GULF SHRIMP, Freshly Grated Horseradish, Red Sauce, and what a Red Sauce 3.25

RIPE MELON 1.25

A RICH ONION SOUP, Swiss Gruyere 1.50

TODAY'S SOUP, the Best of all Goings to Pot .95

salad information

INTERFACE WITH OPEN-FACED, the Roast Beef Sandwich, served with Mustard Pickles 4.95

MATTERS MINCED . . . Meats, Cheeses, and Greens, Julienne 5.50

COLD POACHED STRIPED BASS, Dill Mayonnaise 5.50

CHICKEN SALAD with Pineapple Sticks 5.50

SPINACH AND MUSHROOMS, Mushrooms and Spinach, a Salad 4.95

Prices, Items and Hours Subject to Change

WHAT BUTTERFIELD ATE

ROAST PRIME RIBS OF BEEF
Natural Juices
8.95

Served with Salad, Vegetable and Potato

"He says he never dines on an empty stomach."

Person to Person

Nice ways to keep your favorite company

SEAFOOD STEW CIOPPINO, Herbed Toast, the Super Bowl of Seafood Stew 8.95

LONG ISLAND DUCKLING, Orange Honey Basted 8.25

GRILLED BONELESS SIRLOIN STEAK, Herb Butter 9.50

CHICKEN FILETS, sauteed with Mushrooms 7.50

FILET OF SOLE — Filled with Baby Shrimp 7.25

FILET MIGNON, Red Wine Sauce 9.50

SAUTEED KING CRAB MEAT, Spiced Rice, your direct line to the Crustacean King 8.95

CLAMS, SHUCKED, Stuffed with Sherry-shallot-clam-meat, placed back in the Shell and Baked 5.50

the conference call

Shrimp Prepared Three Ways and served with Spiced Rice

(1) Deep Fried in Ale Batter, Honey Mustard Dipping Sauce 7.50
(2) Sauteed with White Wine and Garlic 7.50 (3) Crabmeat Herb Stuffing 7.95

Main Courses served with Salad, Vegetable and Potato

...and before you hang up

Desserts, Delish, Delightful

MA BELL'S TITANIC TRIFLE, Sponge Cake Soaked in Wine on a Bed of Strawberries, with Old Fashioned Custard and Cream . . . A Trifle not to Trifle with! 1.50

NEW YORK CHEESE CAKE 1.50

EXTRA HIGH APPLE PIE, Good Reason to go off the Deep end 1.25

VERY CHOCOLATE CHOCOLATE ICE CREAM 1.50

BANANA TOPPED FRUIT CAKE 1.50

STRAWBERRIES IN GRAND MARNIER 1.50

ALMOND VANILLA CAKE 1.25

RUM RAISIN and variety of Ice Creams served with bakeshop cookie .95

IRISH COFFEE . . . eliminates static 1.75

BRANDIED COCO COFFEE 1.75

Coffee .75 Tea .60 Milk .60 Sanka .60

"Holy Bazooka! There's live entertainment at Ma Bell's from 7:00 to 12 p.m.!"

Minimum $3.00 per person

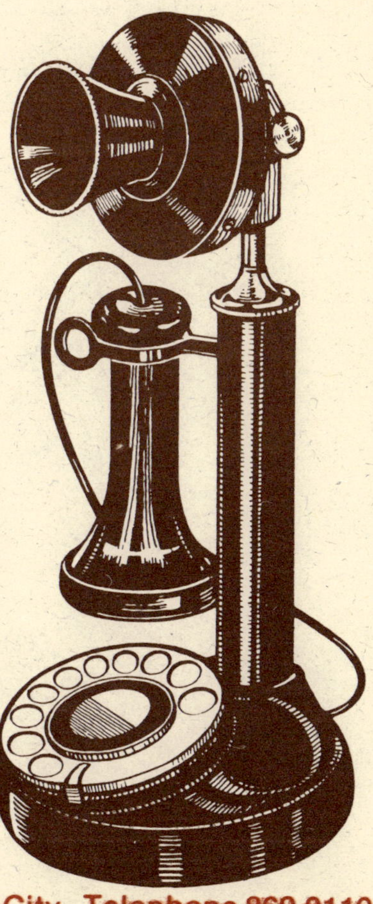

45th Street West of Broadway & Shubert Alley New York City Telephone 869-0110

Promenade Cafe

Address: Rockefeller Center
Location: West of Fifth Avenue, between 49th & 50th Stree
Telephone: 757-5731
Credit Cards: All Major Credit Cards Accepted
Reservations: Recommended, excluding December
Hours: 11:15 a.m. to 10:30 p.m. daily

Wines

IMPORTED

WHITE	BOTTLE	HALF BOTTLE
Macon Blanc Villages	9.00	4.75
Bertani Soave	7.50	4.00
Fogi-Battaglia Verdicchio	7.50	4.00
RED		
Beaujolais-Primeur	8.50	4.75
St. Julien	9.75	5.25
Bolla Valpolicella	6.50	
ROSE		
Lancers Rosé	6.75	3.75
Bolla Rosé	7.50	3.75

DOMESTIC

WHITE		
Inglenook Chenin Blanc	4.00	2.25
Navalle Chablis	4.25	
RED		
Ruby Cabernet	4.75	
Pinot Noir, L. Martini	6.75	3.50
ROSE		
Inglenook Gamay	4.25	2.50
SPARKLING		
Taittinger	19.50	9.00
André	9.50	5.00

WINES BY THE LITRE

Quarter Litre	1.75
Half Litre	2.75
Full Litre	4.75

BEERS

Domestic	Imported
1.35	1.60

DINNER

Appetizers

Fresh Orchard Fruits	1.25
Seafood Crêpe, with Mornay Sauce	1.95
Melon in Season or Today's Fruit with Prosciutto	2.25
Jumbo Gulf Shrimp Cocktail, Freshly Grated Horseradish, Red Sauce	3.95
Country Pâté with Lingonberries	1.75

Soups

Onion Soup Gratinée	1.75
Sherried Black Bean	1.50

Grills

CHOPPED SIRLOIN, Crisped Onions, Red Wine Sauce	6.95
ROAST PRIME RIBS OF BEEF, Promenade Popover	**9.95**
GRILLED BONELESS SIRLOIN, Herb Butter, A Full Pound	9.95
CALF'S LIVER, BACON or SAUTÉED ONIONS	8.50
SKILLET STEAK, Sauce of Crushed Peppercorns	9.50
FILET MIGNON, Sautéed Mushrooms	10.25
TWO DOUBLE RIB LAMB CHOPS, Minted Pear	9.25

Salads Three

Choice of Salads Three Included with All Main Courses
à la Carte 1.50

Beefsteak Tomato and Onions, Freshly Ground Pepper
Light Mixed Greens, Vegetables
Spinach, Bacon and Mushrooms

Homemade Dressings

Liquor: Full Liquor Service
Recommended or listed in: Cue, Where Magazine, Host, Theatre & Events
Seating Capacity: 310
Private Rooms: Private Room Available for Large Groups
Outside Catering: Call 997-1406
Cuisine: American/Continental

PROMENADE CAFE Right in the heart of Rockefeller Center facing the famed Prometheus Statue. Our two dining rooms view the ice skating pond in winter and the outdoor cafe in summer. Famous Saturday and Sunday brunch.

Promenade Cafe

Rockefeller Center - 757-5731

Main Courses

SAUTÉED MEDAILLONS OF BEEF, with Mushrooms, Spaetzle 7.50
DOUBLE BREAST OF CHICKEN, Sauce Diablo 6.75
BOURBON GLAZED FRESH HAM 7.50

TONIGHT'S FRESH FISH 8.25
KING CRAB CLAWS AND PRAWNS, in Ale Batter, Honey Mustard Dipping Sauce 9.50
SEAFOOD STEW CIOPPINO, Herbed Toast Crabmeat, Scrod, Clams, Mussels in Tomato Broth 9.50

LONG ISLAND DUCKLING-TWO WAYS
Orange Honey Basted or with Peaches and Cassis 8.95

QUICHE OF BACON
and Gruyère 6.25

Dinner Salads

Chef's Salad 6.25 Salad Niçoise 6.25
Poached Striped Bass, Dill Mayonnaise, Tomatoes 7.25

Desserts

Deep Dish Apple Pie 1.75 Almond Honey Pound Cake 1.25
Creamy Cheesecake 1.75 Hot Fudge Sundae 1.75 Seven Layer Cake 1.75
Chocolate Chocolate Ice Cream 1.75 Baked Alaska 1.75
Peach Shortcake 1.75 Orange Mousse 1.75
Vanilla, Chocolate, Strawberry, Rum Raisin Ice Creams & Lemon Sherbet 1.25

Beverages

Coffee .60 Tea .55 Sanka .60 Milk .60

Prices, Items and Hours Subject to Change

The Ground Floor Cafe

51 W 52 ST
NEW YORK

appetizers

Clams on the Half Shell or Baked 3.50
Cut Fresh Fruits 1.75
Jumbo Shrimp Cocktail 4.50
Mousse of Chicken Liver, Mimosa 1.95

soups

Chilled Vichyssoise 1.25
French Onion Soup 1.50
Beef and Bourbon 1.25

cold kitchen

Chef Salad Bowl 5.95
Shrimp Salad 6.95
Sliced Prosciutto and Melon 2.50
Tomatoes and Onions 1.75
Seasonal Mixed Green Salad 1.25

House Dressing (Creamy Tarragon), Russian, Oil and Vinegar (Little Garlic),
Blue Cheese .25 Extra

broiler

Chopped Sirloin with Mushroom Gravy 6.25
Sliced Steak, Delmonico 8.75
Broiled or Sauteed Calf's Liver with Crisp Bacon 7.50
A Trio of Lamb Chops 8.50

ground floor specialties

Theatre Toast Veal Scallopine,
Sauteed Bananas with Curry and Chutney 7.95
Deep Fried Shrimp in Coconut Batter 6.95
Quiche Lorraine 5.95
Today's Fishermen's Net 7.50

The Above Items Served with Ground Floor Potato and Vegetables or Seasonal Greens

desserts / beverages

Dessert Cart 1.50
Our Apple Grunt and Ice Cream 1.25

Espresso 1.00
Cappuccino 1.50
Sanka .50
A Pot of Coffee or Tea .75
Milk .50
Great Irish Coffee 1.95

IMPORTED WINES

White
Fazi Battaglia Verdicchio 7.50 / 4.00
Bertani Soave 7.50 / 4.00
Macon Blanc Villages 9.00 / 4.75

Red
Bolla Valpolicella 6.50
Beaujolais Brouilly V. 8.50 / 4.75
St. Julien 9.75 / 4.75

Rose
Lancers Rose 6.25 / 3.25
Bolla Rose 7.50 / 3.75

Sparkling
Korbel 9.00 / 4.50

DOMESTIC WINES

White
Inglenook Chenin Blanc 4.00 / 2.25
Navalle Chablis 4.25 / 2.25

Red
Pinot Noir, L. Martini 6.25 / 3.50
Ruby Cabernet 4.25

Rose
Inglenook Gamay 4.25 / 2.50

Sparkling
Taittinger 19.50 / 9.00

The Ground Floor Cafe

COMPLETE DINNERS

Raw Vegetables and Dipping Sauce
Baked Clams — French Onion Soup
Mousse of Chicken Liver Mimosa

	Dinner	A La Carte
Filet of Beef Stroganoff with Golden Noodles	8.75	7.25
Roulade of Sole, Sauce Mornay Fresh Sole Stuffed with Seafood and Mushrooms	8.95	7.50
Sauteed Chicken Cutlet Dipped in Egg and Parmesan Cheese, Tomato Sauce	8.50	7.25
Roast Prime Ribs of Beef, Natural Juice with Individual Popover	10.50	8.95
Crisp Duckling Poivrade, Pepper Sauce	8.95	7.50
Twin Tournedos of Beef, Sauce Bearnaise	10.95	9.50
Veal Schnitzel a la Holstein Breaded, Sauteed with Traditional Garnitures	9.50	8.00

Complete Dinners are Complemented with Vegetables,
Famous Ground Floor Potato or Baked, Seasonal Green Salad,
and a Selection from the Dessert Cart.
Coffee or Tea Service

served after 9:00 p.m.

Eggs Benedict 5.25

Omelettes Folded or Pancake Style 4.95
Plain, Western or Bacon and Cheese

Giant Burger Platter 4.95

Smoked Salmon on Pumpernickel 6.50
with Cream Cheese and Garnished with Shrimp

Wines by the Litre

(Red, White and Rose)
Full Litre 5.50
Half Litre 3.25

Wine Punch

Sangria Goblet 1.35
Sangria Wine Punch 4.75 / 2.75
Red Wine & Peaches 4.50 / 3.00

Beers on Tap

Heineken 1.50
Michelob 1.35

Bottled Beers

Labatt Ale 1.50
Lowenbrau (Light) 1.50
Lowenbrau (Dark) 1.50
Miller 1.35
Budweiser 1.35
Miller Lite 1.35

Prices, Items and Hours Subject to Change

The Ground Floor Cafe

Address: 51 West 52nd Street
Location: In CBS Bldg. between 5th & 6th Avenues
Telephone: 751-5152
Credit Cards: All Major Credit Cards Accepted
Reservations: Accepted at Dinner Only
Hours: Monday through Friday: Lunch 11:30 to 5 p.m. Dinner 5 p.m. to 11 p.m.
Liquor: Full Liquor Service; Large Bar Facility
Recommended or listed in: Cue, Where Magazine, Host, Theatre & Events, New York Magazine
Seating Capacity: 248
Private Rooms: No; special attention given to groups
Outside Catering: Inquire of Management
Cuisine: American/Continental

THE GROUND FLOOR CAFE When you want an American "Brasserie", come to the Ground Floor. Smart people have discovered this beautiful spot in the landmark CBS Building. A bustling bar and imaginative menu for lunch, dinner and after-theatre dining. Popular priced.

May We Suggest

Yard of Ale 3.00 ½ Yard of Ale 2.00
An Oversized Whiskey Sour 2.75
Or a Long Island Manhattan 2.75
The John Peel Giant Martini (A Gentleman's Drink) 2.75

Complete Dinner at

Includes
Appetizer
Main Course
John Peel Salad
Dessert
Pot of Coffee

Appetizers

Baked Clams with Sherry and Shallots
Chicken Livers, Chopped and Seasoned
Iced Gulf Shrimp, Fresh Horseradish, Cocktail Sauce, 2.50 Add.
Melon and Prosciutto 1.75 Add.
Tiny Little Neck Clams or Giant Blue Point Oysters 2.25 Add.
Tonight's Soup

Crocked Onion Soup

Herring in Cream and Onions
Seasonal Chilled Cut Fruits
Crusted Mushrooms, Tangy Sauce
Mussels in Tomato Vinaigrette
Service of Nova Scotia Salmon Garnished with Tiny Shrimp 2.95 Add.

Sweets

Tipsy Sherry Trifle
Strawberry Cloud
Fresh Orchard Fruits
Minted Chocolate Souffle (1.25 add.)
Orange Mousse

Warm Deep Dish Apple Pie (.75 add.)
Served with Vanilla Bean Ice Cream
Cream Filled Chocolate Pie
Fresh Strawberries and Whipped Cream 1.00 Add.
Chilled Melon
Old Fashioned Cheese Cake
Peach, Black Raspberry, and other Ice Creams Served with Bake Shop Cookie

Wine List

WHITE	FULL	HALF
Pinot Chardonnay	7.00	3.50
Chablis, Premier Cru	8.95	4.50
Liebfraumilch, Blue Nun	8.00	4.25
Grey Riesling, Inglenook	5.50	3.00
Chenin Blanc, Inglenook	6.25	
RED		
Ch. Montbousquet St. Emilion 70	9.25	4.75
Beaujolais Villages 70/72	7.00	
Ch. Des Tours, Brouilly 71/72	7.00	3.75
Pinot Noir, L. Martini	5.00	
Zinfandel, Inglenook	6.25	
ROSE		
Almaden Grenache	5.00	2.75
Mateus	7.50	4.00
SPARKLING		
Bollinger, N.V.	18.00	8.50
Chauvenet Red Cap, N.V.	16.00	7.75
Gold Seal, N.V.	9.00	
Asti Spumante, Cinzano	8.75	4.50

John Peel

Address: Old Country Road, Westbury, Long Island
Location: At the Island Inn
Telephone: (516) 741-3430
Credit Cards: All Major Cards Accepted
Reservations: Suggested; required Saturday Evenings and Sunday Brunch
Parking: Available
Hours: Monday through Friday: Lunch 12 noon-3 p.m. Dinner 6 p.m.-11:00 p.m.
Saturday: Dinner 5 p.m.-12:30 a.m.
Sunday: Brunch 12 noon-3 p.m.
Dinner: 5 p.m.-11 p.m.
Liquor: Full Liquor Service; Separate Bar
Recommended or listed in: Cue Magazine
Seating Capacity: Dining Room 155; Pub 65
Private Rooms: Four Private Rooms
Outside Catering: Inquire of Management
Cuisine: American–English–Continental

JOHN PEEL An English style pub convenient to Roosevelt Raceway and Nassau Coliseum, serving up hearty fare and continental specialties seven days a week. Join us for an evening of dining and dancing, and our taste tempting Sunday brunch is fantastic.

Salads

John Peel Dinner Salad
Chopped Beefsteak, Tomato and Onions .75
Caesar Salad .95
Marinated Mushrooms .75

CHILDREN'S PORTION
Half Price for Portion Served to Children Under 12.

Main Courses

Shrimp-Fried in Ale Batter, Orange Mustard Dipping Sauce 9.95

Baked Shrimp with Tomato & Basil 9.95

Shrimp Stuffed with Scallops, Herbs and Bread Crumbs 9.95

All Shrimp Dishes Served with Spiced Rice

BROILED FILET OF SOLE with Lemon Butter and Capers 7.95
TODAY'S CATCH 7.95
LOBSTER TAILS Stuffed with Tiny Shrimp 13.25
SAUTEED KING CRAB MEAT, Spiced Rice 10.25

Roast Prime Ribs of Beef
John Peel Popover 11.50

BEEF BROCHETTE, Bell Peppers, Sweet Onions 10.50
GRILLED BONELESS SIRLOIN STEAK, Herb Butter 12.50
FILET MIGNON 12.50
CHOPPED SIRLOIN STEAK, Crisped Onions, Vegetables 8.50
TWO DOUBLE RIB LAMB CHOPS 10.50
TOURNEDOS OF BEEF, Brandy, Red Wine and Mushrooms 12.75

STRIPED BASS, Baked Tomato 8.95
FILET OF BEEF, Crushed Pepper Sauce 10.95
VEAL CUTLET, Peppers, Mushrooms, and Onions 10.75

Filet Mignon For Two Carved Table Side
Selected Vegetables, Red Wine Sauce
John Peel Popover 12.75 Per Person

Skillet Steak
with Cracked Peppercorns, Red Wine and Smothered Onions 11.75

Festive Duckling 9.75
Orange Honey Basted

DOUBLE BREAST OF CAPON, Cordon Bleu 8.50

Madras Curries Mild Or Spicy
Chicken 7.75 **Shrimp** And Scallops 9.25
Served With Steamed Rice And Mango Chutney, Peach Chutney, Toasted Coconut, Onion and Peanuts

Prices, Items and Hours Subject to Change

Epilogue

Hearty Meals To Savor While Reviewing Tonight's Show

Fresh Ground Beef Burgers

5 oz. Beef Burger served on Onion Roll with French Fried Potatoes, Seasonal Garnish

JUMBO BEEF BURGER
Fresh Ground Beef Burger grilled to order 2.50
with sliced Bermuda Onion 2.60

CHEDDAR CHEESE BEEF BURGER
Fresh Ground Beef Burger smothered with
Wispride Cheddar Cheese 2.60
and Crisp Bacon Rasher 2.75

BLEU CHEESE BEEF BURGER
Fresh Ground Beef Burger smothered with
Bleu Cheese Pieces 2.70
and Crisp Bacon Rasher 2.90

LO-CAL BEEF BURGER
Char-broiled Fresh Ground Beef Burger with
Peach Half, Cottage Cheese, Ry Crisp 2.70

(All Beef Burgers may be Char-broiled on Request)

Grilled Sandwiches

THE REUBEN GRILL SPECIAL
Corned Beef, Swiss Cheese, Sauerkraut, Russian Dressing
on Grilled Pumpernickel 3.25

GRILLED AMERICAN CHEESE
with slices of Tomato 1.75
with crisp Bacon Rasher 1.95
(Grilled Swiss Cheese add 15¢)

THE RACHEL GRILL
Slices of Turkey, Swiss Cheese, Corned Beef
topped with Coleslaw on Grilled Rye Bread 3.25

Hearty Deli Sandwiches

BAKED HAM, SWISS CHEESE on rye bread
with cole slaw and russian dressing 2.95

SLICED TURKEY AND BACON SANDWICH
with lettuce, tomato and russian dressing 2.95

CHICKEN SALAD AND BACON SANDWICH
with lettuce, tomato, cole slaw and russian dressing 2.95

LIVERWURST DELUXE SANDWICH
sliced liverwurst, bacon, onion, russian dressing 2.95

Salad Items

JUMBO SHRIMP COCKTAIL, seafood dressing 2.75
SMOKED SALMON ON PUMPERNICKEL BREAD with
fresh cream cheese, seasonal garnish 3.95

Selected Side Dishes

FRENCH FRIED IDAHO POTATOES .... .75
FRENCH FRIED ONION RINGS .... .95
TOSSED GREENS AND TOMATO SALAD
Choice of our Salad Dressings .... .95

CAFE

Coffee Cafe Specialties

A SELECTION OF OUR FAMOUS DELICACIES

Exotic Coffees

Gathered from around the World

Freshly Ground and Brewed at your Table.

COLOMBIAN EXCELSO fine flavor and body rich and mellow
KENYA A.A. rich and winey taste, full flavor
GUATEMALA-ANTIGUA flavorful, with a mild body
MOCHA-JAVA combination of two coffees
with one sharp and the other smooth, deep flavor
COSTA RICAN rich, toasted flavor
MEXICAN ATURA full bodied after dinner blend
VIKING BLEND, sharp distinctive
POT OF COFFEE (approximately 4 cups)
priced according to market conditions

Fountain

JUMBO ICE CREAM SODA 1.35
BANANA FUDGE ROYALE 1.75
STRAWBERRY ICE CREAM SHORTCAKE 1.75
ICE CREAM SUNDAES 1.45
HOT FUDGE SUNDAE 1.45

Frozen Yogurt

Vanilla or Strawberry Yogurt

YOGURT SUNDAE with fresh fruit topping 1.75
PEACH MELBA, raspberry topping 1.75
BANANA BOAT ROYALE 1.95
LARGE CUP YOGURT 1.00
with strawberries 1.35
with bananas & raisins 1.45

Desserts

CHOCOLATE LAYER CAKE 1.15
COCONUT LAYER CAKE 1.15
COFFEE CAFE CHEESECAKE 1.35
APPLE CAKE . .95 a la mode . .40 extra
CARROT CAKE with Butter Icing 1.00
COFFEE CAFE PARFAIT 1.35
ASSORTED FRUIT COBBLERS 1.15

Beverages

Coca Cola, Root Beer or Apple Cider .50 Tab or 7-Up .50
Milk .50 Hot Chocolate .50 Sanka .40 Tea .35
COFFEE CAFE SPECIAL BLEND OF COFFEE

Coffee Cafe

Address: 1515 Broadway
Location: Between 44th & 45th Streets
Telephone: 997-1359
Credit Cards: None Accepted
Hours: Monday: 7:30 a.m. to 8 p.m., Tuesday through Friday: 7:30 a.m. to 11 p.m., Saturday: 9 a.m. to 11 p.m., Sunday: 12 noon to 6 p.m.
Liquor: Cocktails Available
Recommended or listed in: Where Magazine, Host, Playbill

Seating Capacity: Dining Room: 100; Counter: 36
Private Rooms: No; special attention to groups
Outside Catering: Call 997-1406
Cuisine: American; full fountain service; coffee specialties

Prices, Items and Hours Subject to Change

COFFEE CAFE Enjoy freshly ground coffee from far away places brewed right at your table. Coffee Cafe has simply delicious dinners, big burgers, and heavenly desserts perfect for those after-theatre hungries.

DINNER AT JAKE'S

6905 Main Street,
Stratford, Connecticut 06497

THE TALL DRINKS

PINA COLADA 1.95
BLOODY MARY 1.95
SANGRIA 1.95
PLANTER'S PUNCH The Jamaican Way 2.25
SINGAPORE SLING 2.25

Wine by the Carafe

Red, White & Rose
½ Carafe 2.50 Full Carafe 4.50

Appetizers

Fresh Seasonal Fruits 1.50
Melon 1.50 Chilled Tomato Juice .60
Pickled Mushrooms, Wine and Herbs 1.75
Homemade Pate, Sauce Cumberland 1.50
Baked Clams w. Sherry and Shallots 2.50
Tiny Bay Shrimp, Freshly Grated Horseradish, Red Sauce 2.50
Blue Point Oysters or Cherrystone Clams on the Half Shell, Red Sauce 2.75

Hearty New England Clam Chowder 1.25
Today's Hot Soup .95
Crocked Onion Soup w. Swiss Gruyere 1.75

Side Orders

Sauteed Mushrooms in Butter w. Lemon and Herbs 1.25
Crispy Fried Onion Rings 1.25

Salads Three

Choice of One:

Light Greens & Vegetables
JAKE'S Salad
Beefsteak Tomato & Onions w. Fresh Pepper

Your Selection of Dressings

Specialties

Pink Shrimp Deep Fried in Ale Batter, Honey Mustard Dipping Sauce 7.75

Shrimp and Scallop Curry, Eastern Relishes 7.95
Tonight's Fish 5.95
Boneless Idaho Trout Sauteed in Lemon Butter 6.95
Fresh Filet of Sole 7.25
Lobster Tails Stuffed with Tiny Shrimp 10.50

Roast Prime Ribs of Beef, JAKE'S Popover 8.95

Grilled Boneless Sirloin Steak, Herb Butter 9.50
Old Fashioned Pot Roast w. House Special Buttered Noodles 6.25
Giant Beef Brochette, Bell Peppers, Sweet Onions 8.75
Filet Mignon, Sauteed Mushrooms 9.95
Chopped Sirloin Steak, Vegetables 6.75
Stuffed Roast Duckling with Black Cherry Sauce 8.75
Thin-sliced Calf's Liver, Crispy Onions and Apple Ring 6.95
Wiener Schnitzel (Breaded Veal Cutlet) Sauteed in Butter, Anchovies and Capers 7.50
Double Breast of Capon, Filled w. Mozzarella, Mushrooms in Cream Sauce 7.25

Main Courses Served w. Jake's Bread Basket, Choice of Salads Three, Vegetable & Potato

Sweets

JAKE'S Cake 1.25 Apple Strudel Parfait 1.00
Ice Creams and Sherbets, Sugar Cookie .75
Frozen Chocolate Mousse 1.25
Rum Lime Cheesecake 1.25 Chocolate Chocolate Cake 1.10
Hot Homemade Deep Dish Apple Pie, Ice Cream 1.50
Old Fashioned Bread and Butter Pudding .95
Fruit Jello, Whipped Cream .75

Irish Coffee 1.95 Cafe Diablo 1.95
Coffee .75 Tea .50 Sanka .60 Milk .50

Children's Portions Half Price

Prices, Items and Hours Subject to Change

Jake's

Address: 6905 Main Street, Stratford, Connecticut
Location: At Stratford Motor Inn–Exit 32 Conn. Turnpike or Exit 53 Merritt Pkwy.
Telephone: (203) 377-0000
Credit Cards: All Major Credit Cards Accepted
Reservations: Accepted
Hours: Daily–Lunch: 11:00 to 2:30 p.m., Dinner: 5:30 to 10 p.m.
Liquor: Full Liquor Service; Separate Bar Facility
Recommended or listed in: Fairfield Guide
Entertainment: Tuesday through Saturday
Seating Capacity: 600
Private Rooms: Large Banquet & Conference Rooms
Outside Catering: Inquire of Management
Cuisine: American & Continental specialties

JAKE'S Restaurant and Bar is located at the Stratford Motor Inn in scenic Stratford, Connecticut. Jake's dining rooms command a superb view of the countryside.

INAGIKU

Address:	111 East 49th Street
Location:	49th Street at Lexington Avenue (in Waldorf-Astoria Hotel)
Telephone:	355-0440
Credit Cards:	AE; CB; V; DC; MC
Reservations:	Required
Hours:	12 Noon to 2:30 PM and 5:30 PM to 10:30 PM Monday thru Friday; 5:30 PM to 10:30 PM Saturday; 5:30 PM to 10:00 PM Sunday
Days Closed:	Major holidays
Liquor:	Full bar service
Recommended or Listed in:	Gourmet; New York Times; Cue
Maitre d's:	Andrew Kaburaki and Heidi Yokota
Seating Capacity:	140
Cuisine:	Japanese
Specialties of the House:	Tempura; Sukiyaki; Steak; Sushi
Dress:	Jackets required
Party Facilities:	2 Japanese-Style Rooms; capacity: 4-6/4-8 Large private room (with partition); capacity: 20

Private dining rooms are available for large groups. For private parties there is an additional room charge of $15 for Japanese style seating and $10 for Western style seating.

New and richly decorated, Inagiku offers the best in Japanese cuisine and ambience. Each of the three separate dining rooms is different in cuisine and atmosphere. There's both traditional "tatami" dining and the more American approach to food. Located in the Waldorf-Astoria, Inagiku is politely formal as befits its surroundings.

Inagiku

continued on next page

continued

LUNCHEON MENU

(Luncheon entrees are served with soup, rice, salad and green tea.)

APPETIZERS & SOUPS:
Sunomono (sliced cucumber with crabmeat) (2.50); Zensai (Chef's seasonal selection) (4.00); Negima Yaki (broiled beef with scallions) (4.00); Yakitori (broiled chicken on bamboo skewers) (2.75); Tempura (deep-fried shrimp and vegetables) (3.75); Sashimi (specially seasoned raw fish) (3.75); Shrimp Brochette (broiled shrimp on bamboo skewers) (3.75); Akadashi (soybean soup, spiced) (1.50); Soup of the Day (1.50).

DESSERTS:
Ice Cream (.85); Sherbet (.85); Fruits in Season (. . .); Yokan (1.25).
(Luncheon appetizers, soups and desserts are identical in all dining rooms.)

ENTREES:
Kamakura Room:
Assorted Tempura 7.75
(Selected seafoods deep-fried)
Lobster Tempura 9.00
(Lobster in crispy light batter)
Tempura and Kushiage 8.50
(Skewered beef, fish, vegetables, deep-fried)
Sirloin Steak Teriyaki 8.75
(Charcoal-broiled beef with teri sauce)
Sashimi 7.50
(Raw fish, seasoned in horseradish and soy sauce)
Chicken Teriyaki 7.50
(Broiled select cuts in teri sauce)
Fish of the Day 6.50
(With teri sauce or seasonings)
Shokazen 12.00
(Broiled chicken with teri sauce, seafood, vegetable and dessert)
Sushi .... 8.50 & 10.00
(Raw fish served on marinated rice)
Sukiyaki 8.75
(Sliced beef and vegetables cooked at table, served with Sukiyaki sauce)

Kinkaku Room:
Tempura Inagiku 7.75
(Shrimp and other shellfish, fish, vegetables, deep-fried)
Lobster Tempura 9.00
(Lobster deep-fried)
Tempura and Kishiage 8.50
(Tempura and skewered beef and vegetables, deep-fried)

Hida Room:
New York Steak Yaki Yaki 8.75
Filet Mignon Yaki Yaki 9.25
Chicken Yaki Yaki 7.50
Shrimp/Beef Brochettes Yaki Yaki 7.75

DINNER MENU

APPETIZERS & SOUPS:
Assorted Cold Tidbits (5.00); Assorted Hot Platter (5.00); Sushi (raw fish, rice marinated in vinegar) (4.50); Shrimp Tempura (deep-fried in light batter) (4.50); Sunomono Salad (crabmeat and sliced cucumber) (3.50); Steamed Clams (In broth with sake and scallion) (3.50); Yakitori (grilled chicken on bamboo skewers) (4.00); Sashimi (selection of fresh fish) (4.50); Yaki-Hama (broiled cherrystone clams) (3.50); Shrimp Brochette (broiled shrimp on bamboo skewers) (4.50); Sumashi (clear soup) (1.50); Akadashi (spiced soybean soup) (1.50).

DESSERTS:
Green Tea Ice Cream (1.00); Vanilla Ice Cream (1.00); Sherbet (1.00); Fruits in Season (. . .); Yokan (1.25).
(Dinner appetizers, soups and desserts are identical in all dining rooms.)

ENTREES: *(a la carte; served in Kamakura, Nikko, Hakone and Imperial Rooms):*
Assorted Tempura 9.75
(Seafoods deep-fried)
Lobster Tempura 12.75
(Lobster in crispy light batter)
Tempura and Kushiage 10.75
(Skewered beef, fish, vegetables deep-fried)
Beef Teriyaki 10.75
(Charcoal-broiled beef with teriyaki sauce)
Chicken Teriyaki 8.25
(Charcoal-broiled chicken, sauced with teri)
Sukiyaki 9.75
(Beef and vegetables for cooking Inagiku style)
Shabu Shabu 9.75
(Beef sliced, browned in broth, served with vegetables and two sauces)
Sashimi Moriawase 8.75
(Assorted Fresh Fish)

Sushi .... 8.50 & 10.00
(Raw fish, rice marinated in vinegar)
Fish of the Day 8.00
(Selection of seasonal varieties)
Broiled Fresh Mainland Lobster 23.75
(3 pound broiled lobster)
Assorted Broiled Seafood, Chicken and Beef 11.75
(Baked clams, skewered shrimp, scallops and Yakitori sauced with teri)
(A la carte entrees are also served as complete dinners including soup, salad, rice, pickles, sherbet or ice cream, and green tea for an additional charge of 2.00.)

Kamakura Room: *(complete dinners):*
Tempura and Kushiage Dinner: (14.75)
- Soup of the Day
- Sunomono Salad (crab meat & sliced cucumber)
- Sashimi (selection of fish fillets)
- Tempura and Kushiage (skewered beef, fish & vegetables in secret blend of deep fry with separate butters for tempura and meats)
- Rice and Green Tea
- Dessert (sherbet or ice cream)

Chef's Gourmet Kaiseki: (23.75)
- Tsuki-dashi
- Zensai (seasonal appetizer)
- Soup of the Day (clear soup)
- Sashimi (selection of fish filets)
- Yakimono (broiled fresh fish)
- Nimono (selected seafood & vegetables
- Sunomono
- Tempura (shrimp, fish & vegetables deep-fried in light batter)
- Beef Teriyaki (broiled tender beef with teri sauce)
- Akadashi, Oshinko pickles & rice, soy bean soup with mushrooms
- Dessert

Inagiku Dinner: (18.50)
- Soup of the Day (clear soup)
- Sunomono Salad (crab meat & sliced cucumber)
- Tempura (shrimp & vegetables, deep-fried in light batter)
- Nimono (selected seafood & vegetables)
- Beef Teriyaki (charcoal-broiled beef with teri sauce)
- Rice and Green Tea
- Dessert

Hida Room: *(complete dinners including soup, salad, rice, pickles, sherbet or ice cream and green tea)*

New York Steak 12.75
Filet Mignon 13.25
Chicken Teri Yaki (broiled) 9.25
Beef and Tempura 13.25
(Broiled beef and deep-fried seafoods)
Broiled Fresh Mainland Lobster 23.75
Assorted Broiled Seafood, Chicken and Beef . 11.75
(Baked clams, broiled skewered shrimp, scallops, and Yakitori in teri sauce)

Kinkaku Room: *(complete dinners including soup, salad, pickles, rice, green tea, sherbet)*

Tempura Inagiku 13.75
(Shrimp and other shellfish, fish, vegetables, deep-fried)
Lobster Tempura 13.75
(Lobster, deep-fried)
Tempura and Kushiage 13.75
(Tempura, skewered beef, vegetables, deep-fried)
Tempura and Steak 13.75
(Light seafoods deep-fried and broiled beef)

Note: Prices for luncheon and dinner are expected to be slightly higher as of April, 1978.

LONG ISLAND CULINARY ASSOCIATION *The name of this organization is slightly misleading since its members actually come from all over the New York area, not just Long Island. Founded 16 years ago, this is also one of the newest organizations for people in the culinary field. The prime concern of the Association is the promotion of the future of the culinary arts in this country . . . it is oriented toward helping young people interested in pursuing careers in the field. With an emphasis on youth, it has active junior chapters on the campuses of the culinary schools in the New York area, and members devote time to raising money for scholarships for both high school and college-level students. The organization is also concerned with helping women make their way in a field which up to now has been almost exclusively reserved for men. The President of the Long Island Culinary Association is Matthew Ryan, Executive Chef at the Yale Club.*

ITALIAN PAVILION

Address:	**24 West 55th Street**
Location:	**55th Street between Fifth Avenue and Avenue of the Americas**
Telephone:	**JU 6-5950**
Credit Cards:	**AE; CB; DC**
Reservations:	**Essential**
Hours:	**12 Noon to 3:00 PM and 5:30 PM to 10:30 PM**
Days Closed:	**Saturday; Sunday; major holidays**
Liquor:	**Full Bar Service**
Recommended or listed in:	**Gourmet, New York Times, Cue**
Seating Capacity:	**207**
Cuisine:	**North Italian**
Specialties of the House:	**Ossobuco alla Milanese; Costoletta di Vitello Milanese; Suprema di Pollo (prepared to order in a variety of ways)**
Dress:	**Jackets Required**
Party Facilities:	**Garden room (dinner only); capacity: 100**

The ambience at the Italian Pavilion exudes class and dignity. You have a choice of a formal dining room or glass-enclosed garden room (heated in winter) with a view of vines and greenery outside. Professional service, gracious captains and North Italian cuisine assure your dining contentment.

LUNCHEON

(a la carte)

APPETIZERS:
Fonduta (3.00); Coppa di Frutta (2.50); Melone (2.50); Prosciutto e Melone (5.75); Salame di Milano (3.50); Paté Maison (3.50); Gamberetti in Remolata (5.00); Salmone Affumicato (5.75); Trota Salsa Rafano (3.50); Oysters (4.00); Cherrystones (4.00); Little Necks (4.00).

SOUPS:
Tortellini in Brodo (2.00); Minestrone (2.00); Riso in Brodo (2.00); Vichyssoise (1.50); Zuppa Pavese (2.00); Zuppa di Verdura (2.00); Pastina in Brodo (2.00); Madrilene (1.50).

PASTA:

Gnocchi alla Piemontese (Wednesday Only)	5.00
Spaghetti al Pomodoro	4.50
Spaghetti alla Bolognese	4.50
Linguine alle Vongole	6.50
Gnocchi alla Romana or Verdi	5.00
Tortellini al Sugo	5.00
Lasagne Casalinga	5.00
Ravioli	5.00
Canelloni	5.00
Fettuccine alla Julian	7.50

ENTREES:

Crepes Pavilion	5.00
Crepes Nino (Friday only)	7.00
Ossobuco alla Milanese	7.00
Rollatini di Vitello alla Milanese	6.75
Suprema di Pollo alla Bolognese	6.75
Fegato alla Veneziana	7.00
Paillard di Manzo	9.00
Costolette D'Agnello	9.00
Filet Mignon	10.00
Paillard di Vitello	8.50
Pollo alla Griglia	6.50
Sirloin Steak	10.00
London Broil with Mushroom Sauce	8.00
Vitello Tonnato	7.00
Lobster Salad	10.00
Crab-Meat Salad	11.00
Shrimps Salad	9.50
Fruit Salad with Cottage Cheese	6.25
Frittata Campagnolo	5.00
Uova al Rognone	5.75
Uova alla Fiorentina	5.00
Omelette Pavilion	5.00
Omelette ai Fegatini di Pollo	5.00
Uova Benedettina	6.50

Filetti di Sogliola alle Mandorle 7.50
Gamberetti alla Provinciale 7.50
Trotelle al Burro .... (...)
Scampi alla Veneziana 8.00
Zuppa di Pesce alla Marinara (Friday only) .... (...)
Scaloppine di Vitello Cacciatora 7.00
Saltimbocca alla Romana 7.00
Cervella Dorata alla Milanese 7.00
Fegato di Vitello all'Inglese 7.00
Rognone Trifolato 7.00
Pollo alla Serpentaglia 8.00
Costoletta di Vitello alla Milanese 9.00

VEGETABLES:
Broccoli (2.50); Zucchini (2.25); Spinaci (2.25); Fagliolini (2.25); Sedani al Sugo (2.25); Pisellini (2.25); Insalate (2.00); Melanzane alla Parmigiana (3.75).

DESSERTS & CHEESES:
Cheese: Gorgonzola, Taleggio, Bel-Paese, Camembert, Provolone, Brie (2.50); Gelati Assortiti (1.75); Zuppa Inglese (2.75); Pasticceria (1.75); Spumoni (1.50); Crema al Caramello (1.75); Pere al Vino Rosso (...); Macedonia di Frutta (2.50); Fresh Strawberries (2.50).

DINNER MENU

(a la carte)

APPETIZERS & SOUPS:
Scampi alla Griglia (6.50); Salmone Affumicato (6.50); Trota Salsa Rafano (5.00); Gamberetti in Remolata (6.00); Cherrystones (4.25); Oysters (4.25); Salami di Milano (4.00); Antipasto Misto (5.25); Prosciutto e Melone (6.00); Coppa di Frutta (3.00); Little Necks (4.25); Baked Clams - Arreganata or Cassino (5.00); Tortellini in Brodo (2.00); Minestrone alla Milanese (2.00); Vichyssoise (1.75); Madrilene (1.75).

PASTA:
Lasagne al Forno 5.50
Canelloni Bolognese 5.50
Ravioli al Sugo 5.50
Spaghetti al Pomodoro 5.50
Tortellini Bolognese 5.50
Linguine alle Vongole 7.50
Spaghetti alla Bolognese 5.50
Fettuccine Pavilion 8.00
Risotto alla Milanese 6.00
Risotto alla Piemontese 7.00

ENTREES:
Medaglione di Bue alla Rossini 10.50
Costoletta di Vitello alla Magenta 10.00
Ossobuco alla Milanese 8.75
Veal Cutlet Parmigiana 9.00
Suprema di Pollo alla San Remo 8.00
Fegato di Vitello alla Veneziana 9.00
Rack of Lamb Bouquetiere (For Two) 26.00
Sirloin Steak 10.50
Fiorentina di Manzo 10.50
Costolette D'Agnello 10.00
Filet Mignon 10.50
Paillard di Vitello 9.50
Pollo alla Griglia 7.00
Filetti di Sogliola Argo Dolce 8.00
Sogliola Inglese alla Mugnaia 8.00
Trotelle al Burro e Salvia 8.00
Scampi Pavilion 8.75
Rane Provinciale 8.00
Sea Bass al Brodetto 9.00
Aragosta Fra Diavolo .... (...)
Saltimbocca alla Romana 8.00
Scaloppine al Marsala 8.00
Scaloppine ai Funghi 8.75
Piccata alla Milanese 8.00
Pollo alla Cacciatora 7.50
Pollo alla Romana 7.50
Pollo alla Piemontese 8.00
Pollo all'Aglio e Olio 7.50
Costoletta di Vitello Milanese 10.00

VEGETABLES:
Broccoli (2.50); Zucchini al Pomodoro (2.25); Spinaci (2.25); Fagiolini (2.25); Carote (2.25); Piselli (2.25); Melanzane alla Parmigiana (3.75); Insalate (2.00).

DESSERTS & CHEESES:
Cheese: Gorgonzola, Swiss, Brie, Taleggio, Provolone, Bel-Paese, Camembert (2.50); Gelati Assortiti (1.75); Spumoni (1.50); Fresh Strawberries (2.50); Zuppa Inglese (2.75); Zabaglione (3.00); Pasticceria (1.75); Crema al Caramello (1.75); Macedonia di Frutta (3.00).

Want more information about New York restaurants? Send your name and address to: Manhattan Menus, P.O. Box 5217, FDR Station, New York, N.Y. 10022.

JEANNINE

Address: 323 West Broadway
Location: West Broadway between Grand and Canal Streets
Telephone: 966-6155
Credit Cards: AE; MC; V; DC
Reservations: Recommended
Hours: Lunch from 12:00 Noon to 3:30 PM, Monday thru Friday; Café from 3:30 PM to 2:00 AM daily; Dinner from 6:00 PM to 12:00 Midnight daily; Saturday and Sunday Brunch from 12:00 Noon to 3:30 PM
Days Closed: None
Liquor: Full bar service
Recommended or Listed in: New York Magazine; Cue
Maitre d': Jeannine
Seating Capacity: Dining Room, 70; Café, 30
Cuisine: French and American
Specialties of the House: St. Jacques en Croûte, Beurre Rouge; Côte de Veau Normande
Dress: Casual

If you're looking for a perfect cap to an expedition of the downtown art galleries, or for dinner before or after that off-off-Broadway show, try Jeannine's, just off Canal Street. The owners, Artie and Jeannine, have taken the best of an old New York building and by incorporating their own personalities—an oak and slate bar designed and executed by Artie and some classically good dishes from Jeannine's native France—have turned Jeannine's into a specially favored local spot. The prices are reasonable; the selection of food will match any palate mood. The brunch menu, served on Saturday and Sunday from 12:00 Noon to 3:30 PM, is definitely worth investigating.

DINNER MENU

(a la carte)

APPETIZERS & SOUPS:
Quiche Lorraine (1.75); Duck Pâté (2.95); Salmon Mousse (3.10); Shrimp in Wine Cream Sauce in a Pastry Shell (3.45); Escargots Smitane or Bourguignonne (3.75); Soupe du Jour (1.50); Onion Soupe (2.00); Cold Cucumber Soupe (1.50).

ENTREES:
St. Jacques Baked with Spinach and Mushrooms in a Pastry Shell 6.95
Veal Scallopini in Brandy and Cream Sauce .. 7.25
Beef Wellington with Truffle Sauce 10.50
Duck with Fresh Apples and Green Peppercorns 7.75
Boneless Breast of Chicken in Garlic Butter and Tomato 6.75
Calf's Liver 6.95
Striped Bass, Butter Lemon Sauce 5.75
Sirloin Steak with French Fries 9.95
Filet Mignon with French Fries, Béarnaise Sauce 10.50
Shell Steak with French Fries 6.95
Ground Sirloin 4.00

SALADS:
Tossed Salad (.75); Endives, Spinach and Romaine (1.25); Your Salad (You begin with a large bowl of spinach and mix our selected ingredients) (5.25).

DESSERTS:
Coffee Mousse (2.25); Amaretto Mousse (2.25); Cheese Cake (1.50); Berries in Wine (2.25).

LUNCH & MIDNIGHT SUPPER MENU

(a la carte)

Omelettes (Ham, Swiss, Mushrooms, Spinach, Onion, Bacon, Sour Cream) 2.65
Mushrooms and Chicken Crêpe 3.45
Hamburger with French Fries 2.65
Sliced Steak with Mushrooms 4.25

(Luncheon and Dinner specials are added to the menus daily; Luncheon specials range from 3.75 to 4.75; Dinner specials are similar in price to other dinner entrees.)

(A Brunch menu is offered on Saturday and Sunday.)

JEFFRIES

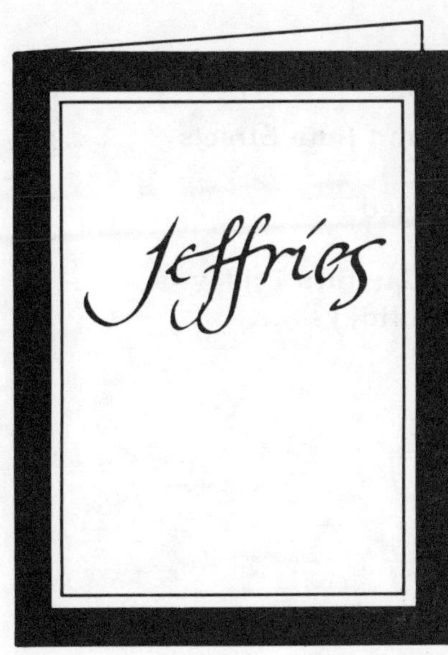

Address: 362 2/3 West 23rd Street
Location: 23rd Street between Eighth and Ninth Avenues
Telephone: 929-1778
Credit Cards: V; MC
Reservations: Required
Hours: 7:00 PM to 12:00 Midnight, Monday thru Thursday; 7:00 PM to 1:00 AM, Friday and Saturday; opened occasionally for special Sunday brunches (call for information)
Liquor: Bring your own wine
Recommended or Listed in: New York Magazine; Christopher Street
Maitre d': Jeffrey
Seating Capacity: 30
Cuisine: International
Specialties of the House: Traditional and Regional British Dishes
Dress: Informal
Entertainment: Gilbert & Sullivan and selections from other operettas with piano accompaniment - occasionally
Party Facilities: Special dinners and parties can be arranged upon request

Restaurants frequently take on the personalities of their owners and this is probably nowhere more clearly the case than at Jeffries. Jeffrey is not only the owner but maitre d', entertainer and designer of his own restaurant. He has combined indirect lighting with an exposed beam ceiling, wood and brick walls, and rich copper tableware, to produce a warm and intimate ambience. The candles on each table are a pleasingly romantic addition. When the mood is mellow, Jeffrey takes over the small stage and sings excerpts from Gilbert and Sullivan. Dining out at Jeffries makes any evening a special occasion.

Jeffries

DINNER MENU

Your meal at Jeffries will consist of five courses at a fixed price of $15 per person (excluding tax and gratuity). The menu changes daily, offering a choice of soup, appetizer, entree and dessert. Please allow two to three hours to relax and dine, and please bring wine if you wish to drink it with your meal. Parties and special dinners may be arranged in advance. Jeffries will be pleased to prepare your choice of menu for such occasions.

JOE'S CHINATOWN

Address: 196 Broadway
Location: Broadway between Fulton and John Streets
Telephone: 227-2345
Credit Cards: All major credit cards accepted
Reservations: Required
Hours: 11:00 AM to 8:00 PM, Monday thru Friday
Days Closed: Saturday; Sunday; major holidays
Liquor: Full bar service
Recommended or Listed in: Cue
Maitre d': Mr. Harrison
Reservations Manager: Joe
Seating Capacity: 275
Cuisine: Szechuan and Mandarin
Specialties of the House: Baby Scallops with Garlic Sauce; Chicken with Brown Sauce; Joe's Chinatown Steak; Baby Shrimp Szechuan Style; Szechuan Beef
Dress: Casual
Party Facilities: Private rooms on request; capacity: 40

Joe's Chinatown is the next best thing to Chinatown in the heart of the financial district. The lunch and dinner menu includes more than 130 Mandarin and Szechuan dishes, expertly prepared and skillfully served. The only North American influence on an otherwise authentic Chinese menu is a ''Dietwatchers' Special'' which includes such dishes as Beef with Broccoli and Shrimp with Chinese Vegetables. The decor combines fragile Chinese screens and bamboo-style wallpaper with a luminous tile ceiling to achieve a pleasant dining ambience.

Joe's Chinatown

MENU

(a la carte)

(The menu is extensive; the following is a representative selection.)

APPETIZERS & SOUPS:

Egg Rolls (2 for 1.65); Shrimp Toast (2 for 2.50); Chicken Balls (4 for 2.50); Fantail Shrimps (4 for 2.75); Fried Wontons (10 for 2.75); Chinese Roast Pork (3.75); Barbecued Spare Ribs (3.75); Po Po Hot Plate (3.50); Egg Drop Soup (.75); Chicken Rice or Noodle Soup (.75); Wonton Soup (.85); Hot and

Sour Soup (1.00); Beancurd with Meat & Vegetable Soup (for two - 2.50); Joe's China Town Special (for two - 2.75).

ENTREES:

Beef with Broccoli 4.95
Shrimp with Black Bean Sauce 5.75
Crabmeat with Straw Mushrooms 5.95
Beef with Oyster Sauce 5.50
Beef with Chinese Mushrooms and Bamboo Shoots 5.50
Joe's Chinatown Steak .... (...)
Chicken with Brown Sauce 5.50
Pork with Scallions 5.25
Pork Szechuan Style......................... 5.25
Hot Spicy Beef 5.50
Hot and Spicy Chicken with Peanuts 5.50
Ta Chien Chicken Special Style 5.50

DESSERTS:

Cookies (Almond or Fortune) (.50); Ice Cream (.75); Pineapple (.95); Kumquats (.95); Lichee Nuts (1.75).

APFELSTRUDEL: *This well-known confection is made with large sheets of* Blatterteig *(puff pastry) dough filled with apples, raisins, cinnamon, sugar and ground almonds. The sheets are rolled about three times and then baked; strudel is served in slices.*

BAUMKUCHEN: *This cake, literally "tree cake," can only be made in a pastry shop, not at home, since it requires a special apparatus. The batter, made with eggs, heavy cream and almond flavoring, is gradually poured on to a long, rotating spindle. As the spindle turns, the batter cooks over gas jets. The resulting cake is long and round, like the trunk of a tree; its concentric layers look very much like the rings you see in the cross-section of a tree. The Baumkuchen is cut into variously sized pieces, usually two or three pounds each, and iced with a white sugar icing when it has been baked—a process that may take up to three hours.*

KAMEHACHI

Address:	**14 East 47th Street**
Location:	**47th Street between Fifth Avenue and Madison Avenue**
Telephone:	**765-4737 or 682-2120**
Credit Cards:	**AE; DC; CB; MC; V**
Reservations:	**Recommended**
Hours:	**Lunch from 12 Noon to 2:30 PM and dinner from 5:30 PM to 9:30 PM Monday thru Saturday; Supper from 10:00 PM to 3:00 AM Monday thru Friday**
Days Closed:	**Sundays; New Year's Day and Labor Day**
Liquor:	**Full bar service**
Recommended or Listed in:	**New York Times; Cue; Esquire; New York Post**
Maitre d':	**Sakai**
Seating Capacity:	**170**
Cuisine:	**Japanese**
Specialties of the House:	**Sushi; Tempura; Makunuchi; Nabemono**
Dress:	**Casual**
Party Facilities:	**Private room; capacity: 60**

Especially popular with Madison Avenue advertising executives, Kamehachi offers a comfortable and typically Japanese atmosphere. The decor in the two dining rooms and the sushi bar features red carpeting, blue ceilings, contemporary lighting and over stuffed chairs and banquettes. The walls are hung with a variety of decorations from Japan. The food is graciously served by women in traditional kimonos. Other Kamehachi restaurants are located in Tokyo and Chicago.

LUNCHEON MENU

(A partial listing from the a la carte menu.)

Sushi 4.50
Inari-Zushi 2.40
Tekka-Don 4.50
Chirashi 2.25
Sashimi 4.50
Futomaki 2.50

Tekka-Maki 4.50
Tempura 4.50
Kakiage 4.00
Vegetable-Tempura 3.00
Tendon 3.25

DINNER MENU

(a partial listing)

SOUPS:

Misoshiru (Bean Soup) (1.00); Osumashi (Clear Soup) (1.00); Clam Soup (1.75); Shrimp Soup (1.75); Squid Soup (1.75).

SUSHI:

Sushi .... (A) 6.00
(Vinegared rice balls, topped with filet of fresh fish) (B) 8.00

Sashimi 4.50
(Filet of fresh fish served with bowl of rice)

Chirashi .... (A) 3.50
(Vinegared rice served in a lacquer bowl, topped with filet of various fresh fish) (B) 5.50

Tekka-Maki 4.50
(Laver rolled with tuna fish)

Tekka-Donn 4.50
(Bowl of vinegared rice topped with filet of fresh tuna)

Futomaki 2.50
(Laver rolled with various fish)

Inari-Zushi 2.50
(Rice-filled bean curd pockets – 6 pieces)

ENTREES:

Beef-Kushiyaki 5.75
(Beef shish-kebab, Japanese style)

Beef-Teriyaki 6.75
(Broiled steak with our special teriyaki sauce)
Filet Mignon 8.75
Chicken-Furai 4.75
(Deep fried tender chicken)
Chicken-Teriyaki 5.00
(Broiled chicken with our special teriyaki sauce)
Yakitori 5.00
(Chicken shish-kebab, Japanese style)
Kushikatsu 4.75
(Deep fried breaded pork tenderloin & onion on skewer)
Tonkatsu 5.75
(Deep fried tenderloin pork)
Unaju 9.95
Tempura .... (A) 5.25
(Fried shrimp, vegetable) (B) 6.25
Yakizakana 4.00
(Broiled fish)
Ebi Teriyaki 5.25
(Broiled shrimp with our special teriyaki sauce)
Kaibashira Butter Yaki 4.75
(Scallops & vegetable with butter)
Ebi-Furai 4.75
(Deep fried shrimp)
Kaki-Furai 5.75
(Deep fried oyster)

NABEMONO:

Sukiyaki 7.95
(Tender beef sliced, green vegetables)
Yose-Nabe 7.95
(Seafood with green vegetable, etc.)
Mizutaki 7.95
(Tender chicken with vegetable, etc.)
Chiri-Nabe 7.95
(Seasoned fish with vegetable, etc.)
Kaki-Dotenabe 7.95
(Oyster with vegetable, etc.)
Hama-Nabe 7.95
(Clams with vegetable, etc.)
Shabu-Shabu 7.95
(Tender beef with green vegetable, etc.)
Makunouchi 8.50

DESSERTS:

Fresh Fruit in Season (1.25); Yokan (.75); Ice Cream (.75); Pudding (1.00); Cream Anmitsu (1.50).

COMPLETE DINNERS:

Sashimi Dinner 7.95
Tempura Dinner 7.95
Sukiyaki Dinner 7.95
Tonkatsu Dinner 7.95
Kamehachi Dinner (8 dishes) 10.00
Kamehachi Dinner (10 dishes) 15.00
Kamehachi Dinner (12 dishes) 20.00

(Complete dinners include appetizer, soup, small dishes, rice, salad, tea and dessert.)

MOSELLE (MOSEL): *The greatest of the German white wines, produced from vineyards bordering the Mosel. Moselles are almost water white with a gleam of green in color and usually have far more bouquet than body. Shipped in distinctive green fluted bottles, these wines possess an apple-like freshness and a flowery, spice-like flavor.*

MOULIN-A-VENT: *The best red wine of the Beaujolais area north of Lyon. Deep colored and sturdy, Moulin-à-Vent improves in the bottle for 8 to 10 years (far longer than the 2 to 3 year life of a typical Beaujolais).*

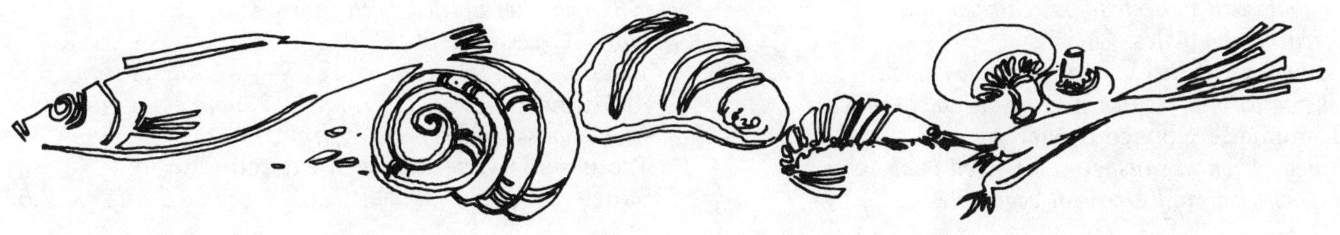

KENERET

Address: 296 Bleecker Street
Location: Bleecker Street and Seventh Avenue South
Telephone: OR 5-9587; 243-0866
Credit Cards: AE; DC; MC; V
Reservations: Required
Hours: 5:00 PM to 1:00 AM, Tuesday thru Sunday
Days Closed: Monday
Liquor: Full bar service
Recommended or Listed in: New York Times; Village Voice
Seating Capacity: 95
Cuisine: International (Middle Eastern)
Specialties of the House Algerian Couscous; Shish Kebab; Shrim Saganaki; Mussaka; Pitinjian-Yarik; Tajeen Mussels (Syrian Style); Escargot; Falkusha
Dress: Informal
Party Facilities: Private room; capacity: 35

A mouth-watering selection of Syrian and Armenian dishes is offered to diners at Keneret. Located in Greenwich Village, Keneret is an ideal place to visit before or after the off-Broadway theatre. The menu is moderately priced and the wine list includes a number of Greek table wines. The decor, as well as the cuisine, captures the atmosphere and flavor of the Middle East. Whether you're looking for an introduction to this flavorful cuisine or are already one of the committed, enjoy a dinner at Keneret.

MENU

(a la carte)

APPETIZERS & SOUPS:
Escargot Bourguignon (½ doz: 4.50) (1 doz: 7.50); Mussels (2.50); Oriental Vegetable Soup (1.45); Chomos (1.95); Tahina (1.95); Dulma (1.95); Phetta Cheese (3.50).

SPECIALTIES:
Tahina 2.95
(Spicy dip of crushed sesame seeds)
Chomos 2.95
(Ground chick peas with Tahina)
Baba Ganoush 3.45
(Broiled eggplant, spices and Tahina)
Chomos and Phalaphel Combination 3.95
Phalaphel Special: Tahina, Chomos, Salad & Phalaphel 5.50
Steamed Mussels, Syrian Style 6.50

ENTREES:
Couscous Algerian 6.95
(Halbata sauce, beef, lamb, chicken and Oriental vegetables)
Couscous Montmartre 8.95
(Skewered lamb, chicken with vegetable sauce)
Homemade Couscous Mergas 9.95
(Spicy Oriental sausages, skewered lamb, beef, chicken and Oriental vegetables)
Dajash Mash-We 6.75
(Chicken legs (3) roasted, marinated in Greek wine sauce)
Chicken Tamates 6.75
(Chicken cooked in sherry, tomatoes, mushrooms and spices)
Mussaka 6.75
(Ground beef with Greek cheese, pistachios, raisins and layers of fine dough)
Mah-shi 6.75
(Zucchini stuffed with chopped spiced lamb and mint)
Pitinjian-Yarik 7.50
(Broiled eggplant stuffed with prime sirloin, almonds, mushrooms, raisins, cinnamon, tomatoes and baked in sherry)
Karaimi 8.95
(Fish filet baked a la Parmigienne)
Samakiia 8.95
(Snapper filet broiled with raw sesame seed sauce, Greek cheese)
Tajeen 8.95
(Baked fish — jumbo shrimp, red snapper, white striped bass, mussels or escargot)
Trout—a la Oriental with Melted Cheese Sauce 7.50

Veal Siniia 7.75
(Veal filet mignon with Sultan sauce, artichokes and pimentoes)
Shish Kebab 9.45
(Marinated lamb broiled with onions, peppers, tomatoes, rice)
Felkusha 9.45
(Marinated lamb, beef and shrimp skewered with onions and peppers)
Veal Shish Kebab 8.45
Ajel Karshoof 9.45
(Vealfilet mignon with Sultan sauce, artichokes and pimentoes)

Broiled Scampi in Garlic Salamtek and Butter Sauce 10.95
Shrimp Saganaki broiled with Saganaki Cheese 11.95

(A variety of salads is offered, ranging in price from 2.50 to 6.50.)

DESSERTS:
Homemade Baklava (1.25); Strawberries a la Creme (1.45); Homemade Cheese Cake (1.45); Grand Marnier (Chocolate Mousse) (1.50).

BAUMSTAMM: *This means "log" and it is a sponge cake roll with either pineapple or strawberry butter cream filling. It is iced with chocolate and sliced to serve.*

BERLINER PFANNKUCHEN: *This "pancake from Berlin" is really a round jelly doughnut. It is filled with apricot jam and covered with powdered sugar.*

BIENENSTICH: *This Bavarian cake is made from a yeast dough; it is cut in half and filled with vanilla custard. Bienenstich means "sting of the bee" and refers to the topping which is made from honey, ground almonds and butter. The topping is baked with the dough.*

DOBOSCH: *This Hungarian cake's name means "drum" and it does, in fact, look like a drum. Seven layers of sponge cake are filled with chocolate butter cream. The topping is made from caramelized sugar and is difficult to make since the sugar can burn so easily. The Dobosch must be cut while it is still warm or else it will crumble.*

THE KING'S WHARF

Address:	**160 Central Park South**
Telephone:	**247-0300, ext. 6240**
Credit Cards:	**All major credit cards accepted**
Reservations:	**Recommended**
Hours:	**Breakfast, lunch and dinner from 7:00 AM to 11:30 PM, daily; Sunday brunch from 10:30 AM to 3:00 PM**
Days Closed:	**None**
Liquor:	**Full bar service; wines to complement any meal**
Maitre d':	**Mr. Gregory**
Seating Capacity:	**240**
Cuisine:	**Continental and American**
Specialties of the House:	**Aged Prime Beef; Fresh Seafood; French Pastry**
Dress:	**Jacket Required**
Party Facilities:	**Upon request; capacity: 95**

As the name implies, the King's Wharf is nautical in decor; the added attraction of its dramatic Central Park view makes dining in this restaurant a feast for the eyes as well as the culinary senses. Breakfast is served at the King's Wharf, in addition to luncheon and dinner, and the restaurant hosts "New York's best brunch buffet" on Sundays. This is a good spot for pre-theatre dinner or a nightcap after the show.

King's Wharf

LUNCHEON MENU

(a la carte)

APPETIZERS & SOUPS:
Salty Tomato Juice (1.55); Chilled Seasonal Melon (2.00); Clam Chowder (2.05); Fresh Oysters on the Half Shell (3.55); Cherrystone Clams on Ice (3.20); Nova Scotia Smoked Salmon (4.55); Escargots Chablaisienne (3.90); Shrimp Cocktail (4.55); Coquille Saint Jacques (3.95); Crab-Stuffed Shrimp (4.95); Crepe à la Reine (3.00); Soup of the Day (2.05).

ENTREES:
Roasted Rib of Beef, au Jus 9.65
London Broil 7.50
English-Style Fish and Chips 5.90
Fried Long Island Bay Scallops 7.50
Rack of Baby Lamb (for Two) 15.50
New York Sirloin Steak Sandwich 7.50
Eggs Benedict 6.50
Crabmeat Benedict 7.30
Long Island Bay Scallops 7.50
(The above entrees are served with french fried potatoes and include the Wharf's Salad Bar.)
Business Luncheon 5.50
Salad Bar Only 4.25
Seasonal Fruit Sampler 5.65
Chef's Garden Salad 5.05
Steak Tartare, Danish-Style 5.95
Shrimp-Stuffed Avocado 7.60
Tuna Salad Cold Plate 4.55
Delicate Thin Pancakes with Strawberry Sauce and Crisp Bacon Strips 5.35
Marriott Club Sandwich 4.25
Broiled Hamburger Platter 4.05
The Grilled Reuben 5.35
Broiled Hamburger Platter with Cheese 4.25
Chicken Salad Sandwich 3.75

DESSERTS:
Strawberry Tart Prosperi (1.60); Praline Chocolate Cheesecake (1.45); Chocolate Mousse (1.45); Orange à la Rose (2.05); Peach Melba (1.75); English Trifle (1.75); Vanilla, Strawberry, Chocolate or Coffee Ice Cream (1.35); Spiced Carrot Cake (1.60); Chocolate Fudge Cake (1.60); Double Crust Apple Pie (1.45); Double Crust Apple Pie à la Mode (1.90).

DINNER MENU

(a la carte)

APPETIZERS & SOUPS:
Clam Chowder (2.25); Fresh Oysters on the Half Shell (3.90); Nova Scotia Smoked Salmon (5.00); Cherrystone Clams on Ice (3.50); Escargots Chablaisienne (4.25); Crab-Stuffed Shrimp (4.95); Shrimp Cocktail (5.00); Coquille Saint Jacques (4.35); Eggs à la Russe (3.00).

ENTREES:
Roasted Rib of Beef, au Jus, with Yorkshire Pudding and Horseradish Cream 13.50
Filet Mignon, Sauce Bearnaise 14.25
Dover Sole Meuniere 11.00
Chicken Ballotine 11.00
Broiled Sirloin Steak 14.50
Veal Oscar 11.25
Steak au Poivre 15.00
Rock Cornish Hen Shenandoah 9.75
(Stuffed with savory brown rice, then finished with port-flavored glaze)
Red Snapper, Sauce Mousseline 10.25
Crab-Stuffed Shrimp 9.75
Double Rib Lamb Chops 14.50
Veal Scaloppine Marsala 10.25

(All entrees include the Wharf's Salad Bar.)

(Desserts are the same as those on the Luncheon Menu.)

DRYNESS: *Very simply, this is the absence of the taste of sweetness. Some popular dry wines are Chablis, Muscadet, Verdicchio and Graves.*

FINESSE: *This word refers to the breeding or style of a wine. It is a very subjective term which attempts to combine the qualities of body, color and finish. Finesse is that highly elusive element which is found in a superior wine, as opposed to very good or excellent ones.*

FINISH: *The sensation that lingers after the wine is swallowed is the "finish." If a wine "finishes well," there is no unusual aftertaste, no unpleasant bitterness, no excess of acidity. What remains, instead, is a general feeling of warmth in the mouth. A good finish is a difficult characteristic to achieve.*

KLEINE KONDITOREI

Address:	**234 East 86th Street**
Location:	**86th Street between Second and Third Avenues**
Telephone:	**RE 7-7130**
Credit Cards:	**AE; DC**
Reservations:	**Recommended**
Hours:	**10:00 AM to 12:00 Midnight, Monday Thru Friday and Sunday; Saturday to 2:00 AM**
Days Closed:	**None**
Liquor:	**Full bar service**
Recommended or Listed in:	**New York Times; Cue; Where**
Maitre d':	**Karl Stroh**
Manager:	**Christa Lober**
Seating Capacity:	**150**
Cuisine:	**German**
Specialties of the House:	**Natur Schnitzel; Beef Roulade; Beef Steak a la Tartare**
Dress:	**Informal**
Party Facilities:	**Private room; capacity: 35**

For over 50 years, Kleine Konditorei has been offering fine German dishes to old and new patrons. Located in the heart of New York's Yorkville district, the restaurant is famous for its fine food and pastries. Walk past the pastry counter into an old world dining room, tastefully accented with panelled walls and brass sconces. You'll enjoy many German specialties in a relaxed European atmosphere.

Kleine Konditorei

MENU

(a la carte)

APPETIZERS & SOUPS:

Chilled Tomato Juice (.95); Fresh Fruit Cocktail (1.10); Filet of Marinated Herring (1.85); Rollmops (1.35); Supreme of Jumbo Shrimps (3.35); Homemade Suelze (1.85); Ochsenmaul Salad (1.95); Soup du Jour (.85); Consomme with Egg Drop (.85); Soup without Entree (1.15).

ENTREES:

Broiled Half Spring Chicken 4.95
Sauerbraten 6.75
Corned Pig's Knuckle 4.55
Wiener Roast Braten 8.25
Grilled Chopped Beef Tenderloin Steak 4.85
Kasseler Rippchen 6.75
Wiener Schnitzel 6.75
Schnitzel a la Holstein 6.95
Rahm Schnitzel 7.25
Bratwurst (Pork) 3.95
Knockwurst (Beef) 3.95
Weisswurst (Veal) 3.95
Hot Turkey Sandwich 3.15
Hamburger Sandwich 3.15
Golden Brown German Pancake 3.55
Plain Apple Pancake 3.65
Potato Pancakes with Applesauce 3.45

(All entrees are served with vegetables, potato and salad.)

(Special German assorted cold cuts, salads, eggs, omelettes and sandwiches are also available.)

SPECIALTIES OF THE HOUSE:

Natur Schnitzel 7.95
(The tenderest Milk Fed Veal Steak Sauteed, with Mushrooms in a light sauce, served with Potato, Vegetable and Salad)
Prime Sirloin Steak 9.25
(One pound of the finest Prime Beef aged to perfection and grilled to your exact order, served with Potato, Vegetable and Salad)
Beef Roulade 6.75
(A delicately seasoned slice of Prime Beef rolled and filled with Onions, Pickle and Bacon, served with homemade Spaetzle and Red Cabbage)
Beef Steak a la Tartare 6.25
(Finely scraped Raw Tenderloin of Prime Beef with Garnitures)

CAKES AND PASTRIES:

Mocca Torte (1.30); Gugel Hupf (1.05); Trueffel Torte (1.40); Haselnuss Torte (1.30); Hippen Rollen (1.65); Rigo Torte (1.40); Linzer Torte (1.05); Schiller Locken (1.65); Schwarzwalder Kirsch Torte (1.60); Marzipan Cherry Torte (1.60); Fuerst Pueckler Torte (1.60); Punch-Rum Torte (1.40); Cream Cheese Cake (1.35); Bienenstich in Season (1.50); Cherry Cake (1.05); Berliner (1.00); Apple Cake (1.00); Plum, Peach, Blueberry or Strawberry Cake in Season (1.55); Cakes and Pastries with Whipped Cream (.65 extra).

(Complete luncheons and dinners are available.)

KYOTO JAPANESE STEAK HOUSE

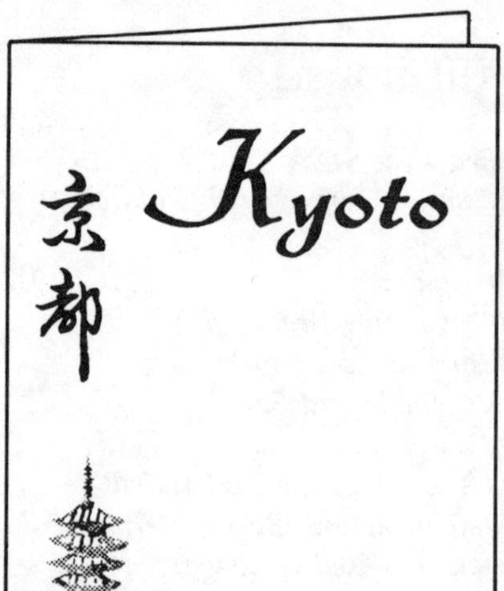

Address: 148 West 46th Street
Location: 46th Street between Seventh Avenue and Avenue of the Americas
Telephone: 265-2345
Credit Cards: AE; CB; V; DC; MC
Reservations: Recommended
Hours: Lunch from 12 Noon to 2:30 PM Monday thru Friday; Dinner from 5:30 PM to 11:00 PM Monday thru Thursday, 5:30 PM to 12 Midnight Friday and 5:00 PM to 12 Midnight on Saturday
Days Closed: Sundays
Liquor: Full bar service
Recommended or Listed in: Cue; Where; Playbill
Reservations Manager: Walter Endo
Seating Capacity: 75
Cuisine: Japanese Steaks and Seafood
Specialties of the House: Teppan Chicken; Teppan Steak; Teppan Seafood; Tempura
Dress: Casual

In the midst of the hustle and bustle of the theatre district is Kyoto, a haven for quiet dining in the Japanese tradition. Kyoto is entered through an open entranceway with a low L-shaped bar on one side. Wood and other natural materials predominate throughout the bar and dining room. The large tables in the dining room each contain a Teppan grill where all entrees, except tempura, are cooked. The cooking of Teppan cuisine is a fascinating procedure to watch and assures piping hot food. The staff of Kyoto is particularly accommodating to theatre-going patrons who must dine quickly to make their curtain.

Kyoto Japanese Steak House

DINNER MENU

(table d'hote)

(Dinner includes Kyoto Soup, Kyoto Green Salad, Rice, Green Tea and Dessert—ice cream or sherbet.)

ENTREES:

Teppan Chicken 6.50
(Teppan Shrimps, Filet of Chicken, vegetables and Special Kyoto Sauces)

Teppan Teriyaki Steak 7.50
(Teppan Shrimps, sliced Beef and Mushrooms, marinated in our Special Teriyaki Sauce, and vegetables.)

Teppan Sukiyaki Steak 9.00
(Teppan Shrimps, thin slices of Prime Beef, vegetables and Special Kyoto Sauces.)

Teppan Sirloin Steak 9.25
(Teppan Shrimps, Prime Beef, vegetables and Special Kyoto Sauces)

Teppan Filet Mignon 9.50
(Teppan Shrimps, Filet Mignon, vegetables and Special Kyoto Sauces)

Teppan Sea Food 11.00
(Shrimps, scallops, lobster tail, vegetables and Special Kyoto Sauces)

Tempura 7.75
(Japanese style deep fried shrimps and assorted vegetables with Special Tempura Sauce)

Teppan Seafood Special 15.00
(Teppan Shrimps, scallops, lobster tail, Filet Mignon, vegetables with Special Kyoto Sauces)

Teppan Kyoto Special 15.00
(Tempura Shrimps, Teppan Shrimps, Filet of Chicken, Sirloin Steak, Vegetables with Special Kyoto Sauces)

Vegetarian Dish 5.50

(A luncheon menu is also available.)

FLOWERY: *A flowery wine has a soft, floral nose that can remind one of violets, roses or spring mountain flowers. Northern Italian wines often have very definite flowery qualities, as do several outstanding German Moselles.*

FOXY: *This interesting term has nothing to do with foxes—it refers to the pungent grape flavor of native American grapes. New York State Concord wines—made from the species* vitis labrusca*—are "foxy" . . . reminding one of jelly or jam.*

FRUITY: *The element of the wine's "nose" reminiscent of fresh fruits. This element is found in most young wines, such as those of Beaujolais. New York State wines, especially the "foxy" types, are very fruity.*

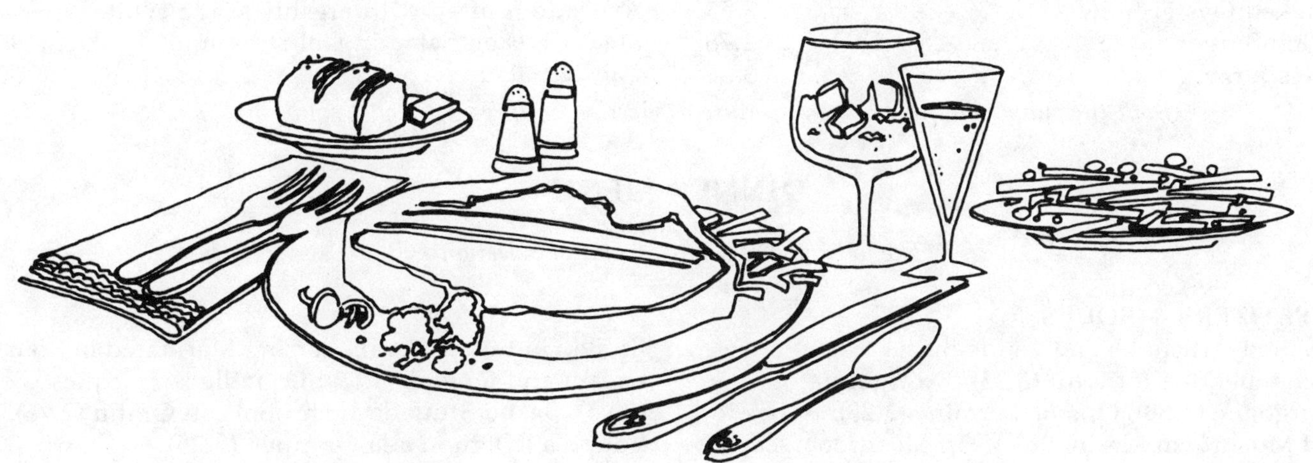

LADY ASTOR'S

Address: 430 Lafayette Street
Location: Lafayette Street near Astor Place
Telephone: 228-7888
Credit Cards: Personal checks accepted with major credit card identification
Reservations: Recommended for dinner
Hours: Lunch from 12:00 Noon to 4:30 PM, Monday thru Saturday; Dinner from 5:00 PM to 12:00 Midnight, daily; Supper from 5:00 PM to 1:00 AM, daily; Sunday Brunch from 12:00 Noon to 4:00 PM
Days Closed: Christmas and Thanksgiving Days
Liquor: Full bar service
Seating Capacity: 135
Cuisine: Continental/American
Specialties of the House: Filet of Lemon Sole with Mustard Hollandaise; Boneless Breast of Chicken à l'Orange; Coquilles St. Jacques; Veal Kidneys in Cognac, Cream and Shallots Sauté; Steak au Poivre Extraordinaire
Dress: No restrictions

While the decor at Lady Astor's is hard to classify, the effect is one of Old World charm and elegance. The dining room is centered around the bar and decorative appointments include rich floral patterned carpeting, green velvet fabrics, magnificent crystal chandeliers, art deco lamps and antiques. It's a fine setting for the gourmet food and the selection of top-quality wines at bistro prices. Right across the street is the N.Y. Shakespeare Festival Theater and those attending find Lady Astor's a perfect spot for before or after theater dining.

LUNCH & SUPPER MENU

(a la carte)

(Lady Astor's menu is extensive and varied; the following is a representative selection.)

ENTREES:

Eggs Benedict 3.95
Soupe à l'Oignon à la Gratinée 2.25
Quiche Lorraine .... 2.25 and 4.50
Steamed Artichoke and Garlic Butter 3.25
Smoked Oyster Stew 3.75
SirloinBurger 2.75
JarlesBurger 3.15
Roast Beef Sandwich on Pumpernickel with Dijon Mustard 3.75

SALADS:

Avocado Stuffed with Freshly Made White Meat Chicken Salad in Dill Dressing 5.95
Caesar Salad 4.75

Both the supper and lunch menu feature a selection of burgers, salads, soups and quiche.

DINNER MENU

(a la carte)

(The following is a representative selection.)

APPETIZERS & SOUPS:

Steamed Artichoke and Garlic Butter (recommended for two) (3.25); Escargot de Bourgogne (4.50); Quiche Lorraine (2.25); Avocado and Mushroom Marinade (1.95); Mushroom Caps Broiled in Butter (1.95); Herring Marinated in Sour Cream and Onions (1.95); Coquille St. Jacques (3.95); Baked Stuffed Mushrooms au Gratin (2.75); Soupe à l'Oignon à la Gratinée (2.25).

ENTREES:

Veal Kidneys in Cognac, Cream and Shallot Sauté 8.75
Boneless Breast of Chicken à l'Orange 7.95
Filet of Lemon Sole in Mustard Hollandaise Sauce 7.95
Filet of Boneless Chicken Breasts Sauté with Lemon and Butter 7.95
Medalion of Veal à la Marsala 9.75
Boneless Sirloin Steak in English Mustard Sauce 11.50
Steak au Poivre Extraordinaire (cut from the Chateaubriand) 13.50

(A Sunday Brunch Menu is also available.)

Menu Note: Lady Astor's menu is extensive and varied. Carefully prepared gourmet entrees and prime beef dinners are complemented by a serving of the house salad, black Russian pumpernickel with sweet butter and a freshly prepared vegetable.

ELEFANTENKOPF: *This "elephant's head" is made from a butter cream-filled cake, covered with marzipan. Chocolate is poured over the marzipan and the result is a small cake that looks like an elephant's head—ears, trunk, tusks and all. At Easter time, frogs and rabbits replace elephants.*

GUGEL HUPF: *This is a light vanilla yeast cake, baked in a fluted tube pan and shaped somewhat like a cone. It is usually sprinkled with powdered sugar; it may also be served with a glaze.*

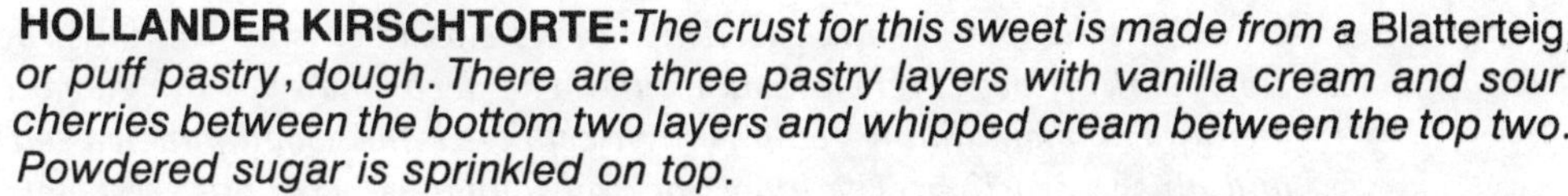

HOLLANDER KIRSCHTORTE: *The crust for this sweet is made from a* Blatterteig, *or puff pastry, dough. There are three pastry layers with vanilla cream and sour cherries between the bottom two layers and whipped cream between the top two. Powdered sugar is sprinkled on top.*

LINZERTORTE: *This is very much like a* wiener waffeln *but it is made with two round pieces of butter dough, with raspberry jam filling. The top round has a hole cut in the middle so the jam can show through. A linzertorte usually has cashews or almonds on top as well as powdered sugar.*

LAURENT

Address: 111 East 56th Street
Location: 56th Street between Park Avenue and Lexington Avenue
Telephone: PL 3-2729
Credit Cards: AE; DC
Reservations: Required
Hours: Lunch from 12 noon to 3:30 PM Monday thru Saturday; Dinner from 6:00 PM to 10:30 PM Monday thru Saturday and 5:00 PM to 10:30 PM Sunday. Cocktail lounge open from 11:30 AM until 12 midnight Monday thru Saturday
Days Closed: Major holidays
Liquor: Full bar service
Recommended or Listed in: Gourmet; Cue; many others
Maitre d': James
Seating Capacity: 174 in main dining room
Cuisine: French
Specialties of the House: Steak au Poivre Flambe à l'Armagnac; Fricassee de Peche Mariniere; Filet de Poulet a la Viennoise Nouilles Fraiches; Seasonal Specialties
Dress: Jackets and ties required
Party Facilities: 3 private rooms; capacity: 10-100

Laurent is famous for the excellence of its classic cuisine and must be rated among New York's finest French restaurants. The decor matches the elegance of the menu. The main dining room is high ceilinged and wood paneled with draperies and plush carpeting. The huge cocktail lounge is luxurious, resembling a private club, and the appointments throughout are of the finest sort. Three private dining rooms, capable of accommodating from 10 to 100 persons, are available for private parties.

LUNCHEON MENU

(table d'hote)

(Menu changes daily. The following is representative.)

APPETIZERS:

Coupe de Fruits; Grapefruit; Little Necks; Cherrystones; Avocado; Tomato Juice; Clam Juice; V-8 Juice; Mortadelle; Shrimp Cocktail (3.50); Hors d'Oeuvre Assorties (3.50); Artichaut Vinaigrette; Melon de Saison; Terrine de Mallard et Faison; Saumon Fumé (4.75); Mousse de Saumon Dill Sauce (3.00); Melon and Prosciutto (4.25); Moules Mariniere (4.00); Blue Points or Wellfleets (4.50).

SOUPS:

Madrilene en Gelée; Consomme en Gelée; Vichyssoise; Gazpacho (2.00); Consomme Celestine; Chicken Gumbo Creole.

ENTREES:

Omelette Opera 11.00
Supreme de Bass Grille Bearnaise 13.00
Bay Scallops Frites, Sauce Remoulade 14.00
Coquilles of Crab Meat and Lobster Gratin . 16.00
Sugar Cured Ham Madere, Beignets de Pommes 12.50
Poulet de Grain Grillé, Courgettes Fine Herbes 13.00
Saute de Veau Marengo Brown Rice 12.50
Le Chopped Steak Laurent 11.00
Foie de Veau aux Raisins, Fond d'Artichaut Farci 12.50
Ris de Veau Grille Diable, Sauce Robert Pointes d'Asperges 13.00
Tournedos de Boeuf Bourguignonne 16.00
Cold Roast Beef, Salade Parmentier 14.50
Salade Niçoise 11.00
Salade Laurent 10.00

DESSERTS:
Patisserie Française; Tarte aux Fruits; Gateau St. Honoré; Mousse au Chocolat; Meringue Glace; Macedoine aux Liqueurs; Fruits de Saison; Compote de Fruits; Les Fromages (1.75); Glaces: Vanille, Chocolat, Cafe, Fraise, Pistachio, Citron, Framboise.

DINNER MENU

(a la carte)

(Menu changes daily. The following is representative.)

APPETIZERS:
Grapefruit (2.75); Little Necks (3.75); Cherrystones (3.75); Blue Points or Wellfleets (4.75); Sardines Francaises a l'Huile (2.75); Saumon Fumé (6.00); Crepes Laurent (4.75); Moules Mariniere (5.50); Mousse de Saumon à l'Arreth (4.50); Caviar Malossol (21.00); Petits Pots d'Escargots Laurent (5.50); Terrine de Faison et Canard aux Pistaches (4.50); Crab Meat Cocktail (6.75); Broiled Spanish Shrimps (7.00); Melon (2.75); Melon au Jambon d'Italie (5.00); Truite Fumé (4.50); Choix des Hors d'Oeuvres (4.50).

SOUPS:
Vichyssoise (2.75); Madrilene (2.75); Consomme en Gelée (2.75); Gazpacho Andaluz (3.00); Petite Marmite (3.50); Soupe à l'Oignon au Gratin (3.00); Creme de Broccolis Amandines (3.00).

ENTREES:
Bay Scallops Meuniere, Tomates et Champignons 12.75
Goujonettes de Sole Sauce Moutarde 12.50
Crab Meat Monte Carlo 13.00
Shrimp Imperiale Riz Pilaff 14.00
Broiled Red Snapper with Lime Butter 13.00
Grenouilles Provencale 12.00
Coq au Vin de Bourgogne, Riz Sauvage 10.00
Long Island Duckling au Poivre Vert, Compote de Poires or à l'Orange 11.75
Royal Squab Grille à l'Americaine 11.50
Cote de Veau Cordon Bleu, Ratatouille Niçoise 13.00
Rack of Lamb aux Herbes de Provence 13.00
Foie de Veau aux Raisins Fond d'Artichaut Farci 10.50
Steak au Poivre Flambe à l'Armagnac 16.00
Filet de Faison aux Marrons et Champignons Riz Sauvage 14.50
Tournedos de Venaison, Grand Veneur, Purée de Marrons 16.00
Roast Prime Ribs of Beef Garni 12.00

(A variety of a la carte vegetables and salads are also available.)

DESSERTS:
Petits Fours (1.75); Compote de Fruits (3.00); Mousse au Chocolat (3.00); Souffles Tous Parfums (4.00); Glaces Variees (2.50); Fruits Rafraichis aux Liqueurs (3.75); Plateau des Fromages (2.75); Coupe aux Marrons (3.00); Crepes Suzette (for 2) (8.50); Le Chariot de Patisserie Maison (2.75).

(There is a cover charge of 1.75 at dinner.)

Laurent

LE LAVANDOU

Address: 134 East 61st Street
Location: 61st Street between Lexington Avenue and Park Avenue
Telephone: 838-7987
Credit Cards: AE
Reservations: Essential
Hours: Lunch from 12 Noon to 2:30 PM; Dinner from 6:00 PM to 10:00 PM
Days Closed: Sunday
Liquor: Full bar service
Recommended or Listed in: Gourmet; Cue
Maitre d': Francois
Seating Capacity: 70
Cuisine: French
Specialties of the House: La Ballotine de Sole Lobster Sauce; La Darne de Saumon Chambord; La Cote de Veau Glacee Normande
Dress: Jackets required

Elegance and sophistication mark the ambience at Le Lavandou, a restaurant which takes its name from a resort village on the French Riviera. Mirror-lined walls, paintings and fresh flowers help to create surroundings appropriate to the excellent haute cuisine provided by Chef-Propriétaire, Jean-Jacques Rachou. The truly educated palate will find many delights here.

LUNCHEON MENU

(prix fixe: 10.50)

APPETIZERS:
Consomme de Volaille; Quiche Lorraine; Creme Saint Germain; Fruits Rafraichis; Saucisson Chaud en Croûte; Melon de Saison; Paté de Campagne; Sardines à l'Huile; Moules a la Moutarde; Maquereaux au Vin Blanc; Oeufs Mimosa; Artichaut en Feuilles; Melon Bayonne (1.25); Bouquet de Crevettes (1.75); Saumon Fumé (1.75); Escargots Chablisienne (2.25); Asperges de France (1.50); Crab Meat Cocktail (3.50).

ENTREES:
L'Omelette aux Cêpes "Manon"
La Truite au Four Provençale
La Suprême de Sole B. Meuniere
Les Rognons de Veau Bordelaise
Le Cassoulet du Chef Toulousain
Les Escalopines Arlésienne
Les Oeufs Poches "Vieille Auberg"
Le Bass Rayé Braise aux Arômates
Les Scallops en Coquille Vin Blanc
Le Foie de Veau Sauté Lyonnaise
Le Poulet en Feuilletage Lavandou
Le Navarin d'Agneau Printanier
La Poire d'Avocado "Maître Jacques"
Le Tournedos Sauté Rossini .... supp 2.50
Les Cotes d'Agneau Vert Pré .... supp 2.50

DESSERTS & CHEESES:
Les Bons Fromages de France; La Tarte au Fruits du Jour; La Mousse au Chocolat; Les Fruits Rafraichis; La Coupe au Grand Marnier; Bavarois au Kirsch; Bombe au Pralin; Le Sorbet au Cassis; Le Granité a la Menthe; Les Fraises Romanoff (1.25); Le Biscuit Glace aux Trois Couleurs.

DINNER MENU

(prix fixe: 19.50)

APPETIZERS:
Melon et Jambon Bayonnaise; Paté de Campagne; Coupe de Fruits Rafraichis; Bouquet de Crevettes (1.00); Terrine de Canard Truffée; Demi Grapefruit Suprême; Saumon Fumé (2.25); Huitres en Saison

continued on next page

(1.50); Avocado Maitre Jacques (4.25); Asperges de France Hollandaise (1.75); Melon Glace; Crab Meat Sauce Savoy (4.25); Foie Gras de Strasbourg (8.00); Le Caviar de Beluga (16.00); Escargots Chablisiens (2.50); La Ballotine de Sole Lobster Sauce; La Quenelle de Brochet au Pernod (1.00); La Creme de Petits Pois Poysanne; Le Consomme de Volaille Béarnaise; Le Bisque de Homard aux Croûtons.

ENTREES:
La Sole Anglaise Des Provencaux
Les Saint Jacques Aux Amandines
La Darne de Saumon Chambord
Le Bass Raye Aux Chasselots
La Sole de la Manche B. Meuniere
La Croustade Nantua "Vieille époque"
La Cote de Veau Glacée Normande ..... supp 2.00
Le Steak au Poivre des Iles Maxim's .... supp 2.00
La Dojine Gintadotte Périgourdine
Les Delices de Veau Aux Chanterelles
Les Rognons en Casserole Bordelaise
Le Canteon Roti Aux "Belles Cerises"
La Suprême de Volaille Biarrotte
Le Ris de Veau Braisé Varoise
Le Tournedos Aux Cêpes Sauce Truffe .. supp 2.00
Le Mignon de Boeuf en Feuilletage ..... supp 2.50

DESSERTS:
Les Bons Fromages de France; La Tarte Aux Fruits; L'Entremet Parisien; La Coupe de Fruits Aux Liqueurs; Le Sorbet au Cassis; Le Granite à la Menthe; La Bombe Glacé au Pralin; La Coupe au Grand Marnier; La Mousse au Chocolat; Le Succes au Cointreau; Les Fraises au Sucre et Grand Marnier (1.25).

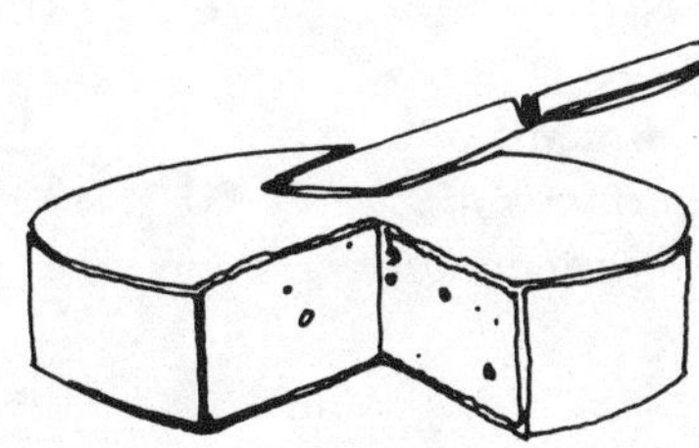

EMMENTHAL: *Made in Switzerland's Emme Valley, this is the great classic of "Swiss"-type cheeses. Formed in huge wheels weighing upwards of 145 pounds, it is a very hard cheese with a nutty and slightly sweet flavor. Pale yellow in color and laced with the holes typical of "Swiss" cheeses, Emmenthal is usually aged for four to ten months before it is sold but may be aged much longer to achieve peak flavor.*

FETA: *The best known of the Greek cheeses, Feta is made of ewe's milk. It is soft and pure white in color. The flavor is sharp and spicy and, because it is cured in brine, Feta is slightly salty.*

MUSCADET: *The charming and delicious light white wine of the lower Loire Valley. Muscadet has a small flavor, when compared to white Burgundies, but it is pleasantly dry and fruity.*

MUSIGNY: *Recognized as one of the best Côte d'Or red Burgundies, Musigny has a haunting delicacy that increases in the drinking. Only slightly lighter than a Chambertin, it is often thought of as being "feminine".*

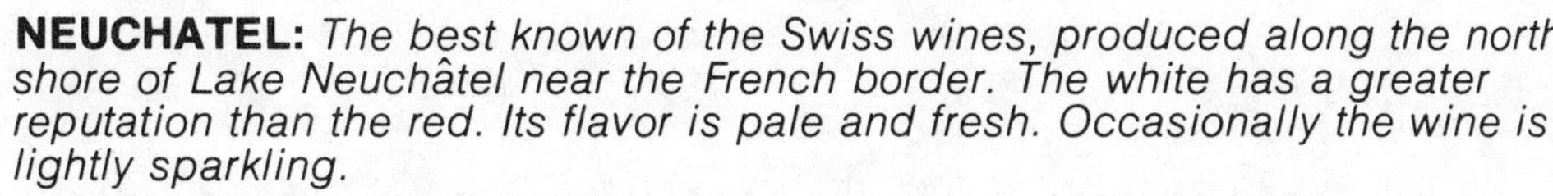

NEUCHATEL: *The best known of the Swiss wines, produced along the north shore of Lake Neuchâtel near the French border. The white has a greater reputation than the red. Its flavor is pale and fresh. Occasionally the wine is lightly sparkling.*

We've spared neither effort nor expense to make this edition of Manhattan Menus *as useful, accurate and up-to-date as possible. If you have suggestions or comments, we'd like to hear them. Drop us a note at: P.O. Box 5217, FDR Station, New York, N. Y. 10022.*

THE LEFT BANK

Address: 1220 Second Avenue
Location: Second Avenue and 64th Street
Telephone: 759-8369
Credit Cards: AE; DC; MC; CB
Reservations: Recommended
Hours: Dinner from 5:00 PM; Sunday Brunch from 11:30 AM to 5:00 PM
Days Closed: None
Liquor: Full bar service
Recommended or Listed in: Cue; New York Magazine; Our Town; New York Times
Reservations Manager: Mr. Al
Seating Capacity: 100
Cuisine: Continental/Cafe
Specialties of the House: Chicken Kiev; Duck with Cherries; Beef Bourguignone; Fresh Florida Stone Crabs
Dress: Casual

The Left Bank is café, bistro and modern design establishment rolled into one—a moderately priced and most pleasant package. Centrally located on the eastside of Manhattan, The Left Bank offers lunch, dinner and brunch menus that provide excellent value in spacious surroundings. The atmosphere is relaxed, informal and comfortable. If you're looking for old-fashioned dining value and contemporary design decor, try The Left Bank.

DINNER MENU

(a la carte)

APPETIZERS & SOUPS:
Paté Maison (2.50); Quiche Lorraine (2.50); Artichoke (Cold vinaigrette or hot seasoned butter) (2.25); Crudites (Fresh raw vegetables with sour cream and garlic dressing (3.00); Melon and Prosciutto (2.50); Escargot (3.25); Baked Clams (2.75); Onion Soup Gratinée (1.75); Soup du Jour (1.35); Cold Vichyssoise (1.50); Fresh Florida Stone Crabs (4.50).

ENTREES:

Hamburger Superb	3.15
Cheeseburger	3.50
Bankburger	3.75
Marinated Spareribs	5.50
Spaghetti Bolognese	4.95
Fish du Jour	(. . .)
Filet of Sole Meuniere	6.95
Grilled Bass or Grenobloise	7.95
Broiled Shrimp Papillon	8.25
Fresh Florida Stone Crabs	10.95
Cold Poached Salmon with Dill Sauce	7.95
Breast of Chicken a la Kiev	6.75
Grilled Chicken	5.95
Roast Duckling with Cherries	7.65
Veal Parmigiana	6.50
Veal Marsala or Piccata	7.25
Beef Bourguignone	6.50
Marinated Shish Kebab, Rice Pilaff	7.25
Chopped Sirloin of Beef	5.50
Double Lamb Chops	8.95
Prime Aged Sirloin Steak	10.95
Steak au Poivre	11.50

(All the fish and meat entrees are served with a choice of potato or rice and a vegetable.)

SALADS:
Nicoise (4.65); Chef (4.75); Spinach (3.50); Caeser's Salad for two (3.50); Mixed Greens (1.50).

DESSERTS:
Chocolate Mousse (1.35); Creme Caramel (1.25); Cheese Cake (1.95); Fruit Tarts (1.75); Chocolate Cake (1.95); Strudel (Apple, Cheese or Cherry) (1.95); Ice Cream (Vanilla, Chocolate, Coffee) (1.25).

LION'S ROCK

Address: 316 East 77th Street
Location: 77th Street between First Avenue and Second Avenue
Telephone: 988-3610
Credit Cards: V; MC; DC; AE
Reservations: Recommended
Hours: Dinner from 5:00 PM to 1:00 AM Monday thru Sunday; Sunday brunch from 12 Noon to 4:00 PM
Days Closed: None
Liquor: Full bar service
Recommended or Listed in: Cue; New York; New York Times; Playbill
Seating Capacity: 90 in winter; 150 in summer
Cuisine: Continental
Specialties of the House: Breast of Chicken with Wild Mushrooms; Grilled Red Snapper with Vermouth Sauce; Fresh Pastas
Dress: Casual
Party Facilities: Private room; capacity: 50

Lion's Rock is perhaps the most sophisticated and stylishly romantic garden restaurant in the city. The wood paneling, brick fireplaces, and glass doors which give way to the outdoor garden, all contribute to the feeling of being far from the crowded city. In summer, the patio is used for alfresco dining. More than 100 years ago, the garden's imposing rock formation marked the site where New Yorkers would pause to picnic after a Sunday outing in Jones Wood (a rustic region extending from 65th to 77th Streets). The food is anything but rustic country fare. The sophisticated continental dishes are prepared with expertise and dedication to quality.

DINNER MENU

(a la carte)

APPETIZERS:
Escargot (3.50); Baked Mushrooms Croustade (2.50); Beurrecks a la Turque (2.50); Carpaccio (2.75); Shrimp Cocktail (3.25); Pate Crudites (2.75).

SOUPS & SALADS:
Potage (1.75); Soup a l'Oignon (2.00); Salade Vinaigrette or Bleu Cheese (1.00); Salade Romaine with Caesar Dressing for Two (3.00).

ENTREES:
Fettucine Alfredo with Green Noodles 4.75
Linguini Primavera 5.75
Breast of Chicken with Wild Mushrooms 7.25
Scampi Saute a la Anthony 7.75
Brochette of Lamb Orientale 6.75
Striped Bass or Red Snapper Casino 8.25
Paillard of Beef au Poivre Vert 8.25
Veal Scallopine Marsala 8.25
Prime Sirloin Steak Maitre d'Hotel with Baked Potato 11.50
Filet Mignon with Baked Potato 11.50
Poulet Saute Lion's Rock 7.25

(A number of daily specials are also offered.)

DESSERTS:
Our Own Cheesecake (2.00); Creme Brulee (1.50); Meringue Chantilly (1.50); Frozen Yogurtberry Shortcake (1.75); Mousse au Chocolat (1.75); Ice Cream, Cassis Sherbet or Frozen Yogurt (1.75).

(This is a seasonal menu; it changes periodically.)

continued on next page

Lion's Rock

SUNDAY BRUNCH

(Entree price includes orange or tomato juice, hot rolls and butter, a selection of fresh cakes and coffee.)

ENTREES:

French Toast with Bacon, Ham or Sausage . . . 3.60
Eggs (3, any style) with Bacon, Ham or Sausage . . . 3.60
Omelettes (Western, Spanish or Cheese) with Bacon, Ham or Sausage . . . 3.75
Sirloin Steak and Eggs . . . 5.25
Eggs Benedict . . . 4.25
Eggs Florentine . . . 4.25
Fresh Nova Scotia Salmon with Cream Cheese on Bagel . . . 5.50

MAKRONENTORTE: *This three-layer sponge cake is filled with apricot and raspberry jelly. It gets its name from its macaroon frosting made with almond paste, macaroon paste and egg whites. Cashew nuts are sprinkled on the sides of the cake and the top is decorated with a criss-cross pattern made from the frosting and raspberry jam.*

MANDELECKE: *This is an almond cake covered with chopped almonds, then dipped in chocolate on all four sides or corners—an "ecke" is a corner.*

MANDELKIRSCH: *Like the* sachertorte, *this cake is made from a batter which is almost completely ground almonds. It has a filling of sour cherries (kirsch) and the top is sprinkled with powdered sugar.*

MANDELROLLE: *Similar to a* Schokoladenrolle, *the dough for this pastry is rolled onto a wooden stick while still warm. The dough has almonds in it. When cooled, it is filled with whipped cream and both ends of the roll are dipped in melted chocolate.*

THE LUCCHESE HOUSE OF SEAFOOD

Address:	**1700 Hylan Boulevard, Staten Island**
Telephone:	**979-1330**
Credit Cards:	**MC; CB; DC; AE**
Reservations:	**Not necessary**
Hours:	**11:00 AM to 2:00 AM, 7 days a week**
Days Closed:	**None**
Liquor:	**Full bar service**
Maitre d':	**Dick Lucchese**
Reservations Manager:	**Joe Lucchese**
Seating Capacity:	**120**
Cuisine:	**Italian-Seafood**
Specialties of the House:	**Shrimp Franchese; Stuffed Fillet Special**
Dress:	**Casual**
Entertainment:	**Pianist every evening; Singing Host and Waiters**
Party Facilities:	**Skylight Room; capacity: 25**
Parking:	**Restaurant parking lot**

Lucchese's is an Italian restaurant specializing in unusual seafood dishes, prepared in the Italian style. The undersea motif is carried out in the nautical decor with tropical aquariums adding an intriguing color. A special feature is Lucchese's "Skylight" room, a sun-filled alcove which makes luncheon dining there a particular pleasure. And every evening, Host Dick Lucchese doubles as an entertainer when he's joined by enthusiastic singing waiters in a rousing Italian repertoire.

MENU

(a la carte)

(The following is a representative selection.)

APPETIZERS & SOUPS:

Steamers (3.00); Soup de Jour (.50 & .75); Antipasto (2.95); Tomato Juice (.50); Clam Broth (.50); Clam Chowder (Manhattan) (.50 & .75); Clam Cocktail (1.75); Shrimp Cocktail (2.25); Clams Oreginata (2.75); Marinated Herring (2.25); Mussels (3.00); Mussels Oreginata (1.75); Crabmeat Cocktail in Season (3.50); Lobster Meat Cocktail (3.75); Longostino (3.95); Clams Casino (2.75); Salmon Garni (3.25); Fruit Cup (.75); Fresh Melon (1.25); Escargot (4.50); Oysters (3.75).

ENTREES:

Lucchese Special 6.50
(Shrimp, Clams, Mussels, Calamari cooked in our own Sauce, with Linguine)

Big "L" Special 6.75
(Crab, Clams, Scallops, Shrimp and Fillet)

Chef's Special 5.25
(Deep Fried Shrimp, Fresh Fried Calamari and Fresh Cut Scungili, served with Biscuit and Hot or Regular Sauce)

Fried Fillet Platter 3.75

Broiled Scallops 5.50

Golden Fried Shrimp Platter 4.95

Broiled Red Snapper 5.25

Crabmeat au Gratin 4.75

Deep Fried Oyster Platter 4.50

Scungili Salad 3.75

Mussels with Sauce 3.00

Calamari with Sauce 3.25

Shrimp Parmesan with Linguine 6.95

Broiled Lobster Tails (2) .... 13.75 and up

Lobster Fra Diavolo (For Two) .... 13.75 and up
(Cooked in Wine Sauce with Shrimp, Clams and Mussels)

Stuffed Fillet Special 5.75

Shrimp Franchese 6.95
(Shrimp Sauteed and Cooked in Our Famous Recipe)

Linguine with Red or White Clam Sauce 3.75

Deviled Crab 4.75

Homemade Baked Lasagne 3.25

(A selection of desserts is also available.)

LUTÈCE

Address: 249 East 50th Street
Location: 50th Street between Second Avenue and Third Avenue.
Telephone: PL 2-2225
Credit Cards: AE
Reservations: Essential
Hours: Lunch from 12:00 Noon to 1:45 PM, Tuesday thru Friday; Dinner from 5:45 PM to 9:45 PM, Monday thru Saturday
Days Closed: Sundays
Liquor: Full Bar Service
Maitre d': Roger Benjamin
Seating Capacity: 80
Cuisine: French
Specialties of the House: Ballotine de sole au buerre blanc; Feuillete St. Jacques; Mignon de boeuf en croute
Dress: Jacket and tie required

This is real "haute cuisine," where the ambience is intimate and charming and the food superb. Lutece takes up two floors of a narrow brownstone, with the lower dining area part of an enclosed garden, and the upstairs composed of several little rooms. Completing the French decor are a crystal chandelier, floral art, a few tapestries and assorted mirrors. Now owned by the chef, André Soltner, Lutèce must be classed at the very top. Expensive, but well worth the money.

LUNCHEON MENU

(prix fixe – 16.00)

APPETIZERS:
Consommé de Volaille; Tarte à l'Óignon; Potage Germiny; Madrilène Froid; Quiche Lorraine; Crème Saint Germain; Oeuf à la Gelée; Escargots; Pâtes Assortis; Saumon Fumé, Champignons, Artichauts Provençale; Saucisson Chaud en Croûte; Brioche de Brochet, Sauce Cresson.

ENTREES:
Omelette aux Girolles
Coquilles St. Jacques Provencale
Poussin Rôti aux Fines Herbes
Mousseline Nantua
Filets de Sole Amandine
Escalope de Veau du Chef
Rognon de Veau à la Bordelaise
Poulet en Croûte Lutèce
Morilles à la Crème
Cèpes à la Bordelaise
Cotes d'Agneau Vert-Pré 16.75
Tournedos Chasseur 17.50

DESSERTS:
Fromage de France; Fruits Rafraîchis; Sorbet au Cassis; Tarte aux Fruits; Soufflé Glacé; Mousse au Chocolat; Crème Renversee au Café; Bavarois; Glace au Pralin; Tarte à la Tatin; Succès Maison.

DINNER MENU

(a la carte)

(Lutèce provides only the host of a dinner party with a menu which includes prices. Please be advised that this is among New York's most expensive restaurants.)

APPETIZERS & SOUPS:
Consommé de Volaille Bressane; Bisque de Homard; Crème Saint-Germain; Consommé Tortue Claire; Champignons et Coeurs d'Artichauts à la Grecque; Saumon Fumé d'Écosse; Foie Gras en Brioche; Perles de la Volga aux Blinis, avec la

Vodka; Pâtè en Croute et Terrines; Brioche de Brochet; Timbales d'Escargots à la Chablisienne; Escalope de Saumon Frais; Demoiselle du Maine; Truite Fraîche a l'Oseille; Pélerines à la Méridionale; Cervelas de Fruits de Mer; Terrine aux Trois Poissons; Saumon Farci en Croûte (Pour 4); Mousseline de Grenouilles à l'Alsacienne; Tourte Régence; Soufflé aux Fruits de Mer (Pour 2); Truffe en Pâté Lucullus.

ENTREES:

Turbot de Dieppe Poché, Hollandaise
Sole Farcie Elzévir
Cassolette de Crabe "Vieille France"
Sole de la Manche Belle Meunière
Poussin Rôti Basquaise
Coquelet à la Crème aux Morilles
Canard aux Pêches (Pour 2)
Pigeonneau Clamart
Côte de Boeuf, Marchand de Vin (Pour 2)
Médaillons de Veau aux Morilles
Ris de Veau Financière
Délices de Veau aux Girolles
Tournedos la Fontaine
Carré de Pauillac Caramelisé (Pour 2)
Mignon de Boeuf en Croûte Lutèce

VEGETABLES:

Haricots Verts; Épinards en Branche; Coeur de Céleri au Jus; Carottes Nouvelles Glacées; Salsifis Meunière; Petits Pois à la Francaise; Timbale de Morilles à la Creme; Asperges Fraîches en Saison; Cèpes à la Bordelaise.

DESSERTS:

Fromages de France; Entrement Parisien; Pèches Blanches Flambées au Kirsch; Coupe de Fruits Rafraichis; Succés a l'Orange; Sorbet au Cassis; Bombe Glacée au Pralin; Mousse au Chocolat; Crêpes Flambées à l'Alsacienne; "Soufflé Glacé" aux Framboises.

NUITS-ST.-GEORGES: *A fine red Burgundy produced around the town of the same name on the southern end of the Côte de Nuits. Nuits-St.-Georges is a generous, soft, well-balanced red; as a Côte de Nuits red, it has a longer life and deeper color than the reds of the Côte de Beaune to the south.*

ORVIETO: *An Italian light white wine produced near the town of the same name in central Italy, between Florence and Rome. Orvieto's "vineyards" actually mingle with trees and crops. This typically sweet wine is shipped in a truncated, Chianti-like straw-covered flask.*

PAUILLAC: *The "classic" red Bordeaux, named for the Médoc town and commune encompassing such celebrated chateaux as Lafite, Latour and Mouton-Rothschild. Pauillac reds are full-bodied and long-lasting, with a great bouquet and the essential Bordeaux flavor – dry with a suggestion of sweetness.*

FONTINA: *Fontina was first made in the Aosta Valley in Italy's Piedmont district. It was originally made from goat's milk but is now more commonly made from cow's milk. A relatively firm cheese with a pale yellow hue, Fontina has a full, nutty flavor and aroma.*

GJETOST: *A dark brown cheese made in Norway from 90% cow's milk and 10% goat's milk, Gjetost has a sweet-sour taste very different from that of any other cheese. Sugar is added while it is being made which accounts, in part, for its unusual flavor.*

MME. ROMAINE DE LYON

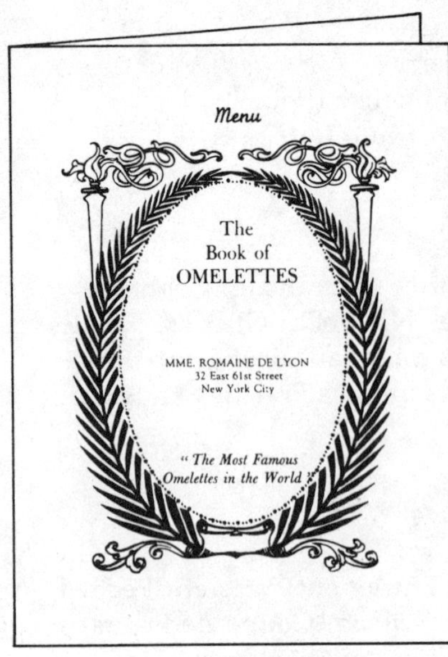

Address:	**32 East 61st Street**
Location:	**61st Street between Madison and Park Avenues**
Telephone:	**758-2422**
Credit Cards:	**Not accepted**
Reservations:	**Recommended for parties of 4 or more**
Hours:	**11:00 AM to 3:00 PM, daily**
Days Closed:	**Some holidays**
Liquor:	**Wine and beer only**
Recommended or Listed in:	**New York Times; Gourmet; Cue**
Seating Capacity:	**75**
Cuisine:	**French**
Specialties of the House:	**Omelets of all kinds**

Without trying to be stylish, this small restaurant has become one of the most fashionable luncheon places in New York. It combines wonderful food, gracious service and comfortable surroundings. Don't drop your fork if you look up to see Paul Newman. Or Joanne Woodward. Or Candice Bergen. Or any of a host of other celebrities who frequent Madame Romaine's.

MENU

Mme. Romaine serves only omelets along with accompaniments (breads, salad, desserts, beverages). Omelets are offered in almost bewildering variety with more than 600 kinds listed in over 17 pages of the menu. Only a representative sampling can be listed here.

ENTREES:

Plain Omelet	3.20
Sausage Omelet	5.25
Chicken Livers Omelet	5.65
Cheese Omelet with Potatoes in Cream Sauce	4.50
Cheese Omelet with Eggplant, Fines Herbes, Garlic and Tomato Sauce	4.80
Cheese Omelet with Asparagus Tips and Parsley	4.70
Spinach Omelet with Mushrooms, Croutons, Garlic and Cheese	5.10
Tomato and Bacon Omelet with Onions, Peppers, Garlic and Fines Herbes	5.35
Tomato and Potato Omelet wih Fines Herbes	4.75
Cauliflower and Bacon Omelet with Onions, Cream Sauce and Cheese	5.40
Mushrooms and Cheese Omelet	4.90
Ham and Potatoes Omelet	5.45
Ham, Foie Gras and Mushrooms Omelet with Croutons and Spinach	6.75
Truffles and Cheese Omelet	10.95
French Bacon Omelet with Potatoes, Fines Herbes	5.75
Ham Omelet with Tomatoes, Olives, Croutons	5.60
Ham Omelet with Mushrooms, Noodles, Olives and Fines Herbes	5.70
Chicken Omelet with Artichoke Hearts and Mushrooms	6.05
Calf Brains Omelet with Croutons, Fine Herbes, Cheese	5.35
Veal Kidney Omelet with Tomatoes and Fines Herbes	5.75
Beef Omelet with Bacon, Spinach, Onions, Croutons, Garlic and Cheese	6.40
Sweetbreads Omelet with Tomatoes, Peas, Noodles, Croutons and Sherry Sauce	6.85
Lobster Omelet with Spinach and Cheese	5.60
Caviar Omelet with Sour Cream	12.95
Tuna Fish Omelet with Tomatoes, Onions, Croutons, Fines Herbes	5.40
Salmon Omelet with Potatoes, Spinach and Cheese	5.35

GIVE A BOOK YOU LIKE TO SOMEONE YOU LIKE.

Manhattan Menus makes a handsome and thoughtful gift — for birthdays, anniversaries, holidays, other occasions. Use the special coupons below to order copies now. Elegant gift cards will be sent to those you designate, inscribed with your personal message and signed with your name.

manhattan menus

Yes! Enclosed is my check for $__________. Please send __________ gift(s) of *Manhattan Menus* @ $8.95 each, plus $1.00 each for postage and handling, to the person(s) listed. Include a personalized gift card with each, signed with my name and inscribed as indicated.

My Name __________

My Address __________

City __________ State _____ Zip _____

Mail to: Manhattan Menus, P.O. Box 5217, FDR Station, New York, N.Y. 10022.

B

Send Gift Copies to:

Name

Address

City State Zip

Inscribe gift card as follows:

Name

Address

City State Zip

Inscribe gift card as follows:

Name

Address

City State Zip

Inscribe gift card as follows:

manhattan menus

Yes! Enclosed is my check for $__________. Please send __________ gift(s) of *Manhattan Menus* @ $8.95 each, plus $1.00 each for postage and handling, to the person(s) listed. Include a personalized gift card with each, signed with my name and inscribed as indicated.

My Name __________

My Address __________

City __________ State _____ Zip _____

Mail to: Manhattan Menus, P.O. Box 5217, FDR Station, New York, N.Y. 10022.

A

Send Gift Copies to:

Name

Address

City State Zip

Inscribe gift card as follows:

Name

Address

City State Zip

Inscribe gift card as follows:

Name

Address

City State Zip

Inscribe gift card as follows:

GIVE A BOOK YOU LIKE TO SOMEONE YOU LIKE.

Manhattan Menus makes a handsome and thoughtful gift — for birthdays, anniversaries, holidays, other occasions. Use the special coupons below to order copies now. Elegant gift cards will be sent to those you designate, inscribed with your personal message and signed with your name.

Send Gift Copies to:

Name
Address
City State Zip
Inscribe gift card as follows:

Name
Address
City State Zip
Inscribe gift card as follows:

Name
Address
City State Zip
Inscribe gift card as follows:

Send Gift Copies to:

Name
Address
City State Zip
Inscribe gift card as follows:

Name
Address
City State Zip
Inscribe gift card as follows:

Name
Address
City State Zip
Inscribe gift card as follows:

Send Gift Copies to:

Name
Address
City State Zip
Inscribe gift card as follows:

Name
Address
City State Zip
Inscribe gift card as follows:

Name
Address
City State Zip
Inscribe gift card as follows:

Send Gift Copies to:

Name
Address
City State Zip
Inscribe gift card as follows:

Name
Address
City State Zip
Inscribe gift card as follows:

Name
Address
City State Zip
Inscribe gift card as follows:

LE MADRIGAL

Address:	**216 East 53rd Street**
Location:	**53rd Street between Second and Third Avenues**
Telephone:	**355-0322**
Credit Cards:	**AE; DC**
Reservations:	**Required**
Hours:	**Lunch from 12:00 Noon to 3:00 PM, Monday thru Friday; Dinner from 6:00 PM to 10:30 PM, Monday thru Saturday**
Days Closed:	**Sunday**
Liquor:	**Full bar service**
Recommended or Listed in:	**Gourmet; Town & Country**
Seating Capacity:	**74**
Cuisine:	**French**
Specialties of the House:	**Coeur de Filet en Chemise au Poivre Vert; Sole de la Manche au Gratin**
Dress:	**Jacket and tie recommended**
Party Facilities:	**Garden; capacity: 20**

Le Madrigal is a bright, cheerful French restaurant that carries you back to the days of the troubadours who are depicted in the restaurant's unique murals. You dine in a charming room which extends back to a green "garden" area; the illusion of dining outside, while inside, is effective and pleasing. The food is urbanely served on the very finest plates and glassware. Le Madrigal has been redecorated recently, and the ambience is fresh, attractive and welcoming. This is one of the most distinctive restaurants in town.

DINNER MENU

(table d'hote)

APPETIZERS & SOUPS:
Jambon de Pays et Melon (2.00); Saucisson Chaud; Truite Fumée (1.50); Caviar de la Caspienne sur Glace (20.00); Feuilleté Jambon et Fromage; Les Trois Terrines; Saumon Fumé de Gaspé (2.25); Blue Points; Foie Gras des Landes (9.50); Bouquet de Crevettes (2.25); Little Necks; Celestines de Fruits de Mer (3.00); Vichyssoise; Billi-Bi; Potage du Jour; Consommé aux Profiterolles; Gratinée.

Le Madrigal

continued on next page

Menu continued

ENTREES:

Suprême de Bass du Jour 18.50
Sole de la Manche au Gratin 20.00
Saumon Condorcet 21.00
St. Jacques Nîmoise 18.50
Le Plat du Jour 18.50
Escalope de Veau à l'Orange 20.00
Mignon de Veau aux Morilles 23.00
Escalope de Ris de Veau aux Girolles 20.00
Pojarsky au Vieux Bordeaux 18.50
Rognons de Veau au Champagne 19.00
Carré d'Agneau aux Primeurs 23.00
Poularde Châtelaine 18.50
Canard aux Pommes et Poivre Vert 22.50
Pigeonneau en Cocotte au Sauterne 22.00
Coeur de Filet en Chemise au Poivre Vert .. 22.50
Steak au Poivre Clermont 22.50
Tournedos Forestière 23.00

DESSERTS:

Tarte aux Fruits; Gâteau du Jour; Salade de Fruits Frais; Oeufs à la Neige; Mousse au Chocolat; Sorbet au Cassis; Glaces; Sabayon aux Fruits de Saison (3.00); Biscuit Glacé (3.00); Soufflés tous Parfums (for two: 6.00); Fromages.

(An a la carte Luncheon menu is also offered with prices ranging from 6.25 to 13.25.)

PINOT CHARDONNAY: *Probably the best white table wine made in the U.S. today, Pinot Chardonnay is produced primarily in the California North Coast Counties. The name is derived from the grape that produces the best white Burgundies and champagnes of France.*

POMEROL: *One of the most attractive red Bordeaux, from a single township of the same name 25 miles east of Bordeaux. Recognized as the gentlest yet richest of Bordeaux reds, Pomerol matures quickly (typically in 5 years, versus the 8 to 10 of a Médoc) and possesses a lustrous, red color, a velvety texture and great depth of flavor.*

GORGONZOLA: *Italy's great veined cheese, Gorgonzola originated in a village of that name not far from Milan. It has a flavor somewhat akin to that of Roquefort but is creamier in texture. It is, also, not as salty as the king of French bleu cheeses.*

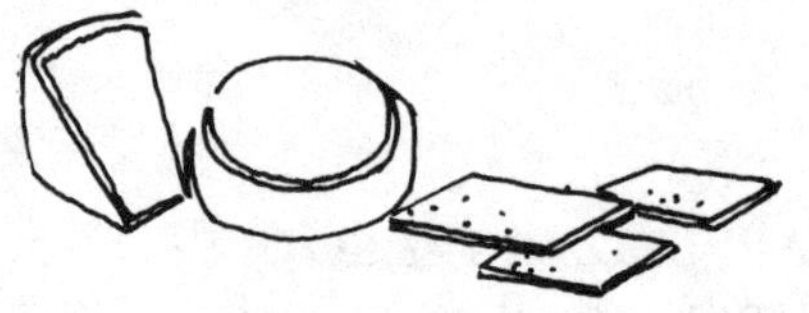

We'd like to make Manhattan Menus even more useful to you, and would welcome hearing any comments or suggestions you may have. Write to: Manhattan Menus, P.O. Box 5217, FDR Station, New York, N.Y. 10022.

THE MAGIC PAN

Addresses: 149 East 57th Street; 1409 Avenue of the Americas (between West 57th and 58th Streets)
Telephones: 371-3266 (149 East 57th); 765-5080 (1409 Avenue of the Americas)
Credit Cards: AE; V; MC; DC
Reservations: Not accepted
Hours: 11:30 AM to 12:00 Midnight, Monday thru Friday
11:30 AM to 10:00 PM, Saturday and Sunday
Days Closed: Some major holidays
Liquor: Full bar service
Recommended or Listed in: New York Magazine; Gourmet; New York Times; New Yorker; Playbill; Cue; Where; Stagebill; Promenade
Seating Capacity: 150-225
Cuisine: French and Hungarian Creperie
Specialties of the House: French and Hungarian Crêpes and Palacsintas; Various Seafood Crêpes; Dessert Crêpes; Crêpes Beignets
Dress: Casual
Party Facilities: Private rooms available on request; capacity: 25-100

This unique crêperie originated in San Francisco and now has locations in New York City and elsewhere in the Metropolitan area. The diner may enjoy either elegant and charming French country dining rooms or the garden room with trees and fresh greenery. The Magic Pan's unusual crêpe-making process can be viewed from most tables. Waitresses are garbed in native costumes in these informal and charming settings.

MENU
(a la carte)

(The following is a representative selection from The Magic Pan's Luncheon, Dinner and Brunch Menus.)

CRÊPE & SALAD LUNCHEONS:

Shrimp Gourmet Crêpe and Salad 4.25
(Tender Louisiana shrimp with a delicate béchamel sauce and a dash of sherry. Served with a mixed green salad.)

Crêpe Ratatouille and Salad 3.30
(A medley of vegetables simmered together and folded in a crêpe. Tomatoes, zucchini, bell pepper, onion and eggplant, topped with melted Gruyère cheese. Served with a mixed green salad.)

Crêpe St. Jacques and Salad 4.50
(Magic Pan's special version of a Coquille St. Jacques; scallops, shrimp and fresh mushrooms in a sherry sauce with Gruyère cheese. Served with a fresh spinach salad.)

CRÊPE DINNERS:

Creamed Chicken, Spinach Soufflé & Salad . . 5.75
(Three of our all-time favorites, served as a complete dinner. First, our orange almond salad bowl. Then the Chicken Élégante Crêpe: tender pieces of chicken in a cream sauce. Served with our famous Spinach Soufflé Crêpe.)

Maritime Crêpe Dinner 6.50
(From the shores of the Canadian provinces: Maritime Crêpe with tender Canadian scallops and tiny shrimp in a smooth cream cheese sauce with bacon bits. Served with a Spinach Soufflé Crêpe and an orange almond salad.)

French Bistro Dinner 6.25
(A very European dinner you might order in a sidewalk café. Start with a mixed green salad, then a Beef Bourguignon Crêpe: tender chunks of beef in red wine sauce. Served with a Crêpe Ratatouille.)

continued on next page

The Magic Pan

BRUNCH CRÊPES: *(Served on Saturday and Sunday)*

Crêpe Benedict 4.40
(Classic combination of Canadian bacon and two poached eggs, served in a crêpe with freshly made hollandaise sauce. Orange almond salad: Romaine lettuce, mandarin oranges, toasted almonds and sweet/sour dressing.)

Maple Butter Crêpes and Bacon 3.30
(Folded hot crêpes, fresh from the Magic Pans, covered with melted butter and maple-flavored syrup. Served with crisp bacon slices and your choice of fruit juice.)

Ham and Apple Crêpes 3.30
(Magic Pan's famous Crispy Ham Palacsintas (the Hungarian crêpe). Served with our apple sizzle: chunky spiced apples in a crêpe topped with toasted pecans and cinnamon sugar.)

(A variety of soups, salads and dessert crêpes is also available at Luncheon and Dinner.)

A Special Supplement to Manhattan Menus

Fish & Shellfish Are Delivered Fresh Each Day

We sell our coffee, all Colombian, in one-pound bags. Ask the headwaiter.

Our Specialties:
Shell-roasted clams
Butcher cuts, charcoal broiled
Fulton Market seafood stew
Vegetables steamed to order
Charlotte Russe cake

APPETIZERS
CLAMS

		Doz	½ Doz
Iced: w. dill mayonnaise & red sauce			
	Littlenecks	5.75	3.25
	Topnecks	5.75	3.25
	Cherrystones	5.75	3.25
Hot:	Stuffed & baked	5.95	3.35
	Shell-roasted	5.95	3.35
	Casino	5.95	3.35
	Any combination	5.95	3.35

OYSTERS

We serve only Cotuits

Iced: w. mignonette sauce & fresh horseradish		5.95	3.35
Baked:	w. saffron & tomato	5.95	3.55
	Devilled	5.95	3.55
	Thermidor	5.95	3.55
	Any combination	5.95	3.55

OTHER FIRST COURSES

Cold:	Pickled herring steaks in cream	3.25
	Large shrimp & chinese radish	4.50
	Meatmarket paté w. brandied mushrooms	3.25
Hot:	Pate of spinach in gnocchi	3.25
	Fettucini in cream w. peas & broccoli (for two)	6.95
	Chicken soup w. soup greens & dill	2.25

BUTCHER CUTS

Grilled over charcoal

20-oz Sirloin, New York Cut	16.95
3-lb Kansas City Strip, for two	26.95
12-oz Rump Steak	12.50
Leg of Lamb, butterflied & charcoal broiled	11.95
Calf's Liver Steak, grilled or sauteed	10.75
Charred Ground Round, rosemary	8.25
2 Double Rib Lamb Chops	15.95
Sirloin Steak, skillet grilled on coarse salt/smothered mushrooms	14.50

Sauces & Garnishes:
Bearnaise sauce
Devil Sauce
Bordelaise sauce
Smothered onions

MARKET

Prepared from seasonal pl
established first-class purveyor

JOS. KENNEY & CO.
Purveyors of fine meats & meat products
BRAISED SHORT RIBS w. CARROTS & KNOB CELERY 9.95

DeBRAGGA and SPITLER
Meats, poultry, provisions

BARRY PACKING CO.
Meats & provisions
VEAL SCALLOPS w. mushrooms & cream 9.75

M.H. GREENEBAUM INC.
Importers, exporters, purveyors, packers

H&H PURVEYORS
Prime meats, poultry
Crisp Duck w. brown Tarragon sauce 11.50

H.N. PITCHAL INC.
Cured and pickled meats

DROHAN CO. INC.
Food specialists, poultry, game

Free parking is avail

SPECIALS

entifuls that are supplied by
s in the city's wholesale markets.

WINANT & CO.
Fine quality fish

HYGRADE FISH PRODUCTS
Fresh & Portioned

Poached Red Snapper w. fresh tomato Sauce 11.50

CALEB-HALEY & CO.
Serving the seafood industry since 1859

B. EISNER
Fresh fruit & produce

WATERMAN LEDER CORP
Purveyors of fruits and vegetables

BROCKFLOWER w. Brown Butter 2.25

HOLLAENDER, GOULD & MURRAY CO.
Purveyor of fine foods

Braised FENNEL glazed w. cheese 2.25

able for dinner guests.

Reservations accepted for evening parties and special events.

We are not responsible for articles lost or exchanged on the premises, nor for deals and bargains struck during meal periods.

CLAM HOUSE COOKING

All fish can be pan-broiled or grilled over charcoal

Steamed Whole Lobster & Shellfish Stew, for two	29.50
Tilefish done two ways:	
charcoal broiled or	9.95
baked on fennel	10.50
Filet of Sole, broiled or sauteed	9.95
Shrimp & Oysters, pan-fried w. smoked sausage & tomatoes	11.75

FRESH VEGETABLES

Potatoes: fried in their skins	1.50
baked crisp	1.50
hashed brown	1.50
Platter of Winter Vegetables, steamed & sauteed	7.45
Fried onion crisps, malt vinegar	1.60
Green beans, hot vinaigrette	1.75

COLD DISHES

Tomatoes & onions, cracked pepper dressing	1.95
Mixed green salad	1.95
w. roquefort-cognac dressing	2.75
Broccoli & garlic-roast pepper	2.75
Lobster Salad, shellfish-mayonnaise	11.25

DESSERTS

Our cakes & pastries are baked here every day.

Double chocolate cake	2.50
Hot fresh pineapple & vanilla ice cream	2.95
Frozen Chocolate Souffle, burnt-almond sauce	2.95
Apple-almond tart	2.50
Bread pudding, warm custard sauce	2.00
Basset's vanilla ice cream, maple syrup	2.25

BEVERAGES

We pour heavy cream with our coffee.

Pot of tea, Earl Grey's or Darjeeling	1.00
Coffee, all Colombian	1.00
Espresso	1.25
Cappucino	1.50
Iced tea	1.00

Our Matches & Ash Trays Are Put Up In Sets For Sale

MARKET BAR AND DINING ROOMS

Address:	On the Concourse, World Trade Center Enter via 5 W.T.C. on Vesey Street (between West Broadway & Church Street)
Telephone:	938-1155
Credit Cards:	AE; DC; CB; MC; V; BA
Reservations:	Recommended
Hours:	Dining Rooms: Lunch from 11:30 AM to 3:00 PM, Monday thru Friday; Dinner beginning at 5:00 PM and still seating at 10:30 PM, Monday thru Saturday; Bar Room & Cafe: 11:30 AM to 1:00 AM, Monday thru Saturday
Parking:	Free parking inside building for dinner guests (West Street parking entrance)
Days Closed:	Sunday
Liquor:	Full bar service
Recommended or Listed in:	New York Times; Gourmet; Cue; SoHo News
Seating Capacity:	Dining Rooms: 200; Bar Room & Cafe: 250
Cuisine:	American Market Cooking
Specialties of the House:	Steamed Whole Lobster & Shellfish Stew; Butcher Cuts Grilled over Charcoal; Shell-Roasted Clams; Seasonal Vegetable Platter; Fettucini in Cream with Vegetables; Potatoes Fried in their Skins; Frozen Chocolate Souffle, Burnt Almond Sauce
Dress:	Jackets required in the Dining Rooms

The Market Bar and Dining Rooms is built upon the site and in the spirit of those great restaurants that flourished in downtown Manhattan during the delectable days of the old Washington Market. It is a restaurant where the top of each day's market determines each day's menu. Where the menu is filled with the dishes you love, the fine full flavor of food at its peak enhanced by careful, straightforward preparation. Everything about the look bespeaks a restaurant that cares about the pleasures good food can bestow, from the big plates and glasses to the starched, pressed, button-holed napkins. There is no mistaking The Market Bar and Dining Rooms' intentions toward you.

Photograph by Burt Glinn

MARY'S

Address:	**42 Bedford Street**
Location:	**Bedford Street, one block east of Seventh Avenue South**
Telephone:	**741-3387**
Credit Cards:	**AE; DC; CB; MC**
Reservations:	**Recommended**
Hours:	**Lunch from 12 Noon to 2:00 PM; Dinner until 12 Midnight Sunday thru Thursday, and until 1:00 AM on Friday and Saturday**
Days Closed:	**None**
Liquor:	**Full Bar Service**
Recommended or listed in:	**New York Times; Gourmet; Cue; After Dark; Village Voice; Women's Wear Daily; New York Magazine; Show Business; Genesis; Madison Avenue; Host; Gentlemen's Quarterly; Esquire**
Maitre d':	**Giorgio Migliaccio**
Seating Capacity:	**65**
Cuisine:	**Italian—Abruzzi Style**
Specialties of the House:	**Chicken Imperiale; Veal Ducale; Beef Barbaresca**

Mary's is in what was once a comfortable home, now converted into a cozy dining place with two dining rooms, one upstairs and one down. Its direct, simple approach is refreshing in this day of carefully preconceived "concept" restaurants. The menu, which features very good food at reasonable prices, changes slightly from time to time and the wine cellar is stocked with excellent Italian vintages. Special orders are often available upon request.

MENU
(a la carte)

APPETIZERS:
Mixed Green Salad (1.75); Mussels Oreganate (3.00); Hot Antipasto (3.95); Clams Cassino (3.95); Stuffed Mushrooms (3.95).

PASTA:

Cannelloni 4.75
Spaghetti Carbonara 4.75
Spaghetti Matriciana 4.95
Spaghetti Pink Clam Sauce 4.95
Spaghetti Squid Sauce 5.50
Spaghetti Shrimps Sauce 6.25

ENTREES:

Eggplant Imperiale 6.25
Wild Pork 6.25
Chicken Maria 6.25
Chicken Tre Mari 6.25
Chicken Imperiale 6.25
Chicken Castellana 6.75
Chicken Parmigiana 6.25
Chicken Scarpariello 6.25
Chicken Cacciatore 6.75
Veal Imperiale 7.25
Veal Bolognese 7.25
Veal Casalinga 7.25
Veal Ducale 7.75
Veal Parmigiana 7.25
Veal Milanese 7.25
Veal Piccata 7.25
Veal Marsala and Mushrooms 7.75
Granadina 8.50
Contadina 8.50
Beef Uccelletti 8.50
Beef Barbaresca 8.50
Beef Abruzzese 10.00
Mussels Posillipo 6.25
Mussels Marechiaro 6.25
Shrimps Maria 7.25
Shrimps Marinara 7.25
Fish Pescatore 7.25
Broil Bass 7.50
Bass al Sughetto 7.50

DESSERTS:
Zabalione (2.00); Cannoli (1.25); Rum Cake (1.25).

MAXWELL'S PLUM

Location: First Avenue at 64th Street
Telephone: 628-2100
Credit Cards: All major credit cards accepted
Hours: 12:00 Noon to 2:00 AM, daily
Days Closed: None
Liquor: Full bar service
Seating Capacity: 240
Cuisine: American and Continental

Maxwell's Plum is a spectacular and elaborately decorated restaurant, a Warner LeRoy creation, with no peer except perhaps LeRoy's Tavern on the Green. The design surprises and glories that abound in this restaurant range from genuine antiques and artifacts from the last century to an illuminated Tiffany stained glass ceiling. Maxwell's Plum is an immensely popular and busy place, and the menu as well as the decor is the attraction. For quality of cuisine, Maxwell's Plum rates with the best and is one of the few four-star dining experiences in town.

DINNER MENU

(The Back Room)
(a la carte)

APPETIZERS:
Céleri Remoulade with Spiced Beets, Tomato and Onion (2.55); Tomato Vinaigrette (1.55); Avocado and Tomato Vinaigrette or à la Russe (2.45); Artichoke with Hot Butter or Hollandaise (2.55); Asparagus in Season with Hot Butter or Hollandaise (3.25); Pâté Maison with Asparagus (3.65); Pâté Maison (2.45); Cold Terrine of Sole with Scallops and Herbed Tomato Sauce (2.45); Melon (2.45); Melon with Prosciutto (3.45); Garlic Sausage with Hot Potato Salad (2.65); Scallop Coquille Paprikas (3.95); Mussels Poulette (3.95); Escargots Bourguignonne (3.95); Baby Shrimp Suprême (4.95); Shrimp and Avocado Guacomole with Tostados (4.95); Maryland Crabmeat Cocktail (5.85); Pacific Dungeness Crab with Mustard Mayonnaise (9.50); Lobster, Avocado and Pineapple à la Russe (8.45); Scottish Smoked Salmon (6.85); Iranian Golden Caviar (2 oz) with Blinis (30.50); Little Neck Clams (2.75); Cherrystone Clams (2.75); Blue Point Oysters (3.25).

SOUPS:
Onion Soup Gratinée (2.45); Fish Soup with Rouille and Garlic Croutons (2.45); Black Bean Soup (2.25); Gazpacho Andaluz (1.95); Vichyssoise (1.95).

ENTREES:
Roast Duckling Normande 9.65
Roast Wild Boar with Gingered Apples and Lingonberries 10.25
Noisettes of Venison au Poivre Vert with Cherries and Chestnut Purée 14.85
Shish Kebab with Rice Istanbul 8.95
Rack of Lamb Persillé (for two) with Fresh Vegetables 27.50
Veal Piccata Sautéed with Lemon Butter 8.85
Veal Parmigiana 7.85
Lime Grilled Chicken with Chinese Spices 7.45
Chicken Curry with Assorted Sambals 7.85
Chicken Mornay in Sherry with Wild Rice 7.95
Chicken Mornay in Deep Fried Bread Crust Topped with Poached Egg 7.25
Sweetbreads Braised with Sherry Vinegar 7.45
Calf's Liver with Sage Butter and Bacon 8.25
German Sausages with Sautéed Onions and Chestnut Purée 6.85
Roasted Marinated Spareribs in Honey, Pineapple and Spiced Barbecue Sauce 6.45
Spaghetti: Bolognese, a Pesto, Clam Sauce 6.45
Steak Tartare 6.95
Sauerbraten with Spaetzle and Pickled Red Cabbage 7.65

Maxwell's Plum

Dutch Apple Pancake 5.65
(Apples Sautéed in Butter, Cinnamon and Sugar with Apricot Preserves and Sour Cream)
Roast Rib of Beef with Yorkshire Pudding and Roast Potatoes 13.50
Russian Beef Stroganoff with Noodles 9.65
Steak au Poivre, Poivrade or à la Crème 13.85
Sirloin Steak 13.85
Filet Mignon Béarnaise 13.85
Chateaubriand with Fresh Vegetables 26.00
Red Snapper Grillé Dijonnaise 12.50
Sole Maxwell 8.85
Filet of Sole Amandine with Green and White Noodles 7.85
English Dover Sole Amandine, Fines Herbes, Meunière, Portuguese 12.95
Poached Salmon with Baby Shrimp, Braised Cucumber and Beurre Blanc 10.25
Shrimp Curry 7.95
Scallops Paprikas......................... 7.65
Sautéed Bay Scallops 7.65
Coquille St. Jacques with Julienne of Vegetables and Beurre Blanc 7.75
Clams and Spinach au Gratin 5.85
Sautéed Flounder Meunière, with Lemon and Capers 6.85
Broiled Lobster.......................... 21.00

SALADS:
Spinach, Bacon and Mushroom (2.55); Caesar (2.55); Endive and Beet (2.55); Limestone and Stilton Cheese (2.95); Avocado, Tomato, Bacon and Roquefort (2.95); Watercress and Tomato (1.95); Tossed (1.70); Tomato (1.75); Chef (5.85).

VEGETABLES:
French Fried Onion Rings (1.75); Asparagus in Season (2.65); Broccoli (1.85); String Beans (1.65); Glazed Carrots (1.45); Artichoke (1.95); Tomato Provençale (1.45); Creamed Spinach (1.75); Sautéed Mushrooms (1.75); Sautéed Onions (1.75); Wild Rice (1.50); Mélange of Sautéed Vegetables (2.45).

POTATOES AND CHILI:
Potatoes Gratinée Dauphinoise (1.65); Baked Potato with Sour Cream, Chives, Bacon (1.65); Baked Potato (1.45); French Fried Potatoes (1.45); Hash Browns (1.65); Maxwell's Mexican Chili with Sour Cream and Diced Onions (1.95).

DESSERTS:
Apple Tarte Tatin with Schlag (2.55); Chocolate Cake (2.55); Chocolate Cake with Ice Cream (3.25); Pecan Pie with Schlag (2.55); Cheesecake (2.45); Cheesecake with Bananas or Strawberries (2.65); Hazelnut Cheesecake with Strawberries (2.65); Banana Fritters with Cinnamon Sauce (1.95); Banana Fritters with Praline Ice Cream and Schlag (2.65); Praline and Strawberry Ice Cream Cake with Chocolate Sauce (2.45); Chocolate Soufflé with Whipped Cream and Chocolate Sauce (3.25); Baked Alaska (for two) (4.75); Maxwell's Fresh Fruit Sorbets (1.85); Creme Caramel (1.65); Chocolate Mousse (1.65); Banana Split (2.85); Fresh Strawberries with Schlag or Sour Cream and Brown Sugar (2.45); Ice Cream: Vanilla, Chocolate, Strawberry, Pralines 'n Cream, Mocha Almond Fudge (1.85); Ice Cream with Chocolate or Butterscotch Sauce (2.45); Seasonal Variety of Cheeses (2.55); Cheese with Fruit Basket (2.95).

(Maxwell's Plum has three different menus: the more elaborate Back Room, the Cafe Menu and a Luncheon Menu. Most items on the Back Room dinner menu are also offered at lunch at lower prices. A wide selection of sandwiches and egg dishes are also offered at lunch.)

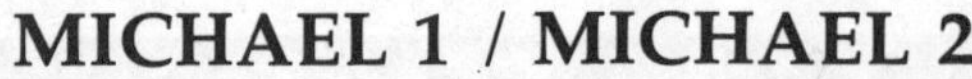

MICHAEL 1 / MICHAEL 2

Addresses: Michael 1, 25 Trinity Place (at Rector Street); Michael 2, 10 Hanover Square (between Water and Pearl Streets)
Telephone: Michael 1 - 344-7270; Michael 2 - 943-6767
Credit Cards: All major credit cards accepted
Reservations: Required
Hours: 11:30 AM to 10:00 PM, Monday thru Friday
Days Closed: Saturday and Sunday
Liquor: Full bar service
Seating Capacity: 225
Cuisine: International
Specialties of the House: Danish Lobster Tails; Veal Francaise; Seafood Mediterranee, Steaks
Dress: Jackets required
Party Facilities: 3 private rooms; capacity: 25-150

Michael 1 and 2 bring sophisticated dining comfort and a carefully selected menu to the heart of the financial district. The lighting is the design catalyst in these two award-winning restaurants by Forbes-Ergas and the mood evoked is subtly opulent. Windowed alcoves and wing-backed chairs are touches that add to the dining enjoyment of the Wall Street clientele. You will probably meet Michael himself, who takes a personal interest in his customers and whose cordial welcome is very much in keeping with the graceful atmosphere of his two restaurants.

DINNER MENU

(a la carte)

(The host of the lunch or dinner party is provided with a menu which includes prices.)

APPETIZERS & SOUPS:
Marinated Beef or Shrimp on Skewer; Middleneck Clams on the Half Shell; Fresh Clams Casino or Oreganato; Jumbo Shrimp Cocktail; Melon with Prosciutto; Escargots de Bourgogne; Danish Lobster Tails; Fresh Lump Crabmeat Cocktail; Onion Soup; Black Bean Soup (in season).

ENTREES:
Prime Sirloin Steak
Junior Sirloin Steak
T-Bone Steak
Deluxe Club Steak
Eye of Filet with Mushroom Caps
Sliced Steak au Jus
Chopped Sirloin of Beef
Roast Prime Ribs of Beef
Shish Kebab with Seasoned Rice
Spring Rib Lamb Chops
New Jersey Pork Chops
Barbequed Spare Ribs
Chateaubriand for Two
Michael's Specialty of the Day
Eggs Benedict Michael
Seafood Mediterranee
Filet of Sole Almondine
Shrimp Scampi with Seasoned Rice
Fresh Brook Trout with Drawn Butter
Danish Lobster Tails with Seasoned Rice
Broiled Maine Lobster with Lemon Butter
Baked Stuffed Lobster
Dover Sole Sautée Meuniere
Crabmeat Baltimore
Veal Francaise

SALADS & VEGETABLES:
Fresh Cut French Fried Potatoes; Stuffed Idaho Potatoe de Fernando; Green Salad with Michael's Dressing; Beefsteak Tomatoes with Bermuda Onions; French Fried Onion Rings; Broiled Bermuda Onions.

DESSERTS:
Strawberry Cream Cheese Cake; Fresh Fruit in Season; Pastry Selections.

NAT SIMON'S PENGUIN

Address: 21 West 9th Street
Location: Ninth Street between Fifth and Sixth Avenues
Telephone: 777-2670
Credit Cards: DC; AE; CB; MC
Reservations: Recommended
Hours: 5:00 PM to 12:00 Midnight, Monday thru Friday; 5:00 PM to 1:00 AM on Saturday; 5:00 PM to 11:00PM on Sunday
Days Closed: None
Liquor: Full bar service
Seating Capacity: 110
Cuisine: American
Specialties of the House: Prime Ribs; Steaks; Seafood
Dress: No requirement
Entertainment: Piano music, Tuesday thru Saturday
Party Facilities: 3 Private rooms; capacity: 36 each
Parking: 3-hour free parking at 20 East Ninth Street

For 30 years, Nat Simon's Penguin has been serving quality steaks, seafood and prime ribs to a large and loyal following. Three intimate dining rooms, subdued lighting, rich wall hangings and tasteful art combine to create a romantic atmosphere. Book-lined shelves surround a wood-burning fireplace; if you get the feeling that you are dining graciously in a private home, the penguin pictures throughout the restaurant will remind you that you're enjoying the excellent cuisine at Nat Simon's Penguin.

DINNER MENU

(a la carte)

APPETIZERS & SOUPS:
Chopped Pure Chicken Livers, Garni (1.95); Marinated Herring in Cream Sauce (1.95); Chilled Sacramento Tomato Juice (.95); Fresh Fruit Cocktail (1.25); Cherrystone Clam Cocktail (2.50); Jumbo Shrimp Cocktail (4.50); Grapefruit or Melon (in season) (1.50); Shrimp Scampi (4.75); Barbecued Baby Spare Ribs (4.50); Cold Vichysoisse (1.50); French Onion Soup (1.95); Chicken Consomme with Noodles (1.25).

ENTREES:
Roast Prime Ribs of Beef 10.95
Roast Prime Ribs of Beef (for more moderate appetites) 8.50
Prime Sirloin Steak — Extra Thick 12.95
Prime Sirloin Steak (for more moderate appetites) 10.95
Prime Filet Mignon 12.95
Prime Sirloin Steak for Two 21.00
Prime Sliced Sirloin Steak 6.95
Double Bone Spring Lamb Chops 12.50
Chopped Sirloin Steak 6.25
Calf's Liver Steak with Bacon 7.95
Half Broiled Spring Chicken 6.50
Jumbo Fisherman's Platter 11.95
Southern Fried Half Spring Chicken 6.50
Yankee Pot Roast with Crisp Potato Pancakes 6.25
Roast Long Island Duckling 7.95
Fresh Fish du Jour 7.50
Fresh Fish du Jour (for more moderate appetites) 6.50
Fresh Filet of Red Snapper 9.95
French Fried Jumbo Shrimp 8.25
French Fried Jumbo Shrimp (for more moderate appetites) 6.75
Shrimp Scampi on Rice 8.75
Shrimp Scampi on Rice (for more moderate appetites) 7.25
Broiled South African Lobster Tails 14.95
Broiled South African Lobster Tails (for more moderate appetites) 11.95
Broiled Maine Lobster .... (...)

(Entrees are served with potatoes and tossed green salad.)

DESSERTS:
Fresh Strawberries and Cream (2.50); Hot Apple Pie (1.50); Penguin's Special Cheesecake (1.95); Peach Melba (1.50); Parfait (1.50); Ricciardi's Ice Cream (1.25); Chocolate Mousse Chantilly (3.50); Cappucino Mousse Chantilly (3.50); Biscuit Tortoni (.95); Melon (in season) (1.50).

NICOLA'S

Address: 146 East 84th Street
Location: 84th Street and Lexington Avenue
Telephone: 249-9850
Credit Cards: Not accepted
Reservations: Recommended for parties of 3 or more
Hours: 6:00 PM to 12:30 AM
Days Closed: Saturdays during July and August
Liquor: Full bar service
Seating Capacity: 117
Cuisine: Italian
Specialties of the House: Tortellini alla Panna or Bolognese; Broiled Scampi Chef's Style; Veal Scaloppine Emiliana; Veal Scaloppine Pizzaiola; Duckling Bigarade; Sauteed Lobster Pescatore; Fettucine Alfredo

This very chic Italian restaurant is especially popular with artists and writers, actors and actresses. Framed photographs of Nicola's famous patrons, past and present, line the dark wood paneled walls and are reflected in the mirrors that add spaciousness and sparkle to the decor. Owner Nicola is usually available to greet her dinner guests and her hospitality contributes to the warm atmosphere. The menu is varied, well-prepared and impeccably served.

DINNER MENU

(Dinner with wine costs approximately 15.00 per person.)

APPETIZERS & SOUPS:
Shrimp Cocktail; Blue Points; Clams on the Half Shell; Clams Casino or Oreganata; Squid Salad; Mussels Mariniere; Mussels a la Dijonnaise; Marinated Filet of Herring; Fresh Roasted Pepper with Anchovies; Melon and Prosciutto; Genova Salami; Stuffed Mushrooms; Stuffed Avocado; Avocado Vinaigrette; Pate Maison; Escargots; Onion Soup; Stracciatella.

ENTREES:
Spaghetti/Linguine
(Tomato Sauce, Bolognese, Matriciana, Meatballs, Carbonara, Clam Sauce – White or Red, Fruitti di Mare or al Pesto)
Cannelloni
Manicotti
Filet of Sole Broiled or Meuniere
Scallops Poulette
Shrimp Marinara
Broiled Lobster Tail
Veal Scaloppine Piccata
Veal Scaloppine Fresh Mushrooms
Saltimbocca
Veal Parmigiana
Tripes
Sweetbreads
Calves Liver, Any Style
Chicken al Limone
Sirloin Steak
Filet Mignon
Lamb Chops
Chop Steak
Pepper Steak
Steak Tartare
Paillarde of Beef or Veal
Veal Chop, Broiled or Sauteed
Wienerschnitzel
Pork Chops

(A variety of vegetables, potatoes and salads is also available.)

DESSERTS:
Cheeses; Desserts of the House.

THE OAK ROOM

Address:	The Plaza Hotel
Location:	Fifth Avenue at 59th Street
Telephone:	PL 9-3000
Credit Cards:	AE; MC; V; DC; CB; United Airlines; Western International Hotels
Reservations:	Required
Hour:	Lunch from 12:00 Noon to 3:00 PM, Monday thru Friday; Dinner from 6:00 PM to 10:00 PM, Monday thru Friday; from 6:00 PM to 11:00 PM, Saturday and Sunday
Days Closed:	None
Liquor:	Full bar service
Maitre d':	Mr. Louis Zalesjak
Seating Capacity:	95
Cuisine:	Gourmet Continental
Specialties of the House:	Scampi Barcelona; Pheasant Alsacienne; Steak Tartare
Dress:	Jacket and tie recommended

Dining in the Oak Room at The Plaza Hotel is an experience not to be missed by anyone who appreciates gourmet cuisine in old-world surroundings. It's a wood-paneled club house that might have been transplanted straight from the Union League and a grand place for expense account entertaining. The vaulted arches and carved dark oak interior are reminiscent of a more gracious era, fortunately preserved for our contemporary enjoyment in this world-renowned restaurant.

The Oak Room at The Plaza

continued on next page

DINNER MENU

(a la carte)

APPETIZERS:
Iced Blue Point or Cape Cod Oysters (4.50); A Service of Nova Scotia Salmon (5.75); A Tureen of Country Pâté (3.50); Platter of Cherrystone or Little Neck Clams (4.25); Jumbo Shrimps, Princess Presented on Tiger Shell (4.95); Chilled Melon and Prosciutto Ham (4.75); The Plaza Marinated Herring (3.95); Escargot in Pot Provencale — Sautéed with Shallots, Tomatoes, White Wine and Herbs (4.95); King Crab Remick — A Specialty of the Plaza (4.50).

SOUPS:
Consommé Bristol (2.50); Chicken Broth with Rice (2.50); Potage St. Germain (2.50); Bisque of Lobster Cardinal (3.00); Vichyssoise (2.50); Gazpacho Andalouse (2.50).

ENTREES:

Scampi Barcelona 13.95
(Sautéed in Butter with a touch of Garlic and Sherry. Served with Rice)

Paillard of Fresh Salmon 11.95
(Sauce Béarnaise — An Oak Room Specialty)

Médaillons of Tender Beef 15.95
(Prepared with Brandy Sauce Topped with Foie Gras)

Steak Tartare 12.95

Roast Ring-Necked Pheasant, Alsacienne (For Two) 29.75

New York Cut Sirloin Steak, Florentine 15.50

Filet Mignon crowned with Fresh Mushrooms 16.50

Double French Lamb Chops, Cressionnière . 15.25

Double Entrecôte, Bouquetière (For Two) ... 24.95

Roast Rib of Beef au Jus 15.95

Breast of Capon, Eugenie 10.95

Veal Scaloppine alla Trevy 13.75

Our Dinner Gueridon 16.75
(The Chef's Special Entrée of the Evening or Broiled Filet of Boston Sole; Entrée includes Choice of Appetizer or Soup, Crisp Green Salad, Selection from the Pastry Cart and Pot of Coffee or Tea.)

SALADS:
Hearts of Palm Salad (3.50); Caesar Salad (3.95); Mimosa Salad (2.75).

DESSERTS:
Baked Alaska (For Two) (8.50); Crêpe Suzette (For Two) (9.00); Coupe aux Marrons (2.75); Pear Hélène (2.75); Fruit Sherbet (2.75); Cherries Jubilee (For Two) (8.00); French Ice Cream (2.75); Continental Cheese Tray (4.50); Selections from the Pastry Cart (2.75).

POMMARD: *The most popular of the red Burgundies, grown between the more distinguished communes of Volnay and Beaune. The best Pommards carry, in addition to the name Pommard, the name of their vineyard, and are gracious, well-balanced, fruity and not too deep in color.*

GOUDA: *The town of Gouda, where this cheese originated, is in the south of Holland. The cheese made there resembles Edam, being a bland, fairly firm table cheese with a smooth consistency. Goudas are ball shaped but are not waxed in red as are Edams. With age, Gouda develops a stronger flavor.*

GRUYÈRE: *Gruyère, made on both the Swiss and the French sides of the Jura mountains, closely resembles that other great "Swiss" cheese, Emmenthal. Both are hard cheeses with a sweet, nutty flavor. Gruyère, however, is made in smaller wheels and has smaller "eyes".*

Nominate your favorite restaurants for inclusion in Manhattan Menus. Send cards or letters to: Manhattan Menus, P.O. Box 5217, FDR Station, New York, N.Y. 10022.

OENOPHILIA

Address:	**473 Columbus Avenue**
Location:	**83rd Street, 2 blocks from Museum of Natural History**
Telephone:	**580-8127**
Credit Cards:	**AE; DC; MC; BA; Telecredit**
Reservations:	**Recommended**
Hours:	**Monday to Thursday, 6pm-11pm; Friday & Saturday to 11:30pm; Sunday, 5-10pm; Brunch Saturday & Sunday 12pm-3:30pm.**
Days Closed:	**None**
Recommended or Listed in:	**New York Times, Village Voice, New York Magazine, After Dark**
Liquor:	**Bring Your Own**
Seating Capacity:	**60**
Cuisine:	**Continental Eatery**
Specialities:	**Country Appled Quails; Baby Pheasant in Fruit Sauce; Rabbit St. Julien, Fettuccine Oenophilia; Oysters Casino**
Party Facilities:	**Private Room; Capacity 20**

Oenophiles with a passion for good food will be delighted by a visit to Oenophilia. Located on New York's new upper west side, the restaurant has become known city-wide for its creative menu, elegantly casual decor, and moderate prices. Palm and ficus trees create a lush interior in which to enjoy Oenophilia's gallery art and live music at weekend brunches. The restaurant also features an outdoor garden for spring and summer dining.

BRUNCH MENU

(a la carte)

Eggs Girondine 4.95
Eggs Georgette 4.95
Eggs Mirabou 4.95
French Toast Oenophilia 3.95
Lasagne Bolognese 4.95

(All Brunch Entrees served with complementary large glass of freshly squeezed orange juice).

DINNER MENU

(a la carte)

APPETIZERS

Country Pate or Chicken Liver Pate (2.25); Fresh Smoked Eel (2.95); Oysters Casino (3.50); Escargot (3.50); Fettuccini Oenophilia (2.95); Coquille (3.25); Fresh Smoked Sturgeon, Salmon or Brook Trout; Artichoke Bearnaise (in season) (2.50); Stuffed Avocado Neptune (3.50); Cold Split Devilled Lobster for Two (8.95); Xerxes (cold cucumber-yogurt-dill soup) (1.75); Two Hot Soups Daily (1.75).

ENTREES

Baby Pheasant in Fruit Sauce 8.95
Country Appled Quails with Nut Stuffing ... 9.75
Fettuccini Oenophilia 4.95
Filet Mignon Bearnaise 9.75
Rabbit St. Julien 8.95
Veal Scalloppini (Allegro, Costelli Romani, or Marengo 7.50
Fresh Whole Stuffed Boneless Brook Trout ..... *
Grey Sole Stuffed w/Fresh Crabmeat & Walnuts 8.95
Flounder Stuffed w/Shrimp, Almonds & Mushrooms 7.95
Jumbo Shrimp & Scallops Verdoux or Provencal 7.50
Striped Bass in Mustard-Dill Sauce .... *
Salmon in Lemon Sauce 8.75
Tuna Steak Provencal .... *
Florida Pompana Al Cesare 8.50

*(Fish dishes and prices vary according to what is available fresh at the market).

DESSERTS...2.00

Dark Chocolate Mousse Cake; Baked Apple Amondine with Vanilla Sauce; Old Fashioned Apple Cake with Vanilla Sauce; Vicarage Pie; French Chocolate Silk Pie; Pecan-Date Pie; Fresh Strawberries (in season) with Freshly Whipped Cream; Fresh Fruit Salad (in season) Grand Marnier.

continued on next page

Oenophilia

MARZIPAN KARTOFFEL: *This is a look-alike for a potato, made from marzipan-covered cake. The cake is rolled in cinnamon and looks remarkably like the real thing.*

MOHRENKOPF: *To make this pastry, a sponge cake layer is cut with a round cake cutter. Whipped cream is put between two of these cake rounds and the top round is dipped in melted chocolate.*

RIGO SQUARE: *This Hungarian dessert is named after a famous gypsy violinist and composer. It is made with two sponge cake layers that have had chocolate and nuts mixed into their batter. The filling is chocolate whipped cream—much like a mousse in texture—and the top is brushed with melted chocolate. A rigo square can be recognized immediately because of the wavy pattern made in its chocolate topping.*

OLD KING COLE RESTAURANT
At The St. Regis-Sheraton Hotel

Address: Fifth Avenue at 55th Street
Telephone: 753-4500
Credit Cards: All major credit cards accepted
Reservations: Recommended
Hours: 7:00 AM to 2:00 AM, Monday thru Saturday; 7:00 AM to 12:00 Midnight, Sunday; Champagne Hour from 5:30 PM to 7:00 PM; Saturday and Sunday Brunch from 12:00 Noon to 3:00 PM
Days Closed: None
Liquor: Full bar service
Seating Capacity: 170
Cuisine: Classical American
Specialties of the House: Billi-Bi; Rack of Lamb stuffed with Spinach; T-Bone Steak of Veal
Dress: Jacket and tie required
Entertainment: Live piano music from 5:30 PM to 8:00 PM; Continuous music for dancing by two bands including the Peter Duchin Orchestra (every night except Sunday)
Party Facilities: 16 private rooms; capacity: 8-400

The new Old King Cole Restaurant in the St. Regis-Sheraton continues to enchant New Yorkers with its grand 70-year-old-plus history. The newly renovated restaurant still focuses on the famous mural of Old King Cole by the American illustrator Maxfield Parrish, which was commissioned by Nicholas Biddle as a gift for his friend Colonel John Jacob Astor. Old King Cole now holds court in a lovely terraced room designed in greens, burgundys and white, and is illuminated by a massive crystal chandelier and romantic cove lighting in an art deco ceiling. Tradition is a trademark of the restaurant—Peter Duchin's Orchestra plays nightly as did his father's orchestra in the '30's, and the "Red Snapper" (or Bloody Mary) is still the popular drink it was 40 years ago when it was invented by the head bartender of the St. Regis. And new traditions are in the making—a Champagne Hour features a variety of specially priced imported champagnes to add a gracious accompaniment to a grand dining experience.

Old King Cole Restaurant at the St. Regis-Sheraton Hotel

continued on next page

continued

LUNCHEON MENU

(a la carte)

APPETIZERS & SOUPS:
Malpeque, Bluepoint, Local, Virginia Oysters (6 for 3.75) (12 for 7.00); Chipolata Sausages and Six Oysters (4.50); Cherrystones, Little Necks (6 for 3.75) (12 for 7.00); Oysters Rockefeller (4.75); Clams Casino Baked in Rock Salt (4.50); Ballotine of Lake Fish, Watercress Sauce (4.50); Four Large Shrimp on Ice (4.75); Smoked Salmon and Sturgeon (6.25); Le Pâté de Cerdagne (3.75); Celery Victor (3.00); Melon or Pear (3.00); Melon or Pear with Westphalian Ham (5.00); Beef Broth with Quenelles (2.25); Billi-Bi, Hot or Cold (3.00); Maryland Cream of Crab Soup (3.25); Vichyssoise Louis Diat (2.50).

ENTREES:
Omelette Carlton 6.50
Eggs Gratiné Castaybert 6.75
Eggs Benedict 6.75
The King's Omelette 7.25
Boston Scrod, Cape Cod 8.25
Seafood Plate Sandy Hook 8.75
Nest of Shrimp and Sole, Tartar Sauce 9.25
Grilled Filet of Sole 9.75
Paillard of Veal 10.25
French Lamb Chops 10.50
Medallion of Beef with Bourbon Sauce 11.50
T-Bone Steak of Veal 10.75
St. Regis Mixed Grill 9.50
Sirloin Steak Cliff House 10 oz 12.50
Sirloin Steak Cliff House 16 oz 14.50
Twin Hamburger and Cheeseburger 6.50
Cold Meats, Cheese and Relish Platter....... 8.75
Filet of Beef Tartar 10.50
Palace Court Shrimp Salad................. 9.50
Sliced Fruit Salad, Yogurt and Sesame Dressing, Cottage Cheese or Sherbet 7.25
Cobb's Salad, Tapenade Dressing 7.50
Chef's Salad 7.25
Salade Niçoise 6.75
Trio of Open Faced Sandwiches 7.25
Club Sandwich 6.50

(Desserts served at luncheon are similar to dinner dessert menu.)

DINNER MENU

(a la carte)

APPETIZERS & SOUPS:
Malpeque, Bluepoint, Local, Virginia Oysters (6 for 4.00) (12 for 7.25); Chipolata Sausages with Six Oysters (4.75); Cherrystone, Little Necks (6 for 4.00) (12 for 7.25); A Sampler: Beluga, Sevruga, Eggplant-Caviar Salad (26.00); Baked Potato à la Neva, topped with Caviar and Sour Cream (10.50); Caviar à la Ward McAllister, served with Smoked Salmon and Great Lakes Sturgeon (16.50); Little Pots of Snails au Chablis (4.75); Oysters Rockefeller (4.75); Clams Casino, Baked in Rock Salt (4.75); Ballotine of Lake Fish, Watercress Sauce (4.75); Celery Victor (3.25); Four Large Shrimp on Ice (5.00); Smoked Salmon and Sturgeon with Leeks (6.75); Parfait of Bay Scallops, George Lamaze (4.50); Melon or Pear with Westphalian Ham (5.25); Le Pâté de Cerdagne (4.00); Beef Broth with Quenelles (2.50); Maryland Cream of Crab (3.50); Essence of Onion with Cheese Crust, Flambé (3.50); Billi-Bi, Hot or Cold (3.00); Vichyssoise Louis Diat (3.00).

APPETIZERS OR ENTREES:
Lobster and Oyster Delmonico (Ramekin 8.50) (Casserole 14.50); Quail, Lime Broiled (Single 8.25) (A Brace, Sauce Aigre-Douce 14.50); Filet of Beef Tartare (7.50) (Buffet Platter 10.50); Palace Court Shrimp Salad (Hors d'Oeuvre 6.50) (Main Course 10.50).

ENTREES:
Red Snapper en Papillotte 10.75
Dover Sole, Meunière 14.50
Fresh Sturgeon, Sauté, Watercress Sauce ... 12.50
Poached Filet of Sole with Crisp Fried Oysters à la Gould 12.00
Escalope of Veal, Cape Cod 14.50
Chicken Sauté, Lady Astor 10.75
Baby Calf's Liver Sauté with Tomato and Eggplant 10.75
Squab Chicken stuffed with Sweetbreads ... 10.50
Mignonettes of Beef, Bourbon Sauce 13.50
Roast Prime Rib of Beef, Traditional Garnish 14.50
Three French Lamb Chops, Minted Hollandaise 12.50
The Carpetbagger Steak 16.50
Sirloin Steak, Cliff House 16.50
T-Bone Steak of Veal 12.50
Game in Season .... (...)
Rack of Lamb, stuffed with Spinach, Béarnaise Sauce, for Two 28.00
A Roasted Duckling, "Iridium," for Two ... 28.00

DESSERTS:
Fresh Stewed Fruits (2.50); A Selection from our Dessert Table (2.50); Bombe Glacée au Praline (3.00); Ice Creams and Water Ices (2.00); Individual Frozen Soufflés with Liqueurs, Fruits and Other Flavors (4.00); Frozen Yogurt, Raspberry (2.00); Timbale of Dark Chocolate (2.50); Mille-feuille with Hazlenuts (2.50); Lemon and Sour Cream Pie (2.50); Mocha Chiffon Pie (2.50); Banana Foster, Flambé (5.25); Confiture Bar-le-Duc et Triple Crème (2.50); Fresh Fruit Tart (2.50); Domestic and Imported Cheese with Seasonal Fruits (3.50); Fried Camembert with Lingonberry Sauce (3.25); Crêpe Salle Cathay (5.25).

OLD MEXICO RESTAURANT

Address: 115 Montague Street, Brooklyn Heights
Telephone: MA 4-9774
Credit Cards: Not accepted
Reservations: Required
Hours: 12:00 Noon to 10:00 PM, Monday thru Saturday
Days Closed: Sunday
Liquor: Full bar service
Recommended or Listed in: Cue; New York Magazine; Village Voice; New York Times
Manager: Richard McMullen
Seating Capacity: 42
Cuisine: Mexican
Specialties of the House: Fiesta Mexican Deluxe Combination (Tostada, Enchilada, Tamal, Taco, Rice and Refried Beans)
Dress: Casual

Brooklyn Heights is one of New York's most picturesque neighborhoods, affording as it does the best view of Manhattan and tree-lined streets of federal houses. It also features Old Mexico, an authentic and reasonable excursion into South of the Border cuisine. Old Mexico's bar is authentic, too, with more imaginative tequila concoctions than you may have thought possible. Good food, good drinks and a very unhurried dining atmosphere.

MENU

(a la carte)
(A representative selection)

SOUPS, APPETIZERS & SIDE DISHES
Mexican Soup of the Day (.95); Black Bean Soup (.95); Fresh Shrimp Cocktail (2.25); Nopalito Salad (1.75); Chalupas (2.25); Mixed Salad (2.00); Guacamole (1.75); Broiled Spanish Chorizo (1.75); Queso Fundido (2.25); Refried Beans with Cheese (1.50); Order of Mexican Rice (1.00); Mexican Chiles Jalapenos (1.00); Fried Beans (1.25); Order of Tortillas (3) (.75); Chile con Carne (cup 1.50); Burrito or Flauta (1) (2.50).

ENTREES:
Tostada, Enchilada and Soft Taco Combination 4.50
Tostada, Enchilada and Crisp Taco Combination 4.50
Tostada, Enchilada and Tamal Combination 4.50
Taco, Enchilada and Burrito Combination 4.75
Taco, Enchilada and Chile Relleno Combination 4.75
Tacos (3) Crisp or Soft 4.25
Enchiladas (3) 4.50
Chicken Mole Poblano 5.25
Flautas (2) 5.25
Chicken and Rice 5.25
Steak a "la Ranchera" 5.75
Chiles Rellenos (2) 4.75
Chilaquiles 4.50
Carne a la Michoacana 5.75
Shrimps al Diablo 5.50
Burritos 4.75
Enchiladas Suizas 5.25
Fiesta Mexican Deluxe Combination 5.50
Spanish Paella 7.25
Pollo con Mole Verde 5.50

(Minimum per person: 3.50)

OLIVER'S

Address: 141 East 57th Street
Location: 57th Street near Lexington Avenue
Telephone: 753-9180
Credit Cards: AE; V; DC; CB; MC
Reservations: Recommended
Hours: 11:30 AM to 11:30 PM; Bar open until 1:00 AM
Days Closed: Sundays and major holidays
Liquor: Full bar service
Recommended or Listed in: Cue; Village Voice; Gentlemen's Quarterly; Genesis; Madison Avenue; ANNY
Proprietor: C. Michael Wharton
Cuisine: American/English
Specialties of the House: Prime Ribs of Beef; 1¼ lb Broiled Maine Lobster; English Trifle; Chocolate Mousse
Dress: Casual
Entertainment: Piano entertainment daily from 2:00 PM to 11:00 PM; on Friday from 2:00 PM to Midnight; on Saturday from 5:00 PM to Midnight
Party Facilities: Private room; capacity: 50

This cozy bistro features good American food at surprisingly moderate prices in a distinctly European atmosphere. The wood paneled room is filled with brown and white checker-clothed tables with fresh flowers. The restaurant is named for the proprietor's son, Oliver, whose photograph is prominently displayed. In addition, the walls are covered by photographs and drawings of other famous Olivers – Oliver Twist, Oliver Cromwell and the recent film production of "Oliver."

LUNCHEON MENU

(a la carte)

APPETIZERS & SOUPS:
Artichoke vinaigrette (1.75); Shrimp cocktail (2.25); Mushrooms a la Grecque (1.50); Eggs a la Russe (1.50); Tossed green salad (1.50); Soup du Jour (.95); Lobster Bisque (Thurs., Fri., Sat.) (1.25); Chili, served with salad (2.95); Steamed Clams (2.95).

ENTREES:
Eggs Benedict 2.95
Broiled Fresh Filet of Sole, Boiled Potato, Vegetable 4.50
American Cheese Bacon Burger *(Sliced Bermuda Onion, French Fries)* 2.95
Russian Burger 2.95
(Lettuce, Caviar, Sour Cream, French Fries)
Aussie Burger 2.95
(Fried Onions, Fried Egg, Sliced Tomato, French Fries)
Burger a la Francaise 2.95
(Lettuce, Tomato, Bearnaise Sauce, French Fries)
New York Cut Sirloin Steak, Salad, French Fries 7.95

SALADS:
Chef Salad (3.95); Shrimp Salad (4.95); Salad Niçoise (3.95); Spinach, Mushroom, Bacon Salad (3.95).

DESSERTS:
Chocolate mousse (1.25); Melon in season (1.50); Creme caramel (1.00); Oliver's own Cheesecake (1.50); English Trifle (1.75).

DINNER MENU

(a la carte)

APPETIZERS & SOUPS:
Artichoke vinaigrette (1.95); Little necks on half shell (2.25); Shrimp cocktail (3.25); Mushrooms a la Grecque (1.95); Eggs a la Russe (1.50); Tossed green salad (1.50); Soup du Jour (1.25); Chili served with salad (3.50); Steamed Clams (3.50).

ENTREES:
Broiled Filet of Sole 5.25
Filet of Sole Stuffed with Crabmeat 6.25
Broiled 1¼ lb Lobster 7.95
Roast Half Spring Chicken 4.95
Chopped Sirloin Steak, Fried Onions 4.95

Roast Prime Ribs of Beef 7.95
Sirloin Steak, Fried Onions 8.95
American Cheese Bacon Burger
(Sliced Bermuda Onion, French Fries) 3.50
Russian Burger 3.50
(Lettuce, Caviar & Sour Cream, French Fries)
Burger a la Francaise 3.50
(Lettuce, Tomato, Bearnaise Sauce, French Fries)

SALADS:
Chef Salad (4.50); Salad Niçoise (4.50); Spinach, Mushroom, Bacon Salad (4.25).

DESSERTS:
Melon in season (1.50); Chocolate mousse (1.75); Creme caramel (1.00); Oliver's own Cheesecake (1.75); English Trifle (1.95).

(Entrees are served with mixed green salad and baked potato.)

SACHERTORTE: *This famous Austrian cake is all chocolate and what makes it unique is that its batter is made with ground almonds and just the slightest bit of flour. It is a round cake, about two inches high; it always has a thin layer of apricot jelly just below its chocolate icing.*

SCHOKOLADENROLLE: *To make this pastry, marzipan dough is baked and, while still warm, wrapped around a wooden stick. When the dough cools and the stick is removed, the tubular shape is brushed with melted sweet chocolate and filled with whipped cream.*

SCHWARZWALDER KIRSCHTORTE: *This is the most popular German cake of all in the United States. Schwarzwalder is German for "from the Black Forest," "kirsch" means sour cherry and "torte" is cake. This rich chocolate cake has a vanilla custard and sour cherry filling with chocolate whipped cream frosting and shaved sweet chocolate on top for decoration. It is often used for special occasions—birthdays, weddings, holidays, etc.*

WIENER WAFFELN: *This sweet is made from a rich butter dough to which ground walnuts are added. It is baked in sheets and between two of the sheets the baker spreads raspberry jam (the jam must have seeds). The top is sprinkled with powdered sugar and the sheets are then cut into squares.*

ONE FIFTH

Address:	One Fifth Avenue
Location:	Fifth Avenue at Corner of 8th Street
Telephone:	260-3434
Credit Cards:	All major credit cards accepted
Reservations:	Recommended
Hours:	Lunch from 12:00 Noon to 3:00 PM, Monday thru Friday; to 4:00 PM, Saturday; Dinner from 6:00 PM to 2:00 AM, daily; Sunday Brunch from 11:00 AM to 4:30 PM
Days Closed:	None
Liquor:	Full bar service
Maitre d's:	Donn and Keith
Seating Capacity:	200
Cuisine:	Continental
Specialties of the House:	Steak Amoureuse; Shrimp with Dill and Capers; Caesar Salad
Dress:	Casual
Entertainment:	Live music: piano and bass, Monday thru Wednesday; piano, Friday thru Sunday

One Fifth is a stunning recreation of the first class dining room of the sunken Cunard Liner Caronia. The decor consists of the ship's classic art deco furnishings, and the portholes look out on a photographic rendering of a stormy sea. The menu is continental and the ambience could have been imported directly from the Paris-famed La Coupole. The huge 1920's bar is as distinctive in its way as the dining room. Rescued from a once plush Hoboken saloon, it is a favorite meeting place for Villagers and uptowners alike. One Fifth is a very popular establishment and if you have to wait for a table, visit the cocktail lounge, whet your appetite with the special clam bar menu and enjoy the live music.

One Fifth

DINNER MENU

(a la carte)

APPETIZERS & SOUPS:

Blue Point Oysters on the Half Shell (3.25); Little Necks on the Half Shell (2.75); Prosciutto and Melon or Figs (3.50); Seafood Cocktail Mariniere (3.25); Pate Maison (2.25); Marinated Scallops Seviche (2.95); Smoked Scottish Salmon (4.95); Fresh Beluga Malossol Caviar (1 oz for 15.00); Oysters Rockefeller (3.75); Escargots Bordelaise (3.50); Turkish Cheese Beurrecks (2.95); Fisherman's Clam and Oyster Soup (1.95); Soupe du Jour (1.95).

ENTREES:

Special Caesar Salad 4.75
Avocado and Seafood Aurore 7.75
Caronia Seafood Salad 8.25
Vitello Tonnato 8.95
Danish Crabmeat Salad 10.75
Steak Tartare Garni 7.50
Shell Steak Bearnaise or Maitre d'Hotel 11.50
Filet Mignon Amoureuse 11.75
Chateaubriand Sauce Perigord (for two) 25.00
Alaskan King Crab Legs 11.50
Shrimp with Dill and Capers 8.50
Scampi Provencale 8.25
Scallops Bonne Femme 7.75
Sole Caprice or Meuniere 7.95
Chicken Kiev 7.95
Chicken Bombay 7.75
Duck a l'Orange 10.75
Brochette of Shrimp and Scallops 8.95
Viennese Schnitzel 7.25
Beef Stroganoff 7.95
Rack of Lamb, Herbes de Provence 12.00
Noisettes of Veal with Wild Mushrooms 10.25
Sauteed Calf Liver Bercy 7.95
Spaghetti Finocchio 5.75
Spinach and Cheddar Omelette 3.95
Mushroom and Herb Omelette 3.95
Quiche du Jour 4.95
Hamburger Garni 3.25
Hamburger with Cheese, Spinach or Bearnaise 3.95

(A variety of desserts is included on a separate Dessert menu.)

(An a la carte Luncheon menu is also available.)

PORT: *A very sweet dark red dessert wine traditionally shipped from Oporto, a port town in northern Portugal. Often a fortified as well as a blended wine, port is shipped in a variety of types:*

Vintage port *is the unblended wine of a single year, matured primarily in the bottle and requiring decanting to remove the sediment crust. Usually poured when it is about 20 years in the bottle, it has an incomparable fatness of flavor and fragrance.*

Tawny port *is blended and matured in oak casks, and is consumed shortly after bottling. It is lighter in color, with a brownish tinge, and is mellower, with a more moderate sweetness than vintage port.*

Ruby port *is blended and matured in casks, then bottled for consumption 4 to 5 years later; it is the youngest and fruitiest of the ports.*

White port *is the less highly esteemed variety made from white grapes.*

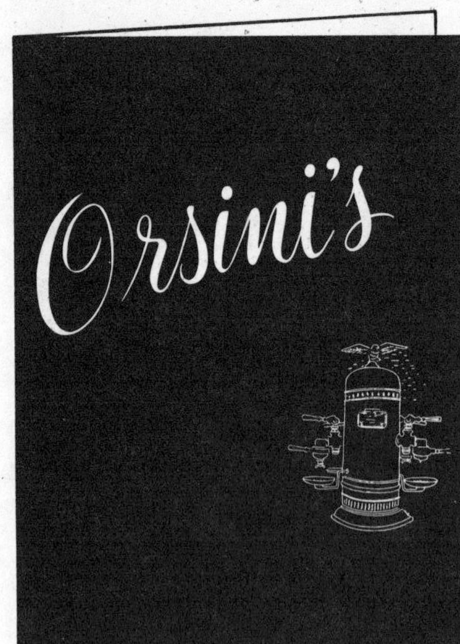

ORSINI'S

Address: 41 West 56th Street
Location: 56th Street between Fifth Avenue and Avenue of the Americas
Telephone: 757-1698
Credit Cards: AE; CB; DC; MC.
Reservations: Essential
Hours: 12 Noon — 3 PM; 5:30 PM — 1:00 AM
Days Closed: Sundays
Liquor: Full bar service
Maitre d': Nino
Seating Capacity: 150
Cuisine: Italian
Specialties of the House: Scampi Orsini; Fettuccine Alfredo; Veal Piccata
Party Facilities: 2 private rooms; capacity: Lunch—30-80, Dinner—50-80

Orsini's is among New York's most fashionable and romantic Italian restaurants. The intimate and romantic atmosphere of the downstairs dining room is created by soft lighting and luxurious red velvet walls and seating. In the upstairs dining room the old brick, lush greenery and Italian tile tables provide a garden setting. The traditional elegance of Orsini's is reflected in a "ladies' menu," which does not list prices. Special care is taken in arranging private parties.

Orsini's

DINNER MENU

(a la carte)

APPETIZERS & SOUPS:

Shrimp Cocktail (4.25); Melone e Prosciutto (4.25); Scampi Orsini (4.25); Beluga Malossal Caviar (S.Q.); Mozzarella in Carrozza (4.25); Crostini alla Romana (4.50); Mozzarella e Pomodori (4.00); Vongole Oreganate (4.25); Zuppa Spinaci e Uova (3.00); Zuppa di Vegetali (3.00); Tortellini in Brodo (3.00).

PASTA:

Fettuccine Alfredo 8.50
Tortellini Alla Panna 8.50
(Dumplings filled with chicken meat; butter and cream sauce)
Linguine alle Vongole 8.50
(With white or red clam sauce)
Cannelloni 8.50
Spaghettini alla Chitarra 8.50
(Great sauce; peas, prosciutto and mushrooms)
Fettuccine Capri 9.00
Rigatoni alla Baronessa 8.50
(Sauce made of tomatoes, fresh mushrooms and chicken livers)
Crespelle alla Fiorentina 9.00
(Delicate crêpes filled with spinach, prosciutto and bechamel)
Linguine al Pesto 8.50
Risotto Ammiraglia 10.00
(Rice with seafood and cognac sauce)
Spaghetti alla Carbonara 8.50
Fettuccine al Porcino 12.00
(Sauce made with Italian wild mushrooms)

ENTREES:

La Pescatora for two 30.00
(Clams, lobster, scampi with our own sauce)
Spigola 10.00
(Filets of fresh striped bass broiled)
Scampi alla Romana 10.00
Dover English Sole 11.00
Spigola in Brodetto 10.00
(Filets of fresh striped bass, tomato sauce, wine)
Crespelle Barcaiola 10.00
(Delicate crêpes filled with sea food; marinara sauce)
Fegato alla Veneziana 9.50
(Calf liver, Venetian style)
Cuscinetti di Vitello 12.50
(Pillows of veal; prosciutto, Gruyere cheese, wine sauce)
Mignonette Peperonata 11.50
(Sliced filet mignon with peppers and spiced tomato sauce)
Cotoletta alla Milanese 9.50
(Breaded veal cutlet)
Pollo all'Arrabbiata 9.00
(Recipe from Rome; chicken white wine sauce)
Piccata al Limone 9.25
(Veal, lemon and butter sauce)
Vitello alla Sorrentina 9.50
(Veal, mozzarella cheese, eggplant, wine sauce)
Pollo alla Margarita 9.00
(Boneless breasts of chicken, Gruyere cheese, white wine sauce)
Uccelletti all'Abbruzzese 9.00
(Rolls of beef filled, mushrooms, proscuito and sauce)
Pollo Scarpariello 9.00
(Pieces of boneless chicken, mushrooms, black olives, wine sauce)
Paillard di Vitello 10.00
Pollo alla Griglia 9.00
Sirloin Steak 12.50
Mignonette of Beef 12.50

DESSERTS:

Zabaglione al Marsala (4.25); Zuppa Inglese (3.00); Chocolat Mousse Torte (4.00); Homemade Cheese Cake (3.00); Crepes Suzette for two (14.00); Coppa ai Marroni (Marrons glacés, ice cream and Grand Marnier) (4.00); Gelato (ice cream) (2.50); Saint Honoré (3.00).

THE OTHER PLACE

Address: 1650 Hylan Boulevard
Staten Island
Location: Hylan Boulevard and Alter Avenue
Telephone: 987-3700
Credit Cards: AE; DC; CB; V
Reservations: Required
Hours: 12 Noon to 2:00 AM, Sunday thru Thursday; to 4:00 AM Friday and Saturday
Days Closed: None
Liquor: Full bar service
Maitre d': John Berteroli
Manager: John Coppotelli
Seating Capacity: 110
Cuisine: American — Italian
Specialties of the House: Prime Rib au Jus; Veal Ambrose; Barbecued Baby Back Pork Ribs
Dress: Casual
Entertainment: Organist, Wednesday thru Saturday Evenings
Party Facilities: Private room; capacity: 50
Parking: Restaurant parking lot

The Other Place boasts a uniquely blended decor of cedar panelling and large stained glass windows. The airy, spacious room makes dramatic use of geometric design, and Art Deco appointments vividly recreate the Belle Epoque era. In addition to a wide menu selection, unusual combination plates are also available, with the barbecued ribs and chicken breast a special favorite. You'll enjoy a visit to The Other Place.

DINNER MENU

(a la carte)

(The following is a representative selection.)

APPETIZERS, SOUPS & SIDE DISHES:
Shrimp Cocktail (3.95); Fresh Clams on a half shell (2.75); Baked Clams à la Dee (3.25); Chopped Chicken Livers (1.75); Melon and Prosciutto (2.95); Alaskan King Crab Cocktail (3.95); Egg à la Russe (1.25); Fresh Fruit Cocktail (1.45); French Fried Mushroom Caps (2.50); Seasoned Fried Onion Rings (1.50); Deep Fried Zucchini (1.50); Fresh Fried Idaho Chips (1.35); Herring in Wine with Sour Cream (2.25); Crab Stuffed Mushroom Caps (4.95); Soup of the Day (.80); Zuppa de Mussels (3.95); Crock of French Onion Soup (1.75).

ENTREES:
Hearty Prime Rib au Jus 9.95
Prime Rib au Jus 8.25
Roast Half Long Island Duck 7.25
London Broil with Mushroom Sauce 7.95
Calf's Liver with Onions and Canadian Bacon 7.75
Double Rib Lamb Chops 8.95
Veal Parmigiana with Pasta 7.25
Veal Ambrose with Asparagus and Crabmeat au Gratin 7.75
New York Strip Sirloin 10.50
Steak Marion with Our Mustard Sauce 9.50
Filet Mignon 10.50
Petite Filet Mignon 8.95
Polynesian Steak Teriyaki 9.75
Chopped Sirloin Steak 6.25
Fillet of Sole Stuffed with Crabmeat 8.75
Broiled Fillet of Sole 7.25
Broiled Bay Scallops 7.25
Fried Seafood Combination 6.95
Shrimp Scampi 8.75
Deep Fried Shrimp 7.25
Alaskan King Crab Legs 10.95
Maine Lobster .... (....)
Lobster Fra Diavolo .... (....)
Lobster Tails stuffed with Crabmeat 13.95
Barbecued Baby Back Pork Ribs 7.95
Barbecued Half Long Island Duckling 7.25
Filet Mignon and Shrimp Scampi 9.95
Barbecued Ribs and Chicken Breast 7.50
Barbecued Ribs and Duckling 7.75

(Entrees include a house salad and choice of potatoes.)

(Omelettes, crêpes, hot or cold sandwiches and salads are also served.)

PAMPLONA

Address: 822 Avenue of the Americas
Location: Avenue of the Americas between 28th Street and 29th Street
Telephone: 683-4242
Credit Cards: AE; CB; DC; MC
Reservations: Recommended.
Hours: Lunch from 12 Noon to 3:00 PM, Monday thru Friday; Dinner from 5:30 PM to 11:00 PM, Monday thru Thursday and until 12 Midnight Friday and Saturday
Days Closed: Sundays
Liquor: Full Bar Service
Recommended or listed in: Cue; Where
Maitre d': Paco
Seating Capacity: 70
Cuisine: Spanish
Specialties of the House: Filet of Sole Marbella; Chuletas de Ternera al Jefe; Tournedos Pamplona
Dress: Casual
Entertainment: Strolling guitarist and singer

This restaurant projects an aura of bullfights, Basques and stomping dancers and the place is so naturally informal that guests may spontaneously break into Spanish song. The cheerful environment is enhanced by Spanish wall posters and fresh red carnations. Featured is a chef of the famous Spanish Pavilion at the World's Fair. Pamplona ranks among the more attractive Spanish restaurants in the moderate price range.

DINNER MENU

(a la carte)

(The following is a representative selection.)

APPETIZERS:
Almejas a la Marinera (3.25); Mejillones en Salsa Verde (2.80); Jamon con Melon Espanol (3.95); Tortilla Espanola (2.95); Cocktail de Mariscos del Mediterraneo (3.75); Tosta de Champinon Segoviana (3.00); Callos Madrilena (3.00); Caracoles en Tazas Pequenas a la Borgona (3.75); Gambas al Ajilo — Nuestra Especialidad (3.75); Ensalada Pamplona (1.95).

SOUPS:
Crema de Alubias Pintas (1.75); Sopa de Ajo (1.75); Gazpacho a la Andaluza Campero (1.75); Sopa de Pescado (2.60); Crema de Langosta (2.50).

ENTREES:

Spec. Merluza a la Vasca	7.50
Filete de Lenguado Molinera	6.50
Carabineros Cardinal	13.50
Lubina al Horno	7.95
Baby Rack of Lamb Segovia Style (For Two)	19.95
Pollo al Grano al Asador	7.50
Steak Maitre d'Hotel	9.95
Solomillo a la Parrilla	9.95
Chuletas de Cordero a la Parrilla	9.50
Chuletas de Cerdo a la Navarra	6.25
Pollo a la Riojana	6.00
Spec. Medallones de Ternera Sevillana	7.50
Escalopes de Ternera Castellana	7.75
Spec. Tournedos Imperial Pamplona	9.25
Pato a la Naranja Valenciana	7.50
Brocheta Mixta Toledana	6.75
Paella a la Valenciana Para Dos	16.50
Spec. Filete de Lenguado Marbella	7.25
Spec. Zarzuela Especial de Mariscos Costa Brava	9.25
Spec. Pollo y Langosta a la Catalana	9.25
Chuletas de Ternera al Jefe	8.95
Spec. Villagodio a las Brasas Para Dos	18.95

(Chef Jose Ibarra)

DESSERTS:
Melon del Tiempo (2.00); Fresones con Nata (2.75); Pasteleria Variada (1.75); Natillas (1.50); Flan de Carmelo (1.50).

(A variety of vegetables and salads is also offered.)

continued on next page

Pamplona

THE PARK ROOM AT THE PARK LANE HOTEL

Address: 36 Central Park South
Telephone: 371-4000
Credit Cards: AE; DC; MC
Reservations: Recommended
Hours: Breakfast from 7:00 AM to 11:00 AM, Lunch from 12:00 Noon to 3:00 PM, Monday thru Saturday; Dinner daily from 5:00 PM to 10:30 PM, Supper daily from 10:30 PM to 12:30 AM; Sunday Brunch from 12:00 Noon to 3:00 PM
Days Closed: None
Liquor: Full bar service
Recommended or Listed in: New York Magazine
Chef: Clement Grangier
Park Room Manager: Mr. Pappas
Seating Capacity: 124
Cuisine: French
Specialties of the House: Crabmeat Imperial; Scallop Florentine; Fillet of Sole Bonne Femme; Baby Rack of Lamb Perselle; Steak au Poivre; Coq au Vin Chambertin
Dress: Jackets required
Entertainment: Piano music during Dinner and Supper, Tuesday thru Saturday
Party Facilities: Private room (with partitions); dining capacity: 200

Here, on the second floor of the luxurious Park Lane Hotel, you'll overlook Central Park through 15-foot-high arched windows. One could virtually dine on the view alone, but the menu provides more substantial fare—grand and gourmet at breakfast, brunch, luncheon, dinner and supper—the creation of the Executive Chef, Clement Grangier, formerly Chef of Le Pavillon. Gold damask, handblown glassware and superb china create a splendid atmosphere, and the swift and unobtrusive service further adds to your dining pleasure.

DINNER MENU

(a la carte)

APPETIZERS & SOUPS:

Prosciutto Ham with Melon (5.50); Smoked Trout, Creamed Horseradish (5.25); Caprice of Fresh Fruit (2.50); Shrimp Cocktail (6.00); Lump Crabmeat (6.50); Chopped Chicken Livers (2.95); Lobster Meat Cocktail (6.50); Melon in Season (2.50); Cherrystone or Little Neck Clams (6) on the Half Shell (3.75); Marinated Herring in Sour Cream (3.50); Coquille St. Jacques au Gratin (7.50); Escargots de Bourgogne (6) (5.00); Potage Saint Germain (2.00); Crock of French Onion Soup Gratinée (2.50); Petite Marmite Henri IV (4.00); Chilled Madrilène (2.00); Chilled Gazpacho (2.50); Cold Vichyssoise (2.00).

ENTREES:

Chateaubriand aux Primeurs for two 32.00
Broiled Double Lamb Chops 12.00
Broiled Filet Mignon 14.50
Grilled Sirloin Steak 14.50
Broiled Chopped Steak, Mushroom Sauce ... 8.00
Broiled Calf's Liver Steak, Bacon or Onions .. 9.75
Broiled Half Chicken Tarragon 9.00

continued on next page

The Park Room (at the Park Lane)

Sirloin Steak au Poivre Flambée au Cognac . 15.50
Broiled Veal Chop 14.00
Broiled Salmon, Bearnaise Sauce 8.50
Roast Capon Derby 10.00
Choice Lamb Steak à la Chef 13.00
Beef Stroganoff 9.50
Breast of Veal à la Génèvoise 10.00

Dover Sole à la Belle Meunière 12.50
Roast Long Island Duckling à l'Orange 12.00
Delicate Frog Legs Sauté à la Niçoise 9.50
Roast Prime Ribs of Beef au Jus 12.00

(A variety of cold platters, salads, side dishes and desserts is also available.)

POUILLY FUISSE: *The superior dry white Burgundy produced exclusively from the Chardonnay grape in the area west of Macon in southern Burgundy. Thought to be between a Meursault and a Chablis in character, a Pouilly Fuissé is green-gold in color, with a fruity flavor, good balance and a fine bouquet; it reaches maturity within three years in the bottle.*

POUILLY FUME: *A dry, white upper Loire Valley wine, made most frequently from the Sauvignon Blanc grape. In its best years, it is smoky, green and spicy, with a metallic fragrance. It should be consumed a year or two after bottling.*

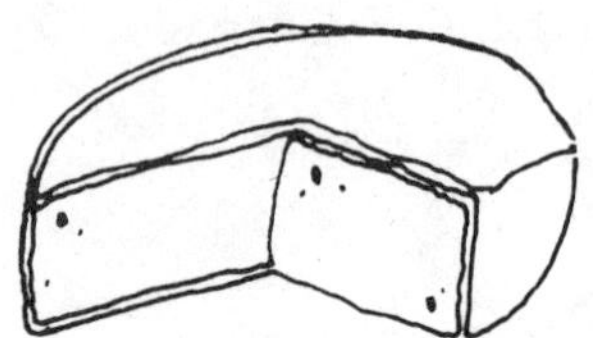

LEICESTER: *This is a Cheddar-type cheese which originated in the English county of Leicestershire. It is made in flat, 40 pound wheels and is dyed in shades ranging from orange to red depending on its age. It is a hard, friable cheese with a rich, strong flavor. Leicester has a higher moisture content and a shorter life span than does Cheddar.*

MAIL THESE CARDS FOR NEWS OF MANHATTAN MENUS' NEXT EDITION.

The Great Restaurant Guide
is revised and expanded every year.
If you'd like to be notified in advance of publication, simply fill-out and mail this postpaid reply card.

The Great Restaurant Guide

Yes! Please let me know when the next annual edition of Manhattan Menus will be available.

Name__________

Address__________

City__________State__________Zip__________

☐ Also send me___copies of the current edition @ $8.95 each, plus $1.00 each for postage and handling. New York State Residents add sales tax.

☐ Check enclosed.
☐ Charge Diners Club
☐ Charge Visa
☐ Charge Master Charge

Card No.__________
Exp. Date__________
Bank No.__________
Signature__________

C

The Great Restaurant Guide
is revised and expanded every year.
If you'd like to be notified in advance of publication, simply fill-out and mail this postpaid reply card.

The Great Restaurant Guide

Yes! Please let me know when the next annual edition of Manhattan Menus will be available.

Name__________

Address__________

City__________State__________Zip__________

☐ Also send me___copies of the current edition @ $8.95 each, plus $1.00 each for postage and handling. New York State Residents add sales tax.

☐ Check enclosed.
☐ Charge Diners Club
☐ Charge Visa
☐ Charge Master Charge

Card No.__________
Exp. Date__________
Bank No.__________
Signature__________

B

The Great Restaurant Guide
is revised and expanded every year.
If you'd like to be notified in advance of publication, simply fill-out and mail this postpaid reply card.

The Great Restaurant Guide

Yes! Please let me know when the next annual edition of Manhattan Menus will be available.

Name__________

Address__________

City__________State__________Zip__________

☐ Also send me___copies of the current edition @ $8.95 each, plus $1.00 each for postage and handling. New York State Residents add sales tax.

☐ Check enclosed.
☐ Charge Diners Club
☐ Charge Visa
☐ Charge Master Charge

Card No.__________
Exp. Date__________
Bank No.__________
Signature__________

A

MAIL THESE CARDS FOR NEWS OF MANHATTAN MENUS' NEXT EDITION.

FIRST CLASS
PERMIT NO. 53760
NEW YORK, N.Y.

BUSINESS REPLY MAIL

NO POSTAGE STAMP NECESSARY IF MAILED IN THE UNITED STATES

POSTAGE WILL BE PAID BY:

P.O. Box 5217
New York, N.Y. 10022

The Great Restaurant Guide is revised and expanded every year. If you'd like to be notified in advance of publication, simply fill-out and mail this postpaid reply card.

FIRST CLASS
PERMIT NO. 53760
NEW YORK, N.Y.

BUSINESS REPLY MAIL

NO POSTAGE STAMP NECESSARY IF MAILED IN THE UNITED STATES

POSTAGE WILL BE PAID BY:

P.O. Box 5217
New York, N.Y. 10022

The Great Restaurant Guide is revised and expanded every year. If you'd like to be notified in advance of publication, simply fill-out and mail this postpaid reply card.

FIRST CLASS
PERMIT NO. 53760
NEW YORK, N.Y.

BUSINESS REPLY MAIL

NO POSTAGE STAMP NECESSARY IF MAILED IN THE UNITED STATES

POSTAGE WILL BE PAID BY:

P.O. Box 5217
New York, N.Y. 10022

The Great Restaurant Guide is revised and expanded every year. If you'd like to be notified in advance of publication, simply fill-out and mail this postpaid reply card.

PARMA

Address:	**1404 Third Avenue**
Location:	**Third Avenue between 79th and 80th Streets**
Telephone:	**535-3520**
Credit Cards:	**AE**
Reservations:	**Recommended**
Hours:	**5:00 PM to 12:30 AM, daily**
Days Closed:	**None**
Liquor:	**Full bar service**
Seating Capacity:	**85**
Cuisine:	**Northern Italian**
Specialties of the House:	**Homemade Pasta; Veal Specialties**
Dress:	**No restrictions**

In the short time that Parma has been in existence, the restaurant has attracted a following appreciative of its good food (especially the homemade pasta), pleasant surroundings and reasonable prices. Wood paneling, rough stone walls and slate floors suggest a rustic ambience, and a profusion of plants in the front window adds color and warmth. Parma is a comfortable spot, either for dining or for socializing at the congenial bar.

DINNER MENU

(a la carte)

APPETIZERS & SOUPS:
Gianchetti (2.50); Mussels Vino Bianco (4.50); Insalata Frutti di Mare (3.00); Mushrooms Genovese (3.00); Fresh Roasted Peppers (2.50); Prosciutto e Melone (3.50); Clams Oreganate (3.00); Clams Casino (3.25); Clams on Half Shell (2.50); Shrimp Cocktail (3.50); Antipasto (3.00); Consommé (1.50); Zuppa del Giorno (1.50).

ENTREES:

Spaghetti di Casa 4.50
Fettuccine Alfredo 5.50
Tortellini alla Panna 5.50
Spaghetti Matriciana 5.50
Linguine Clams Sauce 5.50
Paglia e Fieno 5.50
Scampi 8.00
Sole Meuniere 7.00
Veal Scaloppine Malapaga 7.50
Veal Scaloppine Marsala 7.25
Veal Scaloppine Piccata 7.00
Saltimbocca alla Romana 7.25
Veal Parmigiana 7.00
Veal Chop 8.50
Sirloin Steak 10.25
Filet Mignon 10.50
Calamari Fritti 6.00
Fish of the Day .... (. . .)
Cappone Bolognese 6.50
Chicken Scarpara 6.00
Chicken Francese 6.00
Chicken Parmigiana 6.25
Broiled Chicken 5.75
Calf's Liver 7.75
Chopped Steak 5.00

(All entrees are served with a vegetable of the day.)

SIDE DISHES:
Rugola (2.00); Caesar Salad (5.00); Broccoli (1.50); Spinaci (1.50); Mixed Green Salad (1.50); Fried Zucchini (2.00); String Beans (1.50); French Fried Potatoes (1.50).

(A variety of desserts is available.)

LE PERIGORD PARK

Address: 575 Park Avenue
Location: Park Avenue and 63rd Street
Telephone: PL 2-0050
Credit Cards: AE
Reservations: Recommended
Hours: Lunch from 12:00 Noon to 3:00 PM, Monday thru Friday; Dinner from 6:00 PM to 11:00 PM, 7 days a week
Days Closed: Major holidays
Liquor: Full bar service
Recommended or Listed in: Cue; Gourmet; Promenade
Maitre d': Louis Barbou
Reservations Manager: Louis Barbou; any Captain
Seating Capacity: 280
Cuisine: French
Specialties of the House: Specialties of the Périgord region; Gâteau de Foie de Poularde au Coulis de Homard; Feuilleté d'Huîtres aux Poireaux
Dress: Jacket and tie suggested
Party Facilities: 2 private rooms; capacity: 30/75

The ambience of Le Périgord Park's three dining rooms invites compliments as does its classical French cuisine. Up a few steps from the main dining room is a warm, intimate dining area with curved ceilings and rich beige velvet banquettes. An elegantly mirrored room with gold accents is on the next level. Le Périgord Park is proud of its menu and the specialties it offers from the Périgord region of France.

DINNER MENU
(table d'hote)

SOUPS:
Consommé Julienne Darblay; Longchamps; Bisque de Homard; Potage de Légumes Frais; Le Mourtairol; Soupe aux Moules Safranée (2.50).

SPECIALTIES:
Caviar aux Blinis (21.00)
Tartare de Poissons
Foie Gras d'Oie Gelée Rubis (20.00 Ex.)
Salade de Foie Gras de Canard Pompadour (10.00 Ex.)
Feuilleté d'Huîtres aux Poireaux (3.00 Ex.)
Le Homard aux Racines en Salade (7.00)
Timbale de Champignons aux Quenelles
Terrine de Crabe et Coquille St. Jacques Froide - Mousseline de Cresson
Vol au Vent de Clams au Curry et Julienne de Légumes (3.00)
Notre Assortiment de Légumes à la Grècque
Gâteau de Foie de Poularde au Coulis de Homard
Mousse de Sole les Deux Sauces
Clams aux Fines Herbes et Vin Blanc

ENTREES:
Navarin de Red Snapper et Homard aux Petits Légumes ... 21.00
La Nage de Coquille St. Jacques ... 19.00
Sole Anglaise au Sabayon d'Oseille ... 19.00
Bass Poché aux Aromates et Beurre Rouge .. 18.50
Beurreck de Crab-Meat ... 20.00
Foie Gras de Canard Sauté aux Échalottes et Vinaigre de Framboises ... 21.00
Canard Laqué aux Endives et Truffes Noires ... 20.00
Poularde Poëlée au Porto-Coulis de Cèpes - Pomme Douce ... 19.50
Pigeon Grillé - Diablé à Notre Façon ... 20.00
Côte de Veau à la Crème Aigre - Barquettes Délice - Pruneaux ... 20.00
Poulet Sauté Sauce Rouilleuse ... 18.50

DESSERTS:
Notre Spécialité de Tartes aux Fruits et de Sorbets; Soufflés Tous Parfums (3.50); Poire Belle Françoise (2.50); Glâces: Chocolat, Café, Vanille.

PETE'S TAVERN

Address: 129 East 18th Street
Location: 18th Street and Corner of Irving Place
Telephone: GR 3-7676
Credit Cards: All major credit cards accepted
Reservations: Required
Hours: 8:00 AM to 12:00 Midnight, Monday thru Thursday; 8:00 AM to 1:00 AM, Friday thru Sunday
Days Closed: Christmas, New Year's
Liquor: Full bar service
Recommended or Listed in: Cue; New York Post; The Visitor
Maitre d': Buster Smith
Seating Capacity: 150
Cuisine: Italian-American
Specialties of the House: Chicken Breasts with Artichoke Hearts and Mushrooms; Malaysian Shrimp; Shrimp Scampi; Filet of Sole Stuffed with Shrimp and Crabmeat
Dress: Casual
Party Facilities: Skylight Room; capacity: 50

Pete's Tavern is one of New York's cultural landmarks. Established at its present location in 1864, the Tavern continues to serve drinks at the original bar and to seat customers in polished wooden booths that have been there for more than 100 years. This is "the tavern that O'Henry made famous"—he wrote Gift of the Magi *in Pete's Tavern and most of his other writing also originated in the congenial atmosphere that still flourishes here. Tiled floors, brick walls, subdued lighting and railroad fans beneath the beamed ceilings combine to create a feeling of intimacy and a nostalgic sense of the past. No wonder that this era's writers and artists have continued the rich tradition of Pete's Tavern as a gathering place.*

MENU

(a la carte)

APPETIZERS & SOUPS:
Tomato Juice (.80); Orange/Grapefruit Juice (1.00); Zuppa di Mussels (3.50); Antipasto (Cold) (3.50); Famous Hot Antipasto (4.50); Clam Cocktail (3.00); Clams Casino (3.50); Clams Oreganata (3.50); Clams a la Pete (3.50); Shrimp Cocktail (3.50); Soup du Jour (1.50).

ENTREES:

Chef's Salad a la Pete	4.50
Eggplant Parmigiana	4.00
Chicken Livers with Mushrooms and Onions	4.50
Italian Sausage with Peppers	4.50
Chicken Cacciatora	5.00
Chicken Kiev	5.50
Chicken Parmigiana	5.50
Chicken Tetrazzini with Noodles	5.50
London Broil with Mushroom Sauce	5.50
Veal Parmigiana	6.00
Veal a la Marsala with Mushrooms	6.00
Veal and Peppers	6.00
Veal Salt im Bocca	6.00
Veal Piccata	6.00
Veal Cutlet Milanese with Spaghetti	6.00
Half Spring Chicken	4.50
Pork Chops in Wine Sauce	6.50
Sirloin Steak, New York Cut	11.00
Sirloin Steak Siciliano	12.00
Fresh Filet of Sole	5.50
Fresh Filet of the Day	5.50
Filet of Sole Stuffed with Shrimp and Crabmeat	6.50
Jumbo Fried Shrimps	6.50
Shrimps a la Marinara	6.50
Jumbo Shrimps Scampi	7.00
Shrimp Pizzaiola	7.00
Shrimp Parmigiana	7.00
Shrimp Malaysian	9.00

(The largest—¼ lb each—and finest in the world, broiled in butter and garlic)

(All entrees served with mixed green salad or side spaghetti with tomato or meat sauce.)

DESSERTS:
Spumoni (1.10); Tortoni (1.10); Zabaglione (2.50); Pastry - Assorted (1.00); Cheese Cake (1.30); Rum Cake a la Buster (1.50).

(A variety of pasta dishes is also available, ranging in price from 3.50 to 5.00.)

LA PETITE FERME

Address:	**973 Lexington Avenue**
Location:	**Lexington Avenue between 70th and 71st Streets**
Telephone:	**249-3272**
Credit Cards:	**AE; DC; MC; V**
Reservations:	**Recommended**
Hours:	**Lunch from 12:00 Noon to 2:30 PM; Dinner from 6:00 PM to 10:30 PM**
Days Closed:	**Sunday**
Liquor:	**Full bar service**
Recommended or Listed in:	**New York Times; Gourmet; Cue; New York Magazine; Women's Wear Daily**
Seating Capacity:	**45**
Cuisine:	**French**
Specialties of the House:	**Moules Vinaigrette; Bass Poche, Sauce Chevillot**
Dress:	**Informal**

A welcome addition to the upper eastside, La Petite Ferme brings to its uptown location the same rustic farmhouse charm, cordial service and simple dishes superbly prepared that earned this restaurant its substantial following in Greenwich Village over the past several years. Thick slab tables, fresh garden flowers, plaid napkins the size of dish towels and a pair of duly contented doves add to the charm of La Petite Ferme's interior; in warm weather, quail share the small outdoor garden with patrons who wish to sip an aperitif before dinner. Charles Chevillot, the Proprietor, comes from a family of French restaurateurs, and his well-chosen wine list reflects several excellent selections from his native Burgundy. The cuisine of La Petite Ferme has garnered considerable and justifiable praise for the restaurant and M. Chevillot. Suffice it to say here that you will undoubtedly want to add several superlatives of your own.

DINNER MENU

(a la carte)

(The dinner menu changes daily; the menu includes two appetizers, four entrees and two desserts. The following is a representative selection.)

APPETIZERS & SOUPS:

Petite Marmite (3.00); Asperges au Beurre (3.50); Artichaut Vinaigrette (3.00); Moules Vinaigrette (3.50); Hors d'Oeuvre Varies (5.50); Soupe de Cresson (2.50).

ENTREES:

Cote de Veau Maitre d'Hotel	13.00
Quaille Rotie aux Raisins	13.50
Poussin — Sauce Perigueux	12.00
Foie de Veau Saute	10.00
Entrecote Maitre d'Hotel	13.00
Rognons de Veau Saute	10.00
Pot-au-Feu	11.00
Poulet Aioli	10.00
Saute de Veau Marengo	10.50
Cote de Veau en Croute	13.50
Blanquette de Veau	10.00
Escalope de Saumon — Sauce Chevillot	11.00
Bass Poche	9.00
Brochet Poche	9.00
Truite Meuniere	11.00
Sole Meuniere	10.00
Sole Pochee au Vin Rouge	10.00
Crabes Mous Meuniere	9.50
Homard Poche, Sauce Chevillot	16.00

DESSERTS:

Tarte Tatin (3.50); Tarte aux Framboises (3.50); Mousse au Chocolat (3.00); Framboises Sauce Grand Marnier (3.50); Oranges a l'Arabe (3.50); Souffle au Chocolat (4.50).

La Petite Ferme (Photo by James La Pine, New York Magazine)

(La Petite Ferme offers an excellent, reasonably priced wine list, featuring many wines from M. Chevillot's native Burgundy.)
(Minimum per person: Lunch, 8.00; Dinner, 12.00.)

(A luncheon menu, similar to the dinner menu, is also offered and changes daily. The menu includes two appetizers, four entrees, and two desserts; a la carte prices range from 5.50 to 9.50.)

LA PETITE MARMITE

Address: 5 Mitchell Place
Location: 49th Street at First Avenue (in the Beekman Tower Hotel)
Telephone: 826-1084
Credit Cards: AE; CB; DC; MC
Reservations: Essential
Hours: Lunch from 12 Noon to 3:00 PM Monday thru Friday; Dinner from 6:00 PM to 10:00 PM Monday thru Saturday
Days Closed: Sunday and Major Holidays
Liquor: Full Bar Service
Recommended or listed in: Cue; Gourmet
Maitre d': Jacky Ruette
Proprietors: Jacky Ruette and Gerard Drouet
Seating Capacity: 75
Cuisine: French
Specialties of the House: La Petite Marmite Soup; Foie de Veau aux Raisins; La Cote de Veau Normande
Dress: Jackets preferred
Party Facilities: Semi-private room; capacity: 24

Certainly one of the city's finest French restaurants, and the only one named after a soup, La Petite Marmite is located in the Beekman Tower. Decorations include oil paintings spaced along the walls, mostly bright flowers and landscapes of the French countryside. There are also mirrored partitions, arches and columns. One of the reasons for this restaurant's notable success is that the chef, Gerard Drouet, is part owner. La Petite Marmite is well known throughout the world because it is a favorite among United Nations diplomats.

La Petite Marmite

LUNCHEON MENU

(a la carte)

APPETIZERS:
Pâté Maison (2.50); Jambon de Bayonne (3.25); Saucisson Sec (2.00); Artichaut Vinaigrette (2.50); Salade de Concombres (2.00); Oeuf Froid Mayonnaise (1.75); Pamplemousse (2.00); Coupe de Fruits (2.75); Melon de Saison (2.75); Céleri Remoulade (in season) (2.50); Sardines à l'Huile (2.00); Moules à la Moutarde (2.75); Littlenecks or Cherrystones (3.00); Crevettes Cocktail (3.50); Saumon Fumé (4.25); Filet de Hareng (1.75); Maquereau au Vin Blanc (1.75); Bluepoints (in season) (3.75); Truite Fumée (4.25); Tomato Juice (1.00); Hors d'Oeuvre Assortis (4.00); Escargots (4.00 for 6) (7.95 for 12); Melon Bayonne (4.25).

SOUPS:
Vichyssoise (2.75); Potage du Jour (2.25); La Petite Marmite (2.50).

ENTREES:
La Spécialité du Jour 6.75
Les Omelettes 5.75
(Champignons, Fromage, Fines Herbes)
Le Filet de Sole Meunière 6.75
La Crêpe de Fruits de Mer 6.75
L'Escalopine de Veau au Citron 7.75
Le Foie de Veau à l'Anglaise 8.25
La Poularde Rôtie au Plat 6.75
Les Rognons de Veau Berçy 7.00
La Cervelle Meunière 7.00
La Crêpe de Volaille 6.25
Le Coq au Vin 7.75
Le Filet Mignon 12.75
L'Entrecôte 12.75
La Côte d'Agneau 12.75

SALADS:
Endives (in season) (3.00); Lettuce (2.50); Green Salad (2.00); Roquefort Dressing (.50 extra).

DESSERTS:
Les Fromages (2.50); Les Patisseries (2.50); La Mousse au Chocolat (2.00); La Crème Caramel (2.00); La Pêche Melba (2.75); La Poire Melba (2.75); L'Ananas Melba (2.75); La Coupe aux Marrons (3.00); Les Glaces — Les Sorbets (2.00); Le Melon de Saison (2.75); La Salade de Fruits (2.75); La Poire Belle Hélène (2.75); Les Fraises — Les Framboises (3.50).

DINNER MENU

(a la carte)

APPETIZERS:
(Almost identical to the luncheon appetizers, with no change in prices.)

SOUPS:
Vichyssoise (2.75); Gratinée Lyonnaise (2.50); La Petite Marmite (2.50); Potage du Jour (2.25).

ENTREES:
La Spécialité du Jour 11.25
Le Bass Sauté Amandine 11.25
(Striped bass with almonds)
Les Grenouilles Provençale 13.50
(Frogs Legs)
La Sole Anglaise Pochée Nantua 13.50
(Dover Sole)
La Poularde Poêlée Grand Mère 9.50
(Chicken)
Les Rognons de Veau Beaugé 8.50
L'Escalopine de Veau au Citron 12.50
Le Foie de Veau aux Raisins 12.50
(Calf's Liver)
Le Ris de Veau Sauté Belle Meunière 12.00
Le Caneton Rôti a l'Orange 13.50
Le Pigeon Clamart 13.50
La Côte de Veau Normande 15.75
(Veal Chop)
Le Tournedos au Poivre Vert 15.75
Le Steak Grillé Sauce Béarnaise 15.75
Le Carré d'Agneau "Jardinière" (for two) ... 28.00

SALADS:
Endives (in season) (3.00); Lettuce (2.50); Green Salad (included); Roquefort Dressing (.50 extra).

DESSERTS:
Les Fromages (2.50); Les Patisseries (2.50); La Mousse au Chocolat (2.00); La Crème Caramel (2.00); Les Glaces — Les Sorbets (2.00); La Poire Belle Hélène (2.75); La Coupe aux Marrons (3.00); La Pêche Melba (2.75); La Salade de Fruits (2.75); L'Ananas Melba (2.75); Le Melon de Saison (2.75); La Poire Melba (2.75); Les Fraises — Les Framboises (3.50).

(La Petite Marmite has one of the most extensive and impressive wine lists in the City.)

Inflation affects everyone, including restauranteurs. So look for the prices of menu items listed in this book to rise a bit during the year.

LES PLEIADES

Address:	**20 East 76th Street**
Location:	**76th Street between Fifth and Madison Avenues**
Telephone:	**535-7230**
Credit Cards:	**AE; V; MC**
Reservations:	**Requested**
Hours:	**Lunch from 12:00 Noon to 3:00 PM, Monday thru Saturday; Dinner from 5:30 PM to 11:00 PM, Monday thru Saturday**
Days Closed:	**Sunday**
Liquor:	**Full bar service**
Recommended or Listed in:	**Cue; Gourmet**
Seating Capacity:	**100**
Cuisine:	**Classic French**
Specialties of the House:	**Ris de Veau aux Morilles; Le Pigeon Roti au Riz Sauvage**
Dress:	**Jackets required for Dinner**
Party Facilities:	**Private room; capacity: 20-60**

Classic French cuisine is the luncheon and dinner attraction of Les Pleiades, an elegant restaurant located on the upper eastside and frequented by the neighborhood's antique dealers, artists and gallery owners. The dining room is visually warm and appealing. Attractive paintings of the Provinces of France adorn the walls; burgundy carpets and comfortable red banquettes complete the decor.

DINNER MENU

(a la carte)

APPETIZERS & SOUPS:

Coquille St. Jacques; Champignons a la Grecque; Artichaut ou Poireaux Vinaigrettes; Pate Maison; Celeri Remoulade; Salade Nicoise; Saucisson Sec ou en Croute; Sardines a l'Huile; Grapefruit; Melon; Quiche Lorraine — (3.00); La Truite Fume; Le Saumon Fume; Le Shrimp Cocktail; Le Melon Prosciutto; Les Escargot "Pleiades" — (4.75); La Soupe du Jour; La Vichyssoise; La Madrilene; Le Consomme — (2.50).

ENTREES:

Le Plat du Jour 9.25
La Timbale "Pleiades" 9.25
(Mixed Sea Food, White Wine)
Le Bass a l'Oseille 9.25
Le Navarin d'Agneau Printaniere 9.25
(Lamb Stew, Mixed Vegetables)
Le Poulet Roti a l'Estragon 9.25
Rognon Grille Dijonnaise 9.25
Escalopine de Veau au Citron 9.25
La Sole Anglaise Grillee, Sauce Moutarde .. 10.50
Le Foie de Veau Meuniere 10.50
(Calf's Liver "Saute" Meuniere)
Les Grenouilles Provencales 10.50
Les Crevettes a la Nicoise 10.50
(Scampi Saute, Garlic and Tomatoes)
Le Canard a l'Orange 10.50
Ris de Veau aux Morilles 10.50
(Sweet Bread, White Wine, Morrel Mushrooms)
La Cote d'Agneau Grillee Fine Herbes 10.50
Le Steak Poivre 13.50
Le Pigeon Roti au Riz Sauvage 13.50
Le Steak Grille Bearnaise 12.00
Le Carre d'Agneau Bouquetiere (for two) ... 26.00
(Rack of Lamb, Mixed Vegetables)
Le Bass Braise Beurre Nantais (for two) 26.00

DESSERTS:

Les Desserts "Pleiades" ou Fromage (2.50); Souffle Grand Marnier (for two) (7.50); Peche Melba (3.00); Souffle Chocolat (for two) (6.50); Coupe aux Marrons (3.00).

(Similar luncheon menu available at prices ranging from 6.50 to 7.50.)

(Minimum per person: Luncheon, 6.00; Dinner, 8.00)

PUB THEATRICAL

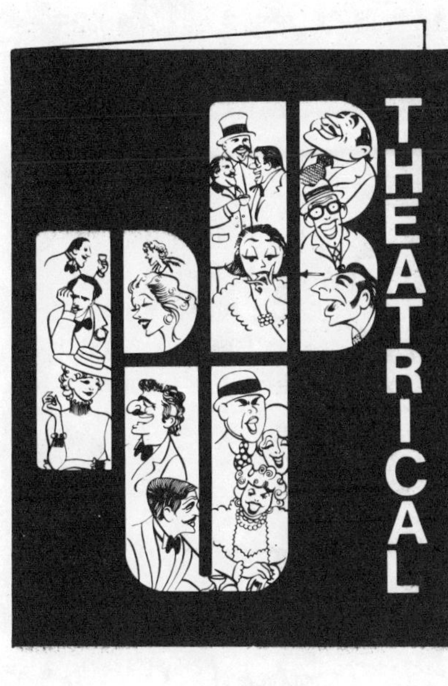

Address: 1633 Broadway
Location: Broadway at 51st Street (concourse level)
Telephone: 581-7700
Credit Cards: AE; DC; MC; V
Reservations: Recommended
Hours: 11:30 AM to 3:00 PM, Tuesday thru Saturday and Monday; 5:00 PM to 11:30 PM, Tuesday thru Friday, to 12:00 Midnight on Saturday
Days Closed: Sunday and Major Holidays; Dinner not served on Monday
Liquor: Full Bar Service
Recommended or Listed in: Cue; Where; Playbill
Maitre d': Jerry Rismiller
Seating Capacity: 175
Cuisine: American and Continental
Specialties of the House: Prime Ribs of Beef; Veal Cordon Bleu; Crabmeat New York
Entertainment: Pianist and singer, Tuesday thru Saturday from 6:00 PM to closing
Party Facilities: The Studio Room (with dance floor); capacity: 25-100

The decor of this contemporary restaurant is highlighted by a fascinating collection of theatrical memorabilia including sketches of costume designs from popular Broadway shows, posters and "Playbills" from the past thirty years. Because of its close proximity to most Broadway theaters, it is a convenient place for dinner before or after curtain. The cocktail lounge features piano music and a singer Tuesday thru Saturday. Look carefully for Pub Theatrical – it's below street level on the concourse of the Uris Building.

DINNER MENU
(table d'hote)

ENTREES:

Scrod New England 9.50
(Cooked with a topping of Buttered Bread Crumbs)

Tenderloin of Beef Madeira 9.50
(Steak Slices and Mushrooms simmered in Wine Sauce, served over Buttered Rice)

Poulet a la Sauterne 9.50
(Boneless Chicken Breast stuffed with an Artichoke-Mushroom-Cognac Filling. Served with Sauterne-Butter Sauce and Rice Pilaf)

Roast Leg of Spring Lamb 9.50

(Dinners include choice of a Cup of Homemade Soup, Fresh Fruits Supreme, Juice or Liver Paté; selection of a Potato or Freshly Cooked Vegetable; Salad with a Cruet of Rosé Wine Dressing; Crusty Breads; Beverage and Ice Cream or Sherbet.)

(Dinner is served until 9:30 PM; a supper menu is available after 9:30 PM.)

DINNER MENU
(a la carte)

APPETIZERS & SOUPS:
Escargots Bourguignonne (3.25); Tureen of Soup (.95); French Onion Soup (.95); Fresh Fruits Supreme (1.25); Chopped Chicken Livers (1.50); Shrimp Cocktail Supreme (3.25); Seafood Cocktail (2.25).

continued on next page

Menu continued

ENTREES:

Bone-In Prime Ribs of Beef au Jus 11.50
New York Strip Steak 12.50
Filet Mignon with Bearnaise Sauce, served with Mushroom Cap 12.50
Pepper Steak a la Maison, served with Mustard Sauce, laced with fine Cognac 11.25
Veal Cordon Bleu 10.95
Crabmeat New York...................... 11.50
(King Crabmeat and Fresh Mushrooms sauteed in fine Chablis, served on a bed of Buttered Rice)
Broiled Filet of Sole, Sesame 9.75
(Lemon Sole coated with Sesame Seeds and broiled in Butter)
Lobster a la Newburg 11.50
(Lobster in a tantalizing Sherry Wine Sauce)
French Fried Gulf Shrimp 10.25
(Entrees include Choice of a Potato or Freshly Cooked Vegetable, Our Distinctive House Salad and Crusty Breads.)

DESSERTS:

Apple Walnut Pie Chantilly (Apples baked in a Flaky Crust with Brown Sugar and Walnuts, topped with Whipped Cream) (1.50); New York Cream Cheese Cake (1.50); Fruits in Season (.95); Our Prestige Ice Cream (.95); Liqueur Ice Cream Parfaits (2.25).

RETSINA: *The resinated wine of Greece. Its taste is unmistakable due to the use of pine resin in the fermentation process. Retsina is predominantly a white wine with a fresh, sappy, turpentine-like flavor.*

RHINE WINE: *Specifically, the strong, complex white wines of the Rhine River in Germany, especially those from the Rhinegau (on the river's right bank from Bingen to Raventhal). Rhine wines are always shipped in a brown fluted bottle and possess a flowery scent and great depth of flavor.*

The term Rhine wine is much misused in the U.S. to describe almost any white wine; the true Rhine wine label usually features the name of both the grower and the shipper.

RIESLING: *In the U.S., the fine dry white wine made in New York and California from the original Riesling grape that is used to produce Germany's Moselle wines.*

LIEDERKRANZ: *Originally developed in an American attempt to copy Scholosskäse, a German relative of Limburger, Liederkranz shares many of the characteristics of these two cheeses. It is soft in texture, golden in color and has a tangy taste. It also has the very strong aroma associated with Limburger.*

LIMBURGER: *A strong cheese with an aroma which has been described as "something between a bouquet and a stink", this cheese was first marketed in Limburg, Belgium whence its name. It is soft in consistency, golden in color and piquant in flavor.*

LEGS: *The "legs" of the wine—or the paths the wine forms when it runs from the "robe" or rim of a glass—tell something about its body. The faster the "legs" drop, and the thicker they are, the more body the wine has. Fairly uniform spacing of the "legs" also indicates wines of fuller body.*

PUERTA REAL

Address: 243 East 58th Street
Location: 58th Street between Second and Third Avenues
Telephone: 758-4756
Credit Cards: All major credit cards accepted
Reservations: Recommended
Hours: Lunch from 12:00 Noon to 3:00 PM, Monday thru Friday; Dinner daily from 5:00 PM to 11:00 PM (11:30 PM on weekends)
Days Closed: None
Liquor: Full bar service
Recommended or Listed in: New York Times; Gourmet; Town & Country; Playbill; Cue
Maitre d': Juan
Seating Capacity: 50
Cuisine: Castilian and Basque
Specialties of the House: Striped Bass Papillote; Stuffed Prawns; Merluza a la Koskera
Dress: Casual

Authentic Castilian and Basque cuisine, attractively presented, is the specialty of Puerta Real, an intimate Spanish restaurant conveniently situated in midtown Manhattan. The restaurant is nicely decorated with wrought iron lamps and colorful ceramics from Toledo which combine to provide a pleasing contrast to the white stucco walls. The menu selections are extensive and are served graciously. Puerta Real is a good choice for pre- and after-theatre dining.

DINNER MENU

(a la carte)

(The following is a representative selection.)

APPETIZERS & SOUPS:

Chorizos de Cantinpalo (Spanish Red Sausage Saute) (2.50); Pequeños Langostinos al Ajillo (Shrimps Saute in Garlic Sauce) (3.25); Caracoles en Cazuela Puerta Real (Snails in Casserole) (3.50); Mejillones en Salsa Verde (Mussels in Green Sauce) (2.75); Pinchitos del Jefe Antonio (Skewered Veal and Pork Bits) (3.00); Salpicon de Mariscos (Cantabrican Seafood Salad Vinagrette) (3.25); Sopa de Ajo Castellana (Castilian Bread and Garlic Soup) (1.75); Gazpacho Campero (Classical Cold Soup) (1.75).

ENTREES:

Langostinos y Lenguado Puerta Real 7.50
(Spanish Prawns and Grey Sole)

Zarzuela de Mariscos del Jefe Antonio 7.95
(Chef's Seafood Casserole)

Gran Villagodio a las Brasas (For Two) 17.00
(Broiled Rib of Prime Beef in Red Wine and Shallots Sauce)

Merluza a la Koskera 6.75
(A Seafood Delight from the Basque Country)

Medallones de Ternera al Jerez 6.95
(Medallions of Veal Simmered Slowly in Tio Pepe Sherry Wine)

Higadillos de Ave al Vino Blanco 5.00
(Sauteed Chicken Livers in Wine)

Langosta Gratinada Puerta Real 10.00
(Lobster Saute in Wine with Lobster Butter, Gratine in Cheese)

Merluza a la Bilbaina 6.50
(Juicy Filet of Hake Marinated with Sweet Red Pepper Stripes)

Pollo al Chilindron 5.95
(Chicken Sauteed with Tomatoes, Red Peppers, Mushrooms and Served with Rice)

Pollo y Langosta al Estilo Catalan 7.95
(A Superb Chicken and Lobster Combination Cooked in a Special Seafood Sauce and Served with Rice)

Brocheta del Jefe 7.50
(Tenderloin in the Spit with Mushrooms, Peppers and Bacon)

Entrecote Diana a las Llamas 9.00
(Steak Diane flambe)

Paella a la Valenciana (For Two) 16.00

Paella de Mariscos Alicantina (For Two) 17.00
(Seafood Paella with Lobster)

Mayordomo al Rioja 9.50
(Prime Sirloin Steak in a Special Sauce)

(A variety of salads and vegetables is also available.)

DESSERTS:

Pasteleria Regia (Our Cake Selection in View on the Cart) (1.75); Naranjas al Caramelo (Caramel Oranges) (2.25).

THE QUILTED GIRAFFE

Address: 3 Academy Street,New Paltz
Location: New York Thruway, Exit 18; Turn left at traffic light, after 3 more lights turn right; restaurant is one more block, on the left
Telephone: (914) 255-9801
Credit Cards: AE; MC; V; DC; CB
Reservations: Required
Hours: 5:30 PM to 10:00 PM daily
Days Closed: Wednesday
Liquor: Full bar service
Recommended or Listed in: Holiday; New York Magazine; Westchester Magazine; Village Voice; Daily News; Cue; Gourmet
Maitre d': Susan
Reservations Manager: Susan
Seating Capacity: 60
Cuisine: French
Specialties of the House: Poisson en Papillote; Duck with Lemon Sauce; Rack of Lamb; Scallop Mousse in Pastry; Homemade Breads, Ice Creams and Desserts
Dress: Jackets not required
Entertainment: Live classical piano music during Dinner
Party Facilities: Private room; capacity: 25
Parking: Restaurant parking lot

If French cuisine in a country setting is to your liking, you certainly will want to experience dining at The Quilted Giraffe. The restaurant specializes in the nouvelle cuisine, and the owner-chef travels to Manhattan regularly to hand-pick first quality provisions. All the baking is done on the premises of the restaurant, and the homemade ice cream is a fitting finale to fine dining at The Quilted Giraffe. The restaurant is convenient to reach via the New York Thruway, and if you wish to prolong the pleasure of dining out of Manhattan, the management can recommend accommodations nearby.

DINNER MENU

(prix fixe — 19.00)

APPETIZERS & SOUPS:
Les Pâtés du Chef; Les Crevettes Aromates; Les Escargots Pernod; La Soupe à l'Oignon; La Truite Fumée; Le Melon de Saison; Le Caviar Béluga for 2 (15.00); Le Saucisson au Beurre.

ENTREES:
Le Poisson en Papillote
(The classical preparation of encasement cooking in which the fish and sauce are baked and served in parchment paper.)
Le Canard au Poivre des Isles
(Duckling first roasted at high temperature to draw out the fat, then more slowly until tender. Flamed again to crisp the skin and served with a spicy green peppercorn sauce.)
Le Filet de Veau aux Cepes
(The finest of white milk-fed veal seasoned with rosemary and thyme and broiled briefly till pink. Served with sauce Bernaise and wild mushrooms from the Swiss forest.)
Le Tournedos au Poivre
(Thick cut rounds of filet of beef tenderloin, pounded with crushed black peppercorns and sauteed in clarified butter. Served with sauce Foyot.)
Les Huitres Frais Sautee du Chef
(Plump fresh oysters removed from the shell and sauteed quickly with onions, shallots and cayenne pepper. Served floating in a broth of heavy cream and butter.)
Le Carré D'Agneau
(Elegant rack of baby lamb, coated with rosemary, mustard and garlic.)

continued on next page

Menu continued

Le Ris de Veau Financière
(Sweetbread medallions seasoned and sauteed for a minute, then truffle-flavored Madeira sauce added and the ensemble simmered gently with mushrooms and olives. Served in pastry.)

Le Foie de Veau à La Moutarde Chinoise
(The crème de la crème of calf's liver. Sliced to your specifications and sauteed to order. Served with crème fraiche mustard sauce.)

Le Filet de Boeuf en Chemise (For Two)
(A six-inch filet cut from the tenderloin, stuffed with pate de foie, wrapped in a pastry crust and baked to order. Served with sauce Perigueux.)

Les Gibiers en Saison (Supplement)
(The chef's preparation of fall and winter game birds and animals as available.)

(Dinner includes salad, dessert and coffee or tea.)

AMARETTI: *The legend about Amaretti is that it was first made by a lovesick baker who wanted to make a special kind of almond cookie. He daydreamed so long about his lady love that he left the cookie in the oven too long and the result was this popular cookie. It is made of pulverized almonds, egg whites and sugar and is quite light and dry. It is served with tea or with a good red wine and, since almonds have always been expensive, is usually reserved for important occasions. A similar cookie is called a* pignoli *and is made of pine nuts as well as almonds. It can be an after-dinner cookie, served with a dessert wine such as Marsala, or served in the morning with coffee.*

BABA: *The best known babá is the babá au rhum. The Neapolitans developed it from the idea of a* brioche *during the time of Ferdinand and Catherine of Aragon in the 1700's. A babá has fewer eggs than a brioche—it is halfway between a brioche and a sponge cake and is in the shape of a cone without a point. The babá au rhum is soaked in rum for a long, long time—a housewife would make them in the early afternoon in order to serve them as a dinner dessert. Babás can also be made in a round shape, cut in half and filled. The babá a crema has a custard cream filling and the babá a ricotta has the same filling as cannoli—ricotta, chocolate chips and candied fruit.*

We'd like to make Manhattan Menus even more *useful to you, and would welcome hearing any comments or suggestions you may have. Write to: Manhattan Menus, P.O. Box 5217, FDR Station, New York, N.Y. 10022.*

RAFFAELA'S

Address: 134 West Houston Street
Location: West Houston Street, between Sullivan Street and Macdougal Street
Telephone: 982-0464
Credit Cards: AE; DC; MC; CB
Reservations: Recommended
Hours: 5:00 PM to 12 Midnight, Sunday thru Thursday; 5:00 PM to 2:00 AM Friday and Saturday
Days Closed: Christmas Day; Thanksgiving Day
Liquor: Full Bar Service
Recommended or listed in: Gourmet; Cue
Maitre d's: Frederick Fiengo and Raffaela
Seating Capacity: 60
Cuisine: Italian
Specialties of the House: Stuffed Artichoke; Calamari a la Napoletana with Mussels and Clams; Chicken Rollatine a la Raffaela; Homemade Italian Cheesecake

Near the Soho district of the West Village, on "Howston" Street, is a friendly Italian bistro called Raffaela's. Host Fred Fiengo presides over a comfortable place, not splashy but appropriately decorated with Peninsular flora and Italian travel posters. It's a family restaurant, intimate in its atmosphere and casual in its style. Ideal for those seeking pleasant dining in the Village.

Raffaela's

DINNER MENU

(a la carte)

APPETIZERS:
Assorted Antipasto (4.75); Fresh Shrimp Cocktail (4.75); Prosciutto and Melon (5.00); Clam Cocktail (3.75); Baked Clams (4.75); Hot Homemade Antipasto (5.50); Stuffed Mushrooms (4.75); Mussels Marinara (4.50).

SOUPS:
Escarole in Broth (2.50); Pasta Fazole (2.75); Lentils and Pasta (2.75); Minestrone (2.75); Stracciatella with Pastina (2.75); Rice or Pastina Consomme (1.75).

ENTREES:
Veal Cacciatore with Green Peppers or Mushrooms 6.75
Veal Cutlet a la Milanese with Spaghetti 7.50
Veal Cutlet Parmigiana with Spaghetti 8.25
Veal Scaloppine a la Margarita 8.50
Veal Scaloppine Pizzaiola with Green Peppers or Mushrooms 8.50
Veal Francese 8.75
Veal Rollantine a la Margarita 10.75
Eggplant Parmigiana with Spaghetti 6.75

continued on next page

Menu continued

Pork Chops with Hot Peppers 8.75
Saltinbocca a la Romano 10.00
Broiled Sirloin Steak 11.00
Sirloin Steak Pizzaiola, Green Peppers 11.50
Broiled Half Spring Chicken 5.75
Half Spring Chicken Cacciatore, Fresh Mushrooms 7.00
Chicken, Oil, Garlic and Lemon 7.00
Chicken Parmigiana, Boneless with Spaghetti 8.25
Chicken Scarpariello 8.75
Chicken Cippolla 7.00
Chicken Breast Rollantine a la Raffaela 9.75
(White Wine, Mushrooms and Prosciutto)
Broiled Veal Chop with Mushrooms Saute ... 9.25
Broiled Pork Chops with Mushrooms Saute .. 9.25
Calamari a la Napoletana with Mussels and Clams 9.75
Clam Soup Posillipo 6.50
Fresh Shrimps Marinara with Spaghetti 9.50
Shrimps Scampi 9.50
Combination of Fresh Shrimp and Calamari en Casserole 9.75
Stripe Bass Filet 9.50
Lobster Fra Diavolo, Oreganato, Broiled or Boiled .... (...)

(A variety of pasta dishes is offered at prices ranging from 4.75 to 8.25.)

(Vegetables and salads are also available a la carte at prices ranging from 2.50 to 4.00.)

DESSERTS:
Spumoni (1.75); Bisquit-Tortoni (1.75); Homemade Italian Cheese Cake (2.50); Fresh Strawberries with Whipped Cream (2.75).

SEDIMENT: *The better wines, usually those that improve with age, deposit a sediment. In white wine it emerges as crystals at the bottom of the bottle; in red it may take the form of a thick crust or appear as large brown flakes. Sediment is a positive sign—an aged wine with no sediment is suspect. If the wine is served properly in a restaurant, the sediment should remain in the bottle and not get into your glass. You can ensure this by asking the wine-steward to decant any bottle of fine red wine for you. This means simply pouring the wine off the sediment in the bottle and into a wide-mouthed decanter for "breathing."*

VANILLA: *This is the flavor imparted to wine from the substance "vanillin" which is present in the oak in which the wine is stored. A young Bordeaux or Burgundy has a mild vanilla flavor derived from the barrel. The younger the barrel, the more apparent the vanilla flavor will be. The influence of this element is most noticeable in the better California Chardonnays.*

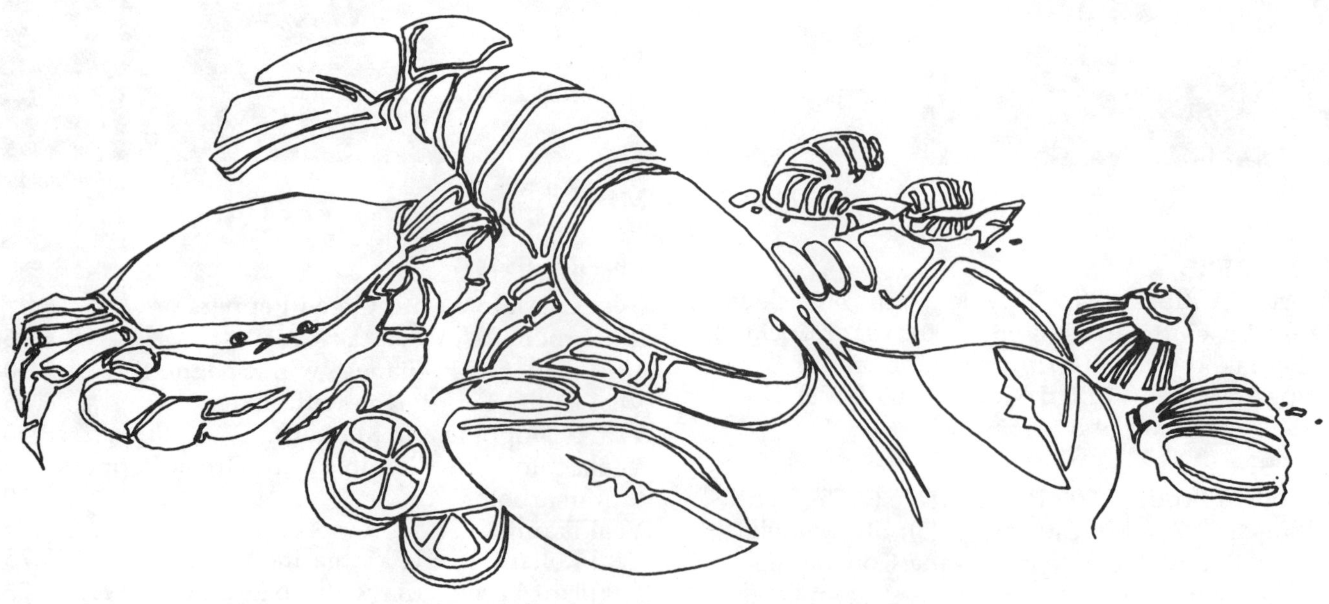

RESIDENCE

Address:	**1568 First Avenue**
Location:	**First Avenue between 81st and 82nd Streets**
Telephone:	**628-4100**
Credit Cards:	**AE; V**
Reservations:	**Required**
Hours:	**6:00 PM to 11:00 PM, Monday thru Saturday**
Days Closed:	**Sunday**
Liquor:	**Full bar service**
Maitre d':	**Primo**
Reservations Manager:	**Primo**
Seating Capacity:	**65**
Cuisine:	**French**
Specialties of the House:	**Specialties vary with the season**
Dress:	**Jacket required**

The Residence is a very special restaurant and as such reflects the care and concern for quality that is its raison d'etre. The Residence is the creation of its proprietor George Colovic, whose own high standards of taste and comfort are always discernible here. All the components of a fine restaurant combine in the Residence: the tastefulness of the decor, the careful attention to the preparation of each individual meal and the very personal service. This is the kind of restaurant that knowing New Yorkers view as their own personal and very special discovery.

DINNER MENU
(a la carte)

(The menu changes daily and according to the season. The following is a representative selection.)

APPETIZERS & SOUPS: *(Prices range from 3.25 to 6.75)*
Pâté Maison; Sea Food Crêpe; Hors d'Oeuvre Residence; Casserolletté d'Escargots Residence; Salmon Fumé; Foie Gras; Mousse de Foie Gras en Brioche; Mousse de Poisson a l'Oseille; Prosciutto and Melon; Salade of the Season; Potages du Jour.

ENTREES: *(Prices range from 11.00 to 15.00)*
Omelette Residence
Oeufs Brouille
Steak Tartar
Mussels Marinière
Écrevisse Provençale
Le Coeur de Filet Mignon Béarnaise
Baby Rack of Lamb Mascotte
Steak au Poivre
Rognon Saute Bordelaise
Riz de Veau Financière
Canard à l'Orange or au Poivre Vert
Striped Bass Etuve "Tout Paris"
Truite Farcie "Fernand Point"
Filet de Sole "Bonne Femme"
Salmon à l'Oseille
Quenelle de Brochet Nantua
Shaslik
Steak Paillard
Cote de Boeuf pour Deux
Médaillion de Veau Vallée d'Auge
Sirloin Steak
Calf's Liver

DESSERTS: *(Prices range from 3.50 to 4.50)*
Pastry; Chocolate Mousse; Fresh Fruit in Wine; Les Crêpe Residence; Coupe aux Marrons; Creme Caramel; Fromage aux Choix; Sorbets Assortis.

continued on next page

continued

Residence

BISCOTTI DI QUARESIMA: *This is a Lenten cookie that is made with almonds, sugar, flour and vegetable shortening—no animal fat, not even butter. After Lent, butter is used and the cookie becomes lighter and is called a Tuscan wine biscuit or, simply,* biscotti. *It is always served with* vin santo, *a wine made from grapes grown only in Tuscany.*

If you own or manage a fine restaurant, and would like to see it included in the next edition of Manhattan Menus, please contact the publisher for information.

RICHOUX OF LONDON

Address:	**Third Avenue and 54th Street**
Telephone:	**753-7721**
Credit Cards:	**AE; V; MC; DC**
Reservations:	**Not necessary**
Hours:	**24 hours,daily**
Days Closed:	**Christmas Day**
Liquor:	**Full bar service**
Recommended or Listed in:	**New York Times; New York Magazine; Cue; Playbill; Sphere**
Seating Capacity:	**75**
Cuisine:	**English**
Specialties of the House:	**English Brunch; Rarebits; Chicken Curry; Daily English Specialties**
Dress:	**Informal**

Richoux of London evokes the feeling of a smart English restaurant in one of New York's newest and most interesting skyscrapers—The Citicorp Building at 54th Street and Third Avenue. The contrast between the quiet understatement of this very British eatery and its bold architectural setting adds another dimension to the experience of eating out. Richoux is open 24 hours a day, offering a variety of dining choices (fresh seafood is flown in from England regularly), from brunch through dinner. It's also a perfect place to stop for a late night chocolate Sundae or a very early breakfast. You can even buy English chocolates, tea, biscuits, cakes and Scotch smoked salmon to take home with you.

Richoux of London

continued on next page

MENU

(a la carte)
(Selections available 24 hours a day.)

APPETIZERS & SOUPS:
Cream of Tomato Soup (1.00); Cream of Chicken Soup (1.00); Cream of Mushroom Soup (1.00); Minestrone (1.00); Vichyssoise (1.25); Chef's Pate served with Hot Toast (1.95); Shrimp Cocktail (2.75); Orange Juice (.65); Tomato Juice (.65); Melon (. . .); Scotch Smoked Salmon Platter (. . .).

EGG DISHES:
Assortment of egg dishes available.

HOT TOASTED SAVOURIES:
Elegant Rarebit topped with Tomato and Crispy Bacon (3.50); Welsh Rarebit (2.75); Buck Rarebit topped with Poached Egg (2.95); Mayfair Rarebit topped with Shrimps and Asparagus (3.95); Quiche Lorraine (4.25); English Style Hamburger or Cheeseburger (3.25).

ENTREES:
English Grilled Dover Sole 10.50
Goujonnettes of Sole (fried pieces of sole) . . . 5.00
Fried English Scampi 6.50
Smoked Haddock with a Poached Egg 6.25
Sirloin Steak dressed with Watercress and Grilled Tomatoes 9.50
Freshly Baked Vol-au-Vent 4.95
(Chicken and mushroom)
Richoux Special Chopped Steak on a bed of Salad 4.95
Chicken Curry 5.50

SALADS:
Chef's Salad Bowl 4.75
Slimmers Salad 4.95
(Fresh Fruit, Apple, Grated Cheese, Raisins, Nuts, Tomato, Lettuce, Plain Yogurt)
Grated Cheddar Cheese Salad 3.95
Niçoise 5.25
Californian 5.25
(Cottage Cheese, Peach, Pineapple, Nuts, Prune, Lettuce, Tomato)
Egg Salad 3.75
(Large variety of sandwiches available, priced from 2.50 to 5.25.)

DESSERTS AND CHEESE:
Knickerbocker Glory (Vanilla Ice Cream, Strawberries, Pineapple, Cherries, Whipped Cream) (1.50); Black Velvet (Vanilla Ice Cream, Black Cnerries in Heavy Syrup, Whipped Cream) (1.65); Strawberry Delight (Vanilla Ice Cream, Strawberries, Chopped Nuts) (1.65); Soft Frozen Yogurt (2.25); Chocolate Imperial (Vanilla Ice Cream, Chocolate Sauce, Chopped Nuts) (1.50); Dusty Road (Coffee and Chocolate Ice Cream, Butterscotch Sauce, Flaked Chocolate, Whipped Cream) (1.65); Yogurt Parfait (Plain Yogurt, Assorted Fruits) (2.50); Cheese with Biscuits or Ryvita and Butter (4.25); Assorted Cakes, Pies, Ice Creams and Sherbets (1.25 to 1.95).

RICHOUX ENGLISH BRUNCH:
Rashers of Bacon, Fried Eggs, Sausages, Grilled Tomato, Fried Bread, Grilled Mushrooms (4.75).

RIOJA: *The most popular Spanish wine, produced in the mountainous area along the Rio Ebro in north-central Spain. Made with the methods of Bordeaux, Riojas are lighter, less alcoholic and drier than Bordeaux, and they are typically inexpensive. Usually only the Rioja reds have distinction. The drier reds are shipped in Bordeaux bottles and the fuller ones in Burgundy bottles.*

ROMANEE-CONTI: *The Burgundian domaine of some of the most celebrated red wines of France, including Romanée-Conti, La Tâche and Richebourg. These wines, traditionally among the highest priced, have a slightly spicy flavor and a soft texture.*

IL RIGOLETTO

Address: 232 East 53rd Street
Location: 53rd Street between Second and Third Avenues
Telephone: 759-9384
Credit Cards: AE; V; MC; DC
Reservations: Requested
Hours: Luncheon from 12:00 Noon to 3:00 PM, Monday thru Saturday; Dinner from 5:30 PM to 10:30 PM, Monday thru Friday; 5:00 PM to 11:00 PM on Saturday
Days Closed: Sunday; Thanksgiving, Christmas, July 4th
Liquor: Full bar service
Recommended or Listed in: Cue; Esquire; Visitors East ; Gentlemen's Quarterly; Where; Host
Maitre d': Mario; Louis
Seating Capacity: 52
Cuisine: Northern Italian
Specialties of the House: Homemade Quadrettini; Homemade Ravioli; Saltimboca a la Romana; Brodetto
Dress: Jackets recommended

This old-country retreat is tucked into the heart of a bustling business community and fashionable residential and recreational neighborhood. Quiet, cozy and comfortable, Il Rigoletto offers authentic Northern Italian cuisine in a gracious, relaxing environment. New (1977) owner-managers, Louis and Mario Orlandi, have between them over 70 years experience in quality food service. Their standards are high, their establishment enchanting.

DINNER MENU

(a la carte)

APPETIZERS & SOUPS:
Roast Peppers and Anchovies (2.50); Crabmeat Cocktail (5.00); Assorted Antipasto (3.50); Baked Clams Parisienne (3.75); Mussels Marinara (3.25); Little Neck Clams (3.50); Avocado with Anchovy Dressing (2.50); Prosciutto and Melon (3.00); Shrimp Cocktail (4.00); Clams Posillipo (4.00); Salami (2.50); Clam, Tomato or Grapefruit Juice (1.25); Half Grapefruit (1.25); Oysters (Blue Point) (3.50); Baked Artichoke alla Diavolo (2.25); Soup du Jour (1.75); Consomme with Rice (1.75); Onion Soup au Gratin (2.00); Minestrone (1.75); Tortellini in Brodo (2.75); Stracciatella (Spinach, Egg Drops in Consomme) (2.75).

PASTA:
Tortellini Bolognese (Stuffed Dumplings with Meat Sauce) 6.75
Spaghetti with Meat or Marinara Sauce 6.25
Fettuccine Alfredo, Bolognese or with Prosciutto 6.75
Lasagna Verdi (Layers of Green Noodles with Meat) 6.75
Manicotti with Cheese served au Gratin 6.75
Cannelloni Stuffed with Meat served au Gratin 6.75
Linguine or Spaghetti with Clam Sauce 7.00
Quadrettini with Spinach Noodles and Prosciutto 6.75
Gnocchi Piemontese (Flour and Potato Dumplings) 6.75
Ravioli Stuffed with Meat and Spinach 6.25

ENTREES:
Broiled Filet of Sole or Meuniere 7.50
Broiled Boston Scrod 7.50
Broiled Striped Bass 7.50
Broiled Pompano Amandine 7.75
Broiled or Sauteed Bay Scallops 7.75
Langustina Marinara 8.00
Crabmeat au Gratin 9.00
Shrimp Fra Diavolo 7.75
Mussels Posillipo 7.25
Boneless Chicken Fiorentina "Maison" 7.75
Boneless Chicken Bolognese with Prosciutto and Cheese 7.75
Chicken Cacciatora with Tomatoes and Mushrooms 7.75

continued on next page

Menu continued

Boneless Chicken Parmigiana 7.75
Half a Broiled Chicken 7.50
Roast Chicken for Two 15.00
Veal Piccata with Butter and Lemon Sauce . . . 8.50
Veal Scaloppine Marsala 8.50
Veal Scaloppine Francese 8.50
Veal Parmigiana 8.50
Veal Rollatine 8.75
Saltimboca alla Romana (Veal with Prosciutto and Cheese) 8.75
Costoletta Milanese (Breaded Veal Chop) 9.50
Veal Chop Paillard 9.50
Sausage Pizzaiola 8.00
Broiled Pork Chops (2) 8.75
Broiled Lamb Chops (2) 8.75
Egg Plant Parmigiana 6.50
Calves Liver Veneziana or Sauteed with Bacon 7.75
Calves Brains au Beurre Noire or Fiorentina . 8.00
Trifolati (Veal Kidney Sauteed in White Wine) 7.50
Rack of Lamb for Two 18.00
Beef and Peppers 8.75
Paillard of Beef 10.00
Broiled Minute Steak 10.00
Sirloin Steak 12.00
Filet Mignon 12.00
Sirloin Steak for Two 24.00
Chateaubriand for Two 24.00

DESSERTS:
Lemon Sherbet (1.50); Ice Cream (Chocolate, Vanilla, Coffee) (1.50); Tortoni (1.75); Spumoni (1.75); Parfaits Tricolor (2.00); Rum Cake (2.00); Cheese Cake (2.00); Crepes Suzette for Two (8.00); Cherries Jubilee (3.00); Zabaglione (3.00); Coupe au Marrons (3.00); Macedonia of Fresh Fruit (2.25); Profiteroles (2.25); Napoleon (1.75); Peach Melba (2.25).

(A table d'hote menu is also available for luncheon and dinner; dinner prices range from 12.00 to 14.75.)

Il Rigoletto

ROSE: *The French word for pink, the color ot these wines. The best rosés are not made from a blend of red and white wines, but rather from black (red wine) grapes whose skins have been removed from the processing shortly after fermentation begins. Rosés, which should be served chilled and drunk young, can be both quite sweet (Anjou) or quite dry (Rhône Valley, particularly Tavel).*

SAINT-EMILION: *The red wines from the most productive of the Bordeaux districts. The chateau-bottled vintages rank with the best wines of the Médoc; in general, St. Emilions are simpler. They are rich, sturdy, warm and generous, maturing less quickly than the neighboring Pomerol, but faster than the wines of the Médoc.*

RIVER'S EDGE

Address: 882 First Avenue
Location: First Avenue between 49th and 50th Streets
Telephone: 758-3258
Credit Cards: AE; MC; V
Reservations: Recommended
Hours: Luncheon from 11:00 AM to 4:00 PM; Dinner from 4:00 PM to 12:00 Midnight; Sunday Brunch from 11:00 AM to 4:00 PM; Bar to 2:00 AM
Days Closed: None
Liquor: Full bar service
Maitre d's: Jerry Maguire; Jay La Mont
Seating Capacity: 70
Cuisine: Continental
Specialties of the House: Chicken Rochambeau; Steak au Poivre; Sole Veronique
Dress: Informal
Entertainment: Live piano music; daily from 7:00 PM to 12:00 Midnight
Party Facilities: Semi-private room; capacity: 25

Nestled on First Avenue, just three blocks north of the United Nations, the River's Edge offers harassed New Yorkers the warmth and leisure of an old-style country inn. Three charming dining areas feature a Buck's County ambience to enhance a tempting, continental menu and an interesting wine list that is in touch with reality. Nightly piano entertainment complements the simple, unrushed hospitality for cocktails or dinner.

River's Edge

continued on next page

continued

LUNCHEON MENU

(a la carte)

APPETIZERS & SOUPS:
Artichoke Mushrooms Vinagrette (1.50); Spinach Crepe, Mornay Sauce (1.50); Sauteed Chicken Livers (1.75); Fresh Berries in Cream (1.50).

ENTREES:
Eggs Benedict 3.95
Eggs Sardou (With Artichoke, Spinach and Hollandaise) 3.95
Eggs Hussarde (With Ham and Hollandaise) . 3.95
Omelettes 3.50
(Mushrooms, Spinach, Cheese)
Filet Mignonettes with Rice Pilaf 4.50
Beef en Brochette with Rice Pilaf 4.50
Quiche Lorraine with Garden Green Salad .. 3.95
Chicken Rochambeau 4.25
(Ham, Boneless Breast of Chicken, Sauce Bourgignonne and Hollandaise)
River's Edge Chef Salad 4.50
Bay Scallops with Lemon Butter, Bacon, Mushrooms 3.95
Roast Beef Hash with Poached Egg 3.95
Steak Sandwich, Mushroom Caps 4.50

DESSERTS:
From the Pastry Tray (1.50); Mousse au Chocolat (1.50); Crepe Fitzgerald (Cream Cheese, Walnuts, Cassis, Raspberries) (2.00).

(Luncheon Minimum per person: 3.95.)

DINNER MENU

(a la carte)

APPETIZERS & SOUPS:
Mushroom Caps Stuffed with Shrimp (2.50); Shrimp Cocktail (3.50); River's Edge Avocado (Madrilene, Sour Cream, Caviar) (2.00); Quiche Lorraine (1.75); Onion Soup au Gratin (2.25); Soup du Jour (1.75).

ENTREES:
Chicken Rochambeau (Ham, Boneless Breast of Chicken, Sauce Bourgignonne and Hollandaise) 6.95
Veal Marsala 7.95
Fettucine Alfredo 5.50
Filet Mignon (Sauce Bernaise) 10.75
Steak au Poivre with Cream Cognac Sauce .. 9.95
Calves Liver with Bacon 7.50
Baked Loin Pork Chops 7.25
Broiled Lobster Tails 9.75
Bay Scallops with Lemon Butter, Bacon and Mushrooms 7.95
Filet of Sole Veronique 6.50

(All entrees are served with a potpourri of fresh vegetables, green salad, bread and butter.)

(Desserts served at Dinner are identical to the Luncheon menu; prices are slightly higher at Dinner.)

(A prix-fixe Brunch is served on Sunday: 4.50 per person, including a Bloody Mary or Screwdriver.)

LIVAROT: *The strongest of the French cheeses, Livarot is named for the village in Normandy where it is made. It is a soft, yellow cheese encased in a brown crust and shares with Limburger and Liederkranz a very powerful aroma. It is also very tangy in flavor.*

ROCK GARDEN OF TOKYO

Address: 34 West 56th Street
Location: 56th Street between Fifth Avenue and Avenue of the Americas
Telephone: 245-7936
Credit Cards: AE; DC; CB; MC; V
Reservations: Recommended for lunch and for large groups at dinner.
Hours: Lunch from 12 Noon to 2:30 PM Monday thru Saturday; Dinner from 5:30 PM to 10:30 PM Sunday thru Wednesday and 5:30 PM to 11:00 PM Thursday thru Saturday
Days Closed: None
Liquor: Full bar service
Proprietor: Shoki Kaneda
Seating Capacity: 90
Cuisine: Japanese
Specialty of the House: Hibachi Yakiniku Steak
Dress: Casual

Rank Rock Garden of Tokyo among the more satisfying and pleasant of the many Japanese restaurants which have joined the New York scene in recent years. Here you'll find the relaxed ambience characteristic of Japanese decor and in the background you'll hear soft and soothing Oriental music. The waitresses are attired in traditional kimonos and each table has individual hibachis for broiling Sekitei specialities.

LUNCHEON MENU

(a la carte)

APPETIZERS:

Tsukidashi (small appetizer): Nambanzuke (Fresh fish pickled in a deliciously unique sweet and sour sauce) (1.50); Sugaki (Fresh oysters with a refreshing vinegar sauce) (1.95); Kushidango (Skewered ground chicken, delicately flavored in sauce) (1.75); Toriwasa (Lightly boiled chicken with a delicate horseradish sauce) (1.75); Sunomono (Fresh seafood garnished with finely sliced cucumbers) (1.95); Sekitei Tsukidashi (Chef's choice - seasoned items) (2.25); Zensai (appetizer): Kushiyaki (Skewered shrimp and mushroom caps boiled till crisp on the outside) (2.50); Sakamushi (Fresh cherrystone clams steamed in sake) (2.50); Tempura (Shrimp and assorted vegetables deep fried in sesame oil) (3.50); Sashimi (Filets of fresh fish in season, served uncooked with green mustard,) (sm. 4.00) (lg. 6.95); Meat Sashimi (Steak tartar, finely chopped sirloin seasoned with exotic spices) (4.25); Sushi (Vinegared rice with fillets of fresh raw fish wrapped in seaweed) (sm. 4.50) (lg. 6.95); Moriawase (Assorted appetizers) (4.50).

SOUPS, SALADS & VEGETABLES:

Sumashi (a light clear soup with mushrooms) (.75); Misoshiru (Traditional soybean soup) (.95); Rock Garden Salad (1.25); Oshinko (Pickled Oriental vegetables) (1.25); Oshitashi (Lightly boiled vegetables with lemon) (1.50); Hibachi Vegetables (Mixed vegetables cooked at your table) (2.50).

ENTREES:

Tatsuta-age 4.50
(Marinated tender chicken deep fried until crisp.)

Tempura 5.50
(Shrimp and assorted vegetables in a light batter, deep fried in oil of sesame.)

Salmon Teriyaki 5.95
(Broiled salmon repeatedly smothered in teriyaki sauce.)

Sukiyaki 6.25
(Thinly sliced prime rib of beef served with a medley of Oriental vegetables in a casserole dish.)

continued on next page

Menu continued

SEKITEI SPECIALTIES:*

Hibachi Yakiniku Liver 4.25
Hibachi Yakiniku Chicken 4.95
Hibachi Yakiniku Beef 5.50
Hibachi Yakiniku Short Ribs 5.95
Hibachi Yakiniku Prime Ribs 6.25
Hibachi Yakiniku Prime Sirloin 6.95
Hibachi Yakiniku Filet Mignon 7.25
(All entrees served with salad, rice and tea.)

DESSERTS:

Ice Cream (.60); Sherbet (.60); Mandarin Orange (.95); Fresh Fruit in Season (1.25).

DINNER MENU

(a la carte)

APPETIZERS:

Tsukidashi (small appetizer): Nambanzuke (Fried fish in a unique sweet and sour sauce) (1.75); Kushidango (Ground chicken flavored in sauce) (1.95); Toriwasa (Lightly boiled chicken with horseradish sauce) (1.95); Sugaki (Fresh oysters with vinegar sauce) (2.50); Ikura Oroshi (Salmon roe with finely grated radish) (2.95); Sekitei Tsukidashi (Chef's choice — seasoned items) (2.95). Zensai (appetizer): Kushyuaki (Skewered shrimp and mushroom caps) (2.75); Sakamushi (Fresh cherrystone clams steamed in sake) (2.95); Tempura (Shrimp and vegetables deep fried) (3.50); Sashimi (Filets of fresh fish in season, served uncooked) (4.00 & up); Usuzukuri (Very thin slices of raw fish with lemon and soy sauce) (5.95); Meat Shashimi (Steak Tartar) (4.50); Sushi (Vinegared rice with filets of raw fish) (sm. 4.50) (lg. 6.95); Tarabagani (Alaskan King Crab Legs) (4.95); Moriawase (Assorted appetizers) (4.95).

SOUPS, SALADS & VEGETABLES:

Sumashi (a light clear soup) with onions and mushrooms (1.50); with clams (1.75); with scallions, egg, and mushroom (1.95); Misoshiru (Traditional soybean soup) (1.75); Oshinko (Pickled Oriental Vegetables) (1.50); Rock Garden Salad (Fresh greens with house dressing) (1.75); Sunomono (Fresh seafood garnished with cucumbers) (2.50); Oshitashi (Lightly boiled vegetables with lemon) (1.95); Yakinasu (Sliced broiled eggplant) (2.50); Hibachi Vegetables (Mixed vegetables cooked at your table) (3.00).

ENTREES:

Tempura 6.95
(Shrimp and assorted vegetables in light batter, deep fried.)

Salmon Teriyaki 7.50
(Broiled salmon in teriyaki sauce.)

Nishikian 7.75
(White fish in season, fried and smothered with a sweet sauce.)

Oroshini 7.95
(White fish in season with sauce of grated horseradish.)

Ise Ebi 12.95
(Live whole lobster boiled or broiled.)

Nabemono *(Japanese One-Pot Cookery) for Two:*

Mizutaki 16.00
(Chicken in a light broth with Oriental vegetables.)

Sukiyaki 18.00
(Thin slices of beef with a medley of Oriental vegetables.)

Shabu Shabu 20.00
(Paper thin slices of beef dipped in a light broth.)

Yosenabe 22.00
(Whole lobster, fish, shrimp, clams and assortment of delicious vegetables for an unforgettable bouillabase.)

Sekitei Specialties:*

Hibachi Yakiniku (Calves) Liver 6.50
Hibachi Yakiniku Chicken 6.95
Hibachi Yakiniku Beef 7.50
Hibachi Yakiniku Short Ribs 7.95
Hibachi Yakiniku Prime Ribs 8.50
Hibachi Yakiniku Prime Sirloin 8.95
Hibachi Yakiniku Prime Filet Mignon 9.50
(Entrees served with rice and tea.)

* Sekitei specialties are sliced and marinated in ten exotic spices and then broiled at your table. It is recommended that the broiling be done by each diner himself to suit his own taste. Each table has individual hibachis for this purpose.

DESSERTS:

Ice Cream (.90); Sherbet (.90); Mandarin Orange (1.25); Melon in Season (1.50); Fresh Fruits in season (. . . .).

ROMA DI NOTTE
Grotte di Bacco

Address:	137 East 55th Street
Location:	55th Street between Third and Lexington Avenues
Telephone:	832-1128
Credit Cards:	AE; CB; DC
Reservations:	Recommended on weekdays; required on weekends
Hours:	Dinner from 6:00 PM to 2:00 AM
Days Closed:	Sunday
Liquor:	Full bar service
Recommended or Listed in:	Cue; Forbes; New York Times; New York Magazine
Maitre d':	Roberto
Seating Capacity:	180
Cuisine:	Roman
Specialties of the House:	Quail; Wild Game; Homemade Pasta
Dress:	Jackets required
Entertainment:	Live music for dancing
Party Facilities:	2 private rooms; capacity: 30/500

Fine Roman cuisine is the attraction at Roma di Notte and a tradition that spans four centuries in owner Armando Mei's family. The restaurant is open for dinner and features live music and dancing throughout the evening. Intimate "caves" where you can hide-away in privacy provide an unusual and romantic addition to dining at Roma di Notte/Grotte di Bacco. The same distinctive cuisine is characteristic of another Mei restaurant at the same location, Iperbole, and can be combined with the private party and meeting facilities of Top of the "I"—the top floor of this triplex restaurant establishment. Westsiders should not feel slighted—Mr. Mei's Fontana di Trevi on West 57th Street offers a similarly delightful dining experience.

Roma di Notte (Grotte di Bacco)

continued on next page

DINNER MENU

(a la carte)

(Roma di Notte's extensive menu features a variety of homemade pasta dishes and special preparations of quail; the following is a representative selection.)

ENTREES:

Green Lasagna alla Lucullo 6.30
Spaghetti with the Sauce of Your Choice 5.20
Homemade Noodles in Butter, Parmesan Cheese 6.00
Linguine Clams, White or Red Sauce 6.00
Large Homemade Macaroni Stuffed 5.90
Gnocchi di Semolina Alla Fiorentina 6.20
Gnocchi di Patate A Piacere 5.50
Homemade Meat Dumpling Gratine 6.50
Tortellini Any Style 5.95
Risotto Mantecato Al Verde 6.40
Risotto Mantecato ai Frutti Di Mare 7.20
Salmon on Green Pepper 9.95
Boston Scrod Livornese 7.95
Assorted Fried Fish 8.50
Grilled Sole 9.50
Wolf of the Sea, Grilled Bass 8.95
Squid Fried or Stewed with Peas 8.10
River Trout Mugnaia Style 8.10
Roast Wild Boar alla Laziale 8.80
Stuffed Baby Pheasant au Crouton 9.30
Rack of Lamb - For Two 19.95
Squab Grilled 9.80
Cutlet of Lamb Grilled 9.50
Assorted Mixed Roast 9.25
Chicken Diable Style - For Two 17.00
Filet Mignon Primitive Style 11.50
Sirloin Steak 11.50
Heart of Filet Mignon with Aromatic Herbs - For Two 24.00
Veal Piccata Sauteed with Lemon 8.70
Veal Scaloppine with Prosciutto Sauteed in Wine 8.80
Breast of Capon Bolognese Style 8.80
Chicken Roman Style, Mushrooms, Peppers . 8.50
Veal Cutlet Parmigiana 8.80
Sliced Filet Mignon Borolo Wine or Pizzaiola 11.00
Milk Fed Veal Chops Sassi Style 8.90
Filet of Chicken Tony Style 8.80
Veal Scaloppine Sorrentina Style 8.95
Milk Fed Veal Loin Paillard 9.50
Quail (Prepared in any of ten different ways) 8.95

(A variety of vegetables and salads is offered at prices ranging from 1.95 to 5.10.)

(Desserts, including a variety of sweets and cheese selections, are also available.)

(Minimum charge per person: 5.00)

SAINT-ESTÈPHE: *The northernmost district of the Médoc, producing red Bordeaux wines that are fuller and more solid with less bouquet than those of the rest of the region. St. Estèphes are the sturdiest of the Médoc wines.*

SAINT-JULIEN: *The smooth and gentle red Bordeaux of the middle and least productive of the Médoc districts. A St. Julien is said to be fuller than a Margaux, more fragrant than a St. Estèphe, and to mature faster than a Pauilloc.*

SANCERRE: *An attractive upper Loire Valley white, with a pleasing pale color, fruitiness and bouquet. Similar in character to Pouilly Fumé, Sancerre matures faster, is shorter-lived and fresher tasting than its regional counterpart.*

RUGGERO'S

Address: 194 Grand Street
Location: Grand Street between Mott and Mulberry Streets
Telephone: 925-1340
Credit Cards: All major credit cards accepted
Reservations: Recommended
Hours: 11:30 AM to 12:00 Midnight, Monday thru Thursday; to 1:00 AM Friday. Dinner on Saturday from 4:00 PM to 1:00 AM. Lunch and Dinner on Sunday from 12:00 Noon to 12:00 Midnight
Days Closed: None
Liquor: Full bar service
Recommended or Listed in: Cue; Playbill
Maitre d': Tony Grassi
Reservations Manager: Tony Grassi
Seating Capacity: 250
Cuisine: Continental Italian
Specialties of the House: Veal Cartuccio; Red Snapper Marechiaro; Chicken Ruggero
Dress: Casual
Entertainment: Guitarist, nightly
Party Facilities: Private room; capacity: 60-150
Parking: Free valet parking available

Located in the heart of "Little Italy," Ruggero's offers an extensive menu with over 100 fine Italian and continental dishes to choose from. Subdued lighting, a wood-burning fireplace and lovely art work contribute to the distinctive decor and the congenial atmosphere. A strolling guitarist provides pleasant background music for dining. The cuisine is the main attraction at Ruggero's but you can also enjoy a drink and conversation in the handsomely appointed cocktail lounge.

MENU

(a la carte)

APPETIZERS:
Hot Antipasto (3.75); Cold Antipasto (3.00); Clam Cocktail (2.75); Shrimp Cocktail (4.25); Clams Oreganate (3.50); Stuffed Artichoke (3.75); Eggplant Rollatini (3.25); Escargots Provencial (4.25); Stuffed Mushrooms (3.50); Prosciutto and Melon (3.75); Mozzarella in Carrozza (3.75); Pimentos and Anchovies (2.50); Spiedini alla Romana (4.50); Clams Posillipo (4.50); Mussels Marinara (4.00); Shrimp Scampi (5.25); Clams Cassino (4.50); Insalada di Pesce (4.00).

SOUPS:
Monday: Pasta e Ceci (2.75); Wednesday: Pasta e Lenticchi (2.75); Thursday: Pasta e Piselli (2.75); Friday: Pasta e Fagioli (2.75); Minestrone (2.00); Stracciatella alla Romana (2.00); Stracciatella alla Fiorentina (2.25); Zuppa alla Pevese (3.50); Tortellini in Brodo (3.00); Escarola in Brodo (2.00); Spinaci in Brodo (2.00); Pastina in Brodo (2.00).

ENTREES:

Spaghetti with Meat Sauce	4.50
Spaghetti with Marinara Sauce	4.25
Spaghetti alla Aglio e Olio	4.00
Linguini with White Clam Sauce	4.95
Linguini with Red Clam Sauce	4.95
Linguini alla Frutti di Mare	5.95
Percatelli al Filetto di Pomodore	5.50
Percatelli alla Puttanesca	5.50
Gnocchi alla Bolognese	4.75

continued on next page

Menu continued

Gnocchi alla Ruggero 4.95
Cheese Ravioli 4.95
Ziti alla Sorrentino 4.95
Ziti alla Siciliana 5.25
Home Made Manicotti 5.00
Rigatoni and Zucchini alla Pepe 4.95
Rigatoni alla Bolognese 4.95
Fettuccini all'Alfredo 4.95
Tagliatelle Verdi alla Bolognese 4.75
Tortellini alla Panna 5.00
Tortellini alla Bolognese 5.00
Cannelloni alla Ruggero 5.50
Veal Pailard 9.50
Broiled Veal Chops 7.95
Broiled Pork Chops 5.95
Broiled Italian Sausages 4.95
Broiled Double Rib Lamb Chops 9.95
Shell Steak 10.95
Filet Mignon 10.95
Broiled Chicken (Half) 5.50
Veal Piccata 6.95
Veal Scaloppine alla Francese 6.95
Veal Scaloppine alla Marsala 6.95
Veal Scaloppine alla Sorrentino 7.50
Saltimbocca alla Romana 7.50
Veal Cutlet alla Milanese 6.75
Veal Cutlet Parmigiana 6.95
Veal Cutlet alla Ruggero 7.95
Veal Rollatini alla Ruggero 6.95
Veal Cartuccio 7.95
Stuffed Veal Chops alla Marsala 9.75
Veal Chops Oreganate 7.95
Veal Chops alla Valdostana 9.95
Chicken Cacciatora 5.95
Chicken Scarpariello 5.75
Boneless Chicken Bolognese 6.50
Boneless Chicken alla Francese 5.95
Chicken Rollatini alla Ruggero 6.50
Pork Chops alla Pizzaiola 6.50
Pork Chops with Cherry Peppers 6.50
Sausages with Peppers and Potatoes 5.95
Sausages Parmigiana 5.75
Sausages with Broccoli Rabe 6.95
Scaloppini of Filet alla Piccota 10.95
Scaloppini of Filet alla Marsala 10.95
Shell Steak alla Pizzaiola 11.95
Filet Mignon Rollatini 10.95
Steak alla Contadina 10.95
Clams and Mussels alla Ruggero 5.95
Zuppa di Pesce 7.95
Fried Calamari 6.50
Calamari in Casserole 6.50
Shrimps Fra Diavolo 7.95
Shrimps Marinara 7.95
Shrimps Oreganate 7.50
Shrimps Parmigiana 6.95
Shrimp Scampi alla Romana 7.95
Filet of Gray Sole alla Marinier 6.95
Filet of Dover Sole Almondine 11.95
Merluzza in Brodetto 5.50
Red Snapper alla Cassalinga 9.95
Broiled Red Snapper 9.50
Striped Bass alla Livernese 9.95
Striped Bass alla Marechiaro 9.95
Broiled Striped Bass 9.50
Fresh Lobster Fra Diavolo .... (...)
Fresh Lobster Marinara .... (...)
Fresh Lobster Oreganate .... (...)
Fresh Lobster Butter Sauce .... (...)
Ruggero's Seafood Special (For Two):
Lobster Marinara served with Linguini alla
Clam and Mussel sauce 29.95
Compagnolo alla Ruggero (For Two) 19.95
(Beef, Chicken and Sausage)
Combination alla Chef Enzo (For Two) 23.95
(Beef, Chicken and Veal)

(A variety of salads and vegetables is also available.)

DESSERTS:

Assorted Italian Pastries (1.00); Italian Cheese Cake (1.50); Zuppa Inglese (2.00); Tortoni (1.00); Spumoni (1.00); Zabaglione (2.50); Zabaglione alla Ruggero (3.50); Assorted Fresh Fruits in Season (1.00); Fresh Melon of the Season (1.75); Fresh Strawberries (2.00); Strawberries with Whipped Cream (2.50); Strawberries alla Ruggero (3.50); Macedonia di Frutta alla Ruggero (3.00); Assorted Imported Cheeses (3.50).

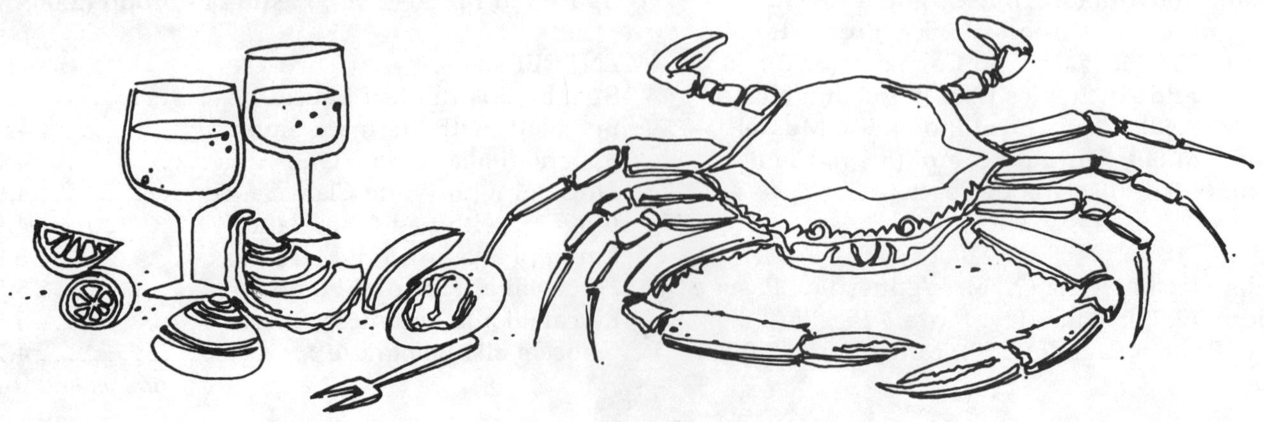

SARDI'S

Address:	234 West 44th Street
Location:	44th Street between Broadway and Eighth Avenue
Telephone:	221-8440
Credit Cards:	Only major credit cards accepted
Reservations:	Required
Hours:	Daily from 11:30 AM to 12:00 Midnight
Days Closed:	None
Liquor:	Full bar service
Recommended or Listed in:	All major magazines
Banquet Head Waiter:	Martin
Maitre d's:	Jimmy; George
Seating Capacity:	230 (First floor); 130 (Club Sardi)
Cuisine:	Continental
Dress:	Optional
Party Facilities:	Belasco Room; capacity: 20-100 (140 for cocktails)

Sardi's is in a class by itself as a theatrical restaurant. It has priceless wall decor—the pictures, prints and drawings of several hundred of the exciting and glamorous theatrical figures of the past half century. Many diners come early just to walk around and look for stars they remember from bygone Broadway hits. You'll dine extremely well here, of course; but the theatrical gallery is by all odds a feature attraction.

SPÉCIALITÉS DE LA MAISON

APPETIZERS & SOUPS

Cold Creme Vichyssoise—1.95
Hot Shrimp a la Sardi with Garlic Crouton—4.95
Avocado Pear or Melon and Prosciutto Ham—3.75
Smoked Brook Trout with Sour Cream and Horseradish Sauce—4.95

ENTREES

Cannelloni au Gratin with Sardi Sauce—7.95
Lump Crabmeat a la Sardi with Asparagus Tips—11.95
Supreme of Chicken Sardi with Asparagus Tips and Duchesse Potatoes—9.95
Scallopine of Milk Fed Veal Saute Eugenia, with Fresh Mushrooms, Fine Herbs, Cream Sauce and Rice Pilaff—9.95
Sliced London Broil on Toast, Home Fried Potatoes and Peas—8.95
Roast Prime Ribs of Beef au Jus, Sardi Sized Cut with Baked Potato and Mixed Green Salad—11.95

DESSERTS

Boccone Dolce—2.50
Frozen Cake, Zabaglione Sauce—2.50
Baked Apple with Vanilla Ice Cream—1.75
Fresh Strawberries with Sour or Sweet Cream—2.95

(Sardi's offers an a la carte menu with a selection of 60 dishes. Brunch is served on Sundays from 12:00 Noon to 3:00 PM at a prix fixe of 5.95.)

RUSSIAN TEA ROOM

Address:	150 West 57th Street
Location:	57th Street between Seventh Avenue and Avenue of the Americas
Telephone:	265-0947
Credit Cards:	AE; CB; V; DC; MC
Reservations:	Recommended
Hours:	11:30 AM to 1:00 AM Sunday thru Friday; 11:30 AM to 2:00 AM on Saturday
Days Closed:	None
Liquor:	Full Bar Service
Recommended or Listed in:	New York Times; Gourmet; Cue; New York Magazine; Bon Appetit; Travel & Leisure
Seating Capacity:	192
Cuisine:	Classic Russian
Specialties of the House:	Cotelette a la Kiev; Karsky Shashlik; Blini with Caviar; Pelmeny Siberian is featured at luncheon every Wednesday
Dress:	Jackets required in the evening

This lively restaurant, which opened its doors 50 years ago as a haven for Russian immigrants, particularly musicians, features several lengthy menus of authentic Russian cuisine which change daily. In a bustling, friendly atmosphere, the decor is dominated by the closely, yet comfortably, spaced tables with pink tablecloths, and by deep green walls covered with Impressionist art, ballet murals and samovars. Everything combines to create a holiday mood, no matter what day it is.

The Russian Tea Room

continued on next page

MENU

(a la carte)

(Served Saturday and Sunday from 11:30 AM to 5:00 PM; Daily from 11:30 AM to Closing.)

CAVIAR WITH BLINI:
Beluga Malossol Caviar with Blini and Sour Cream (22.95); Red Caviar with Blini and Sour Cream (11.75); Fresh Natural Pressed Caviar with Blini and Sour Cream (13.50); Osetra Caviar with Blini and Sour Cream (18.95); Sevruga Caviar with Blini and Sour Cream (14.95); RTR Especially Imported Irish Smoked Salmon with Blini and Sour Cream (12.25).

SOUPS WITH PIROJOK:
Hot Borscht with Sour Cream (3.50); Cold Borscht with Sour Cream (in season) (3.50); Cold Borscht in a Glass with Iced Vodka (5.00); Consomme (3.50); Soup du Jour (3.50).

APPETIZERS:
Beluga Malossol Caviar (20.00 the ounce); RTR Zakuska (Assorted Hors d'Oeuvres) (8.50); Fresh Shrimp Cocktail (5.75); Pickled Herring in Sour Cream (4.75); Swedish Matjes Herring (5.75); Osetra Caviar (16.00 the ounce); Sevruga Caviar (12.00 the ounce); Natural Pressed Black Caviar (10.00); Red Caviar, Chopped Eggs and Onions (8.50); Chopped Chicken Livers (4.50); Kholodetz (Studen) (4.00); Eggplant Orientale (4.50); Smoked Salmon, Capers (8.00); Melon (in season)(1.75); RTR Especially Imported Irish Smoked Salmon (8.50); Imported Boneless and Skinless Sardines (4.75).

ENTREES:
- Half Roast Duckling, Vereniki ... 9.00
- RTR Sirloin Steak Sandwich on Toast ... 12.25
- Spring Lamb Chops ... 11.50
- Broiled Half Chicken ... 8.00
- Chopped Sirloin Steak ... 8.50
- Broiled Veal Chops ... 10.50
- Sliced Calf's Liver with Bacon ... 8.75

RUSSIAN TEA ROOM SPECIALTIES:
- Eggplant a la Russe, au Gratin ... 7.00
- Mushrooms a la Russe, au Gratin ... 7.00
- Blinchiki with Cheese, Sliced Apples or Cherry Preserves and Sour Cream ... 6.75
- Sirniki with Sour Cream ... 6.25
- Karsky Shashlik Supreme ... 14.75
- Cotelette a la Kiev ... 9.75
- Beef a la Stroganoff ... 9.25
- Shashlik Caucasian ... 10.50
- Cotelettes Pojarsky ... 6.75
- Nalistniki ... 7.00
- Luli Kebab ... 7.00
- Cotelette de Volaille ... 10.50

DESSERTS:
Russian Tea Room Pastries (2.25); Cinnamon Toast (1.75); Cranberry Kissel with Cream (1.75); Fruit Compote (1.75); Ice Cream or Sherbet (1.50); Halvah (2.00); Imported Camembert (1.75); Lodichka (2.25); Yogurt with Cherry Preserves (1.75); Baklava (2.50); Baklava with Sour Cream (2.75); Charlottka (2.25); Blackberry Wine Jello with Whipped Cream (1.75); Kasha a la Gourieff (2.25); Russian Cream (2.50); Strawberries Romanoff (3.50); Sherbet Cassis (2.00).

(Cold Platters, Salads, Sandwiches and Omelettes are also listed on the menu.)

LUNCHEON MENU

(a la carte)

(Appetizers and soups similar to a la carte menu.)

ENTREES:
- Pelmeny Siberian ... 7.25
- Boiled Beef, Horseradish Sauce ... 6.25
- Cotelettes of Top Sirloin with Kasha ... 5.75
- Roast Leg of Spring Lamb ... 6.25
- Broiled Salmon, Lemon Butter Sauce ... 7.00
- Blinchiki with Cheese and Sour Cream ... 6.25
- Sirniki with Sour Cream ... 5.75
- Luli Kebab ... 6.75
- Mushrooms a la Russe ... 6.25
- Eggplant a la Russe ... 6.25
- Blini with Red Caviar and Sour Cream ... 8.00
- Shashlik Caucasian ... 9.25
- Karsky Shashlik ... 11.00
- Beef a la Stroganoff ... 8.50
- Cotelette de Volaille ... 9.25
- Cotelette a la Kiev ... 9.00
- Eggs, Fried or Scrambled ... 4.25
- Eggs with Bacon or Imported Ham ... 5.25
- Eggs with Salami ... 5.25
- Omelettes: Cheese, Tomato or Jam ... 4.75
- Mushroom Omelette ... 5.00
- Eggs with Smoked Salmon ... 6.50
- Red Caviar Omelette ... 7.25
- Tunafish Salad ... 5.75
- Chicken Salad ... 6.00

- Cottage Cheese with Sour Cream ... 4.00
- RTR Chef's Special Salad ... 6.50
- Salmon Salad ... 6.75
- Fresh Fruit Salad with Cottage Cheese ... 6.00
- Shrimp Salad with Russian Dressing ... 7.75
- Fresh Berries (in season) ... 5.25
- Cold Cotelette Platter ... 5.00

SANDWICHES:
Chicken Salad (4.25); Smoked Salmon (5.50); Tunafish (3.75); Egg Salad (3.25); American Cheese (3.25); Imported Swiss Cheese (3.50); Sa
Bacon, Lettuce and Tomato (4.25); Cho
Chicken Livers (4.00); Sliced Turkey (4

DESSERTS:
Assorted Russian Tea Room Pastries (2
(2.25); Fruit Compote (1.75); Ice Crean
(1.50); Kasha a la Gourieff (1.75); Crar
with Cream (1.50); Imported Camemb
Blackberry Wine Jello (1.25); Halvah (1.
Cream (2.00); Charlottka (2.00); Lodicl

DINNER MENU

(table d'hote)

(Includes choice of appetizer or soup and dessert.)

APPETIZERS:
Chopped Chicken Livers; Swedish Matjes Herring; Kholodetz (Studen); Pickled Herring in Sour Cream; Eggplant Orientale; Choice of Juices; Grapefruit or Melon (in season); Zakuska (Hors d'Oeuvres).

SOUPS WITH PIROJOK:
Hot Borscht with Sour Cream; Cold Borscht with Sour Cream (in season); Consomme du Jour; RTR Soup du Jour.

ENTREES:
- Bitochki, Sauce Stroganoff ... 9.75
- Noisette of Spring Lamb ... 10.75
- Cotelettes Boyar ... 9.75
- Kulebiaka ... 10.25
- Pilaff of Spring Lamb ... 10.00
- Cotelettes Pojarsky, Fresh Mushroom Sauce . 9.75
- Filet of Sole Meuniere ... 10.25
- Schnitzel a la Vienna ... 10.75
- Chakhobili of Spring Chicken ... 9.75
- Broiled Striped Sea Bass, Lemon Butter ... 10.25
- Salmon Pojarsky ... 10.25
- Goulash of Beef en Casserole ... 10.00
- Veal Kidneys Saute, Mushroom Wine Sauce 10.00
- Broiled Salmon, Lemon Butter Sauce ... 10.25
- Golubtze (Stuffed Cabbage) ...
- Musaka ...
- Pelmeny Siberian ...

RUSSIAN TEA ROOM SPECIALTIE
- Eggplant a la Russe, au Gratin ...
- Mushrooms a la Russe, au Gratin ...
- Blinchiki with Cheese, Sliced Apples Cherry Preserves and Sour Cream ...
- Sirniki with Sour Cream ...
- Karsky Shashlik Supreme ...
- Cotelette a la Kiev ...
- Beef a la Stroganoff ...
- Shashlik Caucasian ...
- Cotelettes Pojarsky ...
- Nalistniki ...
- Luli Kebab ...
- Cotelette de Volaille ...
- Blini with Red Caviar and Sour Crea

DESSERTS:
RTR Assorted Pastries (1.50 extra); B
extra); Kasha a la Gourieff; Halvah; Cr
with Cream; Russian Cream; Blackbe
Imported Camembert; Ice Cream or
Compote; Grapefruit or Melon (in s

M.O.F. (MEILLEUR OUVRIER DE FRANCE) *This extremely prestigious award is presented to the winner by the President of France himself. Only one M.O.F. is awarded in any field, and only once every four years. Two chefs in the United States have received this coveted award in the culinary arts and are therefore entitled to use the initials "M.O.F." after their names: André Soltner, Chef-Propriétaire of Lutèce in New York who received his in 1968 and Maurice Bonté, Owner, Pâtisserie Bonté in New York who received his in 1972. The competition for the M.O.F. is extraordinary, and it is the most coveted award of all among chefs.*

Sardi's

THE STORY OF A FAMOUS RESTAURANT

Sardi's is undoubtedly the best-known theatrical restaurant in the United States. Eugenia and Vincent Sardi, Sr., its founders, made it headquarters for anybody who is anybody in show business.

When something significant happens on the Coast, Sardi's gets the news first, and when something happens in New York, someone in Sardi's gets on the telephone and flashes the Coast. It is post office, message center, lovers' rendezvous, eating trough, drinking-hole, site of scenes tender, tragic and comic on opening nights—and a psychiatrist's couch for the professional theatre.

This phenomenal place is the creation of a couple who entered the United States as Italian emigrants. Because they understood and sympathized with theatrical people and their eccentricities, they endeared themselves to them and to everyone who loves the theatre.

Vincent Sardi

SEA FARE OF THE AEGEAN

Address: 25 West 56th Street
Location: 56th Street between Fifth Avenue and Avenue of the Americas
Telephone: LT 1-0540
Credit Cards: AE; CB; DC; MC
Reservations: Recommended
Hours: 12 Noon to 11:00 PM, Monday thru Saturday; 1:00 PM to 11:00 PM on Sundays
Days Closed: Thanksgiving, Christmas and New Year's Day
Liquor: Full Bar Service
Recommended or listed in: Cue; New York Times; Gourmet; Holiday
Maitre d': Gus or Nick
Seating Capacity: 240
Cuisine: Seafood; Greek
Specialties of the House: Baked Striped Bass with Wine Sauce and Cherrystone Clams; Mexican Shrimps with Feta Cheese, Santorini Sauce.
Dress: Jackets required

No restaurant does a more panoramic job of creating a luxurious Grecian atmosphere than Sea Fare. There is an assortment of original oil and water color paintings on the walls of this three-level restaurant. Service is brisk and friendly and the waiters seem to know a great deal about the seafoods offered. Although the menu features many dishes that are not of Greek origin, these are just as memorable as the Greek specialties. Only the freshest seafood is served at Sea Fare of the Aegean, and the range and variety of the menu is impressive.

LUNCHEON AND DINNER MENU

(a la carte)

(The following is a representative selection.)

ENTREES:

Imported Dover Sole Sauteed in Garlic Sauce 13.65
Broiled Combination Seafood Platter with Lobster Tail 14.75
Lobster, Crab Meat & Shrimp a la Newburg, Saute or Au Gratin 14.25
Individual Flounder Stuffed with Crab Meat 12.25
Bouillabaisse Marseillaise 14.75
Jumbo Shrimps Stuffed with Crab Meat 13.25
Alaskan King Crab with Melted Butter 13.95
Jumbo Shrimps Broiled or Saute — Mustard Sauce 12.25
Baby Lobster Tails Stuffed with Lump Crab Meat 13.85
Sole Seafare en Casserole with Asparagus au Gratin 10.25
Brook Trout Stuffed with Crab Meat 12.45
Striped Bass en Casserole (Aegean Style) Baked with Wine Sauce and Cherrystone Clams 12.25
Jumbo Shrimps (Santorini Style) Baked en Casserole with Feta Cheese, Grilled Tomato and Santorini Sauce 13.85
Poached Red Snapper with White Avgolemono Sauce (Scorpios Style), served with Young Carrots and Boiled Potato 12.65
Baked Filet of Lemon Sole stuffed with Crab Meat (Skopelos Style), served with Grilled Parmesan Tomato and Green Peas 13.25
Steamed Striped Bass en Casserole (Andros Style) served with its own Avgolemono Soup 12.85
Steamed Filet of Striped Bass en Casserole (Cretan Style) served with Fresh Green Herbs and its own Broth 12.85
Steamed Red Snapper en Casserole (Syros Style) 13.65
Steamed Striped Bass en Casserole (Rodos Style) with Mixed Ground Herbs and Sherry Wine served with its own Soup 12.85

Baby Lobster Tails (Santorini Style) Baked en Casserole with Feta Cheese, Grilled Tomato and Santorini Sauce 14.85
Broiled Live Medium Lobster 1¼ lbs 14.75
Broiled Live Large Lobster 1¾ lbs 16.95
Broiled Live Large Lobster 1¾ lbs — Baltimore Style 19.95
Baby Lobster Tails Saute 13.25
Broiled South African Lobster Tails 15.25
Broiled or Saute Filet of Gray Sole 10.25
Broiled Boston Scrod 8.75
Broiled Filet of Lemon Sole or Saute Meuniere 10.25
Broiled Halibut Steak, Eastern 11.65
Steamed Salmon with Hollandaise Sauce ... 12.35
Broiled Striped Bass 10.45
Broiled Red Snapper 11.75
Lobster Curry 14.95
Shrimp Curry 13.25
Lobster Creole 14.95
Shrimp Creole 13.25
Broiled Deep Sea Scallops 10.65
Sauteed Deep Sea Scallops 10.95
Fried Long Island or Digby Bay Scallops 11.95
Broiled or Sauteed Long Island or Digby Bay Scallops 12.25

(A wide selection of seafood appetizers and soups is available, ranging in price from 1.10 to 6.95; fresh seafood salads are offered, with prices ranging from 9.75 to 16.95. The menu also includes a variety of desserts, ranging in price from 1.50 to 2.55.)

SANTENAY: *The soft, full, dry red and white wines produced around the town of the same name at the southern end of the Burgundian Côte d'Or. Santenay wines are relatively inexpensive; the reds are thought to be more substantial and are somewhat better known.*

SAUMUR: *A pleasant upper Loire Valley wine, usually (when exported) white and frequently slightly sparkling. This wine area is particularly unpredictable, being so far north. Frequently, its less than excellent vintages are converted to sparkling wine.*

MOZZARELLA: *A popular Italian cheese, mozzarella was originally made only from water-buffalo milk but is now more commonly made from cow's milk. It is a soft, white, fresh cheese with a bland flavor. In consistency mozzarella is pliant and slightly elastic.*

MUNSTER: *A classic among German cheeses, Münster has a strong flavor which is often enhanced by adding other flavors such as caraway or anise. It is firm to hard in consistency and is yellow in color beneath a brownish-red rind. Münster is at its best during the winter months.*

PARMESAN: *Perhaps the greatest of Italy's classic cheeses, Parmesan originated near the city of Parma in the Emilia district. It is a very hard cheese which is at its best when aged for two to four years. Parmesan crumbles into fine flakes when grated and is frequently used as a flavorful garnish, especially on pasta.*

SEASCAPE INN

Address:	**Montauk Highway; Islip, New York**
Telephone:	**(516) 665-9595**
Credit Cards:	**AE; V; DC; MC; CB**
Reservations:	**Recommended**
Hours:	**11:45 AM to 3:00 PM and 3:30 PM to 1:00 AM Monday thru Friday; 3:30 PM to 2:00 AM on Saturdays; Brunch from 12 Noon to 3:00 PM and Dinner from 3:00 PM to 12 Midnight on Sundays**
Days Closed:	**None**
Liquor:	**Full Bar Service**
Recommended or listed in:	**Mobil Travel Guide**
Maitre d':	**Peter McLaughlin**
Seating Capacity:	**175**
Cuisine:	**Continental-American**

Among Long Island's multitude of restaurants, both large and small, Seascape Inn has continued to stand only for excellence for over 15 years. As soon as you enter, you know you are somewhere special. The Gillespies have created an instant mood by their tasteful and unique decorating in each of their four rooms. The bar with its overhead mementos is the hub of Seascape and not to be missed. All menu selections are expertly prepared and worth trying. You are in the vanguard of elegant dining when you visit Seascape Inn. Sunday Brunch (Prix Fixe 4.75) is served during the Winter Season from 12 Noon 'til 3:00 P.M.

DINNER

(A la Carte)

APPETIZERS:

Chilled Tomato Juice (.75); Florida Fruit Cup (.95); Head Cheese Vinaigrette (1.10); Chopped Herring Salad, Danish Style (1.25); Chopped Chicken Livers (1.25); Smoked Local Eel (1.25); Asparagus Vinaigrette (1.75); Baked Clams Maison (2.95); Westphallian Ham with Melon (2.75); Fillets of Herring in Sour Cream (1.50); Hearts of Artichoke Vinaigrette (1.75); Escargots Provencale (3.75); Stuffed Jumbo Shrimp (3.50); Clams saute on Toast a la Maison (2.75); Long Island Clams on Half Shell (2.50); Maine Lobster Cocktail (5.75); Broiled Shrimp Scampi (3.95); Icelandic Baby Trout, mustard sauce (2.00); Soused Jumbo Shrimp (2.95); Alaskan King Crabmeat Cocktail (3.95); Jumbo Shrimp Cocktail (2.95); Long Island Oysters, in season (2.95).

SOUPS AND SALADS:

Manhattan Clam Chowder (1.25); Cold Vichyssoise Supreme (1.25); Chef's Soup of the Day (1.25); French Onion Soup au Gratin (1.50); Sliced Ripe Tomato (1.00); Hearts of Lettuce (1.00); Sliced Ripe Tomato with Bermuda Onion (1.50); Caesar Salad, for two (6.00).

COLD BUFFET:

Cold Seafood combination Platter a la Maison, garni 12.75
Maine Lobster Salad Platter, garni 11.50
Alaskan King Crabmeat Salad Platter, garni .. 10.95
Florida Shrimp Salad Platter 10.50
Chef's Salad 8.50

ENTREES:

Today's Ocean Fresh Catch—today's choice priced accordingly .... (. . .)
Fried Gulf Stream Shrimp, sauce Remoulade .. 8.95
Shrimp Victoria, mornay sauce 8.95
Shrimp Curry en Casserole, garni with Rice, Chutney, Coconut, Grated Walnuts 8.95
Stuffed Jumbo Shrimp a la Seascape, sauce Remoulade 9.25
Broiled Shrimp Scampi Eschalatos en Casserole 9.75
Broiled or Fried Fresh Peconic Bay Scallops, sauce Remoulade 8.95
King Crabmeat au Gratin en Casserole 9.75
Broiled tiny Danish Lobster Tails, Eschalatos. 11.25
Broiled Australian Lobster Tails, drawn butter 15.95
Lobster a la Newberg en Casserole 10.25

Seascape Inn

Broiled whole live Maine Lobster with drawn butter ....(. . .)
Veal Cordon Bleu, Sauce Printanier 9.25
Scallopine of Veal a la Francaise 8.95
Scallopine of Veal au Picata with Hearts of Artichokes 8.95
Scallopine of Veal au Madeira, with Fresh Mushrooms 8.75
Roast Prime Rib of Beef, au jus (Fri., Sat., Sun.) 8.95
Breast of Chicken and King Crabmeat Madeira, en Casserole 9.95
Chicken a la Francaise 8.75
Roast Long Island Duckling a l'Orange, boned and served in a savory Orange Sauce 9.25
Tender Young Calves Liver Saute, Bacon Strips 8.95
Aged 1 Lb. New York Cut Sirloin Steak 10.95
Broiled Filet Mignon, with Mushroom Caps . 11.50
Boneless Aged Sirloin Steak Sandwich, open style, garni 8.95
Sliced Steak a la Sea Scape, Sauce Maison 9.75
Chopped Sirloin Steak, Mushroom Sauce 6.75
Broiled French Cut Double Lamb Chops, Crisp Bacon, Broiled Tomato, Mint Jelly 10.95
Broiled Center Cut Pork Chops, apple sauce .. 8.75
Whole Roast Long Island Duckling a l'Orange, flambeed at tableside, carved and boned 19.95

Specialties for Two: (Prepared in Dining Room)
Double Sirloin Steak Bouquetiere, Sauce Bearnaise, Fresh Vegetables, Broiled Tomato . 24.00
Chateaubriand Bouquetiere, bouquet of Fresh Vegetables, Broiled Tomato, sauce Bearnaise 25.00
Steak Diane per person 12.50

DESSERTS:
Assorted Ice Creams (.75); Milk Sherbet (.75); Fruit Jell-O with Whipped Cream (.75); Home Baked Apple Pie (.75); A la mode or with Cheddar Cheese (1.25); Chocolate Sundae (.90); Louisiana Pecan Pie with Whipped Cream (1.10); Savoury rich Cream Cheese Cake (1.25); Caramel Custard (.95); Bisquit Tortoni (.95); Coupe Aux Marrons (1.10); Rainbow Parfait (1.50); Peach Melba (.90); Strawberries Melba (.95); Melon in season (.95); Baba au Rhum (1.25); Fresh California Mammoth Strawberries (in season); Coupe St. Jacque (1.25); Crepes Suzette, expertly flambeed with Brandy and Orange Curacao (6.00); Cherries Jubilee, fragrant sauce aflame over Vanilla Ice Cream (6.00)

(A complete luncheon menu is also offered at prices ranging from 4.75 to 7.25.)

SAUTERNES: *The very sweet, rich textured golden white Bordeaux produced from over-ripened grapes in the district of the same name about 30 miles south of Bordeaux. Traditionally dessert wines, the best Sauternes are known by their chateaux (Yquem being the most renowned). Unlike most white wines, Sauternes can age for years, acquiring a warmer color and deeper flavor as they mature.*

In the U.S., the term Sauterne (without the final "s") is used indiscriminately to describe almost any white table wine.

SHALIMAR

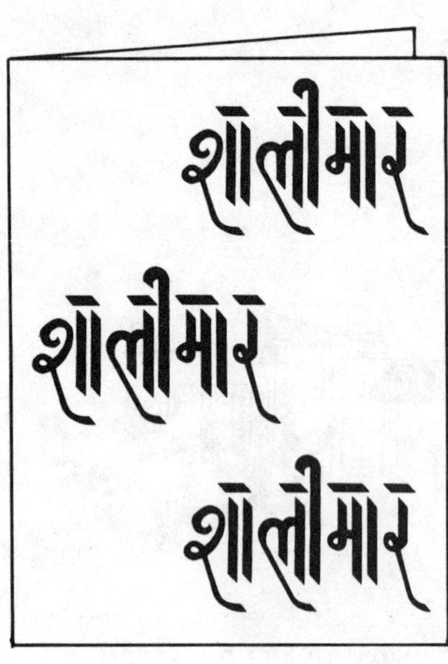

Address:	**39 East 29th Street**
Location:	**29th Street between Park and Madison Avenues**
Telephone:	**889-1977**
Credit Cards:	**All major credit cards accepted**
Reservations:	**Recommended**
Hours:	**12:00 Noon to 12:00 Midnight, daily**
Days Closed:	**None**
Liquor:	**Full bar service**
Recommended or Listed in:	**New York Times; New York Magazine; Cue; Esquire**
Seating Capacity:	**130**
Cuisine:	**Indian**
Specialties of the House:	**Chicken Tandoori; Kati Kabab; Karhai Kabab; Special Luncheon Menu**
Dress:	**Informal**
Party Facilities:	**Private room; capacity: 50-70**

Ten years ago, Shalimar introduced to the Murray Hill section of New York an impressive array of Indian and Pakistani dishes. Loyal and enthusiastic Shalimar patrons include the cognoscenti of Indian cuisine as well as those seeking an authentic introduction to the distinctive flavors of curries and kebabs, biryani and bhaji—and over 60 other Indian specialties. The decor of the restaurant reflects its culinary origin—from the glass mosaics set in the rough stucco walls to the perforated tin lamp shades. The staff is willing and eager to please and the service is excellent.

DINNER MENU

(a la carte)

(The following is a representative selection.)

APPETIZERS & SOUPS:

Bhujia (Vegetable Fritters—Chopped Vegetable Mixed with Chick Pea Flour and Rolled into Small Balls) (.90); Sheek Keebab (Minced Beef with Herbs Rolled into a Sausage Shape and Grilled) (1.25); Cheese Pakora (1.00); Samosa (Meat or Vegetable Pastry Turnover filled with Spiced Minced Meat or Vegetables) (1.20); Madras Liver (Chicken Liver sauteed with Herbs and Spices, with Poori) (1.95); Mulligatawny Soup (.80).

ENTREES:

Bengal Fish Curry 5.50
(Flounder cooked with green vegetables)

Boti Keebab 5.75
(Marinated beef chunks with herbs on skewer; broiled with onions, tomatoes and green peppers)

Kati Keebab 5.25
(Tender chicken pieces flavored with herbs on skewer, broiled with onions)

Biryani 4.50-4.75
(Selected portions of lamb, beef or chicken, sauteed in herbs and spices, served with fragrant rice)

Lamb Kabiraj 5.75
(Lamb chops cooked with onions and tomatoes in aromatic curry sauce)

Aash Kabuli 5.75
(Lamb, chick peas and potatoes cooked Afghan style)

Beef Dolma 5.75
(Ground beef and saffron rice with almond, rolled in a cabbage leaf, topped with curry sauce and broiled)

Chicken Tandoori 5.75
(Tender spring chicken marinated in herbs and spice, oven barbequed)

Duck Kerala Masala 5.95
(Cooked with herbs and spices, served with a thick, lightly spiced gravy)

Dukker ka Vindaloo 5.50
(Pork cooked with spice flavor sauce)
Karhai Kabab 6.50
(Beef, lamb or chicken, marinated and flavored with herbs and spices; delicately cooked in a special pan with onion, tomatoes, green pepper and mushroom)
Pomfret Tandoori 7.50
(Chicken of the Sea Imported from Bay of Bengal, marinated in herbs and spices and oven roasted)

SIDE DISHES:
Cucumber Rayta (1.00); Keema Paratha Stuffed with Spice Flavored Minced Meat (1.95); Alu Paratha Stuffed with Spice Flavored Mashed Potato (1.20).

DESSERTS:
Ras Malai (Homemade cheese cooked in milk with cardamom flavor) (.95); Mango Ice Cream (.95); Rosa Gola (Snow White Succulent Cheese Balls, Rose Water Flavored) (1.00); Firni (Indian Custard) (1.00).

DRINKS:
(Exotic mixture of different liquors served Badshahi style.) Panch Tantra For Two (Champagne Based) (4.95); Amrit Ka Pyala (Rum Based) (3.25); Madira Ho Akbar (Brandy Based) (3.25); Taxila (Rum and Brandy Based) (3.25).

(A special luncheon menu is served from 12:00 Noon to 3:00 PM, with prices ranging from 2.35 to 3.50.)

BISCUIT TORTONI: *This popular Italian dessert classically consists of vanilla ice cream and toasted almonds on a rum-soaked sponge cake.*

CANNOLI: *The singular is* cannolo *but it is rare to hear this pastry ever referred to in the singular. Its name comes from the Italian for "tube" and it is, in fact, tubular in shape. The crust is made with vegetable shortening and just a little flour that is first rolled onto a wooden stick and then fried. When the baking is done, the crust is filled with an incredibly rich filling—typically Sicilian in its lavishness—made of candied fruits, chocolate chips, sugar and ricotta. The result is a crisp outside and a sweet and creamy inside.*

CASSATA: *This is a typically southern-Italian cake—very, very sweet and rich. It is a sponge cake, soaked in rum, filled with ricotta cream and iced. It is always dressed with candied fruits and is popular for weddings, birthdays and other festive occasions.*

SHINBASHI

Address: 280 Park Avenue
Location: 48th Street, between Park Avenue and Madison Avenue
Telephone: 661-3915
Credit Cards: AE; CB; DC; MC
Reservations: Recommended
Hours: Lunch from 12 Noon to 2:30 PM Monday thru Friday; Dinner from 5:30 PM to 10:00 PM Monday thru Saturday
Days Closed: Sundays
Liquor: Full Bar Service
Recommended or listed in: New York Times; Gourmet; Cue
Maitre d's: Tony and George
Seating Capacity: 150
Cuisine: Japanese
Specialties of the House: Sukiyaki; Shabu Shabu; Tempura; Sushi
Dress: Jackets recommended
Party Facilities: Tatami room available for parties: $15 per person, including drinks

A spacious and relatively new establishment, Shinbashi offers the best in traditional Japanese cuisine. Its decor is elaborate and rich without being gaudy and its kitchen turns out traditional Japanese cuisine of a quality satisfying to both Japanese and American tastes. Shinbashi is appropriately classed as one of the very best Nipponese eateries in New York.

DINNER MENU

(Table d'hote; served with clear or bean soup, pickled vegetables, rice, side dish, tea and dessert.)

ENTREES:

Tempura 8.50
(Shrimps, seafood and vegetables, deep fried)
Sashimi 9.50
(Assortment of filet of fresh raw fish)
Sukiyaki 9.50
(Choice of beef, pork or chicken with vegetables, cooked at table)
Shabu-Shabu 11.90
(Beef or pork with vegetables)
Seafood Sukiyaki 11.50
(Bouillabaisse cooked at table, served with lemon soy sauce)
Negimayaki 9.80
(Scallions rolled with sliced beef and broiled)
Teriyaki 9.20
(Choice of Beef, Pork or Chicken)
Tonkatsu 8.50
(Deep fried breaded pork, served with cutlet sauce)
Teriyaki with Tempura 10.90
(Deep fried shrimp, assorted seafood & vegetables; choice of beef, pork or chicken teriyaki broiled)

Omakase
(Formal Japanese dinner of seven to nine courses)
UME 25.00
TAKE 30.00
MATSU 40.00

(a la carte)

ENTREES:

Teriyaki 8.20
(Choice of Beef, Chicken or Pork)
Tempura 7.50
(Shrimps, seafood and vegetables, deep fried)
Shogayaki 7.90
(Sliced Beef or Pork cooked with marin soy sauce & ginger)
Sukiyaki 8.50
(Choice of beef, pork or chicken with vegetables, cooked at table)
Seafood Sukiyaki 10.50
(Bouillabaisse cooked at table, lemon soy sauce)
Shabu-Shabu 11.00
(Sliced beef or pork with fresh vegetables)
Lobster Gusokuni .... 11.90 & up
(Chopped lobster in shell, seafood sauce)

Lobster Sashimi-Kabutoyaki .... 14.00 & up
(Fresh lobster served wth soy sauce)
Kabayaki 12.00
(Japanese eel broiled with mirin soy sauce)
Yosenabe 9.00
(Fish, seafood delicacies with vegetables cooked at table)

Alaskan King Crab 8.90
Tonkatsu 7.50
(Deep fried breaded pork)

(A wide variety of a la carte side dishes is also available.)

Shinbashi

SHERRY: *The most popular aperitif, Sherry is a gold-to-amber-colored fortified wine, traditionally produced and shipped from the district surrounding the town of Jerez de la Fronteyn, in southeastern Spain. Sherry is a "made" wine, a blend of many vintages aged in oak casks to which brandy has been added. It is usually consumed shortly after bottling. Sherry comes in various types (e.g. Amontillado, Fino, and Manzanilla).*

SOAVE: *Probably the best known Italian white wine, Soave is produced in northern Italy, east of Verona, in the foothills of the Alps. It is a plain, dry, pale white wine with a distinctly fresh flavor. It is shipped in tall green "Alsatian" bottles and should be drunk before it is three years old.*

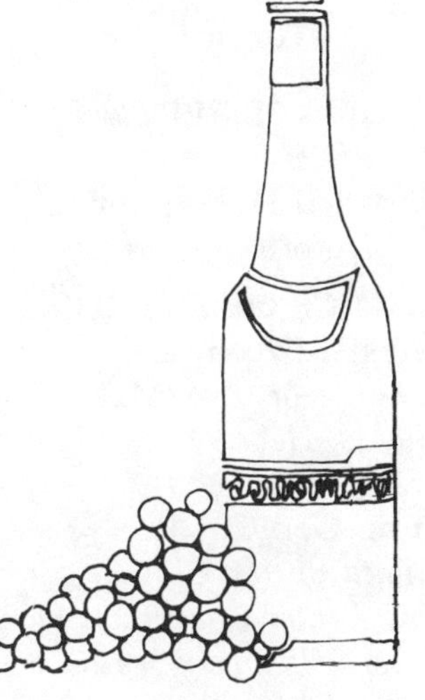

TAVEL: *One of the oldest and most famous rosé wines, produced in the Rhône river valley north of Avignon. Orange-pink in color, with a strong flavor and bouquet, Tavel rosés are usually drunk when less than two years old.*

SHUN LEE DYNASTY/SHUN LEE PALACE

Addresses: Dynasty: 900 Second Avenue
Palace: 155 East 55th Street
Locations: Dynasty: Second Avenue at 48th Street
Palace: 55th Street between Lexington and Third Avenues
Telephones: Dynasty: PL 5-3900
Palace: 371-8844
Credit Cards: DC; AE; CB
Reservations: Recommended
Hours: 11:30 AM to 11:30 PM Sunday thru Thursday; 11:30 AM to 1:30 AM Friday and Saturday
Days Closed: Thanksgiving only
Liquor: Full bar service
Recommended or Listed in: New York Times; Gourmet
Maitre d's: Dynasty: Jimmie Wei;
Palace: Michael Tong
Cuisine: Chinese: Mandarin, Szechuan and Hunan styles
Specialties of the House: Lobster Szechuan; Beef in Housin Sauce; Chicken with Cashew Nuts
Party Facilities: Balcony (Palace), capacity: 30;
5 rooms (Dynasty), capacity: 10-100
Parking: Free parking after 6:00 PM in lot adjacent to Shun Lee Palace, 2-hour limit; Free parking after 5:30 PM for Shun Lee Dynasty patrons at Term Garage (Second Avenue between 48th and 49th streets), 2-hour limit

The two Shun Lee restaurants are famous not only because they are beautifully designed and decorated but also because Chef/Proprietor T. T. Wang is one of the most renowned practitioners of the art of Chinese cooking in America today. Chef Wang was the first to bring Mandarin cuisine to New York 18 years ago. Ten years ago he introduced Szechuan cooking and then, in the early 1970's, he brought the cuisine of Hunan to New York. Only at the Shun Lee restaurants can all three styles be found under one roof.

DINNER MENU

(The following is a representative selection of items on the menus of Shun Lee Dynasty and Shun Lee Palace.)

SHUN LEE SPECIAL DINNER:
(Prix fixe - 13.95)
Assorted Hot Appetizers
Choice of Hot-and-Sour or Velvet Corn Soup

CHOICE OF ENTREES:

Lobster Szechuen
(Chunks of fresh Maine Lobster with Minced Bamboo Shoots, Hearts of Scallions, all Gently Simmered in Szechuen Sauce.)

Tung-Goo Chicken
(Sliced Spring Chicken with Black Mushrooms, Mixed with Water Chestnuts, Bamboo Shoots and Crisp Snow Peas, Deliciously Seasoned and Stir-Fried in Chef Wang's Secret Sauce.)

Fillet of Beef with Umbrella Mushrooms
(Tender Fillet of Beef Cooked with Bamboo Shoots, Umbrella Mushrooms, Green Peas.)

Fresh Pork, Hunan Style
(Sliced Fresh Pork, with Chinese Vegetables Cooked in a Spicy Sauce.)

Five Diced Fish
(Cubed Sea Bass, Cooked with Water Chestnuts, Chinese Cabbage, Black Mushrooms, Snow Peas and Chinese Ham.)

CHOICE OF DESSERT:
Honey Crisp Banana; Sesame Delight; Ice Cream.

Shun Lee Palace

(a la carte)

APPETIZERS & SOUPS:
Spring Roll (1.00); Spare Ribs (5.25); Pearl Balls (3.25); Stuffed Crepe (4.50); Fried Dumplings (2.75); Roast Pork (5.25); Yank Chow Chicken Soon (5.25); Tangy Spicy Shrimp (6.25); Hacked Chicken in Hot Sauce (5.50); Spicy Cucumber (3.95); Hot-and-Sour Soup (1.65); Shark Fin Soup (2.50); Meat Ball Cellophane Soup (1.65); Sizzling Rice Soup (shrimp, chicken or subgum) (1.65); Velvet Corn Soup (1.65).

ENTREES:

Slippery Chicken 6.95
(Shredded Breast of Chicken Dipped in Lotus Flour, Steamed with Rich Brown Sauce, Garnished with Fresh Green Spinach.)

Lemon Chicken 6.95
(Breast of Chicken Marinated in Gin, Coated with Water Chestnut Flour and Eggs, Deep Fried until Crisp, Served with Lemon Sauce)

Mo-Shu Pork 7.25
(Tender Shreds of Pork Mixed with Eggs, Sun-Dried Tiger-Lily Flower, Served with Specially Prepared Thin Crepes.)

Lobster Szechuen 10.95
(Chunks of Fresh Maine Lobster with Minced Bamboo Shoots, Hearts of Scallions, All Gently Simmered in Szechuen Sauce.)

Peking Duck (To be Ordered in Advance) .. 19.00

Steak-Kaw Szechuen 11.95
(Chunks of Sirloin Steak with Bamboo Shoots, Black Mushrooms and Snow Peas Cooked in Hot, Spicy Sauce.)

Sliced Fillet of Veal, Hunan Style 9.95
(Sliced Fillet of Veal Combined with Fresh Mushrooms in a Hot Sauce.)

Velvet Shrimp Puffs 7.95
(Minced Fresh Shrimp, Water Chestnuts and Bamboo Shoots; Dipped in Lotus Flour, Tenderly Fried & Covered with a Velvet Sauce).

Hunan Calves Liver 9.95
(Sliced Baby Calves Liver, Sauteed in a Hot Hunan Sauce, Garnished with Green Spinach.)

General Ching's Chicken 6.95
(Chicken Chunks with Tingling Hot Sauce.)

Sliced Leg of Lamb, Hunan Style 7.95
(Choice Spring Lamb with Scallions and Hot Pepper Sauce.)

Lake Tung Ting Shrimp 7.75
(Giant Shrimp Marinated with Broccoli, Ham, Bamboo Shoots and Mushrooms in a White Sauce.)

Eggplant, Family Style 6.25
(Chunks of Eggplant with Fresh Ginger, Garlic, Scallions in Spicy Hunan Sauce.)

Hunan Duckling with Smoked Flavor 8.95
(Young Duckling Lightly Seasoned with Five Spices Smoked in Hunan Wood.)

Vegetable Duck Pie 6.95
(Crispy Vegetables Served Peking Duck Style. Layers of Vegetable Pie Crispy Fried. Served with a Chinese Pancake, Scallions and Hoisin Sauce.)

Frog's Legs Wang Style 8.95
(A new creation of Chef Wang. Boneless Succulent Frog's Legs Cooked in a Special Tangy, Spicy Sauce.)

Beef with Black Bean Sauce 7.95
(Sliced Fillet of Beef Sauteed with Crisp Chinese Vegetables in Black Bean Sauce.)

(MSG, corn starch, sugar and/or salt will be omitted upon request)

THE SIGN OF THE DOVE

Address:	**1110 Third Avenue**
Location:	**Third Avenue at N.W. Corner of 65th Street**
Telephone:	**861-8080**
Credit Cards:	**AE; DC; MC; V; CB**
Reservations:	**Recommended**
Hours:	**Lunch from 12:00 Noon to 3:00 PM, Tuesday thru Friday; 12:00 Noon to 4:00 PM, Saturday and Sunday; Dinner daily from 6:00 PM to 12:00 Midnight; to 1:00 AM on Friday and Saturday**
Days Closed:	**None**
Liquor:	**Full bar service**
Recommended or Listed in:	**Gourmet; Cue; Mobil Guide; New Yorker**
Seating Capacity:	**150**
Cuisine:	**Continental**
Specialties of the House:	**Prime Filet of Beef Suisse; Pasta; Stuffed Breast of Veal; Medallion de Boeuf Lucullus; Daily Chef's Specials**
Dress:	**Jacket required in Bar/Lounge; Jacket and tie required in Dining Room**
Entertainment:	**Piano in Bar/Lounge; Piano and Violin in Gallery**
Party Facilities:	**Private room; capacity: 60**

For over a decade, people have been enjoying one of the most beautiful dining settings anywhere. Sign of the Dove is made up of several different rooms, including one with a sliding glass roof for starlight summer dining. Each is handsomely decorated and the food at lunch, dinner or weekend Brunch equals the surroundings. While there, ask to visit the wine cellar, stocked with rare vintages.

DINNER MENU

(a la carte)

APPETIZERS & SOUPS:

Beluga Malossal Caviar (28.00); Carpaccio Toscano (8.50); Oysters or Other Mollusks in the shell (5.75); Poached Kennebec Salmon (7.50); Pate Maison (5.75); Prosciutto di Parma, Melone o Fighi (5.75); Smoked Scotch Salmon (6.50); Snails Bourguignonne (5.75); Mussel Salad (5.75); Bibb Lettuce Salad (4.75); Caesar Salad (5.75); Hearts of Romaine Salad (4.75); The Dove's Own Mixed Fresh Green Salad (3.50); Watercress and Belgian Endive Salad (4.75); Wilted Spinach, Bacon and Mushroom Salad (4.75); Cold Cucumber Soup (3.75); Billi Bi (3.75); French Onion Soup (3.75); The Chef's Delight (3.75).

ENTREES:

Trenette Verde, al pesto 9.50
Trenette Verde, Gianvito 9.50
Fettuccine Pope John The Twenty Third 9.50
(Cream Sauce of Butter, Cheese, Prosciutto di Parma, Brandy)
Fettuccine or Trenette Verde, filetto di Pomidoro 9.50
Calf's Liver, Bacon and Apple Fritters 13.50
Caneton a l'Orange et Fruits, Wild Rice 15.50
Poulet du Chef, Madeira 12.50
Scaloppine of Veal with Hearts of Artichokes 14.50
Scalloppine of Veal, Francese, Limone or Marsala 14.00
Stuffed Breast of Veal, Bordelaise 13.50
Medallions de Boeuf Lucullus 16.50
Entrecote au Poivre 15.50
Bouillabaisse Marseillaise 15.50
Dover Sole, Meuniere or Almondine 14.50
Striped Bass Chambord 12.50
Broiled Salmon Steak, Sauce Chauron 14.50
Prime Filet of Beef, Sauce Bearnaise 17.50
Prime Sirloin of Beef, Fiorentina 17.50
Double Lamb Chops 17.50
Chateaubriand, Garni .... (per person) 17.50
(for 2 or 4)

Costata di Sirloin Fiorentina .. (per person) 17.50 (for 2 or 4)
Prime Filet of Beef Suisse .... (per person) 17.50 (for 2 or 4)
Rack of Lamb (for 2 or 4) ...... (per person) 17.50
Hearts of Saddle of Lamb .... (per person) 17.50 (for 2 or 4)

DESSERTS:
Dessert Buffet (4.50).

(Our dessert buffet displays delicious pastries and desserts made daily by our patissier.)

BRUNCH MENU

(a la carte)

APPETIZERS & SOUPS:
Fresh Melon, in Season (3.75); Cold Cucumber Soup (3.75); French Onion Soup (3.75); Billi Bi Soup (3.75); Garden Fresh Asparagus or Leeks, Vinaigrette (4.50); Broiled Honeyed Grapefruit with Kodota Figs (4.50); Snails in Shells Bourguignonne (4.50); Oysters or Other Molluscs in the Half-Shell (5.75); Smoked Scotch Salmon (5.75); Prosciutto di Parma, Melone o Fighi (5.75).

ENTREES:
Poached Eggs, Florentine or Benedictine 9.25
Sunday Eggs, Sarnowska or Colombiane 9.25
Plump Fresh Mushrooms sauteed with Sherry, Scrambled Eggs 9.25
Country Style Omelettes 9.75
Weekend Morning Crepes 9.75
Italian Welsh Rarebit (Poached Eggs, Tomato, Prosciutto di Parma) 9.75
Quiches Extraordinaires 9.75
Trenette, Verde Gianvito, Sauce of Cream, Scotch Salmon, Truffles 11.00
Fettuccine Pope John The Twenty-Third with a Cream Sauce of Butter, Cheese, Prosciutto di Parma and Brandy 11.00
Chicken in Champagne Sauce with Glazed Grapes 11.00
Carpaccio Toscano (Delicate Paper-Thin Filet, Salsa Verde) 13.50
Baby Lamb Chops, Garni 13.50
Calf's Liver with Bacon and Apple Fritters .. 13.50
English Brunch - Prime Sirloin Steak, Topped with Egg, Pommes Frites 15.50
Steak Tartar 15.50

COLD DISHES & SALADS:
Fresh Fruit and Ricotta Cheese Salad 9.50
Chef's Salad 10.50
Caesar Salad 10.50
Salade Nicoise 10.50
Avocado and Crab Meat Salad 12.50
King Crab Salad 12.50
Plump Oysters or Other Molluscs in Half-Shell 11.50

DESSERTS:
Dessert Buffet (4.00); Strawberries, Zabaglione Sauce or in Champagne (4.00).

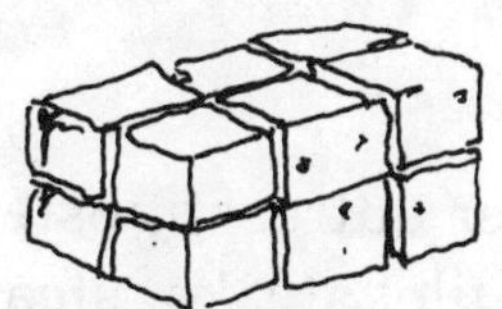

PONT L'EVEQUE: *Named for the small town in Normandy where it is made, Pont l'Evêque is sold in small seven ounce squares which are deep yellow on the outside and pale yellow on the inside. It is semi-soft in consistency and fairly strong in flavor. Pont l'Evêque is best served as a dessert cheese.*

TERLANO: *The best known Tyrolean Italian white wine, produced near the town of the same name near the Austrian border. Terlano is pale green-gold in color, and dry. It is shipped in tall green "Alsatian" bottles bearing Gothic labels which are frequently in German.*

TOKAY: *The extraordinarily long-lasting Hungarian white wines, produced around Tokay in the Carpathian mountains in northeast Hungary near the Russian border. Aged in barrels for six to seven years before bottling in stubby, long-necked bottles, Tokay has a strong and intense grapy flavor.*

VALPOLICELLA: *The distinctive northern Italian red, produced northeast of Verona, in the foothills of the Alps. A beautiful cherry red in color, Valpolicella has a sweet bouquet, a young, fruity, light flavor and smooth body. Typically bottled after 18 months in wood, it improves in the bottle, but should be drunk before it is five years old.*

SMITH & WOLLENSKY

Address:	201 East 49th Street
Location:	49th Street and Third Avenue
Telephone:	PL 3-1530
Credit Cards:	All major credit cards accepted
Reservations:	Recommended
Hours:	12:00 Noon to 11:00 PM, Monday thru Thursday; 12:00 Noon to 12:00 Midnight, Friday; 5:00 PM to 12:00 Midnight, Saturday; 3:00 PM to 10:00 PM, Sunday
Days Closed:	None
Liquor:	Full bar service
Recommended or Listed in:	Promenade; Cue; Focus; Esquire
Maitre d':	Lino Romano
Seating Capacity:	185
Cuisine:	American/Steakhouse
Specialties of the House:	Lobsters; Prime Steaks; Prime Ribs of Beef; Fresh Fish
Dress:	Jacket recommended

Smith & Wollensky is becoming increasingly well-known on Manhattan's eastside for the excellence of its menu (particularly the prime steak and beef selections) and the distinctiveness of its decor. Reminiscent of a turn-of-the-century private men's club, the masculine ambience of Smith & Wollensky is softened by lovely fresh flowers and warm oil paintings. From the gracious antiques to the beautiful bar on a rich marble base, the recently renovated interior is entirely in keeping with the building's designation as an historic landmark. Dramatic floor to ceiling glass separates the kitchen from the dining room and affords diners a view of the meticulous care and attention that characterizes the preparation of Smith & Wollensky's cuisine.

LUNCHEON & DINNER MENUS

Smith & Wollensky offers a variety of a la carte luncheon and dinner entrees, posted daily for diners' convenience. House specialties include sirloin and filet steaks, steak au poivre, chopped steak and prime ribs of beef, at prices ranging from 8.50 to 13.75. Veal, lamb, chicken and fresh seafood entrees are also available from 8.25 to 12.50. A number of special entrees are offered at luncheon only; these include seafood, shrimp, chicken and spinach salads. Steak, chicken, veal and fresh fish dishes are also served at luncheon with prices ranging from 6.50 to 10.75. A selection of a la carte soups, seafood cocktails and other appetizers is also available; cost ranges from 2.00 to 7.00. Desserts include ice cream, cheese cake, fresh fruit and a special House cake.

Only the best prime meats are served at Smith & Wollensky, and the fresh produce on the menu is selected with equal care.

SZECHUAN EAST

SZECHUAN EAST

Address:	**1540 Second Avenue**
Location:	**Second Avenue between 80th and 81st Streets**
Telephone:	**535-4921**
Credit Cards:	**AE; DC**
Hours:	**12:00 Noon to 11:30 PM, Sunday thru Thursday; to 12:00 Midnight, Friday and Saturday**
Days Closed:	**None**
Liquor:	**Full bar service**
Manager:	**Louis Loo**
Seating Capacity:	**120**
Cuisine:	**Szechuan-style Chinese Cuisine**
Specialties of the House:	**Szechuan East Special Beef; Sliced Leg of Lamb; Sliced Prawns with Egg Sauce; Szechuan East Special Chicken; Sliced Fish in Hot Sauce**

Szechuan East is one of the best Chinese restaurants on the upper eastside. Its simple decor and unpretentious service provide an appropriate setting for the flavorful and exotic Szechuan cuisine that is served here. Three dining areas constitute the restaurant, similarly decorated and brightly lit. Szechuan East is always busy—many of the restaurant's customers are "regulars" and it is not unusual for lively conversations to spring up between strangers who have in common an appreciation and enthusiasm for the restaurant's cuisine.

MENU

(a la carte)

(The following is a representative selection.)

APPETIZERS & SOUPS:

Three Delicacy Combination Platter (5.50); Hacked Chicken in Assorted Flavor (4.25); Aromatic Beef (4.25); Assorted Hot Appetizers for Two (Two fan-tail shrimps, two pieces of shrimp toast, two fried dumplings and one piece of spring roll) (4.50); Hot and Sour Soup (1.00); Abalone and Chicken Soup (1.50); Minced Chicken Corn Soup (1.00); Shark Fin Soup (1.50).

ENTREES:

Diced Chicken with Hot Pepper Sauce 5.75
Diced Chicken with Walnuts 5.75
Ta-Chien Chicken 6.50
Sweet and Sour Chicken 5.75
Peking Roast Duck (order in advance) 18.00
Camphor and Tea Smoked Duck (half) 6.95
Szechuan Roast Duck (half) 6.95
Double Sauteed Sliced Pork 4.95
Shredded Pork with Peking Sauce 4.95
Moo Shu Pork (each pancake 25¢) 4.95
Shredded Pork sauteed with Shredded Bean Cake 4.95
Steamed Fish 7.50
Sweet and Sour Whole Fish 7.50
Sauteed Sliced Fish 6.75
Hot Spicy Shrimp 6.75
Sauteed Shrimp with Hot Pepper Sauce 6.75
Sweet and Sour Shrimps 6.75
Prawns with Chili Sauce 6.95
Lobster with Chili Sauce 8.50
Lobster with Black Bean Sauce 8.50
Lobster Cantonese 8.50
Shredded Beef Dry Sauteed, Szechuan Style . 6.95
Beef with Mushroom and Bamboo Shoots ... 6.25
Beef with Snow Peas 6.25
Beef with Scallions 6.25
Egg Plant with Garlic Sauce 4.50
Dried Sauteed String Beans 4.50
Noodles with Sesame and Hot Sauce 3.25
Noodles with Bean Sauce, Peking Style 3.25

DESSERTS:

Honeyed Banana or Apple (for two) (3.50); Lichee Nuts (.85); Ice Cream (.65).

(MSG will be omitted upon request.)

TANDOOR

Address: 40 East 49th Street
Location: 49th Street off Madison Avenue
Telephone: 752-3334
Credit Cards: All major credit cards accepted
Reservations: Recommended
Hours: Lunch from 11:30 AM to 2:30 PM, Monday thru Saturday; Dinner from 5:30 PM to 11:00 PM daily
Days Closed: None
Liquor: Full bar service
Recommended or Listed in: New York Times; Cue; Where; Gourmet; Daily News; ABC/TV; WNEW/TV
Maitre d': Bhushan
Seating Capacity: 220
Cuisine: Tandoori; Indian-Continental
Specialties of the House: Tandoori Dishes; Tandoori Fish Tikka; Spiced Vegetarian Thali; Special Tandoori Dinner; Full Variety Buffet Luncheon
Dress: Casual
Party Facilities: Upstairs room; capacity: 100

Tandoor is one of the finest Indian restaurants in New York. Its menu offers a mouth-watering selection of kababs, biryanis and curries, cooked to perfection and served in generous proportions. Through a large glass window in a corner of the dining room you can watch the chefs cooking Tandoori specialties and baking nan in the Tandoor (large clay oven). Colorful wall hangings and carved wooden beams in the spacious dining room create a handsome and comfortable decor; soft music in the background contributes to the atmosphere. The moderate prices and the quality of the authentic cuisine make this Indian restaurant very special.

DINNER MENU

(The following is a representative selection from Tandoor's extensive a la carte menu.)

APPETIZERS & SIDE DISHES:
Assorted Indian Hors d'Oeuvres (Samosa, Pakoras, Shammi Kebab, Chicken Tikka and Papadum, served with mint chutney) (2.75); Raita (Cool yogurt with cucumbers, tomatoes, potatoes and mint leaves) (1.50).

ENTREES:

Special Tandoori Dinner 8.95
(Tandoori Chicken, Boti Kebab, Sheekh Kebab, Chicken Tikka, Rogan Josh or Beef Kurma and Vegetable Curry, Pillaf, Dal, Nan, Chutney, Pickles)

Tandoori Chicken .... (Half - 4.75) Full - 6.75
(Chicken marinated in yogurt and mild spices with its natural juices, roasted in our clay oven)

Chicken Tikka 4.75
(Thick and juicy cubes of chicken roasted in a clay oven)

Sheekh Kebab 4.75
(Chopped meat mixed with onions and herbs, roasted on skewers)

Tandoor Mixed Grill 7.75

Shrimp Masala 8.75
(Cooked with green peppers, onions and spices)

Fish Masala 5.75
(Cooked in mildly spiced gravy)

Fish Begum Bahar 5.75
(Fresh cut pieces of fish, cooked with eggs and creamy sauce)

Chicken Curry 4.75
(Chicken mildly spiced, cooked in light gravy)

Chicken Palak 4.75
(Chicken cooked with spinach)

Chicken Murg Musalam 5.75
(Chicken cooked in cream, mildly spiced and served with eggs)

Rara Meat 5.95
(Lamb cooked in spices with tomato sauce)

Dal Meat Beef or Lamb 5.75
(Cubes of beef or lamb cooked in lentils, cream and spices)

Special Vegetarian Thali 6.75
(Three varieties of vegetables – Dal, Samosa, Pillaf, Rice, Dhai Raita, Chapati and Papadam)

Navrattan Curry 4.75
(Nine vegetables cooked with nuts, mild spices and cream)

DESSERTS:
Assorted Sweets (1.50).
(Assorted Indian Breads are available from 1.00 to 1.75.)

TAVERN ON THE GREEN

Location: Central Park at West 67th Street
Telephone: 873-3200
Credit Cards: All major credit cards accepted
Reservations: Recommended
Hours: 12:00 Noon to 2:00 AM, daily
Days Closed: None
Liquor: Full bar service
Chef: Daniel Dunas
Seating Capacity: 400 inside; 250 outside
Banquet Facilities: 3 rooms; capacity: 40-1,000 (telephone: 873-4111)
Cuisine: American and Continental
Specialties of the House: Chicken Dunas; Dover Sole Connaught; Rack of Lamb Persillade
Dress: Informal to Elegant
Entertainment: Piano and Base in the Elm Cafe and Bar, 9:00 PM to 1:00 AM, Wednesday thru Sunday
Parking: Parking facilities available

Tavern on the Green is distinctly the creation of Warner LeRoy and bears his imprimatur as surely as Maxwell's Plum, another LeRoy spectacular. The dramatic Crystal Room, completely glass-enclosed, capitalizes on the restaurant's unique location within Central Park. The dazzling effects created by priceless chandeliers and rainbows of Tiffany glass are breathtaking. Countless whimsical and witty manifestations of LeRoy's humor abound in the decor and are best left for the uninitiated to discover and delight in. Suffice it to say that dining here is part of the New York experience.

MENU

The menus at Tavern on the Green are similar to Maxwell's Plum (see page 158). Tavern on the Green offers five different menus: Luncheon, Elm Room Dinner, Crystal Room Dinner; Weekend Brunch and Garden. There is a per person cover charge of $2.50 in the Music Room.

Tavern on the Green

THREE VILLAGE INN

Address:	**Christian Avenue and Dock Road, Stony Brook**
Location:	**Across from the Village Green**
Telephone:	**(516) 751-0555**
Credit Cards:	**AE; MC; V**
Reservations:	**Recommended**
Hours:	**Breakfast from 7:30 AM to 10:30 AM daily; Lunch from 12:00 Noon to 3:00 PM, Monday thru Saturday; Dinner from 5:00 PM to 9:00 PM, Monday thru Thursday, from 5:00 PM to 10:00 PM on Friday and Saturday, from 12:00 Noon to 9:00 PM, Sunday and Holidays. Supper served to 12:00 Midnight, Friday and Saturday**
Days Closed:	**Christmas**
Liquor:	**Full bar service**
Recommended or Listed in:	**Berkshire Traveler; Lovers Guide to America; Mobil Guide; Waterway Guide; Gourmet; Hotel & Motel Association**
Reservations Manager:	**Whitney Roberts**
Seating Capacity:	**275**
Cuisine:	**New England**
Specialties of the House:	**Local Clams (Steamed and Half Shell); Oysters; Mussels; Fresh Long Island Seafoods; Clam Pie; Maine Lobster Stew; Homemade Breads**
Dress:	**Informal; jackets recommended**
Entertainment:	**Live piano music in the "Sandbar," Friday and Saturday Evenings**
Party Facilities:	**Large private room (partitions); capacity: 20-130**

The historical Three Village Inn is housed in what once was the home of a sea captain. The Inn dates back to the 1700's, and its four wood-burning fireplaces provide visitors with a warm welcome during the colder months. The delightful country atmosphere of this charming early American inn encompasses several different dining rooms; the informal, rough-hewn pine-paneled "Sandbar," a more formal room overlooking the Village Green and the Garden Rooms with lovely views of the Harbor and Yacht Basin. The Three Village Inn is an ideal location for pleasant country dining or for a mini-weekend country vacation; overnight accommodations are available. Meals are graciously served by staff in colonial costume who take obvious pride in this restaurant, which has been under the direction of Nelson and Monda Roberts for more than 30 years.

DINNER MENU

(table d'hote)

(The extensive menu changes daily; the following is a representative selection.)

APPETIZERS & SOUPS:
Ratatouille; Chicken Liver Paté; Cold Poached Mussels Epicurean (1.75); Fresh Fruit Cup; Oysters on the Halfshell, Rockefeller, or Stew (2.75); Smoked Eel with Mustard Sauce (1.50); Chilled Long Island Clams on the Halfshell (2.25); Maine Lobster or Fresh Maryland Lump Crabmeat Cocktail (5.25); Platter of Clams Casino or Herbed Clams (3.25); Our Own Home-Made Soups (...); Our Own New England Clam Chowder (.75).

Three Village Inn

ENTREES:

Choice of Special Dishes of the Day . . . 5.50 - 7.00
Baked Finnan Haddie au Gratin in Casserole 8.00
"Lobster Pot" . . . 15.75
Fried Whole Soft Clams with Tartar Sauce . . . 8.75
New England Clam Pie . . . 8.50
Broiled or Fried Long Island Bay Scallops with Tartar Sauce . . . 9.75
Broiled Fresh Fillet of Flounder in White Wine-Butter Sauce . . . 8.75
Lobster, Shrimp & Crabmeat Newburg in Puff Patty Shell . . . 11.50
Baked Colossal Shrimp Stuffed with Crabmeat . . . 11.75
Boiled or Broiled Whole Live Maine Lobster with Drawn Butter . . . (. . .)
"Porpoise Channel" Seafood Platter . . . 9.75
(Fried Flounder, Shrimp, Scallops, Deviled Clam in Shell, Crabmeat Cake and Cole Slaw)
Broiled U.S. Prime Filet Mignon or Sirloin Steak with Sauté Mushrooms . . . 12.50
Grilled Smoked Loin of Pork Chops with Orange-Raisin Sauce and Mustard Pickle . . . 9.75
Broiled Calf's Sweetbreads à la Madeira with Sauté Mushrooms . . . 9.00
Fresh Maine Lobster Salad or Fresh Maryland Lump Crabmeat Salad in Avocado . . . 11.75

DESSERTS:

Old Fashioned Strawberry or Peach Shortcake (in season); Lemon Fromage with Raspberries; Pecan Pie with Whipped Cream; Fresh Cocoanut Ice Cream Ball with Butterscotch Sauce; Lemon or Lime Chiffon Pie with Whipped Cream; Fruit Cordial Parfait; Apple Crisp with Whipped Cream; Baked Indian Pudding à la Mode; Chocolate Ice-Box Cake with Whipped Cream; Black Walnut Layer Cake; Fresh Pineapple Chunks with Sherbet and Cocoanut Macaroon; Baked Pear à la Mode with Ginger Sauce; Ice Cream Meringues with Melba Sauce. *(All desserts are homemade.)*

(A table d'hote luncheon menu is also available; luncheon selections are similar to the dinner menu, at lower prices.)

(Brunch is served on Sunday.)

THURSDAY'S

FRIDAY'S/TUESDAY'S

Address: Thursday's: 57 West 58th Street (58th Street between Fifth and Sixth Avenues)
Friday's: 1152 First Avenue (First Avenue and 63rd Street)
Tuesday's: 190 Third Avenue (Third Avenue between 17th and 18th Streets)

Telephone: Thursday's: 371-7777
Friday's: 832-8512
Tuesday's: 533-7900

Credit Cards: AE; MC; DC; V

Reservations: Recommended

Hours: 11:45 AM to 2:00 AM, weeknights; to 4:00 AM, weekends

Days Closed: None

Liquor: Full bar service

Recommended or Listed in: Where; Cue

Seating Capacity: Thursday's, 250; Tuesday's, 200; Friday's, 95

Cuisine: American

Specialties of the House: Huge Burgers (all varieties); Steaks; Omelettes; Salads

Dress: Informal

Entertainment: Dancing at Tuesday's and Thursday's every night

Party Facilities: Private room; capacity: 30 (Tuesday's and Thursday's). Both restaurants are also available for large functions; capacity: 500 (Thursday's), 250 (Tuesday's)

Parking: Discount parking at Tower Parking, 56th Street and Sixth Avenue (Thursday's)

Each of these three restaurants has in common a high-spirited eastside ambience and good, satisfying fare at reasonable prices. Each has its own distinctive characteristics as well—the lively disco in Tuesday's Bottom, a glass-enclosed, indoor-outdoor cafe at Friday's, and Thursday's multi-level dining and dancing. A profusion of green plants and crisp white tablecloths, Tiffany lamps and sparkling mirrors add to the fresh attractiveness of Thursday's; Tuesday's exudes a warm and comfortable pub atmosphere; and Friday's, with its sawdust covered floors, noteworthy bar and authentic memorabilia never lacks for young and enthusiastic patrons. Any one of these restaurants is a good choice for any night of the week.

MENU

(a la carte)

(The following are representative selections from Thursday's menu.)

SNACKS & APPETIZERS:
Melon (1.45); Shrimp Cocktail (3.75); Fried Fresh Mushrooms with Creamy Horseradish Sauce (1.85); Zucchini Slices (1.75); Onion Soup (1.45); Hot Chili (cup: 1.75).

BURGERS:
(The Burger Plate (3.25) includes lettuce, tomato and pickles; the Platter (3.95) includes french fries and onion rings.)

The Hamburger; Cheeseburger; Friday Burger with Sauteed Onions, Chopped Peppers and Ham; Tuesday Burger with Sauteed Mushrooms, Wine Sauce of Onions, Herbs and Butter; Bacon Cheeseburger; Mexican Burger; Bernaise Burger (.50 extra); Healthy Burger; Cheddar Burger; Bacon Cheddar Burger; Blue Burger; Name Your Own Burger; Onion Burger; Chili Burger; Pizza Burger; Au Poivre Burger (.50 extra).

ENTREES:

Bar-B-Q Chicken and Ribs 5.85
Bar-B-Q Chicken 5.60
Chili by the Bowl 3.25
Honey Fried Chicken Basket 4.75
Barbecued Spare Ribs 5.65
Club Sandwich 3.85
Grilled Bacon and Cheese Extraordinaire 3.25
Jambalaya 3.25
Beer Batter Fried Shrimp 5.75
Fresh Fish .... (...)
New York Sirloin - 16 oz 10.50
Junior Sirloin 8.50
Open Sliced Steak Sandwich 5.85
Filet Mignon Wrapped in Bacon 7.75
Chopped Steak 5.25
Tournado Thursdays 9.75
Roumanian Tenderloin 5.85
Steak and Chili 4.75
Steak Au Poivre 9.75

(All entrees are served with potato or rice, crisp onion rings and a basket of assorted breads.)

(A variety of salads is available with prices ranging from 3.95 to 4.75. Omelette and Egg Dishes are offered, from 3.85 to 4.75.)

DESSERTS:

Cheesecake (1.75); Old-Fashioned Chocolate Pudding with Chunks of Chocolate, Marshmallows and Whipped Cream, Topped with a Cherry (1.45); Our Own Rum Raisin Ice Cream (1.60); Plain Old Melon (1.45); Chocolate Mousse Cake (1.45); Deep Fried Apple Rings (1.65) (with vanilla ice cream, .65 extra).

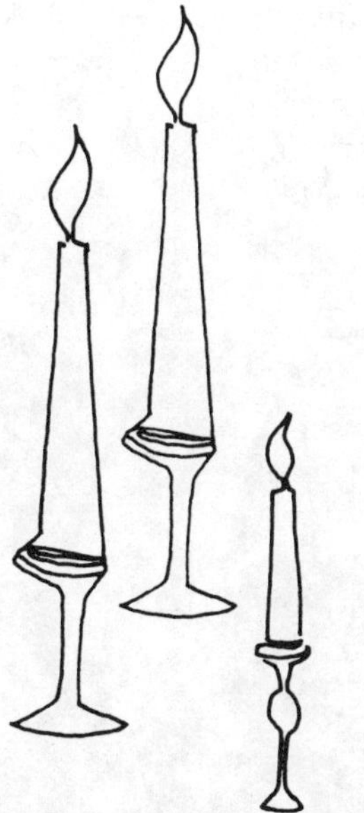

CASSATINA: *This pastry is made in a cupcake tin and has a sponge cake base filled with ricotta, chocolate chips and candied fruits. The filling is used on top of the cake as well and the very top is often garnished with a cherry or other candied fruit.*

CREMOLATA: *This is soft ice cream, creamier than* gelati. *It is made with heavy cream and butter and is often flavored with espresso.*

FARFALLA: *This means "butterfly" and the pastry actually looks like a cupcake with a butterfly perched on top. The base is made of rum-soaked sponge cake. A piece of the cupcake is scooped out and a custard cream is put in its place. The piece of cake that has been removed is then placed on top to look like butterfly wings.*

TIMOTHY

Address:	**127 Lexington Avenue**
Location:	**Lexington Avenue between 28th Street and 29th Street**
Telephone:	**LE 2-7674**
Credit Cards:	**Not accepted**
Reservations:	**For parties over six only**
Hours:	**From 12 Noon to 12 Midnight Monday thru Friday and from 5:00 PM to 12 Midnight on Saturday**
Days Closed:	**Sunday**
Liquor:	**Full bar service**
Recommended or Listed in:	**Esquire; New York Times**
Maitre d':	**Jean Pierre**
Reservations Manager:	**Jesse Wilkins**
Seating Capacity:	**75 plus 40 in the garden during the summer**
Cuisine:	**Thai and International**
Specialties of the House:	**Grilled Satés; Chicken Gai Yang; Grilled Giant Thai Shrimp; Daily Specials**
Dress:	**Casual**

Delightful in decor and atmosphere and refreshingly different in cuisine, Timothy offers a welcome change of pace. Here you'll find two dining rooms plus a charming garden in summer. In the upstairs room the motif derives from the French countryside as evidenced by the high ceiling, tiled floor, hand carved wood and original paintings. In the stucco-walled downstairs room, the theme is Mediterranean. The food is prepared with flair and imagination and the service is excellent.

Timothy

DINNER MENU

(a la carte)

APPETIZERS:
Guacomole served with homemade tortilla chips (2.50); Eggplant Sticks deep fried in seasoned bread crumbs (1.95); Spinach Salade with mustard dressing, crisped bacon and fresh mushrooms (1.75); Romaine Salad with Tomatoes, red onion rings and cucumber (2.50); Cellophane Sea Noodle and Cucumber Salade (1.95); Steak Tartare served on Pumpernickel Slices (2.95); Baked Stuffed Clams (2.50).

ENTREES:

Bucket of Steamed Clams served with drawn butter and broth 4.50

Bowl of Steamed Shrimp with dill and caraway (served in their shells) 5.95

Grilled Giant Thai Shrimp with scallion sauce 7.95

Broiled Filet of Sole with rice pilaf, snow peas, fresh ginger and almonds 5.50

Satés — Chicken, Beef, Shrimp, Pork, or Combination 6.75

(Charcoal broiled on skewers and served with fried rice, cucumber salad and sauces)

Chicken Gai Yang 4.75

(1/2 chicken marinated, broiled over coals, cut into bite-sized pieces, served with a hot and sweet sauce)

Chicken Breasts with water chestnuts, straw mushrooms, peppers, and almonds sauteed in hoisin sauce 5.95

Prime Hamburger Platter 3.50

Steak Kew sauteed cubes of steak with Chinese vegetables 6.50

16 oz Boneless Shell Steak served with French Fries 8.95

Broiled Seafood Platter with Sole, Shrimps, Scallops and Clams 7.95

Oriental Style Pasta 5.95

(Lo mein noodles with sausage, shrimp and chicken breasts in piquant sauce)

Scallops of Beef stir-fried with tomatoes and peppers in oyster sauce 6.95

Oriental Style Spareribs served with pork fried rice and cucumber salade 6.50

DESSERTS:

Rum Mousse au Chocolate (1.75); Carrot Cake (1.50); Chocolate Almond Fudge Cake (1.50); Pecan Pie (1.75); Rum Cream Pie (1.75).

(The luncheon menu is similar to the dinner menu but includes sandwiches and omelettes.)

GATTO: *This Italian pastry has a sponge cake base which is lightly soaked in rum, a layer of custard cream, a layer of chocolate cream and a whipped cream frosting. It is often served on special occasions.*

GELATI: *This is Italian ice cream and has a much higher butter fat content than any other kind. It is folded rather than churned when it's being made, and is so rich that it leaves a glaze on your tongue and palate when you eat it. Vanilla, chocolate and strawberry are the classic flavorings.*

MILLE FOGLIE: *The name of this pastry, "thousand leaves," refers to the crust it has both on top and on bottom. It is a many-layered, flaky crust that, when made correctly, actually looks like many leaves unfolding. Between the crusts of a mille foglie is a sweet sponge cake made from flour, sugar and eggs. The mille foglie is always cut into squares.*

NASPRATA: *This extraordinarily rich pastry got its name from the verb "to ice." It begins with a sponge cake base slightly moistened with rum; it is filled with a cooked custard cream and then iced in pink (strawberry), white (vanilla), or brown (chocolate). The chocolate usually has a ricotta cream filling instead of custard cream. To top it all, there's a candied fruit or two. Some pastry shops call the nasprata a* cassatina.

PANETTONE: *This is the Italian version of raisin bread—it contains chopped raisins and candied fruits, is large and round and is usually served at teatime or for breakfast.*

TINO'S

Address: 235 East 58th Street
Location: 58th Street between Second Avenue and Third Avenue
Telephone: 751-0311 or 751-0312
Credit Cards: AE; V; DC
Reservations: Required
Hours: Lunch from 12:00 Noon to 3:00 PM; Dinner from 5:00 PM to 12:00 Midnight
Days Closed: Major Holidays
Liquor: Full bar service
Recommended or Listed in: New York Times; Cue; Women's Wear Daily
Maitre d': Pietro
Seating Capacity: 80
Cuisine: Northern Italian
Specialties of the House: Linguine with Broccoli; Rigatoni alla Cipullo; Pollo alla Tino; Risotto Milanese al Tartufo; Cheese Cake alla Salvatore; Fresh Fruit and Cheese Daily
Dress: Jackets required
Party Facilities: Private room; capacity: 25

By day Tino's is airy, contemporary and relaxed. By night the mood becomes more formal in the three elegant candlelit dining rooms. Brick walls, partly beamed ceilings and the skylit garden are accented by paintings and tapestries, ceramics, and hanging and potted plants. In this congenial environment, Tino serves up some of the best Northern Italian cuisine in the city. There's a new intimate dining room upstairs for private parties. Mirrors reflect the soft light of the crystal chandelier and a working fireplace adds warmth and charm to the room.

DINNER MENU
(a la carte)

APPETIZERS & SOUPS:
Shrimp Cocktail (4.00); Melone e Prosciutto (3.75); Scampi alla Ligure (Shrimps in Olive Oil and Garlic) (4.00); Mozzarella e Pomodoro (Sliced Mozzarella and Tomatoes) (3.00); Zucchine Ripiene di Carne (Meat Stuffed Zucchini) (3.50); Broccoli al Formaggio (Broccoli with Melted Cheese (3.75); Mozzarella in Carrozza (Baked Mozzarella) (3.75); Vongole Oreganate (Baked Clams) (4.00); Antipasto Misto (4.00); Antipasto Caldo (4.50); Tortellini in Brodo (Dumplings filled with Chicken Meat) (3.00); Stracciatella alla Romana (Chicken Broth with Egg Drops) (3.00); Zuppa alla Pavese (Consomme, Toast, Poached Egg) (3.00); Minestrone alla Milanese (3.00). Beluga Malossal Caviar (. . .);

PASTA:
Fettuccine all'Uovo 7.00
(Egg Noodles with Butter Sauce, as in Rome)
Rigatoni d'Oro alla Cipullo 7.50
Spaghetti al Pomodoro 7.00
Cannelloni alla Bolognese 7.00
(Baked Green Cannelloni Bolognese Style)
Linguine alle Vongole 7.50
(Flat Spaghetti with White or Red Clam Sauce)
Spaghettini al Pesto 7.00
(Genovese Style: Garlic and Basil)
Risotto ai Frutti di Mare 8.50
(Rice with Clams, Mussels, Shrimps & Brandy Sauce)
Bucatini all'Amatriciana 7.00
Spaghetti alla Carbonara 7.00
Rigatoni all'Arrabbiata 7.25
Paglia and Fieno 7.00
(Thin Green and Yellow Noodles, Peas and Prosciutto)
Linguine ai Broccoli 7.50
Risotto alla Trevignana 7.00
(Rice Saute with Onions, Peas, White Wine)
Rigatoni alla Carrettiera 7.50
(Sauce of Tomatoes, Fresh Mushrooms and Chicken Livers)
Conchiglie all'Inferno 7.00
(Shells with Hot Sauce)

Tino's

Spaghettini alla Chitarra 7.00
(Peas, Prosciutto and Mushrooms)
Risotto Milanese al Tartufo 18.00
(Milanese Rice with White Truffles)
Fettuccine alla Salvatore 7.50

ENTREES:
Scaloppine al Marsala 8.00
Pollo alla Margherita 7.50
(Boneless Breasts of Chicken, Bechemel Sauce and Wine)
Mignonette Peperonata 11.50
(Filet Mignon with Peppers and Spiced Tomato Sauce)
Ossobuco alla Milanese 8.50
(Veal Shank with Yellow Rice)
Piccata al Limone 8.00
Saltinbocca alla Sorrentina 8.00
(Veal, Mozzarella Cheese and Prosciutto)
Pollo alla Toscanini 7.50
(Breasts of Chicken, Saute in Wine and White Sauce)
Pollo alla Tino Scarpa 7.75
(Pieces of Boneless Chicken, Mushrooms, Artichokes, in Wine Sauce)
Cotoletta alla Milanese 9.00
(Breaded Veal Cutlet, Milanese Style)
Scaloppina Peperonata 8.00
(Veal, Green Peppers, Tomato Sauce)
Fegato alla Veneziana 9.00
(Calf Liver, Venetian Style)
Bistecca alla Pizzaiola 12.50
(Sirloin Steak Saute, Spicy Tomato Sauce)

Spigola alla Livornese 9.50
(Striped Bass, Livornese Style)
Scampi alla Sorrentina 8.50
(Jumbo Shrimps, Mushrooms, Onions, Tomato Sauce)
La Pescatora (For Two) 29.00
(Lobster, Clams, Scampi with Tino's Sauce)
Vongole alla Livornese 8.00
(Clams in Garlic Broth)
Sogliola-Ripiena 9.50
(Broiled Flounder, Stuffed with Crabmeat and Shrimps)
Aragosta Fra Diavolo 24.00
(Lobster, Spiced Tomato Sauce)
Scampi alla Genovese 8.50
Filets of Sole Genovese 8.50
English Sole 9.00
Sirloin Steak 12.00
Filet Mignon 12.50
Veal Chop 11.00
Paillard of Veal 9.50
Pollo alla Griglia 8.00
Paillard of Beef 12.00
Calf's Liver 10.00

(A variety of salads and vegetables is available a la carte.)

DESSERTS AND CHEESES:
Zabaglione al Marsala (3.25); Bisquit Tortoni (2.00); Spumoni (2.00); Zabaglione and Fresh Strawberries (4.50); Homemade Cheese Cake (2.50); Zuppa Inglese (2.25); Frutta Fresca (2.25); Bel Paese, Gorgonzola, Provolone or Fontina Cheese (3.50).

TOPKAPI PALACE

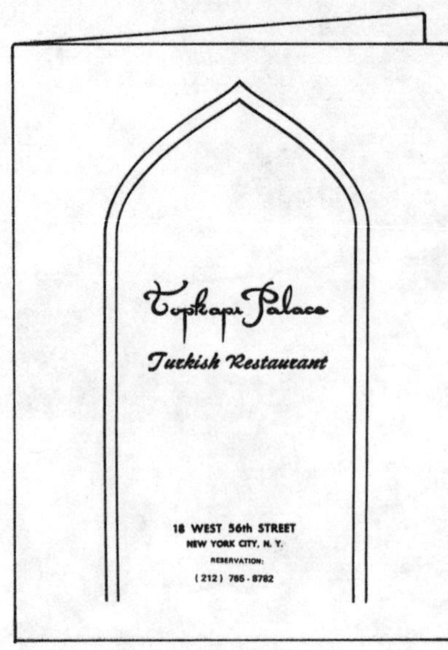

Address: 18 West 56th Street
Location: 56th Street between Fifth Avenue and Avenue of the Americas
Telephone: 765-8782
Credit Cards: AE; DC; CB
Reservations: Recommended
Hours: 12 Noon to 3:00 PM and 5:00 PM to 11:00 PM Monday thru Saturday; 2:00 PM to 11:00 PM Sunday (dinner only)
Days Closed: None
Liquor: Full Bar Service
Recommended or Listed in: New York Times; Gourmet; Cue; Playbill
Seating Capacity: 90
Cuisine: Turkish
Specialties of the House: Yogurt Soup; Patlican Kebab; Lamb with Yogurt
Dress: Casual

If you can't fly off to Istanbul but would like a taste of Anatolia, try New York's oldest authentic Turkish restaurant. Tapestries, brass and hand-painted pottery, all typical of Turkish culture, decorate the walls. Further emphasizing the Byzantine atmosphere are ogee shaped windows and doors and the gaily colored native vests worn by the waiters. Topkapi Palace is truly a Turkish delight.

DINNER MENU

(a la carte)

APPETIZERS:
Enginar (Fresh artichoke cooked in olive oil with onions and carrots) (2.75); Midye Dolmasi (Fresh mussels, stuffed with rice, cooked in olive oil) (2.25); Imam Bayildi (Eggplant, with sliced onion and tomato baked in olive oil) (2.25); Yalanci Dolma (Grape leaves, stuffed with rice, cooked in olive oil) (1.75); Borek (Thin leaves of dough filled with Turkish white cheese) (1.25); Fasulya Piyaz (White boiled beans, garnished with tomato, black olive and onion) (1.75); Tarama (Red caviar spread) (1.75); Cacik (Cucumbers in yogurt) (1.25); Pastirma (Spiced dried beef, sliced thin) (2.25); Turkish White Cheese (Feta cheese) (2.25); Fruit Cup (1.00); Barbunya Plaki (Red Beans cooked in olive oil with carrots) (2.00); Topkapi Special Appetizer (Selected hors d'oeuvres) (7.00).

SOUPS AND SALADS:
Soup du Jour (1.50); Iskembe (Tripe) (2.00); Yayla Corbasi (Yogurt soup) (1.50); Mixed Green Salad (1.75); Coban Salata (a Turkish salad with tomato, cucumber, chopped green pepper and onion) (2.00); Topkapi Salad (a special salad with lettuce, tomato, onion, white beans and white cheese) (2.50).

ENTREES:

Patlican Musakka 5.75
(Baked eggplant layered with chopped meat, topped with an egg sauce)

Patlican Karniyarik 5.25
(Baked sliced eggplant with chopped meat and sliced tomato)

Patlican Kebab 6.00
(Cubed eggplants baked with tender pieces of lamb, pepper, tomato)

Tas Kebab 5.75
(Pot roasted lamb cooked in tomato sauce)

Orman Kebab 5.75
(Pot roasted lamb cooked in oregano sauce)

Yaprak Dolma 5.50
(Stuffed tender grape leaves with chopped meat and rice)

Chicken Topkapi 5.50
(Charcoal broiled tender pieces of chicken leg, onions, tomatoes and peppers)

Tavuk Dolma 5.25
(Chicken, baked with tomato and pepper)

Kiymali Ispanak 5.25
(Spinach cooked with chopped meat, served with or without yogurt)

Kuzu Firin 6.00
(Sliced baked lamb with currants and pine nuts)
Kuzu Kizartma 6.00
(Turkish style baked tender lamb shank)
Hunkar Begendi 6.00
(Pot roasted lamb with eggplant puree)
Turlu 5.75
(Fresh vegetables baked in tomato sauce with tender pieces of lamb)
Etli Bamya 5.25
(Okra cooked in tomato sauce with tender pieces of lamb)
Izgara Kofte 6.00
(Turkish style charcoal broiled lamburgers)
Sis Kofte 6.00
(Charcoal broiled chopped meat on skewer)
Lamb Sis Kebab 6.75
(Charcoal broiled tender pieces of lamb, onions, tomatoes and peppers)
Beef Sis Kebab 7.25
(Charcoal broiled tender pieces of beef, onions, tomatoes and peppers)
Topkapi Kebab 7.50
(Tender pieces of lamb, served with yogurt on a Turkish bread called pide)
Broiled Lamb Chops 7.00

Broiled Sirloin Steak 7.25
Mixed Grill 8.00
Broiled Sea Food Kebab 6.50
Karisik Dolma 6.00
(Stuffed mixed vegetables with chopped meat and rice)

(All above entrees served with Turkish Rice Pilav.)

DESSERTS:
Baklava (Thin layers of dough, filled with chopped walnuts, baked and served with honey syrup) (1.25); Burma (Thin pastry dough, rolled, stuffed with pistachio, baked and served with honey syrup) (1.25); Tel Kadayif (Shredded dough, stuffed with chopped walnuts, baked and served with honey syrup) (1.25); Kaymakli Ekmek Kadayif (Toasted bread pastry, cooked in honey syrup and served with kaymak) (1.75); Sutlac (Turkish rice pudding) (1.25); Ice Cream (1.00); Fruit Compote (1.25); Home Made Yogurt (1.25).

(Table d'hote dinners priced from 7.25 to 9.25 are also available)

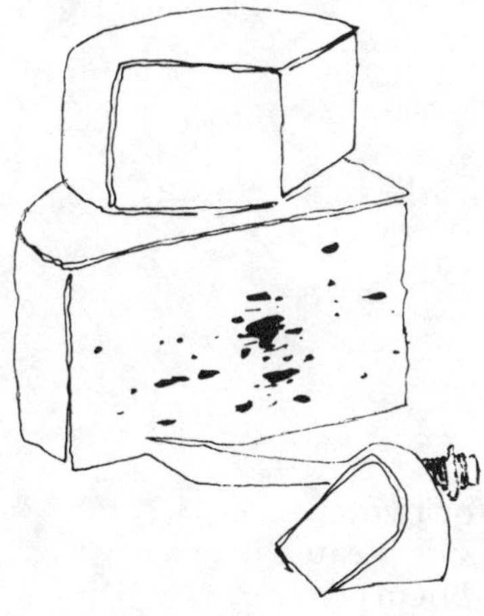

PORT DU SALUT: *Sometimes known as Trappist cheese because it was first made in the Trappist monastery at Entrammes in France, Port du Salut is soft and creamy in texture with a flavor which varies markedly with age. Very young Port du Salut is bland almost to the point of being tasteless but this cheese becomes much stronger with age.*

PROVOLONE: *A classic Italian table cheese, Provolone is firm and pliant in consistency and pale yellow or ivory in color. It is mild in flavor but is often smoked before being dried and salted, giving it a distinctive, smoky taste.*

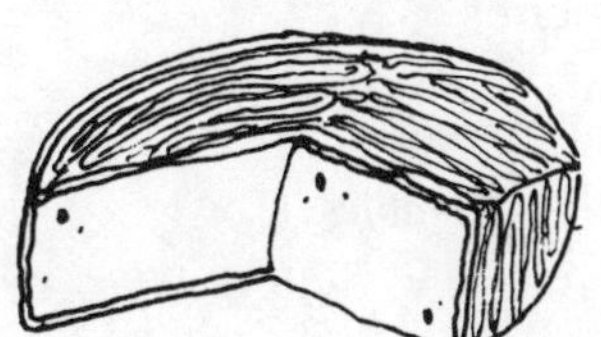

RICOTTA: *The Italian cottage cheese, Ricotta is fresh white curd which is moist with whey and unsalted. It is very bland in flavor and smoothly textured. Ricotta is used frequently in cooking, e.g. in lasagna.*

ROMANO: *This is a black-rinded Italian sheep's milk cheese used mainly for flavoring. It is much like Parmesan in that it is very friable and crumbles into fine flakes when grated. It has a much stronger flavor than Parmesan, however.*

LES TOURNEBROCHES

Address: One Citicorp Center
Location: The Market, Citicorp Center (at 53rd Street and Third Avenue)
Telephone: 935-6029
Credit Cards: AE; DC; V; MC
Reservations: Recommended
Hours: 11:30 AM to 9:30 PM
Days Closed: None
Liquor: Full bar service
Seating Capacity: 60
Cuisine: French
Dress: Casual

Les Tournebroches is a welcome recent addition to The Market, located in the Citicorp Center. It features a unique, open rotisserie for leg of lamb, venison, poultry, pigeon and game. Three roasting grills, made of black iron and mounted on tiles, are visible to those who enjoy this very old and very popular European cooking technique. Mr. Chevillot, owner of Les Tournebroches, has gained a deserved reputation for excellent cuisine, exemplified by his other New York restaurant, La Petite Ferme on the upper eastside. Coming from a family of French restaurateurs, Mr. Chevillot brings to Les Tournebroches his own high standards and his personal philosophy that " a restaurant man has a responsibility to provide affordable good food and friendly, efficient service in warm, comfortable surroundings."

LUNCHEON & DINNER MENU

(a la carte)

(The prices of entrees begin at 6.00.)

APPETIZERS & SIDE DISHES:
Les Hors d'Oeuvre Varies; Salade Verte.

ENTREES:
Le Plat du Jour
Le Poulet Roti
Le Poussin Roti
Le Canard Roti
Bifteck Maison
Les Cotlettes de Porc
La Cote de Boeuf (for two)
Les Cotes d'Agneau
Le Poisson du Jour
L'Entrecote
Le Carre d'Agneau (for two)
Brochette de Rognons de Veau
Brochette de Filet de Boeuf
Brochette de Veau Printanier
Brochette de Fruits de Mer
La Brochette "Tournebroches"

(All entrees are served with vegetables.)

DESSERTS:
Les Tartes Maison.

TRUMAN'S

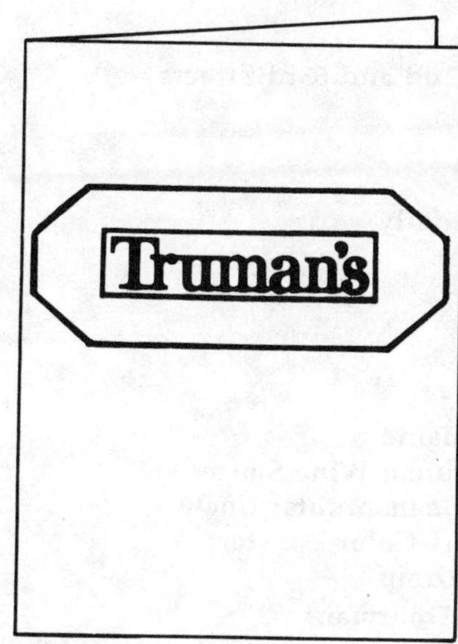

Address: 1401 Old Northern Boulevard, Roslyn
Location: Northern Boulevard and Roslyn Road
Telephone: (516) 621-0778
Credit Cards: MC; AE; CB; DC; V
Reservations: Recommended
Hours: Lunch from 12:00 Noon to 2:30 PM, Monday, Wednesday thru Friday; Dinner from 5:30 PM to 10:00 PM weekdays (except Tuesday), to 11:30 PM on Saturday; from 4:00 PM to 10:00 PM, Sunday
Days Closed: Tuesday
Liquor: Full bar service
Recommended or Listed in: New York Times; Cue; Newsday; North Shore Magazine
Manager/ Hostess: Margaret Olive
Seating Capacity: 110
Cuisine: French and American
Specialties of the House: Lobster Bouillabaisse; Shrimp Tempura; Shell Steak; Duck with Apricots
Dress: Informal; Jackets preferred in upstairs dining room
Entertainment: Concert singer and pianist, Thursday thru Saturday
Party Facilities: 2 private rooms; capacity: 40 each
Parking: Restaurant parking lot

Truman's has something for everyone—bacon cheeseburgers and gourmet house specialties; the informal atmosphere of the downstairs dining room and the stunning decor that enhances dining Upstairs-at-Truman's; an exciting concert singer on weekend evenings and a special businessman's menu for weekday luncheons. Truman's is located in what was once an historic mansion in Roslyn and the graciousness of a bygone era is captured in the silver beaded curtains, dinners served by candlelight and an abundance of fresh flowers.

DINNER MENU

(a la carte)

APPETIZERS & SOUPS:
Onion Soup (1.75); Vichyssoise (1.75); Soupe du Jour (1.50); Quiche Lorraine (2.75); Escargots Bourguignons (3.75); Avocado Vinaigrette (2.25); Clam Cocktail (2.75); Clams Casino (3.50); Baked Clams Maison (2.50); Champignons Farcis (2.50); Mussels (au Vin, Marseillaise, or Marinara) (3.95).

ENTREES:
Bouillabaisse with Lobster 13.50
Shrimp Tempura 8.95
Coq Saute Chasseur 8.95
Prime Sirloin Steak 11.95
Jumbo Shrimp 9.50
Filet of Sole Normande 8.95
Lobster Tails with Caper Sauce 11.95
Roast Duckling à l'Orange 8.95
Roast Duckling au Grand Marnier 9.95
Escalopes de Veau Marsala 7.95
Escalopes de Veau Casimir 8.95
Supreme of Chicken Ambassadrice 9.50
Striped Bass à la Française 9.50
Veal Chops Bourguignons or aux Champignons à la Crême 9.95
Calves Liver Lyonnaise 7.95
Hamburger* 3.50
Cheeseburger* 3.75
Mushroom Burger* 3.75
Bacon Cheeseburger* 4.00
(Starred entrees are not served on Saturday.)

SALADS:
Truman Salad (1.75); Caesar Salad (2.00); Panache Salad (2.00).

DESSERTS:
Chocolate Mousse (2.00); Beignets Banana or Strawberry (2.25); Dame Blanche (2.00); Pecan Pie (1.75); Cheese Cake (1.75); Amaretto Ice Cream (2.00); Fresh Strawberries (2.25); Assorted Fruit Flan (1.75); Chocolate Cake (1.75); Pears Melba (2.25); Creme Brulee (2.00).

(A complete dinner special is also offered every evening except Saturday.)

(An a la carte luncheon menu is available with entree prices ranging from 3.00 to 5.50. A special Business Man's Lunch includes a choice of soup and Truman's Salad in the price of any entree.)

UNCLE TAI'S HUNAN YUAN

Address: 1059 Third Avenue
Location: Third Avenue between 62nd and 63rd Streets
Telephone: 838-0850
Credit Cards: AE; DC
Reservations: Recommended
Hours: 12:00 Noon to 11:30 PM, daily
Days Closed: None
Liquor: Full bar service
Manager: Jack Shar
Seating Capacity: 175
Cuisine: Hunan-Style Chinese Cuisine
Specialties of the House: Fresh Blue Crabs with Hunan Wine Sauce; Shredded Chicken with Beansprouts; Uncle Tai's Beef; Uncle Tai's Tri-Color Lobster; Quick Sauteed Jumbo Shrimp
Parking: 2-hour free parking (see Doorman)

Wen Dah Tai has been cited by Craig Claiborne of the New York Times *as "one of New York's finest Chinese chefs . . .", and Uncle Tai's Hunan specialties are certainly the major attraction of this restaurant which is well-known and respected among those who appreciate the cuisine of the province of Hunan. The distinctive decor of Uncle Tai's creates a pleasant dining atmosphere, and the quality of the service reflects the pride that the staff has in the reputation of the restaurant, designated as a four-star restaurant by the* New York Times.

MENU

(a la carte)
(The following is a representative selection.)

APPETIZERS & SOUPS:
Assorted Special Appetizers (for 2) (6.25); Diced Boneless Squab Packages (6.25); Crispy Walnuts (6.25); Hacked Chicken in Spicy Sauce (6.25); Hot and Sour Fish Broth (1.75); Velvet Corn Soup with Crabmeat (1.75); Sliced Fresh Fish in Chicken Broth (for 2) (5.50); Hot and Sour Soup (1.50).

ENTREES:
Fresh Blue Crabs with Hunan Wine Sauce . . . 8.75
Shredded Chicken with Beansprouts 9.25
Uncle Tai's Beef 11.25
Uncle Tai's Tri-Color Lobster 19.75
Quick Sauteed Jumbo Shrimp 11.25
Lake Tung Ting Shrimp 8.75
Prawns in Chili Sauce (out of shell) 11.25
Steamed Sea Bass with Garlic and Black Bean Sauce, Hunan Style 10.50
Sliced Fish with Vinegar and Wine Sauce 8.25
Lobster with Chili Sauce 11.50
Sliced Prawns with Hot Pepper Sauce 8.25
Sliced Prawns with Garlic Sauce 8.25
General Tso's Chicken 7.95
Diced Chicken with Walnuts 7.95
Shredded Chicken with Straw Mushrooms . . 7.95
Diced Chicken with Hot Pepper Sauce 7.95
Smoked Duck (Half Duck) 9.25
Deep Fried Crispy Duck (Half Duck) 9.25
Twice Cooked Pork Hunan Style with Bitter Melon 7.25
Shredded Beef Tripe 7.25
Sliced Lamb with Scallion 7.25
Sa-Chia Beef 8.25
Sliced Beef with Broccoli 8.25
Shredded Beef with Garlic Sauce 8.25
Uncle Tai's Beancurd 5.95
Winter Bamboo Shoots with Black Mushrooms and Preserved Vegetables 5.95
Dried Sauteed String Beans 5.95
Spicy Bean Curd 5.95
Pan-Fried Noodles 6.50

DESSERTS:
Sesame Apple or Sesame Banana (for 2) (3.50); Fresh Fruit (1.75).

(MSG will be omitted from any order on request.)

Uncle Tai's Hunan Yuan

PRIX TAITTINGER *This prize is awarded in the fall of each year in honor of the founder of Taittinger Champagne who was known as a great gastronome and supporter of the culinary arts. Competition for the Prix is held in France and the winner receives a trip from Paris to New York where he is presented with a silver "coupe" at a reception at The Vatel Club. The most recent winner was Yves Menes, Executive Chef at the Shoreham Hotel in Washington, D.C., whose preparation of turbot was judged the finest of all entries.*

LA SAINT MICHEL SOCIETE MUTUALISTE DES PATISSIERS DE FRANCE *This French organization has a U.S. branch and its representative is Maurice Bonté, M.O.F. The Société, made up of pâtissiers, confiseurs, chocolatiers and glaciers is pledged to support and encourage the best in the field of pastry-making. It awards medals to deserving practitioners of the art.*

THE U.S. STEAKHOUSE COMPANY

Address:	120 West 51st Street
Location:	51st Street between Avenue of the Americas and Seventh Avenue (in Time-Life Building)
Telephone:	757-8800
Credit Cards:	All major credit cards accepted
Reservations:	Recommended
Hours:	12 Noon to 1:00 AM
Days Closed:	Sundays and major holidays
Liquor:	Full bar service
Recommended or Listed in:	New York Times; New York Magazine; Cue; Promenade; Where
Maitre d's:	Teddy Lupo and George Marchese
Seating Capacity:	180
Cuisine:	American
Specialties of the House:	Porterhouse Steak; Steak Salad; Six-Nut Pie; Homemade Saratoga Chips
Dress:	Casual
Party Facilities:	Private room; capacity: 70
Parking:	Free parking at Tower Garage (on 51st Street)

This restaurant heralds America and its food and wine in a way that's bound to make all of us feel proud. The menu consists of a large variety of USDA prime steaks and an interesting array of regional dishes rarely found in this part of the country. To accompany dinner there is an ample selection of fine American wines. The restaurant is handsomely, yet simply, appointed with a long dark oak bar leading into a natural wood and mirrored dining room. And (what could be more patriotic) Old Glory herself looks down upon diners.

DINNER MENU

(a la carte)

APPETIZERS & SOUPS:
Today's Stuffed Vegetable (1.95); A Starter of Tartar (1.95); Local Clams (3.25); Oysters (3.25); Shrimp Cocktail (4.50); Fresh Grapefruit (1.50); Sliced Tomato and Onion (1.95); Cream of Peanut Soup (1.50); Chicken with . . . (1.50); Our Kitchen Soup (1.50).

ENTREES:

Sirloin Steak - 16 oz 13.95
Châteaubriand for Two 26.00
Filet Mignon 13.50
Porterhouse for Two or more .. (per person) 13.95
Our Famous 24 oz T-Bone Steak 16.95
Prime Ribs of Beef - Regular Cut 10.95
Prime Ribs of Beef - Manhattan Cut 13.95
"More than a Pound" Chopped Steak with Sauteed Onions 5.95
"More than a Pound" Chopped Steak with Curried Vegetable 6.50
"More than a Pound" Chopped Steak with Béarnaise Center 6.50
Sliced Beef Steak 8.25
"More than a Pound" Chopped Steak with Red Wine and Cheddar Cheese 6.50
Tartar Steak 7.50
Cold Steak Salad 6.95
Barbecued Beef Bones 6.95
Cold Roast Beef Platter 6.95
Roast Turkey with Two Stuffings (Corn Bread and Cranberry) 6.95
Lamb Chops 10.95
Broiled Herbed Chicken 6.95
(Tarragon, Garlic or Oregano)
U.S. Steakhouse Vegetable Plate 5.95
Deep Fried or Broiled Scallops 7.95
Deep Fried Prawns 7.95
Filet of Sole, Nutted with Walnuts or Almonds 8.25
Today's Fish 7.95
A Large Maine Lobster 17.95

(All steaks, filets and prime ribs are served with baked potatoes or french fries.)

POTATOES, SALADS & VEGETABLES:
Baked Potato (1.25); Potato Skins (1.10); French Fries (1.25); Hashed Browns (1.25); Hashed Browns with Apple (1.50); Baked Stuffed Potatoes (1.50); Fresh Vegetables of the Season (1.95); Mixed Green Salad (1.50); Tomato and Onion Salad (1.95); Spinach Salad (1.95); Onion Rings (1.95); Corn Fritters (1.95); Caesar Salad for two or more (2.95 per person).

DESSERTS:
Six-Nut Pie (1.95); Deep Dish Apple Pie (1.95); Cheese Cake (1.95); Chocolate Cake (1.95); Fresh Grapefruit (1.50); Fresh Strawberries (2.25); Fresh Melon (1.50); Ice Cream or Sherbet (1.25); Real Hot Fudge Sundae (1.95).

(The Luncheon Menu is similar to the Dinner Menu except that entrees are priced approximately 1.00 lower.)

PASTICCIOTO A RICOTTA, PASTICCIOTO A CREMA: *Both of these pastries have a cupcake shape and are made with a short crust dough. The pasticcioto a ricotta crust is filled with ricotta, sugar and farina (traditionally whatever was left over from the preparation of the pasta or second course of a meal). It always has a cross made of crust on top. The pasticcioto a crema is the same dough filled with custard cream. In Naples,* amarena, *or wild cherries, are usually added but not in the U.S.—Americans seem to object to the blackish tint that the amarena gives to the custard. Pasticcio literally means "a mixture."*

PIZZA GRANA: *This cake is similar to a* torta di ricotta *but it is made with whole wheat grain—a symbol of rebirth and resurrection—and is most often eaten during the Easter season. It is whiter and its texture is grainier than the* torta di ricotta.

PIZZA RUSTICA: *Although this is not really a pastry, it is sold in most Italian pastry shops. It is eaten in place of a sweet, often in mid-afternoon. A rustic, peasant-style pie, its double crust is filled with cheese, salami and eggs. It is similar to a French* quiche *but much heavier.*

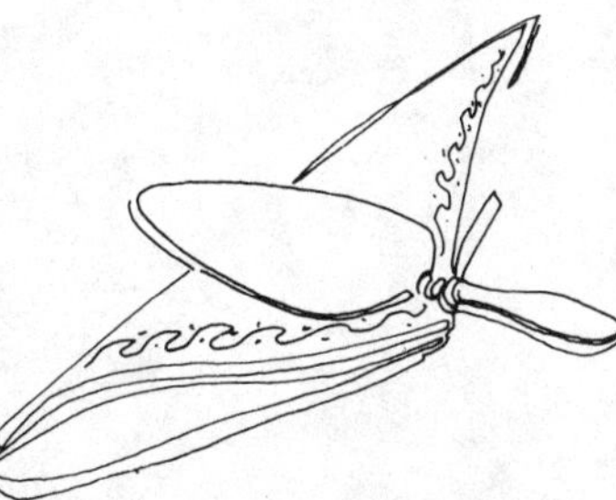

SFOGLIATELLA: *"Foglia" is the word for leaf and "sfoglia" is the opening or unfolding of leaves. This pastry is made from very thin and flaky "sfoglia" dough which is filled with ricotta, eggs, candied fruits, sugar and farina. When it is put in the oven it looks like a clam shell but when its "leaves" open it assumes a triangular shape. The sfoglia dough must be rolled almost 100 times if it is to be as light as it should be.*

SPUMONI: *This is a multi-flavored, multi-colored combination of ice creams laden with candied fruits and pieces of sponge cake.*

TORTA DI RICOTTA: *This is Italian cheese cake made with ricotta, flour and sugar in a pie crust.*

VAGABONDO DI MARE

Address: 1111 First Avenue
Location: First Avenue and 61st Street
Telephone: TE 8-9743
Credit Cards: All major credit cards accepted
Reservations: Optional
Hours: Lunch from 12:00 Noon to 3:00 PM, Monday thru Friday; Dinner from 5:30 PM to 12:00 Midnight, Monday thru Thursday, to 1:00 AM on Friday and Saturday
Days Closed: Sunday
Liquor: Full bar service
Recommended or Listed in: Our Town
Maitre d': Jackie
Seating Capacity: 100
Cuisine: Northern Italian; Seafood
Specialties of the House: Zuppa di Pesce; Shrimp Scampi; Calamari; Veal and Chicken Specials
Dress: Casual
Entertainment: Live music several nights a week

The accent is obviously nautical at Vagabondo di Mare—from the fish net divider between the congenial bar and comfortable booths to the porthole mirrors on the walls. A patterned tile floor, blue and white checked tablecloths and subdued lighting contribute to the comfortable and cheerful dining atmosphere. The menu's seafood selections are varied and moderately priced, and chicken and veal dishes are also specialties here; all are nicely served. If you enjoy dining at Vagabondo di Mare, you will want to try Il Vagabondo and Oggi, the other two restaurants in this triumverate.

DINNER MENU

(a la carte)

APPETIZERS & SOUPS:
Mixed Seafood Salad (3.00); Shrimp Cocktail (3.00); ½ Dozen Clams on Half Shell (2.75); Baked Clams Oreganata (3.00); Baked Mussel Oreganata (2.50); Antipasto Variato (3.00); Roasted Peppers and Anchovy Filets (2.25); Soup of the Day (1.50); Tortellini in Brodo (2.00).

PASTA:
Homemade Spinach-filled Ravioli 6.50
Tortellini 6.50
Tortellini alla Panna 6.50
(Small Meat-filled Ravioli with White Sauce)
Canneloni with Meat and White Sauces 4.75
Manicotti with Tomato Sauce 4.75
Lasagna alla Bolognese 4.75
Spaghetti with Tomato or Meat Sauce 4.50
Linguini with Clam Sauce 6.50
Eggplant Parmigiana 4.75

(The spinach-filled ravioli and tortellini may be ordered with butter, tomato or meat sauce. All pasta dishes may also be ordered as appetizers.)

ENTREES:
Broiled or Sauteed Red Snapper (when available) 9.50
Broiled or Sauteed Striped Bass 9.50
Zuppa di Pesce 10.50
(Seafood Combination, includes Lobster Tail)
Shrimp Scampi in Marinara Sauce or Sauteed 8.50
Broiled or Sauteed Scallops 7.50

Broiled or Sauteed Lemon Filet of Sole 7.50
Broiled or Sauteed Blue Fish 7.00
Broiled or Sauteed Brook Trout 7.50
Broiled or Sauteed Sea Trout 7.00
Mixed Seafood Plate in Vinaigrette Dressing . 7.50
Steamed Clams in Light Red Sauce 7.50
Steamed Mussels in Light Red Sauce 6.00
Calamari 7.00
Sauteed Breaded Chicken Breast 6.50
Boneless Chicken Grilled with Tomato Sauce and Cheese 6.50
Boneless Chicken Cooked in Marsala Wine and Mushrooms 6.50
Boneless Chicken Cooked with Prosciutto and Cheese 6.50
Sauteed Breaded Veal Cutlet 7.50
Vitello alla Parmigiana 7.50
Veal Cutlet Cooked in Marsala Wine with Mushrooms 7.50
Vitello alla Francese 7.50
Vitello Piccata 7.50
Vitello Pizzaiola 7.50
Grilled Veal Steak Paillard 9.75
Beef Paillard 9.75
Prime Shell Steak 11.50

DESSERTS:

Cheese Cake (1.50); Rum Cake (1.50); Tortoni (1.35); Spumoni (1.35).

(An a la carte Luncheon Menu is also offered and is similar to the Dinner Menu; prices for most entrees are lower on the Luncheon Menu.)

SOCIETE CULINAIRE PHILANTHROPIQUE *This is the oldest culinary association in the U.S. Founded in 1865 by a group of French chefs, it now has over 450 members. One of the prime functions of this group is the organization of the Annual Culinary Exhibit or Salon Culinaire that is held every November at the New York Coliseum. To be eligible for membership one must "conform to the fundamental requirements of proven professional ability and irreproachable morality." The Société is also the trustee and administrator of the Jules Weber Foundation and the Culinarians' Home Foundation—La Maison Familiale—which is located in New Paltz, New York and is dedicated to the "welfare of convalescent and aged culinarians and their wives . . ." In 1950, on the 85th anniversary of the Society, members were awarded the Medal of Honor of Foreign Affairs by the government of the French Republic. The current President of the Société is Henri Deltieure, Chef, Colony Club, and Louis Bonnafous is President of the Home Foundation.*

LE VEAU D'OR

Address: 129 East 60th Street
Location: 60th Street between Lexington Avenue and Park Avenue
Telephone: 838-8133 or 838-9649
Credit Cards: Not accepted
Reservations: Recommended
Hours: 12 Noon to 2:30 PM; 6 PM to 10 PM
Days Closed: Sundays and major holidays; also closed during the month of August
Liquor: Full Bar Service
Recommended or Listed in: New York Times; Cue
Maitre d': Joseph and Gerard Rocheteau
Seating Capacity: 60
Cuisine: French
Specialties of the House: Cassoulet Toulousain; Coq au Vin; Navarin d'Agneau

Le Veau d'Or is a very popular, intimate and well patronized East Side French bistro, affording just about the best "cuisine bourgeoise" in the city, thanks to its renowned chef de cuisine, Gerard Vidal. The atmosphere is ingrained French, with tables snuggled closely together, after the manner of a Left Bank cafe.

LUNCHEON MENU

(table d'hote)

APPETIZERS:
Maquereau au Vin Blanc; Artichaut ou Poireaux Vinaigrette; Melon de Saison; Jus de Tomate; Grapefruit; Saucisson Chaud ou d'Arles; Canapé Maison; Melon et Jambon de Parme (2.50); Saumon Fumé de la Nouvelle-Ecosse (3.25); Les Escargots de Bourgogne (2.80 for 6), (5.60 for 12); Blue Points, Cherrystones, Little Necks (2.50); Filets de Hareng, à la crème; Sardines Importées; Céleri Remoulade; Pâté du Chef; Consommé aux Pâtés; Bisque de Homard.

ENTREES:
Filet de Sole Sauté Meunière au Amandines . 7.90
Omelette au Fromage 7.90
Moules de Roches Marinière 7.90
Rognon de Veau, Sauce Moutarde 9.10
Foie de Veau Sauté Meunière ou Lyonnaise . . 9.50
Cervelle au Beurre Noir 8.90
Poulet Sauté Chasseur, Riz Blanc 9.10
"Scampi Baratin" 11.70
Estouffade de Boeuf au Vin Rouge 9.10

SALADS:
Salade de Saison (.90); Endives (2.25).

DESSERTS:
Les Tartes aux Fruits; Les Fromages Assortis; Melon de Saison; Grapefruit; Poire au Vin; Crème Caramel; Mousse au Chocolat; Les Glaces (Vanille et Café); Sorbet au Citron-Cassis; Fraises "Romanoff" (2.25).

DINNER MENU

(table d'hote)

APPETIZERS:
Artichaut ou Poireaux Vinaigrette; Melon de Saison; Jus de Tomate; Grapefruit; Saucisson Chaud ou d'Arles; Coquille "Veau d'Or"; (1.25);Melon et Jambon de Parme (2.50); Saumon Fumé de la Nouvelle-Ecosse (3.25); Les Escargots de Bourgogne (2.80 for 6) (5.60 for 12); Blue Points, Cherrystones, Little Necks (2.50); Filets de Hareng, à la Crème; Céleri Remoulade; Canapé Maison; Pâté du Chef; Sardines Importées; Maquereau au Vin Blanc.

SOUPS:
Potage Cressonière; Consommé aux Pâtés; Soup à l'Oignon Gratinée.

ENTREES:

Filet de Sole Sauté Amandines 11.50
Grenouilles Sautées Provençale ou Meunière 13.50
Homard Grillé au Beurre Fondu (entier) .... (...)
Canard Rôti aux Cerises, Riz Sauvage 13.50
Poussin Rôti en Cocotte, "Grand'Mère" 11.90
Foies de Volaille Poëlés, Lyonnaise 11.90
La Douzaine d'Escargots Bourguignonne ... 13.90
Carré d'Agneau Soissonnais (2) 33.00
Rognon de Veau Sauté Moutarde 12.90
Sauté de Veau Niçoise 12.10
Filet de Boeuf Rôti; Sauce Champignons 14.90
Gigot d'Agneau Rôti Bretonne 12.10
Tripes à la Mode de Caen 12.10

SALADS:

Salade de Saison (.90); Endives (2.25).

DESSERTS:

Parfait au Rhum; Pêche Melba; Meringue Glacée; Crème Caramel; Mousse au Chocolat; Poire au Vin; Melon de Saison; Grapefruit; Les Glaces (Vanilla et Café); Les Fromages Assortis; Coupe aux Marrons (2.00); Sorbet au Citron-Cassis; Fraises "Romanoff" (2.25); Les Tartes aux Fruits.

VERDICCHIO: *One of the most popular Italian white wines, produced in central Italy near the Adriatic port of Ancona. Verdicchio is dry and pale, but full of flavor; it is shipped in a distinctive, slender vase-like bottle.*

VERMOUTH: *A fortified white wine, flavored with herbs, bark, roots, seeds and spices, with a distinct aroma of wormwood. Usually served as an aperitif or cocktail ingredient, vermouth comes in either of two varieties:*

French – *Pale in color and quite dry; usually aged 3 to 4 years before shipping;*

Italian – *Dark red, and sweet, usually aged 2 years before shipping. Both French and Italian vermouths are made in both France and Italy.*

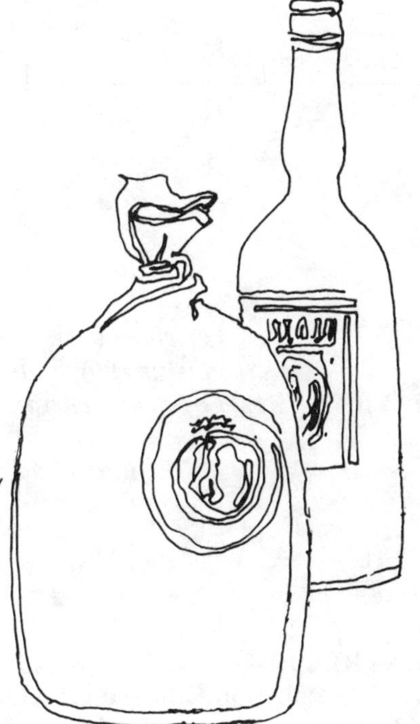

VOLNAY: *A Côte de Beaune red Burgundy produced in the districts of Volnay and Meursault. (Whites from both districts carry the Meursault name.) Volnay is a particularly soft and delicate red, with a round texture and a fragrant aftertaste.*

VOUVRAY: *The best-known of the Touraine wines, produced on the north bank of the Loire River, near Tours. One of the longest-lived white wines, Vouvray can be, in turn, depending on weather and vinting, bone dry and fruity, rich and Rhine-like or pale and sparkling.*

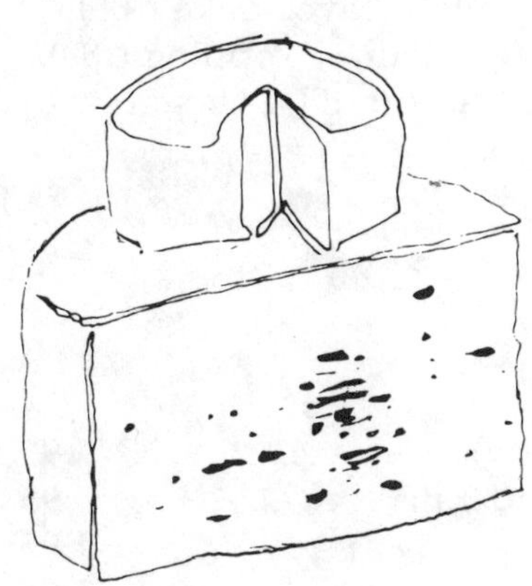

ROQUEFORT: *Roquefort, often called the King of the bleu cheeses, is made from sheep's milk in the Roquefort district of France. It is marbled with blue-green mold and has a flavor which has been described as pleasantly prickly and tinglingly pungent. It is friable but is creamy in the mouth. Roquefort varies considerably in quality depending on age and other factors.*

SAPSAGO: *Made in the Swiss canton of Glarus where it is known by its original name, Schabziger, Sapsago is a hard grating cheese which comes to market in green cones. It is made from skim milk, buttermilk and whey but derives its unusual flavor and aroma from an aromatic clover which is added to the curds when the cheese is made.*

STILTON: *England's outstanding bleu cheese, Stilton differs markedly from other veined cheeses such as Roquefort. In texture Stilton is firmer than Roquefort and in flavor it is much less pungent. In color, too, it is different, being ivory at the center and brownish-yellow near the rind.*

VIRGIL'S, Ltd.

Address:	**115 Main Street, Port Washington**
Telephone:	**(516) 767-6161**
Credit Cards:	**MC; V; DC; AE; CB**
Reservations:	**Recommended**
Hours:	**12:00 Noon to 11:00 PM, Monday thru Thursday; 12:00 Noon to 12:00 Midnight on Friday; 4:30 PM to 12:00 Midnight on Saturday; 3:00 PM to 10:00 PM on Sunday**
Days Closed:	**None**
Liquor:	**Full bar service**
Recommended or Listed in:	**Cue; New York Times; Newsday**
Maitre d's:	**Virgil and Morella**
Seating Capacity:	**200**
Cuisine:	**Steak House**
Specialties of the House:	**Roast Beef; Lobster; Daily Specials, e.g.: Veal Cutlet Parmigiana (Monday)**
Dress:	**Casual**
Entertainment:	**Pianist (5 evenings a week); Big Band (1 night a week)**
Party Facilities:	**Private room; capacity: 180**
Parking:	**Restaurant parking lot**

For eight years Virgil's has been attracting a large and loyal following at its Port Washington location. The atmosphere is informal and relaxed; abundant portions are served at moderate prices, and live music, including a piano bar is offered six nights a week. Children are more than welcome at Virgil's; Sunday is family day and the menu for the under-twelves is half-price. Dining out is still a bargain at Virgil's—try it.

LUNCHEON MENU

(a la carte)

ENTREES:

Ham/Mushroom/Cheese Omelette 2.35
Chopped Sirloin with Onions 2.90
Sliced Steak 3.75
Filet of Sole 2.95
Tuna or Salmon Platter 2.75
Hamburger on Sesame Roll 2.15
Grilled Cheese/Bacon and Tomato 2.15
Daily Special with Beer 3.15

(The above entrees are served with hash brown or french fried potatoes and salad.)

Shrimp Cocktail 2.50
Fettuccine Alfredo with Salad 3.15
Virgil's Salad (by itself) 1.35

DESSERTS:

Hot Apple Pie (.65); Chocolate Layer Cake (.65); Chocolate Layer Cake with Walnut Topping (.80); Creamy Cheesecake (.85); Assorted Ice Cream (.50); Fruit Ices (.50).

DINNER MENU

(a la carte)

ENTREES:

Filet Mignon 7.95
Twin Lobster Tails* 7.95
Sirloin Steak 6.95
Sirloin Steak (heavy)* 7.95
Prime Ribs of Beef 6.95
Prime Ribs of Beef (heavy)* 7.95
"Odd Couple" Steak and Tail 7.95
Chopped Sirloin Steak* 4.95
Barbecued Beef Ribs* 5.25
Beef Kabob with Rice 5.25

Broiled Shrimp* 5.95
Long Island Duckling* 5.95
Skewered Scallops and Shrimp* 5.95
Filet of Sole* 5.50
*(*These entrees are available in junior portions at half price.)*

(All entrees are served with draught beer, salad, Italian bread and butter.)

SIDE ORDERS:
Soup of the Day (Bowl .95); Vegetable of the Day (.65); Sauteed Mushrooms (1.25); Baked Potato (.65); French Fried Potatoes (.65); French Fried Onion Rings (.65); Smothered Onions (.65).

DAILY DINNER SPECIALS:
Monday: Veal Cutlet Parmigiana with Spaghetti (5.50); Tuesday: Seafood Newburgh (6.95); Wednesday: Breast of Capon, Cordon Bleu (5.25); Thursday: Barbecue Platter (6.25); Friday and Saturday: Broiled Live 1 lb Maine Lobster (7.95); Friday, Saturday and Sunday: Broiled Live 1¾ lbs Maine Lobster (12.95).

(Daily specials include salad and beer.)

(A late snack menu is available after 10:00 PM on week nights and after 11:00 PM on Friday and Saturday. Prices range from 1.45 to 3.95.)

THE VATEL CLUB, INC. *This Club was founded in 1913 and named after chef Jean-Francois Vatel (1631-1671) who "sacrificed his life for the honor of the culinary profession while in the service of the Prince de Condé." The membership of the Club includes French chefs and cooks with at least five years of experience. Its motto is "nous maintiendrons"—and members of The Vatel Club are pledged to maintain "the French language, French tradition, culinary and gastronomic art—the ninth art." As part of their dedication to the French language, the Club publishes a review called* Torque Blanches, *"la seule révue culinaire de langue Française en Amérique du Nord" (the only culinary review in French in North America). The Vatel Club is located in the Fisk Building, 250 West 57th Street, New York 10019; its President is Roger Fessaguet, Chef, La Caravelle Restaurant, and owner of Le Poulailler Restaurant.*

WINDOWS ON THE WORLD

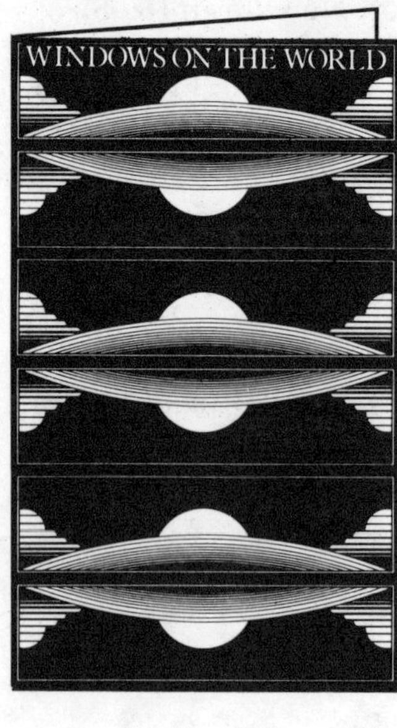

Address: 1 World Trade Center, 107th Floor
Location: West Street between Vesey and Liberty Streets
Telephone: 938-1111
Credit Cards: AE; DC; CB; MC; V; BA
Parking: Free parking for dinner patrons in the World Trade Center garage
Liquor: Full bar service; extensive wine list
Recommended or Listed in: New York Magazine; New York Times; Forbes; Holiday; Promenade; Cue; Women's Wear Daily; many others
Cuisine: American and International
Specialties of the House: Rainbow Trout Stuffed and Baked in Pastry; Rack of Lamb, James Beard; Golden Lemon Tart
Dress: Jacket and tie required in The Restaurant; Jacket required in the Hors d'Oeuvrerie. Jeans? Never!
Party Facilities: 18 private rooms; capacity: 10-300

Hours, Reservations, Seating Capacity, Entertainment, Cover Charge:

THE RESTAURANT: **Monday thru Saturday, dinner 5:00 PM to 10:00 PM; Grand Buffet Saturday, 12:00 Noon to 3:00 PM, Sunday 12:00 Noon to 7:00 PM. Reservations required. 350 seats.**

CELLAR IN THE SKY: **Monday thru Saturday, dinner at 7:30 P.M. Reservations required. 35 seats.**

THE HORS D'OEUVRERIE: **Monday thru Friday, drinks and hors d'oeuvre from 3:00 PM to 1:00 AM. Piano music from 5:00 PM, alternating with an orchestra after 7:30 PM. Cover charge after 7:30 PM: $2.00. Saturday luncheon from 12:00 Noon to 2:30 PM. Hors d'oeuvre from 3:00 PM to 1:00 AM. Entertainment as above. Sunday Brunch from 12:00 Noon to 3:00 PM. Hors d'oeuvre from 3:00 PM to 12:00 Midnight, with dancing from 4:00 PM to 11:30 PM. Cover charge after 4:00 PM: $2.00.**

THE CITY LIGHTS BAR: **Monday thru Friday, 3:00 PM to 1:00 AM; Saturday, 12:00 Noon to 1:00 AM; Sunday, 12:00 Noon to 12:00 Midnight.**

"The most spectacular restaurant in the world."
Gael Greene
New York Magazine

In The Restaurant, the sweep of space is splendidly dramatic; the feeling one of intimacy and celebration. The menu is unique, representing the best of the world's cuisines as well as distinctly American cooking. In the multi-level room, every table has a clear view of the ever-changing city, and of fifty miles beyond.

The Cellar in the Sky is the working wine cellar for all of Windows on the World. Adjoining The Restaurant, it is walled with 10,000 wine bottles, which cast beautiful dappled light patterns on its stone floor. The single seven-course menu ($45.00) is designed to complement a selection of five wines, freely poured throughout the evening. The menu changes frequently. A classical guitarist plays all during the evening.

The Hors d'Oeuvrerie, America's first international hors d'oeuvre restaurant, is a romantic dining room with tiered seating to provide a view of moonlit New York and of the International Cooks' Table. There, cooks in their colorful national dress prepare varied small delights ($.55 to $4.65) to be accompanied by the enthusiastic drinks of The City Lights Bar, and by music for dancing.

Windows On The World

DINNER MENU

(a la carte)
(A table d'hote dinner is also offered: 18.50)

APPETIZERS & SOUPS:
Nearby Clams and Oysters (3.95); Large Gulf Shrimp (5.50); Avocado and Shrimp Salad (4.95); Talmouse with Ham (3.95); Pâté of Duck with Orange (3.50); Truffled Cervelat of Pike, Shrimp and Sole (4.75); Quail Eggs in Tarragon Aspic (2.75); Tortellini of Shrimp in Cream (5.25); Casserole of Snails in Pasta Shells (4.50); Corn and Crab Soup (2.25); Spinach Consommé with Dumplings (1.95).

ENTREES:
Striped Bass Steamed on a Bed of Vegetables 12.95
Frogs' Legs with Tomatoes and Olives, Provençale 12.95
Rainbow Trout Stuffed and Baked in Pastry 12.50
Coquille of Lobster Newburg 14.95
Chicken Stroganoff 9.50
Scallopine of Veal with Wild Mushrooms ... 12.95
Scandinavian Steak Sauté, Dill and Horseradish 14.95
Rack of Young Lamb, James Beard (for two) .... 17.95 p.p.
Côte de Boeuf Marchand de Vin à la Moëlle (for two) .... 17.50 p.p.
Block Island Swordfish Steak, grilled over charcoal with Spice Butter 10.50
Brochette of Sea Scallops, Back Bacon and Scallions, grilled over charcoal with Spice Butter 10.50
Calf's Liver Steak with Grilled Onion, grilled over charcoal with Spice Butter 11.50
Filet Mignon or Sirloin Steak, grilled over charcoal with Spice Butter 14.95
Two Double Thick Lamb Chops, grilled over charcoal with Spice Butter 16.25

VEGETABLES & SALADS:
String Beans Sauté (2.50); Gratin of Sliced Potatoes (2.50); French Fried Zucchini (2.50); Eggplant Grilled with Soy and Ginger (2.50); Baked or Shredded Potato (1.95); Red Onion and Orange Salad (2.50); Watercress and Raw Mushroom Salad (2.75); Beefsteak Tomato and Basil Salad (2.75); Three Green Salad (2.25).

DESSERTS:
Chocolate Pecan Soufflé, Ice Cream Sauce - For Two (3.50 p.p.); Mango and Macadamia Nut Sundae (2.75); Strawberry Bavarian Cream (2.75); The Golden Lemon Tart (2.50); Frozen Soufflé Amaretto (2.25); Floating Island, Caramel Almonds (2.50); Peach and Raspberry Compote (2.50); Crêpe Soufflé of Candied Fruit (3.25); Hazelnut Dacquoise (2.50); Chocolate Pastry Cake (2.50); Canteloupe Sorbet (2.25); Mocha Mousse Praliné (2.50); Kiwi Fruit Parfait (2.50); Ice Creams - Best of Brands (2.25); Vermont Cheddar, Fontina and Soft, Ripe Cheeses (3.25).

YE WAVERLY INN

Address:	**16 Bank Street**
Location:	**Corner of Bank Street and Waverly Place**
Telephone:	**WA 9-4377**
Credit Cards:	**AE; MC; DC**
Reservations:	**Recommended on weekends**
Hours:	**Lunch from 11:45 AM to 2:00 PM, Tuesday thru Saturday; Dinner from 5:15 PM to 10:00 PM, Monday thru Thursday; 5:15 PM to 11:00 PM, Friday and Saturday; 4:30 PM to 9:00 PM on Sunday; Sunday Brunch from 12:00 Noon to 3:30 PM**
Days Closed:	**None**
Liquor:	**Full bar service**
Recommended or Listed in:	**New York Times; Cue; Esquire; New York Post; Host**
Maitre d':	**Murray Sellack**
Seating Capacity:	**100**
Cuisine:	**New England and Southern**
Specialties of the House:	**Chicken Pot Pie; Southern Fried Chicken; Roast Stuffed Duckling with Cherry Jubilee Sauce; Homemade Soups, Rolls and Desserts**
Party Facilities:	**Available on request**

Ye Waverly Inn is a genuinely American restaurant dating back to the early 1920's. Located on the premises of a former carriage house (and an historic landmark), Ye Waverly Inn offers the ambience you would expect to find in a New England roadside hostelry—pegged floors, low ceilings with exposed beams, two working fireplaces and a pleasant outdoor garden. For intimate dining in a candlelight atmosphere, visit Ye Waverly Inn. And if you write in advance of your visit, the restaurant will send you a free map of Greenwich Village which, upon presentation, will entitle you to a 10% reduction in your dining check.

LUNCHEON MENU

(The luncheon menu changes frequently. A representative menu follows.)

(Table d'hote – includes entree and choice of soup or dessert and beverage.)

APPETIZERS:
Mulligatawny Soup; V-8 Juice.

ENTREES:
Boneless Chicken with Lemon and Garlic 4.50
Lamb and Mushroom Casserole 4.50
Broiled Bluefish with Lemon 4.50
Baked Meat Loaf with Brown Gravy 3.75
(choice of potato and vegetable)

DESSERTS:
Walnut Layer Cake; Pecan Pie; Lemon Pudding; Apple Cobbler a la Mode; Custard with Caramel Sauce.

a la carte

SOUPS:
Soup of the Day (cup .75) (bowl 1.25); Cold Gazpacho (cup .75) (bowl 1.25).

ENTREES:
Fresh Garden Salad 3.25
Chef's Salad Bowl 3.25
Fruit Salad Plate 3.10
Quiche Lorraine and Waldorf Salad 3.50
Hamburger 3.25
Cheeseburger 3.50
Blue Cheese Burger 3.50
(Burgers are served with French fries, lettuce, tomato & cole slaw.)

DESSERTS:
Pecan Pie (1.25); Cake of the Day (1.25); Ice Cream (.85); Melon in Season (1.25); Creme de Menthe Parfait (2.00); Creme de Cocoa Parfait (2.00).

DINNER MENU

(Table d'hote – includes soup or juice; salad; two vegetables; dessert and beverage.)

SOUPS & JUICE:
Soup du Jour; Chicken Consomme; Chilled Gazpacho; Chilled Juice; Quiche (1.25).

ENTREES:
Grilled Shell Steak with French Fried Onion Rings 9.50
Shrimp Scampi 9.25
Roast Stuffed Duckling with Cherry Jubilee Sauce 8.95
Roast Sirloin of Beef — Gravy 8.95
Sauteed Calves Liver with French Fried Onion Rings 8.50
Boneless Chicken Breast, Sauteed with Lemon & Garlic 8.50
Broiled Fresh Fish — Lemon 8.25
Chef's Salad Bowl 7.50
Southern Fried Chicken — Gravy 7.50
Individual Chicken Pot Pie with Vegetable & Salad 7.50
Baked Meat Loaf — Gravy 6.95

DESSERTS:
Warm Pecan Pie; Wellesly Fudge; Hot Apple Cobbler a la Mode; Cup Custard — Caramel Sauce; Butterscotch Pudding; Butterscotch Sundae; Chocolate Sundae; Vanilla or Chocolate Ice Cream; Camembert, Gruyere or Blue Cheese and Crackers.
(A la carte service is also available.)

ZUPPA INGLESE: *This cake is so heavily doused with rum that it is called a "zuppa" or "soup." It is so moist that most pastry shops put their Zuppa Inglese in dishes, rather than on doilies or cardboard. The rum-soaked sponge cake is layered with chocolate cream and custard cream. Zuppa Inglese is traditionally eaten with a spoon and is the texture of bread pudding. It is becoming more and more popular with Americans as a special-occasion cake.*

ZUPPETTA: *This sponge cake pastry (its name means "little soup") is soaked in a generous amount of rum. Topped with a light, many-layered* "sfoglia" *crust, it is served in squares.*

YUNNAN YUAN

YUNNAN YUAN

Address:	144 East 52nd Street
Location:	52nd Street between Lexington and Third Avenues
Telephone:	759-8260
Credit Cards:	AE
Reservations:	Recommended
Hours:	Daily from 11:30 AM to 10:00 PM
Days Closed:	None
Liquor:	Full bar service
Recommended or Listed in:	New York Times; Cue; Our Town
Maitre d':	David Liu
Reservations Manager:	David Liu
Seating Capacity:	140
Cuisine:	Chinese (Hunan Style)
Specialties of the House:	Dragon and Phoenix; Beggar's Hunan Ham; Sauteed Lobster Balls with Hot Spiced Ginger Sauce; Shredded Chicken and Abalone (with Pancake)
Dress:	Jackets recommended
Party Facilities:	Private room; capacity: 50

Yunnan Yuan brings to midtown Manhattan an interesting selection of Hunanese cuisine, the spicier relative of the more familiar Cantonese and Mandarin dishes. The dining room is spacious and open with tables amply and generously spaced; the decor is pleasant and unpretentious . The Yunnan Yuan has been cited for the fine quality of its kitchen and the menu. Prices are reasonable particularly for a restaurant in this location.

Yunnan Yuan

DINNER MENU

(a la carte)

(The following is a representative selection.)

SOUPS:

Ham and Asparagus Soup (1.25); Shredded Chicken and Abalone Soup (1.50); Minced Squab Soup in Bamboo Container (1.65); Royal Chinese Bouquet Soup — Shark Fin and Chicken (3.00).

ENTREES:

Marinated Chicken Served with Lemon and Orange Sauce	4.95
Spicy Tai-Chin Chicken	4.95
Diced Chicken with Walnuts	4.95
Sue Tze Chicken	5.95
Chunked Chicken Showered with Ginger Sauce	5.25
Deep Fried Crispy Duck (Half Duck)	5.95
Camphor and Tea Smoked Duck (Half Duck)	5.95
Moo Shu Pork (Pancakes, .25 each)	4.95
Beef with Oyster Sauce	5.25
Beef with Mushroom and Bamboo Shoots	5.75
Sauteed Beef Hunan Style	5.75
Lamb with Scallion	5.95
Lamb Hunan Style	5.95
Honeyed Hunan Ham	6.50
Fried Crispy Shrimp Ball	5.70
General Tso's Chicken	5.95
Shredded Chicken and Abalone	6.75
Chef's Squid with Hot Pepper Sauce	6.95
Sweet and Sour Crispy Fish	6.95
House Special Steak	7.25
Lamb Prepared in Two Styles	7.50
Sauteed Lobster Balls with Hot Spiced Ginger Sauce	9.25
Chicken Prepared in Three Styles	8.75
Dragon and Phoenix	11.75
Peking Duck	18.00
Jumbo Shrimp with Egg White	6.25
Beef with Orange Flavor	6.25
Chicken with Orange Flavor	5.75
Shrimp with Garlic Sauce	5.25
Prawns with Hot Pepper Sauce	6.25
Prawns with Hot Spiced Ginger Sauce	6.25
Carp with Hot Spiced Sauce	6.95
Braised Vegetable Heart and Mushroom with Oyster Sauce	4.50
Bean Curd Hunan Style	4.50

(A selection of desserts is also offered, ranging in price from .75 to 2.50.)

TALEGGIO: *A soft, creamy cheese, Taleggio is named for a small town in Lombardy, Young Taleggio has a bland flavor with just a hint of pungency. The pungency grows stronger with age and some prefer a more mature Taleggio. Its life is brief, however, and timing is important.*

TILSIT: *A German cheese which originated around the town of Tilsit in East Prussia. It has been likened to Port du Salut but is much stronger, being full-bodied and somewhat coarse. Tilsit is semi-soft in consistency and has small "eyes" like Port du Salut.*

menu translator

A French and Italian Dictionary for Restaurant-Goers

The following entries define and explain over 1,300 of the most commonly served dishes and frequently misunderstood food terms you are likely to encounter on menus in New York.
The entries are arranged in alphabetical order, with English explanations following the French and Italian words and phrases.

French Menu Definitions

a

abatis de volaille *chicken giblets*
abricot apricot
agneau *lamb*
agneau de lait persillé *baby lamb grilled and served with parsley*
agneau grillé au thym *lamb broiled with thyme*
aigre *sour*
aigrefin *haddock*
aigrefin à la lyonnaise *haddock prepared with onions*
aigrefin fumé *smoked haddock*
aiguillettes de canard *breast of duck*
aiguillettes de caneton *breast of duckling*
ail *garlic*
aile de poulet *chicken wing*
ailerons *chicken wings*
aiöli *garlic-flavored paste which is the consistency of mayonnaise*
airelles *cranberries*
à la *in the style of*
Albert, sauce *an English sauce flavored with horseradish and mustard; used on braised beef*
alcool *alcohol*
allumettes *potatoes cut to the thickness of match sticks*
alose *shad*
aloyau de boeuf *beef sirloin*
amandes *almonds*
amandine *prepared with almonds; often used for fish fillets*
amoricaine, à l' *see homard à l'américaine*
ananas *pineapple*
ananas à l'orange *oranges and pineapple mixed*
ananas au kirsch *pineapple soaked in kirsch*
anchois *anchovy*
andalouse, sauce *tomato purée, pimentos and parsley*
andouille *large sausage made with tripe and pig's intestines*
andouillettes *in the U.S., called chitterlings; similar to "andouille" but made with the smaller intestines*
anglaise, à la *cooked in either water or stock*
anguille *eel*
arachide *peanut*
archiduc, à la *prepared with a paprika and cream sauce*
artichauts *artichokes*
artichauts à la grecque *artichokes cooked in olive oil and garlic*
artichauts à la vinaigrette *artichokes in a dressing of oil and vinegar*
asperges *asparagus*
asperges à la crème *creamed asparagus*
asperges en branches *whole, boiled asparagus*
asperges mornay *asparagus with a thick cheese sauce*
asperges mouselline *asparagus with a sauce of egg yolks, lemon juice and whipped cream*
assiette *a plate*
assiette anglaise *assortment of cold cuts*
assiette de charcuterie *assorted sausages*
aubergine *eggplant*

aubergines à la niçoise *eggplants with garlic and tomatoes*
au four *baked in the oven*
au jus *in its own juice or gravy*
au lait *with milk*
aveline *filbert*
avocat *avocado*
avocat farci de crevettes *shrimp-stuffed avocado*

b

baba au rhum *cake that has been soaked in rum after it's been baked*
baguette *long loaf of French bread*
ballottine *boned meat, fish or fowl that is rolled into a bundle-like shape and served sliced*
banane *banana*
bananes à la crème chantilly *bananas with whipped cream*
bananes flambées *bananas doused with rum and served flaming*
bar *bass*
barbue *brill; a type of fish*
bar grillé *broiled bass*
bar-le-duc *currant preserves*
bar poché à l'oseille *poached bass with sorrel*
barquette *pastry shell in the shape of a boat*
barquettes ostendaise *pastry shells filled with oysters in a cream sauce*
bar raye *striped bass*
basilic *basil*
basquaise *with a garnish of mushrooms, ham and potatoes*
bavarois *bavarian cream*
béarnaise, sauce *a thick sauce made with shallots, tarragon, thyme, bay leaf, vinegar, white wine and egg yolks; most often served with grilled or sautéed meat or grilled fish*
bécasse *woodcock*
béchamel, sauce *milk blended with a 'roux'– a mix of butter and flour*
beignets *fritters*
beignets de pommes *apple fritters*
beignets niçoise *tuna fritters*
belon *a French variety of oyster*
betteraves *beets*
betteraves à l'orange *beets with an orange sauce*
beurre à la maître d'hôtel *butter melted with parsley, salt, pepper and lemon juice; served with meat or fish or vegetables*
beurre d'ail *garlic butter*
beurre d'anchois *anchovy butter*
beurre d'échalote *butter and shallots together; used on meat or fish*
beurre de citron *lemon butter*
beurre de crevettes *shrimp butter; used as a sandwich spread or filling for eggs*
beurre fondu, au *with melted butter*
beurre noir *brown butter; served with eggs, fish or vegetables and often used in the preparation of brains*
beurre vert *butter mixed with pulverized spinach*
bien cuit *well-done; used to describe meats*
bière *beer*
bigarade, sauce *made from pan drippings of duck, orange juice, lemon juice and a touch of curaçao; used on duckling*
billi-bi *cream of mussel soup (sometimes spelled billy-by)*
biscuits *cookies*
bisque *soup, usually made of puréed shellfish*
blanquette d'agneau à l'ancienne *lamb stew with cream, onions and potatoes*
blanquette de veau *veal stewed in a cream sauce*
bleu *means extremely rare when used to describe meats*
bleu, au *fish that is prepared in this manner is put into a boiling mixture of water and vinegar while it is as fresh as possible or even alive; usually served with melted butter*
blini *thin pancake made with yeast; of Russian origin and often served with caviar and sour cream*
boeuf *beef*
boeuf à la mode *braised beef in red wine*
boeuf bourguignon *braised beef prepared in the style of Burgundy; with small glazed onions, mushrooms and red wine*
boeuf rôti *roast beef*
boeuf miroton *beef stewed with an onion-based sauce*
bolets *boletus mushrooms*
bombe glacée *ice cream dessert*
bon bon *candy*
bonne femme, à la *cooked with bacon, onions, potatoes and a thick brown gravy*
bordelaise, sauce *brown sauce made with wine and bone marrow*
bouchée à la reine *pastry filled with mushrooms and sweet breads in a cream sauce*
bouchées *individual patty shells*
bouchère, sauce *a meat sauce with tomatoes and onions; literally "as the butcher's wife makes it"*
boudin *blood sausage*
bouillabaise *a well-known dish from Provence; made with fish cooked in either water or wine with garlic, parsley, pepper, oil and tomatoes added; the ingredients will vary with the restaurant; one French poet was so inspired by the bouillabaise he ate, that he wrote a poem about it*
bouilli *boiled*
bouillon *stock or broth*
bouillon de boeuf *stock made with a beef base*
bourgeoise, à la *prepared with carrots, onions and bacon*
bourride *fish stew*
braisée *braised*
brandade *salt cod*
bretonne, à la *served with beans*
brioche *a cake or roll made of yeast dough in a circular shape; brioche dough is also used in the preparation of many hors d'oeuvres and some desserts*
brioche de foie gras *brioche dough stuffed with goose liver pâté*
brochette *a skewer; anything cooked on a skewer may be called a "brochette"*
brocoli *broccoli*
brouillé *scrambled*
brugnon *nectarine*
bûche *Swiss roll; sponge cake rolled around a jelly or cream filling*

bûche de Noël *a special Christmas cake made to look like a yule log*

C

cabillaud *cod*
café glacé *ice cream with coffee flavoring*
caille *quail*
caillette *young quail*
calmar *squid*
canapé *a toasted slice of bread; also applied to these slices when topped with a variety of spreads; used as an appetizer*
canard *duck*
canard à l'orange *duck in an orange sauce*
canard aux cerises *duck roasted with black cherries*
canard rôti *roast duck*
canard sauvage *wild duck*
caneton *duckling*
cannelle *cinnamon*
câpres, sauce aux *caper sauce; frequently used on lamb*
carafe *pitcher or bottle often used for wines*
carbonnade à la flamande *beef cooked with beer*
cari *curry*
carottes *carrots*
carpe *carp*
carré d'agneau *loin of lamb*
carré d'agneau aux herbes *loin of lamb with a variety of herbs*
carré de pauillac *loin of milk-fed lamb; the best milk-fed lambs are reputed to be the ones raised in the Pauillac section of France*
carrelet *flounder*
cassis *black currant*
cassoulet *a stew made with white beans and pork; may also include lamb, goose or duck*
cassoulet toulousain *navy bean stew with lamb, pork, sausage or poultry*
céleri *celery*
céleri-rave *celeriac*
cèpes *type of mushroom*
cèpes farcis *stuffed mushrooms*
cerfeuil *chervil (a parsley-like herb)*
cerise *cherry*
cervelles *brains*
cervelles au beurre noir *brains prepared in brown butter*
champagne, au *prepared with a champagne sauce; often used with fish*
champignons *mushrooms*
champignons à blanc *stewed mushrooms*
champignons à la grecque *marinated mushrooms*
champignons farcis *stuffed mushrooms*
chanterelles *a type of mushroom that is extremely popular in France; may also appear on menus as "girolle"*
chapon *capon*
charlotte *cream dessert in a deep mold*
charlotte russe *Bavarian cream in a mold lined with lady fingers and topped with whipped cream*
chartreuse *a dish made from cabbage and partridges*
châteaubriand *thick slice of steak, classically grilled and served with a garnish of potatoes cut in strips and with a béarnaise sauce*
chaudfroid *cream sauce containing aspic*
chausson *turnover*
chèvre *goat*
choix *choice*
chou *cabbage*
chou à la crème *cream puff*
choucroute *sauerkraut*
choucroute garnie *sauerkraut baked with ham, bacon and sausages*
chou frisé *kale*
choux de bruxelles *brussel sprouts*
choux de bruxelles à la grandmère *brussel sprouts sautéed with onions and bacon*
choux rouges *red cabbage*
choux verts *green cabbage*
ciboulette *chives*
citron *lemon*
civet de lièvre *stew made with hare*
clamart *garnish of artichoke hearts and green peas*
cloche *a cover put over food to keep it warm*
coeur à la crème *a rich dessert made in a heart-shaped mold; made with cottage cheese, cream cheese, heavy cream and topped with crushed strawberries*
coeur d'artichauts *artichoke hearts*
coeur de laitue *hearts of lettuce*
coeurs de palmier *hearts of palm*
colin *hake*
compote de fruits *stewed, mixed fruit; may be made from fresh or dried fruits; served cold*
concombres *cucumbers*
confit d'oie *goose that is preserved in its own fat*
confiture *jam*
congelé *frozen*
conserve au vinaigre *pickle*
consommé *meat stock that has been enriched, concentrated and clarified*
consommé à l'alsacienne *consommé with sauerkraut and sausages*
consommé à la bourgeoise *consommé with carrots, turnips, potatoes*
consommé à la madrilène *clear chicken soup with tomato pulp; served chilled*
consommé à la reine *chicken broth served with sliced chicken*
consommé aux abatis *consommé with chicken giblets*
consommé aux perles *barley soup*
consommé Célestine *chicken consommé served with noodles*
consommé de volaille *chicken broth*
consommé froid *cold consommé*
consommé julienne *clear soup served with sliced vegetables*
consommé printanier *consommé with a variety of vegetables added*
consommé queue de boeuf *soup made with oxtails, turnips and carrots*
contre-filet *tenderloin*
coq au vin *chicken prepared in a wine sauce with mushrooms, garlic, small onions and diced pork added*
coquelet *young rooster*
coquillages *shellfish*
coquille St. Jacques *scallops*

coquilles St. Jacques à la parisienne *scallops and mushrooms in white wine sauce*

cochon *pig*

cochon de lait *suckling pig*

cornichon *gherkin*

côte de boeuf grillé *grilled beef rib*

côte de veau *veal chop*

cotriade *stew made with fish*

coulibiac de saumon en croûte *salmon, rice and mushrooms baked in a rectangular pastry shell*

coupe aux cerises noires *ice cream dessert with black cherries*

coupe aux marrons *chestnut dessert*

coupe de fruits frais *fruit cup made with fresh fruit*

courge *pumpkin*

courgette *zucchini squash*

courgettes farcis *zucchini squash, stuffed*

court bouillon *the liquid in which meat, fish and some vegetables are cooked; may contain a variety of spices and vegetables and will vary from dish to dish*

crabe *crab*

crème *custard or cream*

crème brûlée *a rich dessert pudding made with vanilla and cream which is dusted with sugar, placed under the broiler and then allowed to cool for two to three hours before serving*

crème caramel *custard with a burnt sugar flavor*

crème Chantilly *whipped cream*

crème d'asperges *cream of asparagus soup*

crème de volaille *cream of chicken soup*

créole, à la *prepared with rice*

crêpes *thin pancakes*

crêpes alsaciennes *thin pancakes filled with jelly, sprinkled with sugar and put in the oven to glaze*

crêpes de homard *pancakes stuffed with lobster chunks*

crêpes surprise flambée au Kirsch *pancake doused with Kirsch and served flaming*

crêpes Suzette *thin pancakes made with a batter flavored with curaçao and the juice of mandarin oranges; usually served flaming*

crevettes *shrimp*

croissant *crescent-shaped roll made with a puff pastry or yeast dough; most often served at breakfast*

croque madame *grilled chicken and cheese sandwich*

croque monsieur *a ham and cheese sandwich, fried*

croquembouche *a pyramid of tiny, glazed cream puffs*

croustade *a dish made with a flaky puff pastry shell or from bread that has been hollowed out*

croûtons *bread that has been diced and fried in butter; most often used sprinkled on soup but may also be used in a salad*

cru *raw*

crudités *raw vegetables served as an appetizer*

crudités de saison *vegetables of the season, served raw*

cuisses de grenouilles *frogs' legs*

d

darne de saumon *thick slice of salmon*

datte *date*

daube *chunks of meat stewed with vegetables*

délices *strictly speaking this refers to a particular pastry but on American menus it can mean anything that is reputed to be especially tasty*

demi glace *a thick, brown sauce*

demi-tasse *strong, black coffee served in a small cup*

demoiselles de Maine *Maine lobsters*

diable, sauce à la *spicy sauce of white wine, vinegar, shallots, pepper, etc.*

dieppoise, à la *a method for cooking fish in white wine with a mussel garnish and a white wine sauce*

dijonnais, sauce *egg yolks, Dijon mustard, salt and pepper beaten with oil and lemon juice to the consistency of mayonnaise*

dinde *turkey*

dindonneau *young turkey*

dolmas *food wrapped in a vine leaf*

doux *sweet*

duglère, à la *with a cream sauce made with wine, tomatoes, etc., and served with fish*

duxelles *mushrooms chopped and browned in butter and oil, mixed with onions, shallots and a bit of wine and parsley*

échalotte *shallot*

écrevisse *crawfish*

en bordure *served with a border, commonly of duchesse potatoes*

en croûte *baked in a pastry crust*

endives à la normande *endives simmered in cream*

entrecôte *literally "between the ribs"; the steak cut from between two ribs of beef; usually grilled or fried*

entrecôte marchand de vin *steak cooked with red wine and shallots*

épaule *shoulder*

épaule d'agneau *shoulder of lamb*

épaule de mouton *shoulder of mutton*

épaule de veau *shoulder of veal*

éperlan *smelt*

épice *spice*

épinards *spinach*

épinards au beurre noisette *spinach in browned butter*

érable *maple*

escalopes *boneless slices of meat or fish; usually fried in butter*

escalopes de saumon à l'oseille *slices of salmon with sorrel*

escalopes de veau *thin, boneless slices of veal*

escalopes de veau cordon bleu *thin slices of boneless veal with ham and cheese*

escalopes de veau sautées à l'estragon *veal scallops with tarragon*

escargots *snails*

escargots à la bourguignonne *snails baked in their shells and served with garlic butter*

escargots de Bourgogne *snails of Burgundy; famous for their succulence*

espadon *swordfish*

estragon *tarragon*

esturgeon *sturgeon*

étuvé *stewed with just a little liquid*

f

faisan *pheasant*

farces *stuffing*

farci *stuffed*

fenouil *fennel*

fermière, à la *method of preparing meat with carrots, celery, turnips and onions*

feuillette *puff pastry*

feuillette de fruits de mer *puff pastry filled with a variety of seafood*

feuillette de homard *puff pastry with a lobster filling*

feuillette de ris de veau *puff pastry with a sweet bread filling*

figues *figs*

filet de boeuf *tenderloin*

filet de boeuf en croûte *fillet of beef in a pastry crust; beef Wellington*

filet mignon *small, choice cut of beef prepared by grilling or sautéeing*

financière, à la *made with a garnish of sweetbreads, mushrooms and olives*

flageolets *small kidney beans*

flamande, à la *with cabbage, carrots, turnips, bacon and potatoes and sausage*

flambé *describes a dish that has been ignited after it has been doused in a liqueur*

flan *tart*

flet *flounder*

flétan *halibut*

florentine, à la *foods cooked in this style—usually eggs or fish—are put on spinach, covered with mornay sauce and sprinkled with cheese*

foie *liver*

foie de canard *duck's liver*

foie de veau *calf's liver*

foies de volaille *chicken livers*

foies de volaille en brochette *chicken livers, mushrooms and bacon grilled on a skewer*

foie gras *the livers of especially fattened geese and ducks; the "foie gras" of Toulouse and Strasbourg are the most highly prized and may weigh up to four pounds each*

fondue *there are several varieties but the most popular is made with cheese and originated in Switzerland; it is made with melted cheese, white wine and a bit of kirsch added at the last minute; dessert fondues, such as ones made from chocolate, have become popular, too, in recent years*

fondue bourguignonne *beef cut into small pieces and cooked at the table in boiling oil; a variety of sauces accompanies the meat*

forestière, à la *with mushrooms, bacon and diced potatoes*

four *oven*

fourrage à la crème d'orange *orange and butter cream filling for a cake*

frais *fresh*

fraises *strawberries*

fraises à la crème *strawberries and cream*

fraises au sucre *fresh strawberries sprinkled with sugar*

fraises aux liqueurs *strawberries, sugared and sprinkled with a variety of liqueurs*

fraises Chantilly *strawberries with whipped cream*

fraises des bois *wild strawberries*

fraises Romanof *strawberries in a mixture of orange juice and curaçao, topped with whipped cream*

fraises tzarine *strawberries on pineapple ice cream with a whipped cream topping*

framboises *raspberries*

frappé *chilled*

fricassée *meat braised with spices and vegetables and served with a thick sauce; most commonly used to prepare veal and poultry*

frit *fried*

frites *french fries*

friture *a mixture of fried fish*

fromage *cheese*

fromage de tête *head cheese*

fromage rapé *grated cheese*

fruits de mer *sea food*

galantine *boned turkey, duck or chicken stuffed into a sausage shape and cooked in wine-flavored bouillon and chilled; usually served in aspic: according to Julia Child, "a galantine is not built in a day . . ."*

galette *a flat cake*

garni *garnished or decorated; classic French cooking puts a great deal of emphasis on garnishes*

garbure *thick peasant soup made with cabbage*

gâteau *cake*

gâteau de crêpes à la florentine *layered crêpes filled with spinach and topped with a cheese sauce*

gâteau de crêpes à la Normande *layered crêpes with apple slices and macaroons*

gaufre *waffle*

gaufrette *wafer*

gelées *jellies*

gibelotte *fricassee of rabbit*

gibier *game*

gigot d'agneau *leg of lamb*

gingembre *ginger*

glace *ice cream*

glace aux noix *walnut ice cream*

glaces tous parfums *ice cream in all flavors*

grand veneur *brown sauce served with ground game or venison*

granité à la menthe *mint sherbet*

gratin, au *prepared with a crumb topping of toasted breadcrumbs; usually includes grated cheese, most often Parmesan*

gratin dauphinois *scalloped potatoes with browned top*

gratin de homard *lobster in a cream sauce with a cheese and breadcrumb topping*

gratin de volaille *chicken in a cream sauce with a cheese and breadcrumb topping*

grecque, à la *describes a dish made with olive oil and vinegar*

grenade *pomegranate*

grenobloise *with capers, brown butter and lemon*
grenouilles *frogs' legs*
grenouilles à la provençale *frogs' legs in garlic butter*
gribiche, sauce *sauce made with hard boiled egg yolks, oil, vinegar, mustard, capers, gherkins and spices; frequently served with cold fish*
grives *thrushes*
groseilles à maquereau *gooseberries*

h

hareng *herring*
hareng fumé *kippered herring*
harengs salés *salt herring*
haricots *beans*
haricots de Soissons *navy beans*
haricots verts *green beans*
haricots verts à la maître d'hôtel *green beans tossed with butter, parsley and lemon juice*
haricot verts sautés au beurre *fresh green beans sautéed in butter*
herbe *herb*
hollandaise, sauce *hot sauce made with egg yolks and butter; served with vegetables and fish*
homard *lobster*
homard a l'américaine *lobster sautéed in oil with onions and tomatoes*
homard Newburg *chunks of lobster cooked in a sauce of brandy and fish stock*
homard grillé *broiled lobster*
homard sauté *chunks of lobster sautéed in butter with herbs added*
hors d'oeuvres *appetizers, hot or cold*
huile *oil*
huîtres *oysters*

i

igname *yam*
île flottante *literally "floating island"; a dessert of meringue afloat on a pudding*
indienne, à la *prepared with curry*

j

jambon bayonnaise *smoked ham from near Bayonne, a French town in the Pyrénées*
jambon fumé *smoked ham*
jardinière, à la *garnished with fresh vegetables, served with roast, stewed or braised meat and poultry; the vegetables may be boiled or glazed and are placed around the meat*
julienne *meat or vegetables cut into thin strips*
jus de tomate *tomato juice*

l

lait *milk*
laitue *lettuce*
laitues braisées *braised lettuce, usually Boston lettuce*
langoustine *crawfish, small lobster*
langue *tongue*
langue de boeuf *beef tongue*
langue de chat *literally, "cat's tongue;" a thin, flat cookie*
languedocienne, à la *with sausage, parsley and garlic*
lapereau *young rabbit*
lapin *rabbit*
lard *bacon*
lard fumé *smoked bacon*
lentille *lentil bean*
légumes *vegetables*
levrant *young hare*
limon *lime*
longe *loin*
loup *sea bass*
lyonnaise *prepared with onions; onions grow abundantly in the Lyonnais region of France*

m

macédoine *fruit or vegetables, diced and then mixed*
madeleine *sweet made from flour, butter, eggs and sugar baked in shell-like molds*
madère, sauce au *a sauce made with Madeira wine*
madrilène *clear chicken soup with tomato; served chilled*
maigre, au *lean*
maïs *corn*
maison *this term is meant to be applied only to recipes that are exclusive to the restaurant's owner or chef but is usually used more loosely to mean in the style of the restaurant; literally it means house*
maltaise, sauce *mayonnaise with orange juice and orange peel added; used with asparagus*
mange-tout *sweet pea; the pod is eaten as well as the peas*
maquereaux *mackerel*
maquereaux au vin blanc *mackerel in a white wine sauce*
maquereau mariné *pickled mackerel*
marchands de vin, sauce *brown sauce of butter and red wine*
marguery *prepared with a sauce of white wine and stock made from mussels; most often used for fillets of sole*
mariné *marinated*
marjolaine *marjoram*
marron *chestnut*
marrons glacés *candied chestnuts*
marzipan *paste of almonds*
mascotte, à la *garnish of artichoke hearts and small potatoes cooked in butter*
mayonnaise *egg yolks, oil, vinegar or lemon juice thoroughly blended*
menthe *mint*
médaillon *food cut into a round or oval shape*
médaillons de veau *veal, cut in an oval shape*
menthe poivrée *peppermint*
meringue glacée *egg whites and sugar beaten and baked, served with ice cream*
merlan *whiting*
meunière *method of preparing fish; it's first seasoned, floured and fried in butter, then served with lemon juice, parsley and melted butter*

miel *honey*
mijoté *simmered*
mirabelle *a yellow plum*
mirepoix *diced vegetables cooked in butter*
moelle *bone marrow*
montmorency, à la *prepared with cherries; a method used most often with duckling*
morilles *a mushroom, called morel in English*
mornay, sauce *a cream sauce with cheese added*
moules *mussels*
moules à la marinière *mussels cooked in broth and served with a mixture of the broth and melted butter*
moules farcies *stuffed mussels*
mousse *a light and airy dish that is made with cream and eggs; may be of fish, chicken, etc., or fruits and chocolate; served either hot or cold*
mousse de volaille *chicken mousse*
mousseline *a type of mousse made with cream and meat, fish or eggs*
mousseline, sauce *a thick sauce of egg yolks, lemon juice and whipped cream*
moutarde *mustard*
mure *blackberry*

n

nantua, sauce *shrimp sauce*
navets *turnips*
nature *plain; without trim; in its natural state*
neige *literally snow; the name given to the chipped ice that goes along with some cold dishes*
niçoise, à la *prepared with tomatoes, zucchini, garlic, sometimes potatoes, green beans, olives, capers and anchovies; may also mean with tomatoes and garlic*
noisettes *hazelnuts*
noisettes de chevreuil *a cut of venison, round or oval shape*
noix de Brésil *Brazil nuts*
normande, sauce *with oyster juice; used with fillet of sole*
nouilles *noodles*

o

oeuf *egg*
oeufs à la coque *boiled eggs*
oeufs à la Russe *hard-boiled eggs with a mayonnaise sauce of chives, onion and a bit of tabasco*
oeufs à la Richelieu *eggs served with stuffed tomatoes, mushrooms and potatoes*
oeufs argenteuils *scrambled eggs with asparagus*
oeufs bénédictine *classically, eggs over salt cod with a cream sauce; in a New York restaurant this refers to an egg and ham on an English muffin with hollandaise sauce and possibly even a slice of truffle*
oeufs d'alose *shad roe*
oeufs de poisson *fish roe*
oeufs en gelée *eggs in aspic*
oeufs frits *fried eggs*
oeufs Rossini *eggs with truffles and Madeira*
oeufs sur le plat *shirred eggs*
oie *goose*
oignon *onion*
oiseaux sans têtes *rolled sliced meat with a stuffing*
omelette *omelet; an egg dish*
omelette à la confiture *omelet with jam; a dessert*
omelette au fromage *cheese omelet*
omelette au foie de volaille *omelet with chicken livers*
omelette au jambon *omelet with ham*
omelette au lard *omelet with bacon*
omelette aux fines herbes *an omelet made with parsley, tarragon and chives*
omelette aux girolles *omelet with mushrooms*
omelette aux truffes *omelet with truffles*
omelette basquaise *omelet with peppers, ham, garlic, tomatoes and mushrooms*
omelette bonne femme *omelet with onions and bacon*
omelette nature *plain omelet*
omelette norvégienne *our baked Alaska; ice cream covered with meringue that is browned in the oven; served flaming*
omelette parmentier *potato omelet*
omelette provençale *omelet with garlic, tomatoes, onions and olives*
orge *barley*

p

pabrica *paprika*
paillard de boeuf *boned shell steak that is pounded very thin*
pailles *potatoes cut thin and deep fried; literally means "straws"*
pain *bread*
palissade aux marrons *chestnut and chocolate dessert*
palourdes *clams*
pamplemousse *grapefruit*
panaché *mixed*
papillote, en *cooked in a sheet of oiled paper or parchment*
parfait *an iced dessert*
parmentier *with potatoes*
pastenaque *parsnip*
pastèque *watermelon*
patate *sweet potato*
pâte *dough, pastry*
pâté *originally the term pâté was applied only to a meat or fish dish enclosed in pastry and baked; now it describes any dish of ground meat or fish baked in a mold that has been lined with strips of bacon*
pâté maison *a pâté unique to a particular restaurant*
pâtisseries *pastries*
paupiettes de sole *slices of sole, rolled and stuffed*
pavot *poppy seed*
pané *breaded*
pannequets *large, thin pancakes that are filled and rolled*

paysanne *peasant style; with vegetables and bacon*
pêche *peach*
pêches cardinal *stewed peaches on strawberry ice cream topped with red currant jelly*
pêches melba *peaches that have been steeped in vanilla-flavored syrup over vanilla ice cream, topped with raspberry purée; a creation of Escoffier*
perche *perch*
perdrix *partridges ("perdreau" is singular)*
périgourdine *with foie gras and truffles*
persil *parsley*
persillade *chopped parsley, usually mixed with garlic*
petit-beurre *butter cookie*
petite marmite *clear soup made with meat, poultry, marrow bones, stock pot vegetables and cabbage; usually served with toast and sprinkled with grated cheese*
petit mont blanc *dessert made with chestnuts and whipped cream*
petit pain *roll*
petits pois *sweet peas*
pieds de porc *pig's feet; most often prepared by grilling*
pigeon en cocotte *casserole of pigeon or squab*
pigeonneau *squab*
pilaw *pilaf; rice prepared with a variety of other ingredients*
piments *pimentos*
pipérade *omelet with peppers, tomatoes, garlic, ham and onions*
pistaches *pistachio nuts*
plâteau de fromages *choice of cheese*
poêle, à la *fried*
point, à *medium done, refers to beef*
point d'asperges *asparagus tips*
poireaux *leeks*
poires *pears*
poire à la Condé *pear served on vanilla-flavored rice*
poires belle Hélène *poached pears served on vanilla ice cream with hot chocolate sauce*
pois *peas*
pois à la française *peas cooked with lettuce leaves and onions*
pois chiche *chick pea*
poisson *fish*
poitrine *breast*
poitrine de veau *breast of veal*
poivre *pepper*
poivre vert *green pepper (the spice)*
poivron *green pepper (the vegetable)*
pomme *apple*
pommes de terre duchesse *potatoes put through a sieve and mixed with butter, salt and pepper; may be served as is or but through a pastry bag to make a border*
pommes de terre à l'huile *potato salad with vinaigrette sauce*
pommes gaufrettes *apple waffles*
porc *pork*
potage *soup*
potage clair *clear soup*
potage crécy *puree of carrot soup*
potage crème *cream soup*
potage crème de céleri *cream of celery soup*
potage crème d'épinards *cream of spinach soup*
potage de betterave *beet soup; borscht*
potage Dubarry *puree of cauliflower soup*
potage germiny *soup of puréed peas, chicken stock and heavy cream*
potage parmentier *puree of potato soup*
potage St. Germain *green pea soup*
potage tortue *turtle soup*
pot-au-feu *French version of the boiled dinner*
pots de crème au chocolat *rich chocolate pudding*
pouding *pudding*
poudre, en *powdered*
poularde à la hongroise *roast chicken stuffed with rice and flavored with paprika*
poule au pot *chicken stewed with vegetables*
poulet *chicken*
poulet à la Marengo *this method of cooking chicken was created by Napoleon's chef after the general's successful battle against the Austrians at Marengo; he browned the chicken in oil, added wine and served it with a garnish of fried eggs, mushrooms and crawfish; nowadays it is more likely to be served without the eggs or the crawfish*
poulet chasseur *chicken prepared with sautéed mushrooms, shallots and white wine and tomatoes; literally "hunter's chicken"*
poulet de Bresse *a chicken from the Bresse region of France; especially fed and highly prized*
poulet en cocotte *chicken roasted in a casserole*
poulet froid *chicken served cold*
poulet rôti a l'estragon *roast chicken with tarragon*
poulpe *octopus*
poussin *young chicken*
primeurs *early vegetables*
printanière, a la *garnished with a variety of vegetables*
profiterole *eclair-like pastry; may be filled with ice cream or any purée or with a custard, jam or other sweet filling*
profiteroles glacées au chocolat *small eclair-like pastry with chocolate frosting*
provençale, à la *with tomatoes, garlic, olives and eggplant*
prune *plum*
purée *food that has been mashed or put through a sieve or, in more recent days, processed in a blender*
purée de pommes de terre à l'ail *mashed potatoes flavored with garlic*

q

quenelles *dumplings made with either fish or meat*
queue de homard *lobster tail*
quiche lorraine *a tart made with eggs, cream, cheese and bacon*

r

râble de lapin *saddle of rabbit*
raclette *hot, melted cheese; served with baked potatoes and gherkins; a dish of Swiss origin*

radis *radish*
ragout *a dish made from meat, poultry or fish that has been cut up and browned; may or may not include vegetables; a navarin is a popular ragout of lamb*
raifort, sauce *sauce made with horseradish, breadcrumbs, fresh cream and vinegar*
raisins *grapes*
ratatouille *a mixture of eggplant, zucchini, squash, onions, tomatoes and peppers; may be served hot or cold*
ravigote, sauce *a white sauce, hot or cold, which is highly seasoned with thyme and coarsely ground black pepper*
réglisse *licorice*
reine-claude *green gage plum*
reine de saba *cake of chocolate, rum and almonds*
remoulade *mayonnaise with gherkins, capers, parsley, onions, tarragon and anchovies*
ris de veau *sweetbreads*
ris de veau archiduc *sweet breads prepared in a paprika and cream sauce*
risotto *rice braised in chicken stock*
rissole *meat-filled turnover that can be either fried or baked*
riz *rice*
riz à l'impératrice *molded bavarian cream with candied fruits, rice and kirsch*
riz étuvé au beurre *buttered rice that's been steamed*
Robert, sauce *sauce of onion, white wine and mustard; served with grilled pork dishes*
rognons *kidneys*
rognons de veau *veal kidneys*
romarin *rosemary*
Rossini *garnished with truffles and foie gras*
rôti *roast*
rouelle *thick cut of veal*
roulade *rolled, stuffed meat*

s

sabayon *the Italian zabaglione; a frothy dessert made of beaten eggs, sugar and wine*
salade *salad*
salade d'endive aux noix *a salad with endives and nuts*
salade d'épinards aux champignons *spinach salad with mushrooms*
salade de cresson *watercress salad*
salade mimosa *green salad with sieved eggs, herbs and a vinaigrette dressing*
salade niçoise *potatoes, string beans with an oil and vinegar dressing; trimmed with olives, capers, anchovies and tomatoes*
sang, au *with a sauce made from the blood of the meat used*
saucisson *large sausage; sliced for serving*
sauge *sage*
saumon *salmon*
saumon d'Ecosse fumé *smoked Scottish salmon*
saumon fumé *smoked salmon*
saumon glacé *salmon in aspic; served cold*
saumon poché *poached whole salmon*
sauté *cooked over a high heat in butter, oil or other fat*
savarin *molded yeast cake soaked in liqueur-flavored syrup; may be served hot*
sec *dry*
sel *salt*
selle d'agneau *saddle of lamb*
selle de pré-salé desosée *saddle of boned lamb*
sirop *syrup*
soles de douvres *dover sole*
sorbet *sherbet; made from fruit or liqueurs*
sorbet au cassis *sherbet flavored with a black currant liqueur*
soubise, sauce *cream sauce with onion purée added*
soufflé *dish made with pureed ingredients, thickened with egg yolks and stiffly beaten egg whites; the varieties are limitless and may be made with vegetables, fish, meat, fruit, nuts or liqueurs; served as an appetizer, a main dish or a dessert*
soufflé ambassadrice *soufflé made with macaroons and blanched, rum-soaked almonds*
soufflé aux épinards *spinach soufflé*
soufflé aux fraises *strawberry soufflé*
soufflé Mont-Bry *chestnut and vanilla-flavored soufflé*
soupe a l'oignon *onion soup*
soupe au pistou *vegetable soup with garlic, basil and cheese; a specialty of the Riviera*
sous la cendre *cooked in the coals*
specialité de la maison *specialty of that particular restaurant*
steak au poivre *steak made with crushed peppercorns*
steak tartare *uncooked ground meat seasoned with salt and pepper and served with a raw egg yolk on top and with capers, chopped onion and parsley on the side*
sucées *a kind of small cake*
sucre *sugar*
suprêmes de volaille *chicken breasts*
suprêmes de volaille à blanc *chicken breasts poached in butter with a wine and cream sauce*
sur commande *to your special order*

t

tacon *young salmon*
tarte *pie*
tarte alsacienne *an apple flan with a bit of cinnamon flavoring added to the custard*
tartelette *tart*
tartines *slices of buttered bread*
terrine *meat, fish or fowl chopped finely, baked in a dish called a terrine, and served cold; often called a pâté in the U.S.*
terrine de caneton *terrine of duckling*
thé *tea*
thon *tuna fish*
timbale *a dish made in a pie crust*
tournedos *small slice of beef, round and thick, from the heart of the fillet of beef; sautéed or grilled*
tournedos Rossini *tournedos sautéed in butter and arranged on toast; a slice of foie gras and truffles tops the meat and there's a sauce over all*
tourte *sweet tart*
tranche *slice*

tripes à la mode de caen *tripe made with calf's feet, vegetables and cider*
tronçons de homard *lobster chunks*
truffe *truffle, a fungus that grows underground; Périgord truffles are the most highly prized*
truite *trout*
truite saumonée *salmon trout; pink-skinned trout*
turbot *a large, flat fish which is very popular in Europe; similar to halibut*
turbot poché hollandaise *poached turbot served with a sauce of egg yolks and butter*

v

vanille *vanilla*
varié *assorted*
velouté, sauce *smooth sauce of butter, flour, veal or chicken stock*
velouté de volaille à la senégalaise *curried turkey soup*
venaison *venison*
verdurette, sauce *chives, egg yolks, chervil and tarragon with oil, vinegar, salt and pepper*
vermicelle *thin spaghetti*
veronique *with green grapes*
vert-pré, au *garnished with potatoes cut in sticks and watercress*
verte, sauce *green mayonnaise, colored with spinach, watercress, tarragon or other green herbs*
viandes froids *cold cuts*
vichy *garnished with carrots*
vichyssoise *a cream soup of leeks, potatoes and chicken broth; served cold*
vichyssoise à la Russe *leek and potato soup with beets and sour cream*
vin *wine*
vinaigre *vinegar*
vinaigrette *mixture of oil and vinegar, seasoned with salt and pepper and, at times, herbs; a vinaigrette sauce is often served with asparagus, cauliflower or boiled fish or as a green salad dressing*
Vincent, sauce *green herbs puréed and added to mayonnaise with hard-boiled egg yolks*
volaille *fowl, poultry*
vol-au-vent *pastry shell filled with a variety of mixtures bound together with a brown or white sauce*

y

yaourt *yoghurt*

Italian Menu Definitions

a

abbacchio *baby lamb*
abbacchi arrosto *roast baby lamb*
abruzzese, all' *made with red peppers; in the style of Abruzzi*
acciughe *anchovy*
acero *maple*
aceto *vinegar*
acqua *water*
acquacotta *vegetable soup*
adriatico, dell' *marinated in oil and lemon juice and then grilled over a wood or charcoal fire*
affogato *steamed*
affumicato *smoked*
a fuoco lento *braised*
aglio *garlic*
agnello all'arrabbiata *literally "angry lamb"; lamb cooked over a high flame*
agnello in guazetto *lamb stewed in an egg and cheese broth*
ai ferri *grilled*
albicocca *apricot*
al dente *literally "to the tooth", refers to pasta that is cooked firm*
al forno *baked*
ali *chicken wings*
alici *anchovies*
all'amatriciana *prepared with onion, ham and tomatoes; literally means in the style of the women of Amatrice, a town in the Abruzzi*
alla griglia *broiled*
alla salvia *with sage*
alloro *bay leaves*
amaretti *macaroons*
ananasso *pineapple*
anchellini *ravioli stuffed with meat and fried*
aneto *dill*
anguilla *eel*
anice *anise*
animelle *sweetbreads*
anitra *duck*
anitra arrosto *roast duck*
anitra selvatica *wild duck*
antipasti di pesce *appetizers made with fish*
antipasto *hors d'oeuvres; appetizer*
arachide *peanut*
aragosta *lobster*
arancia *orange*
aringa *herring*
aringa affumicata *kippered herring*
aringa marinata *marinated herring*
arista *roast pork loin*
arselle *mussels*
asparagi *asparagus*
asparagi alla fiorentina *asparagus tossed in butter with Parmesan cheese and topped with fried eggs*

b

baccalà *salt cod*
bagna caôda *hot dip for vegetables flavored with anchovies*
balsamella *white sauce made with milk, flour and butter*
barbabietola *beet*
balsamella *sauce of flour and milk cooked in butter*
basilico *basil*
ben cotto *well-done, to describe meat*
bianco *white*
bigné al cioccolato *chocolate puff dessert*
biscotti all anice *anise-flavored cookies*
biscotto *cookie*
biscuit torton *dessert made of egg whites, whipped cream and topped with chopped almonds*
bistecca *beef steak*
bocconcini *small pieces of veal cooked in white wine sauce; also called olivette because the pieces are the size of olives*
bollito misto *mixed boiled meat, served with a tomato or pepper sauce; what goes into the mix depends on the chef and the region of Italy he or she is from; it may include veal, tongue, sausage, calf's head, beef brisket*
bolognese, alla *with a sauce of meat, milk and tomatoes*
braciola *roast pork stuffed with pine nuts, raisins and almond paste; a Sicilian specialty*
broccoletti di Brusselle *Brussel sprouts*
broccoli al formaggio *broccoli with melted cheese sauce*
broccoli all'agro *broccoli served with olive oil and lemon juice*
brodetto *fish stew*
brodo *broth*
brodo di manzo *beef broth*
brodo di pesce *fish chowder*
brodo vegetale *vegetable broth*
brushetta *garlic bread*
bucatini *long noodles*
budino *pudding*
bue *beef*
burro *butter*
burro fuso *melted butter*
burro di acciuga *anchovy butter*
burro maggiordomo *butter melted with parsley and lemon juice*

c

cacciatora, alla *prepared in the style of a hunter; with mushrooms, herbs, shallots, tomatoes, wine, etc.*
cacciucco alla livornese *fish soup with onions, parsley and tomatoes*
caffè cappuccino *coffee with whipped cream topping and cinnamon flavor*
calamaretti *baby squid*
calamari *squid*
calamari affogati *steamed squid*
caldo *hot*
calzone *pastry crust with ham and cheese filling*
campagnola *in the country style; usually with onions and tomatoes*
cannelloni *meat-stuffed rolls of pasta, baked*
cannelloni alla catanese *baked pasta stuffed with meat with a sauce of tomatoes and pecorino cheese*
cannoli *custard filled pastry in a tubular shape with candied fruits and rum flavoring; powdered sugar sprinkled on top*
cantarello *chanterelle mushrooms*
capocollo *spicy, smoked pork*
caponato *mixture of egg plant, onions and tomatoes*
cappelletti *garnish for soup; hat-shaped*
capelli d'angelo *very thin noodle, literally means "angel hair"*
cappero *caper*
cappesante *bay scallops*
capretto *kid*
caramella *toffee*
caramellato *caramelized*
carciofi *artichokes*
carciofi alla romana *artichokes cooked with mint leaves and cloves of garlic*
carciofini *small artichokes*
carne *meat*
carota *carrot*
carpio *carp*
carrettiera, alla *with basil and tomatoes*
casalinga *home-made*
cassata *ice cream with candied fruits*
castagne *chestnuts*
caviale *caviar*
cavolfiore fritto *fried cauliflower*
cavolfiori *cauliflower*
cavolirape *kohlrabi*
cavolo *cabbage*
cavolo riccio *kale*
ceci *chick peas*
ceppatella *mushroom*
cerase *cherries*
cerforglio *chervil (a parsley-like herb)*
cervo *venison*
cetriolini *pickles*
cetriolo *gherkin*
chido di garofano *cloves*
cialda *wafer or waffle*
ciambella *bun*
cibreo *stew*
cicoria *chicory*
ciliegia *cherry*
cioccolato *chocolate*
cipolla *onion*
cipolline in agrodolce *sweet and sour onions*
cervelle *calves' brains*
cervelle dorate alla milanese *calves' brains seasoned with salt and pepper, dipped in egg and bread crumbs and fried in butter*
cocomero *watermelon*
con *with*
conchiglie *pasta shells*
condimento *condiment*
coniglio *rabbit*
coniglio al forno *baked rabbit*
conserva *preserve*
coppa *type of salami*
coppa di ciliege *cherries jubilee*
coscia *leg*

coscia di agnello arrosto *roast leg of lamb*
costola *rib*
costolette *chop*
costolette alla milanese *veal chops that have been breaded and cooked in butter*
costolette alla valdostana *veal or pork chop with ham and fontina cheese*
costolette di agnello *lamb chop*
costolette di vitello *veal chop*
costolettine *baby lamb chops*
cotoletta *slice of veal, turkey or beef or some vegetables like eggplant*
cotoletta di tacchino alla bolognese *turkey breasts cooked with ham, Parmesan cheese and truffles*
cotto a vapore *steamed*
cozze *mussels*
cozze alla marinara *mussels cooked in white wine with garlic and parsley*
crema *cream*
crema al mascarpone *cream dessert made with a soft, yellowish cheese*
crescione *watercress*
crespelle *thin pancakes*
crespelle alla fiorentina *spinach-filled pancake*
crocchette di pollo *chicken croquettes*
crostacei *shellfish*
crostata *pie*
crostata di pere alla milanese *pear tart with apricot jelly and rum*
crostini *rounds of bread, sprinkled with cheese and then toasted or bread fried in garlic oil*
crostini in brodo *croutons in broth*
crudo *raw*
cuore *heart*
cuscinetti di vitello *veal roast*

d

dattero *date*
dattero di mare *mussel*
del giorno *of the day, equivalent to the French "du jour"*
delicatezza *delicacy*
della casa *of the house; in the style of that particular restaurant*
dolci *sweets*
dolci assortiti *assorted sweets*
dragoncello *tarragon*

e

endivia *endive*
erba *herb*
erba cipollina *chive*
espresso *very strong black coffee*

f

fagiano *pheasant*
fagioli *kidney beans*
fagioli in salsa *cold bean salad*
fagiolini verdi *green beans*
fave *flat bean, fava bean*
fegatelli *slices of liver*
fegatelli di maiale con la rete *pork liver wrapped in caul fat and then broiled*
fegato *liver*
fegato ai ferri *broiled liver*
fegato alla veneziana *thinly sliced liver and onions cooked in olive oil; very popular dish*
fetta *slice*
fettucine *ribbon-shaped noodle*
fettucine al burro *noodles with melted butter*
fettucine all'Alfredo *immensely popular dish in New York; noodles tossed with butter, cream and Parmesan cheese; the creation of a Roman chef named Alfredo*
fettucine al sugo di vongole bianco *noodles with a white clam sauce*
fiamma, alla *served flaming, like the French "flambé"*
fico *fig*
filetti di sogliola *fillet of sole*
filetto *fillet*
filetto di bue *fillet of beef*
filetto di sogliole alla parmigiana *fillet of sole baked with Parmesan cheese*
finocchi al burro *fennel cooked in butter*
finocchio *fennel; a green, celery-like vegetable with a slight taste of anise*
fiorentina, la *beefsteak rubbed with crushed peppercorns and broiled over charcoal*
fonduta *a fondue made with fontina cheese and truffles*
formaggio *cheese*
formaggio grattugiato *grated cheese*
fra diavolo *with a spicy, tomato-based sauce; in the style of the devil*
fragole *strawberries*
freddo *cold*
fresco *fresh*
frittata *omelet*
frittata al formaggio *omelet with melted cheese*
frittata alla paesana *omelet with bacon, potatoes and onions*
frittata genovese *omelet with grated cheese, basil and spinach*
fritella *fritter*
fritelle *fritters*
fritto di mare *fried shell fish*
fritto di verdure *fried vegetables*
fritto in padella *sauteed*
fritto misto di pesce *assortment of fried fish; Italian version of the fish fry*
fritto misto alla bolognese *brains, liver, zucchini, cheese-stuffed puffs and pasta stuffed with chopped chicken giblets, all fried*
frutta *fruit*
frutta candita *candied fruit*
frutta composta *compote of fruits; may be made from fresh or dried fruits*
frutta della stagione *fruit that is in season*
frutta fresca *fresh fruit, one of the favorite Italian desserts when served with cheese*
frutti affogate al vino russo *fruits poached in red wine*
frutti di mare *seafood*
funghi *mushrooms*
funghi trifolati *sauteed mushrooms*
fusilli *spiral shaped pasta*

g

gallina *hen*
gallinella *spring chicken*
gamberetti *small shrimp*
gamberi *shrimp*
gamberi fritti *fried shrimp*
garganelli *macaroni made from an egg dough by hand*
garofolato *beef stew with cloves added*
gelantina, in *in aspic*
gelato *ice cream*
gelato agli amaretti *ice cream made with a macaroon mixture*
genovese, alla *with pine nuts, cheese, basil, garlic and other herbs*
ghiaccio *ice*
giardiniera *a mixture of vegetables, marinated*
ginepro *juniper berries*
gnocchi alla romana *dumplings made with semolina*
gnocchi di patate *potatoes, flour and eggs made into dumplings*
gnocchi di riso *rice dumplings*
gnocchi verdi *gnocchi made with spinach*
granchio *crab*
granita di caffè *coffee ice*
granita di limone *lemon ice*
granturco *corn*
grasso *fat*
gratinati *baked with a golden crust; usually of bread crumbs and cheese*
grissini *bread sticks*
guarnito *garnished*

i

il rotolo di pasta *sheets of pasta rolled and stuffed with spinach and then sliced*
imbottito *stuffed*
imbrogliata di uovo con pomidoro *omelet with bacon and tomatoes*
insalata *salad*
insalata alla Lucia *artichoke hearts with an oil and vinegar dressing; served cold*
insalata alla russa *cooked vegetables cut up and mixed with mayonnaise*
insalata di finocchio *fennel salad*
insalata di fruitti di mare *seafood salad*
insalata di pesce *seafood salad*
insalata siciliana *tomatoes with basil and garlic and an oil and vinegar dressing*
involtini *stuffed rolls of veal*

l

lamponi *rampberries*
lardellato *larded*
lardo *bacon*
lasagna *pasta in broad sheets; may be either white or green; also refers to the same pasta baked with a meat and tomato sauce, mozzarella, ricotta and Parmesan cheese*
lasagna verdi al forno *green lasagne baked with a meat sauce*
latte *milk*
lattuga *lettuce*
lattuga romana *romaine lettuce*
lauro *bay leaf*
lenticchie *lentils*
lepre *hare*
lesso *boiled*
lingua *tongue*
lingua in salsa *tongue in a sauce of white wine, capers and anchovies*
linguini *narrow noodles*
liquirizia *licorice*
lombata *loin*
lombatina *tenderloin*
lonza *loin*
lonza di vitello *loin of veal*
lo scrigno di venere *spinach fettucine baked in a pasta bundle*
luganega *a sausage*
lumache *snails*

m

maccarello *mackerel*
maccheroni *macaroni*
maccheroni al forno *baked macaroni*
macedonia di frutta *fruit cup; salad of fruit*
maggiorana *sweet marjoram*
magro *lean, as meat*
maiale *pork*
maigletto *suckling pig*
maionese *mayonnaise*
maltagliati *triangular noodles*
mandorle *almonds*
manicotti *large, pancake-like noodles that are stuffed and baked with a sauce*
manzo *beef*
manzo alla lombarda *pot roast cooked in red wine with parsley, carrots, celery and onions*
marinara *sauce made with tomatoes, olives and garlic; no meat*
marinato *marinated*
marmellata *jam*
medalioni di vitello *fillet of veal*
mela *apple*
melagrana *pomegranate*
melanzana *eggplant*
melanzane alla siciliana *eggplant halves stuffed with pulp, olives, anchovies and capers and then baked*
melanzane fritte *fried slices of eggplant*
menta *mint*
menta peperina *peppermint*
merluzzo *codfish*
miele *honey*
meringa *meringue*
merlango *whiting*
midolla *marrow*
milanese, alla *coated with bread crumbs and cooked in butter*
millefoglie *flaky pastry; like a napoleon*
minestra *term used to describe the first course of an Italian meal; may also mean soup*
minestra di funghi *mushroom soup*
minestra di pomodori *tomato soup*

minestra di riso e fagioli *soup with rice and beans*
minestrone *a thick vegetable soup; the variety of vegetables that may go into a minestrone is endless and as variable as the regions of Italy*
miringhie de castagne *chestnut meringues*
monte bianco *dessert of chestnuts and whipped cream*
montone *mutton*
mortella *cranberry*
mostarda *mustard*
mozzarella ai ferri *grilled mozzarella*
mozzarella in carrozza *two pieces of bread, soaked in consomme, dipped in egg and spread with cheese, then fried, sandwich-like, in olive oil*
muscoli *mussels*

n

nasello *hake*
naturale *plain, as is*
nocciuola *hazelnut*
noce *nut*
noce moscata *nutmeg*
noci di cocco *coconut*

o

oca *goose*
olio *oil*
oliva *olive*
olive nere *black olives*
olive ripiene *green olives stuffed with pimento*
olivette di vitello *boneless veal cut into small pieces and cooked in wine*
ombrina *bass*
oreganato *baked with oregano; appears on menus most often as a way of preparing clams*
orzo *barley*
osso buco *veal shank stewed in tomatoes and wine*
ostriche *oysters*

p

pagello *red snapper*
paglia e fieno *literally, straw and hay; two kinds of noodles, one green, the other white; in a cream sauce with prosciutto and peas*
pagnotta *loaf of bread*
pancetta *bacon*
pan di spagna *light cake covered with cream or jam and soaked in liqueur*
panettone *yeast cake filled with candied fruit; especially popular at Christmas time*
panforte *fruitcake*
panizza *white beans, rice, tomatoes, onions and bacon*
panna *cream*
pann montata *whipped cream*
pan tostato *toast*
paparot *spinach soup*
pappardelle *broad noodles with a crimped edge*
parmigiana, alla *prepared with Parmesan cheese*
parmigiano *Parmesan cheese*
pasta *the first course in a classic Italian meal; dough made into a variety of shapes that may be eaten alone, in a broth or with a sauce*
pasta all'uovo *pasta made with eggs*
pasta e fagioli *soup of beans and pasta; the beans will probably be of the great northern variety in New York restaurants*
pasta verde *spinach noodles; lasagne is often made with spinach added*
pastina *noodles used primarily for soup*
pastinaca *parsnip*
patate fritte *fried potatoes*
patate lesse *boiled potatoes*
patate novelle *new potatoes*
patate stacciate *mashed potatoes*
penne *short, tubular pasta*
peoci *mussels*
pepe *pepper (the spice)*
peperonata *stewed green peppers, tomatoes and onions*
peperoni *sweet peppers*
peperoni alla calabrese *peppers fruit in oil with tomato*
peperoni alla piemontese *peppers stuffed with a mixture of tomatoes, garlic, anchovies, egg and bread crumbs*
peperoni ripieni con ricotta *green peppers stuffed with ricotta cheese*
pera *pear*
perciatelli *elongated macaroni*
perfetto *parfait, an iced dessert*
pernici *partridge*
pesca *peach*
pesca noce *nectarine*
pesce *fish*
pesce al cartoccio *fish baked in oiled paper or parchment*
pesce da taglio *halibut*
pesce fritto *fried fish*
pesce persico *perch*
pesce spada *swordfish*
pesche *peaches*
pesche ripieni *stuffed peaches*
pesto *paste or sauce made from fresh basil, garlic, cheese and olive oil ground in a mortar or, more likely, in a blender*
petonchio *scallop*
petto di pollo *breast of chicken*
piatto *plate*
piccante *highly seasoned*
piccata al limone *veal sauteed in butter and lemon juice*
piccione *pigeon*
pignoli *pine nuts*
piselli *peas*
piselli novelli *sweet, tender peas*
pizzaiola *sauce of tomato, garlic and marjoram; a popular method of preparing veal and beef*
pizza rustica *cheese pie with ham, sausage and hard-boiled eggs*
polenta *cornmeal simmered in water; some like to equate it to cornmeal mush*
polenta al burro e formaggio *polenta mixed with butter and cheese*
pollame *poultry*
pollastina *pullet*
pollo *chicken*
pollo alla diavola *spicy chicken; literally "devilishly hot"*

pollo alla griglia *broiled chicken*

pollo alla romana *chicken sauteed with peppers and tomatoes*

pollo disossato *chicken that has been boned*

pollo in vino bianco *chicken in white wine*

pollo novello *spring chicken*

pollo spezzato alla sabinese *chicken cooked in a sauce of olives, capers and anchovies*

polmone *lung*

polpette *meat balls*

polpettone *meat loaf*

polpettone con ripieni *meatloaf with a stuffing*

polpi alla luciana *octopus cooked in a sauce of oil and hot red peppers*

polpo *octopus*

pomodori *tomatoes*

pomodori ripieni *tomatoes stuffed with rice*

pomodori ripieni alla romana *tomatoes stuffed with rice and mozzarella cheese*

pompelmo *grapefruit*

popone *melon*

porchetta *pork roast*

porri *leeks*

porro *leek*

poverella, alla *method of preparing pasta with eggs and bacon; literally "the way the poor woman makes it"*

prezzemolo *parsley*

profiterole alla cioccolata *cream puff with chocolate frosting*

prosciutto *smoked ham, sliced wafer thin*

prosciutto e melone *smoked ham, sliced very thin with melon; a popular appetizer*

pruna *prune*

puntino, a *medium, used to describe degree of cooking meat*

pure di patate *mashed potatoes with Parmesan cheese added*

q

quadrucci *pasta in the shape of little squares*

quaglia *quail*

r

rabarbaro *rhubarb*

radicchio *radish*

ragno *sea bass*

ragù *may mean a sauce or a meat stew with garlic, tomatoes and herbs*

ragù di fegatini *sauce of chicken livers*

rane in guazetto *frogs' legs in a stew of garlic, tomatoes, etc.*

ravanello *radish*

ravioli *envelopes of pasta that are stuffed with either meat or cheese and eaten in soup or with a sauce*

rigatoni *large, ribbed and tubular macaroni*

rigatoni al forno col ragù *rigatoni baked with a meat sauce*

ripieni *stuffing*

risi e bisi *soup of rice and peas*

riso *rice*

risotto *rice dish prepared by sauteeing raw rice and onion and then cooking the rice by gradually adding broth; to be true risotto, the rice must* not *be boiled*

risotto alla milanese *risotto with saffron, Parmesan cheese and ham added*

rognon *kidneys*

rombo *turbot*

romotaccio *horseradish*

rosbif *roast beef*

rosmarino *rosemary*

rossi *red; to describe a sauce, etc.*

s

sale *salt*

salmone *salmon*

salmone affumicato *smoked salmon*

salsa alla milanese *sauce of ham and veal cooked in butter with fennel and wine*

salsa di burro al gorgonzola *sauce with gorgonzola cheese and melted sweet butter*

salsa di funghi *mushroom sauce*

salsa di pignoli *cream sauce with pine nuts*

salsa di vongole *clam sauce; served on pasta*

salsa verde *green sauce served with fish or boiled meats*

salsiccia *spicy pork sausage*

saltimbocca *slices of veal seasoned with sage, rolled around slices of prosciutto ham and sauteed in butter and Marsala wine; literally means "jump into the mouth"*

sangue, al *rare, used to refer to degree of cooking meat*

sardina *sardine*

sbaglione *see "zabaglione"*

sbira *tripe soup*

scalogno *shallot*

scaloppine *thin slices of meat, most usually of veal*

scaloppine alla bolognese *veal cooked with prosciutto and potatoes*

scaloppine alla fiorentina *thinly sliced veal on spinach with a white sauce*

scaloppine al sedano *veal cooked in butter with prosciutto and celery*

scaloppine di vitello *thin slices of veal*

scampi *shrimp*

scampi o fra diavolo *shrimp in a spicy tomato sauce*

scarola *escarole; a popular side dish when cooked in a chicken broth*

sciroppo *syrup*

scombro *mackerel*

sedano *celery*

sedano alla milanese *celery prepared with white sauce and grated cheese*

sedano e olive *celery and olives*

selvaggina *game*

seme d'anice *anise seed*

sfogliatelle *flaky pastry in the shape of a small fan*

sidro *cider*

sogliola Inglese *Dover sole*

sorbetto *sherbet*

spaghetti al burro *spaghetti with butter*

spaghetti alla carbonara *spaghetti tossed with oil, eggs, bacon and cheese; literally in the style of the charcoal gatherer*
spaghetti alla pommorola *spaghetti with tomato sauce*
spaghetti al pomodoro *spaghetti with tomato sauce*
spaghetti con aglio e olio *spaghetti with garlic and oil*
spaghetti con carne *spaghetti with meat*
spaghettini *very thin spaghetti*
spalla *shoulder*
spalla d'agnello *shoulder of lamb*
spalla di vitello *shoulder of veal*
spalla di vitello ripieno *stuffed veal shoulder*
spezie *spices*
spezzatino di pollo *stewed chicken*
spezzatino di vitello *veal stew*
spiedini *pieces of meat or anything else on a skewer*
spiedini alla romana *mozzarella and bread dipped in a batter, put on a skewer and deep fried*
spiedino di mare *fish roasted on a skewer*
spigola *sea bass*
spinaci *spinach*
spumone *dessert of ice cream, candied fruits, whipped cream and nuts*
stagione *season*
starna di montagna *grouse*
stellette *star-shaped pasta*
storione *sturgeon*
stracatto al barolo *beef cooked in a sauce of red wine and tomatoes*
stracciatella *bouillon with eggs and Parmesan cheese; the Italian version of egg-drop soup; literally means "little rags" because of the shape the eggs take when dropped in the soup*
strappazate *scrambled*
stufato *beef stewed with white wine and vegetables*
stufato misto di carne *mixed meat stew*
succo *juice*
sughi *sauces*
sugo *sauce*
sugo di broccoli e acciughe *anchovy and broccoli sauce*
suppli *rice patties*
suprema di pollo *chicken breast*
susina *plum*
susina verde *greengage plum*

t

tacchino *turkey*
tagliatelle *what the people of Bologna call "fettucine"*
tagliato *sliced*
tagliolini *thin noodles, most often used in soup*
tartaruga *turtle*
tartufo *truffle*
tellina *clam*
testa di abbacchio *sheep's head*
timballo *pudding mold*
timo *thyme*
tonnato *in a sauce made from tuna; veal prepared this way is a popular dish in New York's Italian restaurants*
tonno *tuna fish*
topinamburo *Jerusalem artichoke*
torrone *nougat*
torta *open pie, flan or cake*
torta con formaggio *cheesecake*
trancia *slice*
trenette *fine pasta, the thickness of a match; cut in long pieces*
trifolati *sauteed*
trippa alla bolognese *tripe fried in olive oil, bacon, onion and garlic with egg yolks added*
tritato *chopped*
trota *trout*

u

uccelletti *small birds*
umido, in *stewed*
uova affogate *poached eggs*
uova alla coque *boiled egg*
uova di pesce *fish eggs, roe*
uova mollette *soft-boiled egg*
uovo *egg*
uva *grapes*
uva secca *raisin*

v

vaniglia *vanilla*
veneziana, alla *cooked with onions and white wine*
verde *green*
verdure *vegetables*
verza *green cabbage*
vino *wine*
vitello *veal*
vitello all'uccelletto *veal cut into small, thin slices, cooked in white wine and flavored with sage*
vongole *clams*
vongole al forno *baked clams*
vongole oreganate *baked clams with oregano*

z

zabaglione *dessert made with egg yolks, Marsala wine and sugar beaten to a froth; may also appear as sbaglione or zabaione*
zafferano *saffron*
zampone *stuffed pigs' feet*
zenzero *ginger*
zeppole *a type of fritter*
zeppole alla napoletana *fritters with a brandy flavor*
ziti *large, tubular pasta*
zucca *pumpkin*
zucchero *sugar*
zuppa *soup*
zuppa all'aglio *garlic soup*
zuppa di lenticchie *lentil soup*
zuppa di patate e cipolle *potato and onion soup*
zuppa di pesce *the Italian version of bouillabaisse; a fish soup with ingredients that vary from chef to chef and seaon to season*
zuppa di vongole *clam chowder*
zuppa inglese *sponge cake soaked in rum with candied fruits and either whipped cream or custard*
zuppa pavese *broth with toast and poached eggs topped with grated cheese*

Compiled and Edited by Marjorie Adoff Cohen.